PRAISE FOR THE *SECRETS* SERIES

"*Secrets of the Code* is a veritable *Da Vinci Code* encyclopedia – a lively combination of interviews, commentaries and extracts from Dan Brown's sources which will give you a taste of the issues which have been thrown into the debate."

The Rough Guide to The Da Vinci Code

"Dan Burstein's *Secrets of the Code* ... is the first to break through, snaring a spot on the best-seller list ... What does Burstein's book offer that the other tag-along books don't? For starters, he unravels a hidden message on the dust jacket of the hardcover edition, and, unlike the others, he doesn't attack the book from a religious standpoint."

Wall Street Journal

"*Secrets of the Code* is one of the best of a recent boomlet of books ... a collection of various scholarly and critical opinions. Burstein's bottom line? Brown's book is fun, brainy – and fiction."

Reader's Digest

"Unlike other works cashing in on the Code's success ... Dan Burstein's collection of essays seeks to understand the complexities of gnosticism, Christian origins and the battle over the feminine in Christianity. What the author does is present a range of divergent views about these matters – and about the novel ... In bringing such questions and scholarly voices together and into the wider public domain, Burstein (and perhaps even Dan Brown) has done us a service."

Anthony Egan, *Mail & Guardian*

"*Secrets of Angels & Demons* ... contains eye-opening, thought-provoking essays from noted scholars, thinkers and experts in fields that range from quantum physics to the papal succession process, from modern conspiracy theory to the worlds of Bernini and Galileo."

U.S. News & World Report

"If you're truly Brown obsessed, or if you're just dying to read about the conjunction of Freemasonry, the Founding Fathers and the nation's capital, *Secrets of the Widow's Son* ... is there for you."

The Washington Post

SECRETS *of* MARY MAGDALENE

The Untold Story of History's Most Misunderstood Woman

EDITED BY

Dan Burstein & Arne J. de Keijzer

with an Introduction by Elaine Pagels

CONTRIBUTING EDITOR: Deirdre Good
MANAGING EDITOR: Jennifer Doll

Weidenfeld & Nicolson
LONDON

First published in the USA in 2006
by CDS Books

First published in Great Britain in 2006
by Weidenfeld & Nicolson

1 3 5 7 9 10 8 6 4 2

A CIP catalogue record for this book
is available from the British Library.

ISBN-13   978 0 297 85168 4
ISBN-10   0 297 85168 3

Printed in Great Britain by Mackays of Chatham plc, Chatham, Kent

Weidenfeld & Nicolson

The Orion Publishing Group Ltd
Orion House
5 Upper Saint Martin's Lane
London, WC2H 9EA
www.orionbooks.co.uk

The Orion publishing group's policy is to use papers that are natural,
renewable and recyclable products and made from wood grown in sustainable forests.
The logging and manufacturing processes are expected to conform to the
environmental regulations of the country of origin.

Contents

Appendixes

Preface

She is the Mary of many faces: humble saint, penitent sinner, apostle of the apostles, disciple, exorcist, anointer, Christian idealist, matriarch of a holy bloodline, the female goddess in the sacred union, beneficiary of exorcism by Jesus, independent woman of means, role model, artist's model, muse, feminist icon, pleasure revolutionary, embodiment of feminist spirituality, victim of a male-dominated religion, wife of Jesus, worldly counterpoint to the ethereal Virgin Mary, and much more. "No other biblical figure—including Judas and perhaps even Jesus—has had such a vivid and bizarre post-biblical life in the human imagination," says Jane Schaberg, one of our contributors. Nor has any cultural figure set off more controversy.

Today, we have come to know that much of her image has been contorted, her power as a spiritual figure dismissed. The "true" Mary Magdalene has been kept a secret, in effect, by a church tradition that exiled her from authority and imprisoned her theologically for her sex. For some, she was an inconvenient woman from the beginning. The Romans considered all women to be untrustworthy; the disciples followed suit. "Tell Mary to leave us," Peter tells Jesus in the Gospel of Thomas, "for women are not worthy of life." As the early church evolved, many church fathers began to preach that Jesus had died to rid the world of Adam's sin. The source of that sin, of course, was Eve. In the third century, Tertullian, a prolific defender of the orthodox church, wrote: "On account of [women] . . . even the Son of God had to die."

The next turn of the screw came on an autumn Sunday in 591, when Pope Gregory the Great suggested to the assembled that Mary

Magdalene had been a whore before being redeemed by Christ. Christendom quickly embraced this erroneous but religiously instructive image of the saintly sinner. Despite her allegedly sinful past—or perhaps because of it—this version of Mary Magdalene would become a new heroine to many as she morphed into a popular cult figure in thirteenth-century France, fed by stories of her arrival in Provence in a rudderless boat and the "discovery" of her bones.

During the Renaissance, artists found her a muse of great versatility—she could be buxom and bountiful (Titian), or haggard and ascetic (Donatello). Mary Magdalene even became something of a pious pinup, as can be seen in the painting recently attributed to Leonardo da Vinci.

The great social dislocation brought on by the industrial revolution saw churches invoke her name in an effort to rein in the wayward. Nuns started Magdalene houses in hopes of saving the lost. By the late nineteenth century Wagner, Rilke, and a few other cultural figures began to revive the suggestion that Mary had been an erotic partner to Jesus. By the end of the twentieth, she had become a feminist icon, a role model for women in the church, and a spiritual guide to New Agers. The Vatican, bowing in 1969 to the new scholarship that was emerging even from within, reversed the verdict that had stood for fourteen hundred years by directing that from then on, Magdalene should be identified with her role as witness to the Resurrection and not with the sinful woman in Luke. But one aspect of her old image remains—even the rehabilitated Mary has continued to be defined by her sex. Look no further than the *Da Vinci Code* phenomenon, or what one contributor to this book, the pop singer Tori Amos, calls Mary Magdalene's attractive quality of "sinuality."

Mary Magdalene's real meaning, it seems, often continues to be a reflection of the mirror we hold up to ourselves. For some scholars and religious figures, the master narrative is the received Word of God and must remain in place unchanged, even though, as it turns out, what we have been taught about Mary Magdalene comes out of the Dark Ages of thought, and not from the lips of Jesus. Many others have embraced a Christianity born of diversity, and characterized by egalitarianism and tolerance. For still others, Mary Magdalene is only a nominal figure in the Christian story. Considering how closely

Christianity and Western civilization have been intertwined for the last two thousand years, her mythic evolution is really a meta-commentary on how our culture perceives the role of women.

This book was written to help you, the reader, scrape off the encrusted layers of meaning that have come to obscure Mary Magdalene's fundamental secular and religious importance, and come to your own conclusions about one of the most important and fascinating women in history.

As in previous books in the *Secrets* series—*Secrets of the Code* and *Secrets of Angels & Demons*—we have brought together a stellar group of theologians, scholars, and other experts who bring to our intellectual feast a wide variety of perspectives and experience. We share with you the ideas of those who believe that all we need to know about Mary Magdalene can be found in the New Testament, as well as the opinions of those who find the alternative gospels—with their much greater emphasis on her starring role as disciple and close companion to Jesus—the best way to interpret her. We also bring you the voices of those who connect her to ancient goddess figures and the sacred feminine. And the views of still others for whom Mary Magdalene is the ultimate inspiration for creativity or spiritual community.

We direct you especially to Chapter 5, where six of the world's leading experts on Mary Magdalene engage in a remarkable round-table discussion of the major themes and controversies that surround her within the context of twenty-first-century Mary Magdalene studies. All have published and spoken extensively on Mary Magdalene and related subjects: the historical Jesus; the early Christian movement; Gnosticism and other alternative strains within Christianity; the role of women in the early church; religious art, archaeology, and culture from the biblical era to the present day; and many other topics within the nexus of gender/spirituality/religion/myth/archetype. Their pathbreaking work has uncovered new ideas about the events of two thousand years ago and what they imply for our era.

A word on our editorial approach. We have engaged in an extensive process to identify the most interesting and thought-provoking ideas and experts, and find the right balance of elements—original essays, interviews, and excerpts from previously published material. All original source material has been identified and we have taken care to be clear about when we are presenting original material and when we are speaking in our own editorial voice. For example, the short pieces that introduce the excerpts, interviews, or original essays are set off in a noticeably different typestyle. Permissioned materials that previously appeared elsewhere are identified with bylines and/or copyright and reprint permission notices. We have tended to regularize spelling and naming conventions in our own work while leaving undisturbed the original spelling and conventions in excerpts. Variations in style such as the spellings "Magdalene" and "Magdalen" are inevitable, and we ask your understanding. Short biographical notes are contained within most of the introductions. For fuller biographies, please see the contributors section at the back of the book. We also encourage you to explore the full-length works by each of our contributors.

The story of Mary Magdalene is in some ways one about how we as a society interpret myth, legend, and the unknown when it intersects with the "real world." It can also serve to remind us of the essential value of compassion, openness, tolerance, and respect for individuals that reaches beyond the narrow confines of one gender, one religious group, or one people. We invite you to explore these themes with us.

Dan Burstein
Arne J. de Keijzer
August 2006

Introduction

BY ELAINE PAGELS

Who was she, that elusive—and fascinating—woman in the circle around Jesus of Nazareth? For nearly two thousand years, Mary Magdalene has lived in the imagination of Christians as a seductive prostitute; in our own time, contemporary fiction pictures her as Jesus' lover and wife, mother of his children. Yet the earliest sources that tell of Mary Magdalene—both within the New Testament and outside of it—do not describe either of these sexualized roles, suggesting that the woman herself, and how we have come to see her, is more complex than most of us ever imagined. Was she, then, one of Jesus' followers, whose wealth helped support him, as the earliest New Testament gospel, the Gospel of Mark, says? A madwoman who had been possessed by seven devils, as Luke says? Or Jesus' closest disciple, the one he loved more than any other, as the Gospel of Mary Magdalene tells us? Or, in the words of the Dialogue of the Savior, "the woman who understood all things"?

When we investigate the earliest available records, we find all of these conflicting images, and more. What we discover, too, is that which answer we find depends on where we look. What is probably the earliest story comes from the New Testament Gospel of Mark, written about forty years after Jesus' death. Mark tells us that while Roman soldiers were crucifying Jesus, Mary Magdalene stood among a group of women watching the execution, grieving, although the male disciples had fled in fear for their lives. Standing with Salome and another woman named Mary (the mother of James and Joseph), Mary Magdalene continued her vigil until Jesus finally died; later, along with her companions, she saw his body carefully wrapped in strips of linen, entombed, and sealed into a cave cut out of rock.

Mark explains that Mary, Salome, and "the other Mary" were among those who "followed Jesus and provided for him"—probably meals and a place to stay, perhaps money for necessities—when he was in Galilee. The morning after Sabbath, the women came to offer their teacher the final service, bringing aromatic spices to complete his burial. But Mark's account ends on a note of confusion and shock: finding the tomb open, the body gone, the women, hearing that Jesus "is not here; he has risen," run away, shaking with terror, "for trembling and astonishment came upon them, and they said nothing to anyone, for they were terrified."

Matthew, who wrote his version with Mark's account before him, repeats the same story but changes the troubling ending. What Matthew says instead is that Mary and her companions did leave the tomb quickly, but did so "with fear and great joy." And instead of intending to say nothing, they immediately run "to tell his disciples." Then, while they were on the way, the risen Jesus himself actually met and spoke to them.

Luke, like Matthew, has Mark's story before him, but has something different in mind when he revises Mark. To make clear to the reader that women—*any* woman, much less Mary—could *not* be among Jesus' disciples, Luke initially leaves out Mark's comment that Mary, Salome, and the other Mary "followed Jesus" (since saying this could be understood to place them among the disciples). Then Luke deliberately contrasts "the twelve"—the men whom he says Jesus named as disciples—with those he calls "the women," whom he classifies among the needy, sick, and crazed members of the crowds that pressed themselves upon Jesus and his disciples. Thus Luke, unlike Mark, says that Mary came to Jesus driven by demonic spirits, and as only one among "some women who had been healed from evil spirits and from illnesses." Luke identifies these women as "Mary, called Magdalene, from whom seven demons had gone out, and Joanna . . . and Susanna, and many others," who, he concedes, "provided for [Jesus and his disciples] from their resources."

When Luke tells the story of Jesus' crucifixion and death, he changes three passages in which Mark had named Mary Magdalene, leaving her nameless in each of these stories, standing among an anonymous group he calls "the women."

Only after the anonymous women, horrified at first to find Jesus' grave empty, testify about what they saw to "the eleven" (the inner circle that Luke had called "the twelve" until Judas Iscariot, who betrayed Jesus, had left them) does Luke name the women. For at this point, apparently, their witness matters to validate their testimony and he now names the three that he sees as the most prominent: Mary Magdalene, Mary the mother of James and Joseph, and Joanna. Although Luke, like John, sometimes speaks positively about "the women," we may wonder why, at other times, he denigrates Mary and downplays her role.

Now, thanks to the recent discovery of *other* ancient gospels—gospels not included in the New Testament, and which remained virtually unknown for nearly two thousand years—we may be able to understand what Luke had in mind. For these other gospels, found translated into Coptic in Egypt, originally had been written earlier, in Greek, like the New Testament gospels. Scholars debate *when* they were written, but generally agree that most of them come from the first two centuries of the Christian movement. What we find in these discoveries is surprising: *every one of the recently discovered sources that mention Mary Magdalene*—sources that include the Gospel of Mary Magdalene, the Gospel of Thomas, the Gospel of Philip, the Wisdom of Faith, and the Dialogue of the Savior—unanimously picture Mary as one of Jesus' most trusted disciples. Some even revere her as his *foremost* disciple, Jesus' closest confidant, since he found her capable of understanding his deepest secrets. We can see that Luke apparently did not want to acknowledge that some of those he had simply called "the women" previously were actually regarded as disciples themselves. Although in this introduction we cannot discuss these remarkable texts in detail, let us briefly look at each of these in turn.

First, the Gospel of Mary Magdalene pictures Mary taking a leading role among the disciples. Finding the male disciples terrified to preach the gospel after Jesus' death since they feared that they, too, would be arrested and killed, Mary stands up to speak and encourages them, "turning their hearts to the good." When Peter, acknowledging that "the Lord loved you more than other women," asks Mary to "tell us what he told you" secretly, Mary agrees. After she finishes, Peter, furious, asks, "Did he really speak privately with a woman, and not openly to us? Are we supposed to turn around and all listen to her? Did he love her more than us?" Distressed at his rage, Mary replies, "My brother Peter, what do you think? Do you think that I thought this up myself in my heart, or that I am lying about the Savior?" Levi breaks in at this point to mediate the dispute: "Peter, you have always been hot-tempered. Now I see you contending against the women like [our] enemies. But if the Savior made her worthy, who are you to reject her? Surely the Lord knew her very well; that is why he loved her more than us." The Gospel of Mary ends as the others agree to accept Mary's teaching, and the disciples, including Mary, go forth to proclaim the gospel.

Like the Gospel of Mary, the Gospel of Thomas pictures Mary as one of Jesus' disciples. Strikingly, it names only six disciples, not twelve, and two of these are women—Mary Magdalene and Salome, one of Mary's companions. Yet like the dispute between Peter and Mary in the Gospel of Mary Magdalene, several passages in the Gospel of Thomas indicate that at the time it was written, probably around 90–100 CE, the question of whether women could be disciples had already triggered explosive controversy. In saying 61, for example, Salome asks Jesus to tell her who he is: "Who are you, man, that you have come up on my couch, and eaten from my table?" Jesus answers, "I come from what is undivided"; that is, from the divine, which transcends gender. He thereby rejects what her question implies—that his identity involves primarily his being male, as hers does being female. Salome, instantly understanding what he means, recognizes that the same is true for her and immediately answers, "I am your disciple."

Here, too, however, as in the Gospel of Mary, Peter challenges and opposes the presence of women among the disciples. According to saying 114 in the Gospel of Thomas, Peter says to Jesus, "Tell Mary to leave us, for women are not worthy of [spiritual] life." But instead of dismissing Mary, as Peter insists, Jesus rebukes Peter and declares, "I will make Mary a living spirit," so that she—or any woman—may become as capable of spiritual life as any man would have been in first-century Jewish tradition.

We find yet another account of an argument in which Peter challenges Mary's right to speak among the disciples in the dialogue called

Wisdom of Faith. Here, after Mary asks Jesus several questions, Peter breaks in, complaining to Jesus that Mary is talking too much and so displacing the rightful priority of Peter and his brother disciples. Yet here, too, just as in the Gospel of Mary Magdalene and the Gospel of Thomas, Peter's attempt to silence Mary earns him a quick rebuke, this time from Jesus himself. Later, however, Mary admits to Jesus that she hardly dares to speak with him freely, because "Peter makes me hesitate; I am afraid of him, because he hates the female race." Jesus replies that whomever the Spirit inspires is divinely ordained to speak, whether man or woman.

This theme of conflict between Mary and Peter that we find in so many sources—conflict involving Peter's refusal to acknowledge Mary as a disciple, much less as a leader among the disciples—may well reflect what people knew and told about actual conflict between the two. We know, too, that since women often identified with Mary Magdalene, certain people in the movement told such stories about her—or against her—as a way of arguing about whether, or how, women could participate in their circles.

Note, for example, that the very writers who picture Peter as the disciple whom Jesus acknowledges as being their primary leader— namely, the authors of the gospels of Mark, Matthew, and Luke—are the same ones who picture Mary as no disciple at all, but simply as one of "the women," or, worse, in the case of Luke, someone who had been demon-possessed. What makes their accounts important historically, of course, is that these are three of the gospels that came to be included in the canon of the New Testament—often invoked, even now, to "prove" that women cannot hold positions of authority within Christian churches.

Let us note, too, how this works in reverse: every one of the sources that revere Mary as a leader among the apostles was excluded from the New Testament canon. When these texts came to be excluded—among them the Gospel of Mary Magdalene, the Gospel of Thomas, the Gospel of Philip, Wisdom of Faith, and the Dialogue of the Savior—many Christians excluded as well the conviction that women could—and should—participate in leading the churches.

The Dialogue of the Savior, another ancient text discovered with these other gospels, claims to recount a dialogue between the risen

Jesus and three disciples he chooses to receive special revelation—Matthew, Thomas, and Mary. Yet here, after each of the three engage in dialogue with Jesus, the Dialogue singles out Mary to receive the highest praise: "This she spoke as the woman who understood all things."

Finally, before turning to the fascinating studies that are found in this book, let us look at one of the most intriguing sources of all: the Gospel of Philip. This gospel shows how many early Christians saw Mary Magdalene—as Jesus' constant companion. Certain contemporary readers have taken this literally to mean that she was Jesus' lover and wife. It is true that the Gospel of Philip pictures her as Jesus' most intimate companion, and that the Greek term *syzygos* (companion) can suggest sexual intimacy. Plus, like the other sources we have looked at, the Gospel of Philip attests to a rivalry between Mary Magdalene and the male disciples:

> The companion of the Savior is Mary Magdalene. [But Christ loved] her more than [all] the disciples, and used to kiss her often on her [mouth]. The rest of the disciples were offended by this. They said to him, "Why do you love her more than all of us?" The Savior answered and said to them, "Why do I not love you as much as I love her?"

This statement, in which the Gospel of Philip pictures Mary as Jesus' companion, and perhaps even his partner, helped inspire one of Dan Brown's most controversial plot points in *The Da Vinci Code*. For the purposes of his fiction, Brown tends to take these suggestions literally. But had he gone on to read the rest of the Gospel of Philip, he would have seen that its author sees Mary Magdalene as a powerful *spiritual* presence, as one who manifests the divine as it appears in feminine form—above all as divine Wisdom, and the Holy Spirit.

When Israel's prophets and poets spoke of the divine *spirit* and *wisdom,* they recognized the feminine gender of Hebrew terms. The biblical Book of Proverbs speaks of wisdom as a feminine spiritual presence who shared with God the work of creation:

> The Lord created me at the beginning of his work . . . before the beginning of the earth; when there were no deep waters, I was brought forth . . . before the mountains had been shaped, I was there . . . when

he marked out the foundations of the earth, then I was beside him, like a master worker; and I was daily his delight, rejoicing before him always, rejoicing in his inhabited world, and delighting in the human race.

So the Gospel of Philip sees Mary as divine wisdom—*hokhmah* in Hebrew, *sophia* in Greek, both feminine terms—manifest in the world. Jewish mystical tradition often speaks of God's presence in the world not only as *wisdom,* but also as *shehkina,* as his *presence.* Over a thousand years after the Gospel of Philip was written, kabbalistic tradition, using the language of mystics throughout the world, would celebrate this feminine aspect of God as his divine bride.

Simultaneously, the Gospel of Philip celebrates Mary Magdalene as manifesting the divine spirit, which this gospel calls the "virgin who came down" from heaven. When Christians spoke of Jesus "born from a virgin," this author agrees—but refuses to take it literally. So some people, he says, take this literally to mean that Jesus' mother became pregnant apart from any man, apart from sexual intercourse. But this, he says, is the "faith of fools" who fail to comprehend spiritual matters (although, as we note, it can be seen in the birth narratives offered in the New Testament gospels of Matthew and Luke). Instead, continues the Gospel of Philip, Jesus was born physically, just as all humans, as the son of biological parents. The difference, says the author of this gospel, is that he was also "born again" in baptism—born spiritually to become the son of the Father above, and of the heavenly Mother, the Holy Spirit.

Many other texts discovered with Philip echo the same language. The Gospel of Truth, too, declares that grace restores us to our spiritual source, bringing us "into the Father, into the Mother, Jesus of the infinite sweetness." The Secret Book of John tells how the disciple John, grieving after Jesus' crucifixion, went out into the desert, filled with doubt and fear until suddenly "the whole creation shook, and I saw . . . an unearthly light, and in the light, three forms." As John watched, amazed, he heard the voice of Jesus coming forth from the light, speaking to him: "John, John, why do you doubt, and why are you afraid? I am the one who is with you always; I am the Father; I am the Mother; and I am the Son."

Startling as this may be at first glance, who else would we expect to find with the Father and the Son if not the divine Mother, the Holy Spirit? But this early formulation of the trinity apparently reflects the Hebrew term for spirit, *Ruah,* as a feminine being—a connotation lost when *spirit* was translated into the New Testament's language, Greek, in which the word becomes neuter.

Even this quick sketch suggests the wide range of characterizations and wealth of meanings the early Christians associated with Mary Magdalene, many of which the essays in this book explore and amplify. From the first century through our own time, poets, artists, and mystics have loved to celebrate this remarkable woman whom the Dialogue of the Savior celebrates as the woman "who understood all things." Now, through the research presented here, and through discussions now engaged, we may discover new aspects of Mary Magdalene—and, in the process, of ourselves.

Princeton, NJ
May 2006

1 Mary Magdalene

Outcast No More

Though pedantry denies,
It's plain the Bible means
That Solomon grew wise
While talking to his queens.

—W. B. YEATS

Mary Magdalene is a person, and a representative and symbolic person,
who has been part of the tradition since the very beginning. It's like having
a photograph in which one of the major images has been airbrushed out
and now we're seeing that the image has been there from the beginning,
and belongs as part of the tradition we know.

—ELAINE PAGELS

It has come to me, then, that one must sift through the nonsense and
hostility that has characterized thought and writing about Mary, to find
some images, shards, and fragments, glittering in the rubble.

—MARY GORDON

Our Fascination with
Mary Magdalene
Confessions of a Da Vinci Code *Fan*

BY DAN BURSTEIN

It was about 2:00 a.m. on a warm night in 2003. I had picked up *The Da Vinci Code* earlier that evening, and been speed-reading through its cliff-hanging chapters for several hours. I was utterly fascinated with this novel that was proving to be an intriguing murder mystery and, at the same time, a veritable treasure hunt through the myths, legends, and symbols of thousands of years of Western civilization.

When I came to the scene set in Leigh Teabing's library, where this fictional character explains his thesis that a woman is seated at the right hand of Jesus in Leonardo's *Last Supper*—and that this woman is supposed to be Mary Magdalene who, in turn, is supposed to be the partner and wife of Jesus, not to mention the mother of his child and therefore the embodiment of the Holy Grail—I couldn't resist going to my library and taking a new look at the *Last Supper*. Quietly, in the middle of the night, I pulled down the oversized coffee-table book of Leonardo's works that has been in my family for decades. I looked with new eyes at the familiar masterpiece. In the dim light, under the spell of Dan Brown's conspiratorial *Da Vinci Code* fictions, I discovered to my considerable surprise that what I had always thought to be the figure of John did indeed look like a woman.

That moment proved to be the beginning of my journey to sort out fact from fiction in *The Da Vinci Code* and to explore the scholarship, archaeological finds, and current thinking about how to interpret events and characters of the biblical era.

When I went to my local Barnes & Noble bookstore the next morning, the first thing I discovered was the plethora of recent books about Mary Magdalene. In addition, I found a whole world of books on many topics in which Mary Magdalene figured prominently and in surprising ways: the bestselling *Gnostic Gospels* by Elaine Pagels as well as the works of Karen King, Margaret Starbird, Susan Haskins, Lynn

Picknett, and Tim Freke. And dozens of other titles, from the *Nag Hammadi Library* to *Holy Blood, Holy Grail,* that had been drawing attention for the last three decades. There was Robert Graves on the white goddess, Riane Eisler on the symbols of the chalice and the blade, and Nikos Kazantzakis's novel depicting Jesus' dream about Mary Magdalene as he died on the cross, as I would soon come to know.

As I would soon come to know, in the seventies musical *Jesus Christ Superstar,* the Mary Magdalene character sang the hit song, *I Don't Know How to Love Him.* Odetta performed a fascinating version of the old folk song, *John Henry,* in which the lyrics tell that the heroic John Henry character was married to Mary Magdalene. In the mid-1990s, I learned, there were only a handful of events celebrating Mary Magdalene's official saint day (July 22) in the United States. By last year, that number had grown to more than three hundred. In short, people were thinking about alternative interpretations of the Mary Magdalene story long before there was a *Da Vinci Code.*

Most of us, however, weren't even aware that the Mary Magdalene story was undergoing reinterpretation until *The Da Vinci Code* became a global phenomenon. It has been purchased as a book by more than sixty million people over the past several years, and seen as a movie by several hundred million more. Whatever the critical opinion of *The Da Vinci Code,* it has become one of the defining cultural works of the early years of the third millennium.

From the very first moment of what soon became a fascinating journey—that night, as I read the novel, and as I gazed back through five hundred years of art history at Leonardo's masterwork—to the creation of *Secrets of the Code,* our internationally bestselling guidebook to the issues raised by *The Da Vinci Code,* one thing has been crystal clear to me: Mary Magdalene is the star of the show. Brown's novel became so popular and so controversial for multiple reasons. But if I had to give one reason that explains *The Da Vinci Code* phenomenon, I would say it lies in the novel's provocative arguments about Mary Magdalene (however speculative or fictive they may be) and the deep, resonant chord those ideas struck at that moment in global culture.

Dan Brown didn't originate any of the arguments and theses about Mary Magdalene that are critical to *The Da Vinci Code.* Instead, in creating his pop culture/intellectual stew he mixed in bits and pieces of ideas and arguments that came from the works of those who had spent the last several decades working on new biographies and new ideas about Mary Magdalene. His sources ranged from the occult to Ivy League academics; from mythic folklore to archeological finds, and even to outright frauds and hoaxes. He synthesized and compressed these stories. He stretched and twisted them to make them fit his very compelling plot. In doing so, he helped make Mary Magdalene the new "It" girl of the twenty-first century. Incidentally, he also shone a laser beam back in time on her role as the "It" girl of the first century as well.

Although *The Da Vinci Code* is fundamentally "just a pop novel" filled with fact and fiction, speculation and storytelling, it has nevertheless become the new centerpiece of popular knowledge about Mary Magdalene and the wellspring of today's debates about the historical Jesus, the meaning of the alternate gospels, the role of women in the church, Gnosticism, and the differing trends of thought in the early Christian movement. Even leading academics in the field who are annoyed by *The Da Vinci Code*'s errors and confusions feel compelled to address the arguments in the novel—because they know that it is the novel, and not serious scholarly work, that has attracted the interest and sparked the imagination of millions upon millions of people. Indeed, *The Da Vinci Code* weaves into the physical package of a book hundreds of strands of ideas and arguments that connect it to the spiritual reawakening occurring at the beginning of this new millennium.

At this time of great uncertainty, new religious and spiritual winds are blowing forcefully throughout the world. The experience of living in the twenty-first century is one that highlights for many people the apparent absence of a just and loving God. On the one hand, we live in a world where terrible things happen—from Rwanda to Darfur, from the tsunami to Katrina, ours is a world of widespread political violence, massive natural catastrophes, unexpected disease epidemics, intolerance, and corruption. Sexual abuse and violence continue to erupt within families, communities, and even the church. At the same time, our world has generated amazing material wealth. It has produced immense and profound new scientific discoveries. And it has broken down almost every barrier and every taboo. In the process of building this new world order and freeing postmodern global citizens from the strictures of religion, many people have become separated from their traditional roots and beliefs. Our culture, however rich, productive, and enjoyable, is increasingly vulgar, excessively commercial, and alienating.

In the face of these contradictions, many different religious and spiritual responses have arisen. Traditional religious belief is experiencing a towering revival, no matter the form—from Islamic fundamentalism to Orthodox Judaism to Opus Dei to born-again Protestant evangelism. But while orthodoxy gains adherents, new religions and new spiritual directions of all types are also proving appealing. It is estimated that some two hundred new religions are created in America each year. In our popular culture, this new religiosity is reflected in a continuum of works that runs from Mel Gibson's *The Passion of the Christ* to Dan Brown's *The Da Vinci Code*.

In *The Passion of the Christ,* we are told, in effect: This is exactly the way it was two thousand years ago. We know what happened. It happened just the way traditional scripture says it happened, and we are going to use the powerful tools of modern Hollywood filmmaking to make you feel that you, too, witnessed these apocalyptic events. You will leave the theater with a new commitment to a traditional belief in Jesus and a traditional understanding of the Christian message.

At the other end of the continuum, *The Da Vinci Code* says, in effect: Everything you were told about what happened two thousand years ago is probably wrong. You were never told about some of the most important things, like who Mary Magdalene really was. You should question everything, because powerful people are conspiring to conceal the real history. Those called heretics are the true believers; those who call others heretics are the false prophets.

In *The Da Vinci Code*'s interpretation, Roman pagan emperors, the enemies of Jesus, later hijacked his movement, turned his philosophy inside out, and recast Christianity as the hierarchal, patriarchal, imperialistic state religion of their empire. Along the way, they edited out the role of women as priestesses and prophetesses; they excised the spirit of the goddess and the union of the duality of male and female that had been central to certain religious cults in Egypt, Greece, and elsewhere in the eastern Mediterranean. The Romans overturned the revolutionary anti-materialism of Jesus in favor of using Christianity to justify the accumulation of power and wealth. Rather than encourage the self-actualization embedded in such documents as the Gnostic Gospel of Thomas and Gospel of Mary, they used their approved and accepted gospels to keep serfs, slaves, and soldiers in their place. They eradicated the search for self-knowledge and the ability to approach God individually, superimposing on the simple, unmediated religion of Jesus the infrastructure of priests and popes, churches, confessionals, cathedrals, and crusades. They denounced as heresy the mystery traditions and the Gnostic practices of seeking ever-deeper knowledge of the sacred from within. And they replaced what was a diverse, evolving religious movement with the dogma of flawed and contradictory gospel accounts they declared to be the true word of God.

As *The Da Vinci Code* tells it, Mary Magdalene symbolizes all that was ripped from the heart of Jesus' revolutionary vision. She embodies all the wisdom and knowledge tragically lost to future generations. In the novel, keeping the secret of Mary alive also symbolizes the potential to bring Christian faith back to its true spiritual principles. It is no surprise that some people have taken *The Da Vinci Code* far more seriously than an action-adventure beach book should be. The novel is constructed as a romantic grail quest on the order of a Joseph Campbell–style "hero's journey" to find what has been lost, to slay the demons and dragons of adversity, and to recover the heroine's true identity, thus restoring her to her rightful place. Like Carl Jung's archetypal feminine spirit of the *anima,* Mary Magdalene animates the novel. Whether or not Mary Magdalene is in the *Last Supper,* and whether or not Leonardo da Vinci thought of her as the Holy Grail, she is definitely the Holy Grail of *The Da Vinci Code.*

Much has been made of the sloppy historical errors in *The Da Vinci Code,* of the way its author plays fast and loose with matters of faith, theology, and religious practices, and his seeming inability to discern what for most intellectuals is a clear bright line dividing the factual from the fictional. While all these criticisms are valid to one extent or another, they miss the point. For one thing, it is difficult to get worked up over criticism that *The Da Vinci Code* is an unholy amalgam of fact and fiction when such criticism comes from those who fail to recognize that the same problem is inherent in religious scriptures— Gnostic, Jewish, Christian, or otherwise. For me, the weaving of fact and fiction until they are almost indistinguishable poses no more or less of a logical problem in determining how to react to the story told in *The Da Vinci Code* than it does in determining how to react to the stories told in the Bible.

But perhaps more relevant to us here is the value, and even the validity, of *The Da Vinci Code* at a certain level of abstraction. If you step back, ignore the erroneous details, cardboard characters, sometimes laughable dialogue, and over-the-top plot elements for a moment, and focus on the big picture, you begin to see that *The Da Vinci Code* does a reasonably good job of conveying at least some of the big ideas about Mary Magdalene that pioneering scholars, theologians, and feminists have been articulating for the last several decades.

In *The Da Vinci Code,* we learn most importantly what Mary Magdalene was *not:* she was not a prostitute, repentant or otherwise. Even the self-styled keepers of religious purity—those who have attacked the numerous perceived affronts to theology and history they see in *The Da Vinci Code*—have generally not attacked Dan Brown's "shocking" premise that Mary Magdalene was not the repentant prostitute that the Roman Catholic Church described from the time of Pope Gregory the Great in 591 until 1969. It was only amid the storms of the 1960s and all the other profound changes in church policy that the Vatican itself made a small set of changes in certain documents and recommended scripture readings for her saint's day that disassociated Mary Magdalene from the harlotized image that had dominated the official church story since the time of Pope Gregory I.

Of course, spending 1,378 years institutionalized in Western consciousness as a prostitute has had certain lingering effects. My personal experiences at Catholic services are limited but, as recently as the mid-1990s, I heard a priest deliver a sermon on the meaning of Jesus forgiving the sins of Mary Magdalene, the prostitute. This was almost three decades after the church had supposedly corrected the record.

The Da Vinci Code vision of Mary Magdalene, however radical for the public culture at large, was already commonplace to students in America's leading divinity schools in the 1970s and 1980s, where the alternative scriptures found at Nag Hammadi in Egypt in 1945 were the subject of intense debate and brilliant doctoral dissertations. Those who read Elaine Pagels's pathbreaking book, the *Gnostic Gospels,* and other similar revolutionary accounts of Mary Magdalene, the historical Jesus, and the Gnostic movement were similarly enlightened. Still, among the billion Christians in the world in 2003, statistically very few were aware that Mary Magdalene's biography no longer included a stint as a streetwalker. Unaware, that is, until they encountered *The Da Vinci Code* that year. I find it more than ironic that an obscure novelist from a small town in New Hampshire, now routinely attacked by some as a heretic and blasphemer himself, is responsible for informing far more people of the church's efforts to correct Mary Magdalene's record than the Vatican itself.

Pope Gregory's portrayal of St. Mary from Magdala as the penitent sinner was based on his decision to conflate three distinct female characters referenced within the same gospel passage—Mary Magdalene, Mary of Bethany, and an unnamed woman known only as the "sinner from the city"—and declare them to be one person: Mary Magdalene. In doing so, whether intentionally or not, he changed the Christian (for which you could also read: Western) world's attitude toward Mary Magdalene, women, and sexuality for centuries to come.

Was Gregory's conflation of the three women a simple Dark Ages error of transcription, made in the effort to simplify the story for an illiterate audience and standardize the official canon? Was it a conscious attempt to debase Mary Magdalene's reputation and, in doing so, eviscerate the history of female prophets and leaders in the church? Was it part of a philosophical argument to portray sexuality as a moral vice, with women as temptresses and prostitutes, and therefore the sources of sin? Or was it a way of suggesting the universality and totality of Jesus' capacity for forgiveness, such that even a former prostitute—if she repented—could become a member of the inner circle of the son of God?

In the end, of course, the answers to these and many other questions now being asked by scholars are speculative. Except to Dan Brown, who presumes to know the truth. *The Da Vinci Code* argues there was a deliberate, purposeful conspiracy afoot. In the novel's scenario, Pope Gregory was a conscious opponent of Mary Magdalene's legacy and the inheritor of a male tradition that began with St. Peter and continued through Constantine and the early church fathers such as Irenaeus, Tertullian, and Origen. All these men were the willing tools of a church conspiracy to denigrate Mary, obliterate her central role in the Jesus story, and cut Christianity off from the ancient influences of the sacred feminine she represented. In this context, *sacred feminine* means everything from the sacredness of sexuality and the life-giving power of sex, fertility, and birth to the special nature of female intuition and women's superior access to divine knowledge.

Moving from the sacred to the profane, *The Da Vinci Code* goes on to suggest that Mary ends up cast as history's most famous prostitute, rather than as history's most famous wife and mother, in order to cover up all traces of what amounted to a political coup d'état: Peter, seeking control over the movement for himself, refused to allow a woman's leadership. This coup, according to the novel, explains Peter's threatening gestures and the sharp knife pointed toward the "Mary" figure in *The Last Supper*. It may also explain the reason why the Gospel of Matthew contains a rather awkward and out of context utterance from Jesus, from whence Peter derives his legitimacy: "You are Peter and upon this rock I will build my church." Some scholars think this sentence sticks out like a sore thumb and is a much later addition made to bolster Peter's claim to be the standard-bearer of the Jesus movement, as opposed to, and in place of, Mary.

Next we travel from the profane back to the sacred: *The Da Vinci Code* goes on to suggest that, fearing Peter's threats as much as the Roman soldiers, Mary—the woman Jesus was accustomed to "kiss frequently on the [mouth]" according to the tantalizing words of the Gospel of Philip, the woman to whom Jesus confided his deepest knowledge and most penetrating visions—escapes to France. She is pregnant with his child when she flees the tumult of the post-crucifixion Holy Land. This child from her marriage to Jesus is the real holy blood that she holds in her womb, making her the ultimate bodily chalice—the Holy Grail. Numerous French legends, especially popular during the medieval period, do, indeed, tell stories about Mary Magdalene and a child, or children, arriving on French shores in a small boat without sail and without oars. Mary lives out her days in various locations in the south of France, some of which have claimed to preserve relics of her bones and strands of her famous red hair.

Moving on from the sublime to the almost definitely ridiculous, *The Da Vinci Code* then spins a legendary tale of the offspring of Jesus and Mary seeding a royal bloodline, their child intermarrying with those who go on to become the Merovingian kings of France, the bloodline continuing to this day. All of this highly charged history is said to be rediscovered by the Knights Templar during their occupation of the ruins of the Temple of Solomon for a few brief years during the Crusades. But popes and emperors instigate the massacre and persecution of the Templars on Friday the thirteenth, in October 1307, because these medieval knights have come to know and understand the powerful story of Mary Magdalene and her bloodline, and therefore have to be murdered for fear the secret will get out. The secret continues to be documented and maintained, however, by the so-called grand masters of the Priory of Sion, whose ranks are said to have included a pantheon of great European geniuses. These men— and they are almost all men, which is a bit surprising for an allegedly feminist-tinged cult—know the truth about Mary Magdalene, worship her as a goddess figure, and even engage in the ancient Greek mystery practice of *hieros gamos* (sacred sex) to keep their commitment to the sacred feminine alive. From Leonardo, whose *Last Supper* is supposed to show Mary Magdalene as the Holy Grail, to Disney's *Little Mermaid* (Ariel keeps an image of Mary Magdalene on her undersea dresser), *The Da Vinci Code* claims there is a whole world out there that knows the secret of Mary Magdalene and keeps hiding it in plain sight in the hopes of getting the rest of us to notice.

After three years of studying the source materials for *The Da Vinci Code,* as well as all the controversies and speculations it has provoked, I am reasonably convinced of the following propositions:

One: As I indicated above, when Dan Brown insists that Mary Magdalene is *not* a prostitute and that there is no indication in the earliest scriptures or the early years of the Christian movement to support an interpretation of her as a repentant prostitute, he is historically correct and in the mainstream of the best and most important scholarly work done on this subject in the last half century.

Two: I am equally certain that almost everything in *The Da Vinci Code* having to do with Mary Magdalene as the Holy Grail, or as the chalice responsible for mothering a still traceable bloodline from two thousand years ago, as well as almost everything having to do with a deliberate conspiracy by the Catholic Church to cover all this up, and/or a sustained multi-century effort by an alleged Priory of Sion to keep the truth about Mary Magdalene alive—all of this is far more fanciful than factual. While the success of the novel demonstrates that these elements make compelling and memorable storytelling, I find it hard to assign any historical credibility to these parts of *The Da Vinci Code*. I am quite certain that the Priory of Sion, for example, is a mid-twentieth-century hoax cooked up by Pierre Plantard and his nostalgic, right-of-center royalist friends in France. It is also my considered view that Leonardo da Vinci was a grand master of nothing except the arts and ideas of the Renaissance. The dramatic conspiracy theories and occult-infused parts of *The Da Vinci Code* are extremely interesting on the level of myth and metaphor, archetype and symbolic narrative. But it is important to note that these parts of the story—and in particular this version of who Mary Magdalene was—is not derived from facts, historical evidence, or even serious scholarly speculation.

Three: The more complex and nuanced areas of *The Da Vinci Code* concern not the prostitute that Mary Magdalene wasn't, nor the postmodern conspiracy victim she has become for some. The more interesting questions about Mary Magdalene have to do with who she really was (or at least who she really might have been) and the role she might actually have played in the life and times of Jesus, the role attributed to her in early Christian history by certain Gnostic groups, and the reasons she has emerged today as so central to so many facets of new spiritual thinking. Just as *The Da Vinci Code* was the source from which many readers heard for the first time that Mary Magdalene was not a prostitute, it is also the source from which many readers first learned of the existence of alternative gospels and scriptures besides Matthew, Mark, Luke, and John and the other accepted books of the New Testament. The importance of these alternative scriptures is, in part, that they give more airtime to Mary Magdalene than the accepted gospels do. Indeed, in the alternative texts she has her "own" Gospel of Mary (to my mind, not actually written by Mary Magdalene, but rather written by later Gnostic thinkers, attempting to capture her spirit, wisdom, and story). And it is certainly of significance that in the alternative texts she is called the "companion" of Jesus (from an ancient Greek word that was sometimes used to mean "spouse") and is said to be "frequently" kissed by him, whether on the mouth or elsewhere.

But to me, the greatest significance of the link between the Gnostic Gospels and Mary Magdalene may lie in the relevance of this type of spirituality to our times. To today's loose but rapidly growing neo-gnostic movement there appears to be a more Zen-like, more profound, more spiritual wisdom in the Gnostic Gospels than in traditional Christian theology. There is much more searching to understand the mysteries and magic of life, more sense of the sacred. The Gnostics seemed to have emphasized the processes of self-discovery and self-actualization as lying at the heart of morality and religion. And although extremely contradictory things are said about women in the Gnostic texts, at least a strong pro-feminine trend seems to be one thread running through many of these documents.

In this context, it is interesting to note the "revolution within the revolution" that is now going on in Mary Magdalene studies. Having been so recently rehabilitated from fourteen centuries of identity theft, what identity should Mary assume now? There are those who think that merely making her an important figure in the Jesus movement again—the "apostle to the apostles," as she is sometimes referred to in traditional Christian parlance—is not good enough. Some think she should be seen as a goddess, or at least that stories about her should be interpreted as mythic representations of the spirit of the goddess in eastern Mediterranean culture.

There are those who think Dan Brown's view of Mary as being married to Jesus and the mother of his child is too confining a role (i.e., "Mrs. Jesus") for this deeply spiritual, independent woman who embodies the essence of the sacred feminine principle. Some say she should be seen as fully equal with Jesus in the creation of the Christian revolution. Others think it is not exotic enough to see her as a wealthy Jewish woman from the fishing village of Magdala on the Sea of Galilee, but suggest instead that she was a black woman from a town, also called Magdala, in Ethiopia—perhaps explaining the Cult of the Black Madonna, which is particularly strong in those parts of France where legend holds Mary Magdalene lived after the death of Jesus.

A few Mary Magdalene experts are even unhappy with the idea of taking the role of prostitute away from her. Some evidence exists that so-called temple prostitutes inhabited certain places of religious worship in Egypt, Greece, Israel, and elsewhere in the eastern Mediterranean. These temple prostitutes performed sacred sex rites with kings, princes, warriors, and religious leaders, anointing males with their goddess-like powers through these acts of *hieros gamos.* By bestowing their female gifts, the temple prostitutes caused the men to be successful in the hunt and in battle, in attracting rain for the crops, or in predicting the future. The association of Mary Magdalene with prostitution, a handful of feminist scholars argue, is a corrupted allusion to this glorious goddess-like history of powerful women in the ancient world.

As I discovered wandering among the many titles in Barnes & Noble on that morning in 2003—and as I have continued to discover by reading many of the hundreds of new books and articles about Mary Magdalene published in recent years—Mary Magdalene is like a twenty-first-century Rorschach test for attitudes about women, gender, sexuality, religion, Christianity, the historical Jesus, spirituality, knowledge, self-discovery, intuition, and what is truly sacred and profane in our world. The reality is that Mary Magdalene—like Jesus, Moses, Buddha, Confucius, and virtually all popular icons of religious belief and faith—has become whoever we want her to be.

Who Was Mary Magdalene?

BY JAMES CARROLL

"The whole history of western civilization is epitomized in the cult of Mary Magdalene," begins James Carroll in this provocative essay. Carroll is a former priest, author of 10 novels, columnist for *The Boston Globe,* and author of *Constantine's Sword* and other nonfiction titles. His thesis here is that from the original documents that become the New Testament to the filming of *The Da Vinci Code,* Mary Magdalene's image has been repeatedly conscripted, contorted, and contradicted. But through it all, he says, the essential question has gone largely ignored: who was she?

Carroll's essay sets out to provide an answer by noting that the confusions which have swirled around Mary Magdalene start with the gospels themselves. These, he reminds readers, grew out of "what scholars commonly call the 'telephone game' character of oral tradition," meaning that while the writers of these gospels might agree that she appeared at key events, such as the Crucifixion and Resurrection, they differ on what happened—especially in the subsequent retelling. For example, when, in the garden near the empty tomb, the risen Jesus encounters Mary Magdalene, he says to her, "Don't cling to me." This, says Carroll, is a phrase that rings true for a Jesus who in most biblical accounts is "remembered as treating women with respect, and as equals in his circle." But this interpretation soon began to be subtly altered, Carroll says, and, as with every narrative related to Mary Magdalene, erotic details start to loom large. Thus begins the invention of Mary Magdalene as the repentant prostitute—a manipulation, he says, carried out by men, for men: "A celibate's vision conjured for celibates." But as elements of this religious movement moved from challenging misogyny to confirming it, one result was significant changes in the Mary Magdalene story. Mary, says Carroll, "went from being an important disciple whose superior status depended on the confidence Jesus himself had invested in her, to a repentant whore whose status depended on the erotic charge of her history and the misery of her stricken conscience."

In this piece, a former priest blends his knowledge of biblical thinking with his journalist's eye for detail to paint a nuanced version of Mary's history.

The whole history of western civilization is epitomized in the cult of Mary Magdalene. For many centuries the most obsessively revered of saints, this woman became the embodiment of Christian devotion, which was defined as repentance. Yet she was only elusively identified in Scripture, and has thus served as a scrim onto which a succession of fantasies has been projected. In one age after another her image was reinvented, from prostitute to sibyl to mystic to celibate nun to passive helpmeet to feminist icon to the matriarch of divinity's secret dynasty. How the past is remembered, how sexual desire is domesticated, how men and women negotiate their separate impulses; how power inevitably seeks sanctification, how tradition becomes authoritative, how revolutions are co-opted; how fallibility is reckoned with, and how sweet devotion can be made to serve violent domination— all these cultural questions helped shape the story of the woman who befriended Jesus of Nazareth.

Who was she? From the New Testament, one can conclude that Mary of Magdala (her hometown, a village on the shore of the Sea of

Galilee) was a leading figure among those attracted to Jesus. When the men in that company abandoned him at the hour of mortal danger, Mary of Magdala was one of the women who stayed with him, even to the Crucifixion. She was present at the tomb, the first person to whom Jesus appeared after his Resurrection and the first to preach the "Good News" of that miracle. These are among the few specific assertions made about Mary Magdalene in the Gospels. From other texts of the early Christian era, it seems that her status as an "apostle," in the years after Jesus' death, rivaled even that of Peter. This prominence derived from the intimacy of her relationship with Jesus, which, according to some accounts, had a physical aspect that included kissing. Beginning with the threads of these few statements in the earliest Christian records, dating to the first through third centuries, an elaborate tapestry was woven, leading to a portrait of St. Mary Magdalene in which the most consequential note—that she was a repentant prostitute—is almost certainly untrue. On that false note hangs the dual use to which her legend has been put ever since: discrediting sexuality in general and disempowering women in particular.

Confusions attached to Mary Magdalene's character were compounded across time as her image was conscripted into one power struggle after another, and twisted accordingly. In conflicts that defined the Christian Church—over attitudes toward the material world, focused on sexuality; the authority of an all-male clergy; the coming of celibacy; the branding of theological diversity as heresy; the sublimations of courtly love; the unleashing of "chivalrous" violence; the marketing of sainthood, whether in the time of Constantine, the Counter-Reformation, the Romantic era, or the Industrial Age—through all of these, reinventions of Mary Magdalene played their role. Her recent reemergence in a novel and film as the secret wife of Jesus and the mother of his fate-burdened daughter shows that the conscripting and twisting are still going on.

But, in truth, the confusion starts with the Gospels themselves.

In the gospels several women come into the story of Jesus with great energy, including erotic energy. There are several Marys—not least, of course, Mary the mother of Jesus. But there is Mary of Bethany, sister of Martha and Lazarus. There is Mary the mother of James and Joseph, and Mary the wife of Clopas. Equally important, there are three un-named women who are expressly identified as sexual sinners—the woman with a "bad name" who wipes Jesus' feet with ointment as a signal of repentance, a Samaritan woman whom Jesus meets at a well, and an adulteress whom Pharisees haul before Jesus to see if he will condemn her. The first thing to do in unraveling the tapestry of Mary Magdalene is to tease out the threads that properly belong to these other women. Some of these threads are themselves quite knotted.

It will help to remember how the story that includes them all came to be written. The four Gospels are not eyewitness accounts. They were written 35 to 65 years after Jesus' death, a jelling of separate oral traditions that had taken form in dispersed Christian communi-ties. Jesus died in about the year a.d. 30. The Gospels of Mark, Matthew and Luke date to about 65 to 85, and have sources and themes in common. The Gospel of John was composed around 90 to 95 and is distinct. So when we read about Mary Magdalene in each of the Gospels, as when we read about Jesus, what we are getting is not history but memory—memory shaped by time, by shades of emphasis and by efforts to make distinctive theological points. And already, even in that early period—as is evident when the varied accounts are measured against each other—the memory is blurred.

Regarding Mary of Magdala, the confusion begins in the eighth chapter of Luke:

> Now after this [Jesus] made his way through towns and villages preaching, and proclaiming the Good News of the kingdom of God. With him went the Twelve, as well as certain women who had been cured of evil spirits and ailments: Mary surnamed the Magdalene, from whom seven demons had gone out, Joanna the wife of Herod's steward Chuza, Susanna, and several others who provided for them out of their own resources.

Two things of note are implied in this passage. First, these women "provided for" Jesus and the Twelve, which suggests that the women were well-to-do, respectable figures. (It is possible this was an attri-bution, to Jesus' time, of a role prosperous women played some years later.) Second, they all had been cured of something, including Mary Magdalene. The "seven demons," as applied to her, indicates an ailment (not necessarily possession) of a certain severity. Soon enough, as the blurring work of memory continued, and then as the written Gospel was read by Gentiles unfamiliar with such coded language, those "demons" would be taken as a sign of a moral infirmity.

This otherwise innocuous reference to Mary Magdalene takes on a kind of radioactive narrative energy because of what immediately precedes it at the end of the seventh chapter, an anecdote of stupendous power:

> One of the Pharisees invited [Jesus] to a meal. When he arrived at the Pharisee's house and took his place at table, a woman came in, who had a bad name in the town. She had heard he was dining with the Pharisee and had brought with her an alabaster jar of ointment. She waited behind him at his feet, weeping, and her tears fell on his feet, and she wiped them away with her hair; then she covered his feet with kisses and anointed them with the ointment.
>
> When the Pharisee who had invited him saw this, he said to himself, "If this man were a prophet, he would know who this woman is that is touching him and what a bad name she has."

But Jesus refuses to condemn her, or even to deflect her gesture. Indeed, he recognizes it as a sign that "her many sins must have been forgiven her, or she would not have shown such great love." "Your faith has saved you," Jesus tells her. "Go in peace."

This story of the woman with the bad name, the alabaster jar, the loose hair, the "many sins," the stricken conscience, the ointment, the rubbing of feet and the kissing would, over time, become the dramatic high point of the story of Mary Magdalene. The scene would be explicitly attached to her, and rendered again and again by the greatest Christian artists. But even a casual reading of this text, however charged its juxtaposition with the subsequent verses, suggests that the two women have nothing to do with each other—that the weeping anointer is no more connected to Mary of Magdala than she is to Joanna or Susanna.

Other verses in other Gospels only add to the complexity. Matthew gives an account of the same incident, for example, but to make a different point and with a crucial detail added:

> Jesus was at Bethany in the house of Simon the leper, when a woman came to him with an alabaster jar of the most expensive ointment, and poured it on his head as he was at table. When they saw this, the disciples were indignant. "Why this waste?" they said. "This could have been sold at a high price and the money given to the poor." Jesus noticed this. "Why are you upsetting the woman?" he said to them. . . . "When she poured this ointment on my body, she did it to prepare me for burial. I tell you solemnly, wherever in all the world this Good News is proclaimed, what she has done will be told also, in remembrance of her."

This passage shows what Scripture scholars commonly call the "telephone game" character of the oral tradition from which the Gospels grew. Instead of Luke's Pharisee, whose name is Simon, we find in Matthew "Simon the leper." Most tellingly, this anointing is specifically referred to as the traditional rubbing of a corpse with oil, so the act is an explicit foreshadowing of Jesus' death. In Matthew, and in Mark, the story of the unnamed woman puts her acceptance of Jesus' coming death in glorious contrast to the (male) disciples' refusal to take Jesus' predictions of his death seriously. But in other passages, Mary Magdalene is associated by name with the burial of Jesus, which helps explain why it was easy to confuse this anonymous woman with her.

Indeed, with this incident both Matthew's and Mark's narratives begin the move toward the climax of the Crucifixion, because one of the disciples—"the man called Judas"—goes, in the very next verse, to the chief priests to betray Jesus.

In the passages about the anointings, the woman is identified by the "alabaster jar," but in Luke, with no reference to the death ritual, there are clear erotic overtones; a man of that time was to see a woman's loosened hair only in the intimacy of the bedroom. The offense taken by witnesses in Luke concerns sex, while in Matthew and

Mark it concerns money. And, in Luke, the woman's tears, together with Jesus' words, define the encounter as one of abject repentance.

But the complications mount. Matthew and Mark say the anointing incident occurred at Bethany, a detail that echoes in the Gospel of John, which has yet another Mary, the sister of Martha and Lazarus, and yet another anointing story:

Six days before the Passover, Jesus went to Bethany, where Lazarus was, whom he had raised from the dead. They gave a dinner for him there; Martha waited on them and Lazarus was among those at table. Mary brought in a pound of very costly ointment, pure nard, and with it anointed the feet of Jesus, wiping them with her hair.

Judas objects in the name of the poor, and once more Jesus is shown defending the woman. "Leave her alone; she had to keep this scent for the day of my burial," he says. "You have the poor with you always, you will not always have me."

As before, the anointing foreshadows the Crucifixion. There is also resentment at the waste of a luxury good, so death and money define the content of the encounter. But the loose hair implies the erotic as well.

The death of Jesus on Golgotha, where Mary Magdalene is expressly identified as one of the women who refused to leave him, leads to what is by far the most important affirmation about her. All four Gospels (and another early Christian text, the Gospel of Peter) explicitly name her as present at the tomb, and in John she is the first witness to the Resurrection of Jesus. This—not repentance, not sexual renunciation—is her greatest claim. Unlike the men who scattered and ran, who lost faith, who betrayed Jesus, the women stayed. (Even while Christian memory glorifies this act of loyalty, its historical context may have been less noble: the men in Jesus' company were far more likely to have been arrested than the women.) And chief among them was Mary Magdalene. The Gospel of John puts the story poignantly:

It was very early on the first day of the week and still dark, when Mary of Magdala came to the tomb. She saw that the stone had been moved away from the tomb and came running to Simon Peter and the other disciple, the one Jesus loved. "They have taken the Lord out of the tomb," she said, "and we don't know where they have put him."

Peter and the others rush to the tomb to see for themselves, then disperse again.

Meanwhile Mary stayed outside near the tomb, weeping. Then, still weeping, she stooped to look inside, and saw two angels in white sitting where the body of Jesus had been, one at the head, the other at the feet. They said, "Woman, why are you weeping?" "They have taken my Lord away," she replied, "and I don't know where they have put him." As she said this she turned around and saw Jesus standing there, though she did not recognize him. Jesus said, "Woman, why are you weeping? Who are you looking for?" Supposing him to be the gardener, she said, "Sir, if you have taken him away, tell me where you have put him, and I will go and remove him." Jesus said, "Mary!" She knew him then and said to him in Hebrew, "Rabbuni!"—which means Master. Jesus said to her, "Do not cling to me, because I have not yet ascended to . . . my Father and your Father, to my God and your God." So Mary of Magdala went and told the disciples that she had seen the Lord and that he had said these things to her.

As the story of Jesus was told and told again in those first decades, narrative adjustments in event and character were inevitable, and confusion of one with the other was a mark of the way the Gospels were handed on. Most Christians were illiterate; they received their traditions through a complex work of memory and interpretation, not history, that led only eventually to texts. Once the sacred texts were authoritatively set, the exegetes who interpreted them could make careful distinctions, keeping the roster of women separate, but common preachers were less careful. The telling of anecdotes was essential to them, and so alterations were certain to occur.

The multiplicity of the Marys by itself was enough to mix things up—as were the various accounts of anointing, which in one place is the act of a loose-haired prostitute, in another of a modest stranger preparing Jesus for the tomb, and in yet another of a beloved friend named Mary. Women who weep, albeit in a range of circumstances, emerged as a motif. As with every narrative, erotic details loomed large, especially because Jesus' attitude toward women with sexual histories was one of the things that set him apart from other teachers of the time. Not only was Jesus remembered as treating women with respect, as equals in his circle; not only did he refuse to reduce them to their sexuality; Jesus was expressly portrayed as a man who loved women, and whom women loved.

The climax of that theme takes place in the garden of the tomb, with that one word of address, "Mary!" It was enough to make her recognize him, and her response is clear from what he says then: "Do not cling to me." Whatever it was before, bodily expression between Jesus and Mary of Magdala must be different now.

Out of these disparate threads—the various female figures, the ointment, the hair, the weeping, the unparalleled intimacy at the tomb—a new character was created for Mary Magdalene. Out of the threads, that is, a tapestry was woven—a single narrative line. Across time, this Mary went from being an important disciple whose superior status depended on the confidence Jesus himself had invested in her, to a repentant whore whose status depended on the erotic charge of her history and the misery of her stricken conscience. In part, this development arose out of a natural impulse to see the fragments of Scripture whole, to make a disjointed narrative adhere, with separate choices and consequences being tied to each other in one drama. It is as if Aristotle's principle of unity, given in Poetics, was imposed after the fact on the foundational texts of Christianity.

Thus, for example, out of discrete episodes in the Gospel narratives, some readers would even create a far more unified—more satisfying—legend according to which Mary of Magdala was the unnamed woman being married at the wedding feast of Cana, where Jesus famously turned water into wine. Her spouse, in this telling, was John, whom Jesus immediately recruited to be one of the Twelve. When John went off from Cana with the Lord, leaving his new wife behind, she collapsed in a fit of loneliness and jealousy and began to sell herself to other men. She next appeared in the narrative as the by-then notorious adulteress whom the Pharisees thrust before Jesus. When Jesus refused to condemn her, she saw the error of her ways. Consequently, she went and got her precious ointment and spread it on his feet, weeping in sorrow. From then on she followed him, in chastity and devotion, her love forever unconsummated—"Do not cling to me!"—and more intense for being so.

Such a woman lives on as Mary Magdalene in Western Christianity and in the secular Western imagination, right down, say, to the rock opera *Jesus Christ Superstar,* in which Mary Magdalene sings, "I don't know how to love him . . . He's just a man, and I've had so many men before . . . I want him so. I love him so." The story has timeless appeal, first, because that problem of "how"—whether love should be eros or agape; sensual or spiritual; a matter of longing or consumma-tion—defines the human condition. What makes the conflict univer-sal is the dual experience of sex: the necessary means of reproduction and the madness of passionate encounter. For women, the maternal can seem to be at odds with the erotic, a tension that in men can be reduced to the well-known opposite fantasies of the madonna and the whore. I write as a man, yet it seems to me in women this tension is expressed in attitudes not toward men, but toward femaleness itself. The image of Mary Magdalene gives expression to such tensions, and draws power from them, especially when it is twinned to the image of that other Mary, Jesus' mother.

Christians may worship the Blessed Virgin, but it is Magdalene with whom they identify. What makes her compelling is that she is not merely the whore in contrast to the Madonna who is the mother of Jesus, but that she combines both figures in herself. Pure by virtue of her repentance, she nevertheless remains a woman with a past. Her conversion, instead of removing her erotic allure, heightens it. The misery of self-accusation, known in one way or another to every hu-man being, finds release in a figure whose abject penitence is the con-dition of recovery. That she is sorry for having led the willful life of a sex object makes her only more compelling as what might be called a repentance object.

So the invention of the character of Mary Magdalene as repentant prostitute can be seen as having come about because of pressures in-hering in the narrative form and in the primordial urge to give ex-pression to the inevitable tensions of sexual restlessness. But neither of these was the main factor in the conversion of Mary Magdalene's image, from one that challenged men's misogynist assumptions to one that confirmed them. The main factor in that transformation was, in fact, the manipulation of her image by those very men. The mutation took a long time to accomplish—fully the first 600 years of the Christian era.

Again, it helps to have a chronology in mind, with a focus on the place of women in the Jesus movement. Phase one is the time of Jesus himself, and there is every reason to believe that, according to his teaching and in his circle, women were uniquely empowered as fully equal. In phase two, when the norms and assumptions of the Jesus community were being written down, the equality of women is reflected in the letters of St. Paul (c. 50–60), who names women as full partners—his partners—in the Christian movement, and in the Gospel accounts that give evidence of Jesus' own attitudes and highlight women whose courage and fidelity stand in marked contrast to the men's cowardice.

But by phase three—after the Gospels are written, but before the New Testament is defined as such—Jesus' rejection of the prevailing male dominance was being eroded in the Christian community. The Gospels themselves, written in those several decades after Jesus, can be read to suggest this erosion because of their emphasis on the authority of "the Twelve," who are all males. (The all-male composition of "the Twelve" is expressly used by the Vatican today to exclude women from ordination.) But in the books of the New Testament, the argument among Christians over the place of women in the community is implicit; it becomes quite explicit in other sacred texts of that early period. Not surprisingly, perhaps, the figure who most embodies the imaginative and theological conflict over the place of women in the "church," as it had begun to call itself, is Mary Magdalene.

Here, it is useful to recall not only how the New Testament texts were composed, but also how they were selected as a sacred literature. The popular assumption is that the Epistles of Paul and James and the four Gospels, together with the Acts of the Apostles and the Book of Revelation, were pretty much what the early Christian community had by way of foundational writings. These texts, believed to be "inspired by the Holy Spirit," are regarded as having somehow been conveyed by God to the church, and joined to the previously "inspired" and selected books of the Old Testament to form "the Bible."

But the holy books of Christianity (like the holy books of Judaism, for that matter) were established by a process far more complicated (and human) than that.

The explosive spread of the Good News of Jesus around the Mediterranean world meant that distinct Christian communities were springing up all over the place. There was a lively diversity of belief and practice, which was reflected in the oral traditions and, later, texts those communities drew on. In other words, there were many other texts that could have been included in the "canon" (or list), but weren't.

It was not until the fourth century that the list of canonized books we now know as the New Testament was established. This amounted to a milestone on the road toward the church's definition of itself precisely in opposition to Judaism. At the same time, and more subtly, the church was on the way toward understanding itself in opposition to women. Once the church began to enforce the "orthodoxy" of what it deemed Scripture and its doctrinally defined creed, rejected texts—and sometimes the people who prized them, also known as heretics—were destroyed. This was a matter partly of theological dispute—If Jesus was divine, in what way?—and partly of boundary-drawing against Judaism. But there was also an expressly philosophical inquiry at work, as Christians, like their pagan contemporaries, sought to define the relationship between spirit and matter. Among Christians, that argument would soon enough focus on sexuality— and its battleground would be the existential tension between male and female.

As the sacred books were canonized, which texts were excluded, and why? This is the long way around, but we are back to our subject, because one of the most important Christian texts to be found outside the New Testament canon is the so-called Gospel of Mary, a telling of the Jesus-movement story that features Mary Magdalene (decidedly not the woman of the "alabaster jar") as one of its most powerful leaders. Just as the "canonical" Gospels emerged from communities that associated themselves with the "evangelists," who may not actually have "written" the texts, this one is named for Mary not because she "wrote" it, but because it emerged from a community that recognized her authority.

Whether through suppression or neglect, the Gospel of Mary was lost in the early period—just as the real Mary Magdalene was beginning to disappear into the writhing misery of a penitent whore, and as women were disappearing from the church's inner circle. It reappeared in 1896, when a well-preserved, if incomplete, fifth-century copy of a document dating to the second century showed up for sale in Cairo; eventually, other fragments of this text were found. Only slowly through the 20th century did scholars appreciate what the rediscovered Gospel revealed, a process that culminated with the publication in 2003 of *The Gospel of Mary of Magdala: Jesus and the First Woman Apostle* by Karen L. King.

Although Jesus rejected male dominance, as symbolized in his commissioning of Mary Magdalene to spread word of the Resurrection, male dominance gradually made a powerful comeback within the Jesus movement. But for that to happen, the commissioning of Mary Magdalene had to be reinvented. One sees that very thing under way in the Gospel of Mary.

For example, Peter's preeminence is elsewhere taken for granted (in Matthew, Jesus says, "You are Peter and on this rock I will build my Church"). Here, he defers to her:

Peter said to Mary, "Sister, we know that the Savior loved you more than all other women. Tell us the words of the Savior that you remember, the things which you know that we don't because we haven't heard them."

Mary responded, "I will teach you about what is hidden from you." And she began to speak these words to them.

Mary recalls her vision, a kind of esoteric description of the ascent of the soul. The disciples Peter and Andrew are disturbed—not by what she says, but by how she knows it. And now a jealous Peter complains to his fellows, "Did [Jesus] choose her over us?" This draws a sharp rebuke from another apostle, Levi, who says, "If the Savior made her worthy, who are you then for your part to reject her?"

That was the question not only about Mary Magdalene, but about women generally. It should be no surprise, given how successfully the excluding dominance of males established itself in the church of the

"Fathers," that the Gospel of Mary was one of the texts shunted aside in the fourth century. As that text shows, the early image of this Mary as a trusted apostle of Jesus, reflected even in the canonical Gospel texts, proved to be a major obstacle to establishing that male dominance, which is why, whatever other "heretical" problems this gospel posed, that image had to be recast as one of subservience.

Simultaneously, the emphasis on sexuality as the root of all evil served to subordinate all women. The ancient Roman world was rife with flesh-hating spiritualities—Stoicism, Manichaeism, Neoplatonism—and they influenced Christian thinking just as it was jelling into "doctrine." Thus the need to disempower the figure of Mary Magdalene, so that her succeeding sisters in the church would not compete with men for power, meshed with the impulse to discredit women generally. This was most efficiently done by reducing them to their sexuality, even as sexuality itself was reduced to the realm of temptation, the source of human unworthiness. All of this—from the sexualizing of Mary Magdalene, to the emphatic veneration of the virginity of Mary, the mother of Jesus, to the embrace of celibacy as a clerical ideal, to the marginalizing of female devotion, to the recasting of piety as self-denial, particularly through penitential cults—came to a kind of defining climax at the end of the sixth century. It was then that all the philosophical, theological and ecclesiastical impulses curved back to Scripture, seeking an ultimate imprimatur for what by then was a firm cultural prejudice. It was then that the rails along which the church—and the Western imagination—would run were set.

Pope Gregory I (c. 540–604) was born an aristocrat and served as the prefect of the city of Rome. After his father's death, he gave everything away and turned his palatial Roman home into a monastery, where he became a lowly monk. It was a time of plague, and indeed the previous pope, Pelagius II, had died of it. When the saintly Gregory was elected to succeed him, he at once emphasized penitential forms of worship as a way of warding off the disease. His pontificate marked a solidifying of discipline and thought, a time of reform and invention both. But it all occurred against the backdrop of the plague, a doom-laden circumstance in which the abjectly repentant Mary

Magdalene, warding off the spiritual plague of damnation, could come into her own. With Gregory's help, she did.

Known as Gregory the Great, he remains one of the most influential figures ever to serve as pope, and in a famous series of sermons on Mary Magdalene, given in Rome in about the year 591, he put the seal on what until then had been a common but unsanctioned reading of her story. With that, Mary's conflicted image was, in the words of Susan Haskins, author of *Mary Magdalene: Myth and Metaphor,* "finally settled . . . for nearly fourteen hundred years."

It all went back to those Gospel texts. Cutting through the exegetes' careful distinctions—the various Marys, the sinful women— that had made a bald combining of the figures difficult to sustain, Gregory, standing on his own authority, offered his decoding of the relevant Gospel texts. He established the context within which their meaning was measured from then on:

> She whom Luke calls the sinful woman, whom John calls Mary, we believe to be the Mary from whom seven devils were ejected according to Mark. And what did these seven devils signify, if not all the vices?

There it was—the woman of the "alabaster jar" named by the pope himself as Mary of Magdala. He defined her:

> It is clear, brothers, that the woman previously used the unguent to perfume her flesh in forbidden acts. What she therefore displayed more scandalously, she was now offering to God in a more praiseworthy manner. She had coveted with earthly eyes, but now through penitence these are consumed with tears. She displayed her hair to set off her face, but now her hair dries her tears. She had spoken proud things with her mouth, but in kissing the Lord's feet, she now planted her mouth on the Redeemer's feet. For every delight, therefore, she had had in herself, she now immolated herself. She turned the mass of her crimes to virtues, in order to serve God entirely in penance.

The address "brothers" is the clue. Through the Middle Ages and the Counter-Reformation, into the modern period and against the

Enlightenment, monks and priests would read Gregory's words, and through them they would read the Gospels' texts themselves. Chivalrous knights, nuns establishing houses for unwed mothers, courtly lovers, desperate sinners, frustrated celibates and an endless succession of preachers would treat Gregory's reading as literally the gospel truth. Holy Writ, having recast what had actually taken place in the lifetime of Jesus, was itself recast.

The men of the church who benefited from the recasting, forever spared the presence of females in their sanctuaries, would not know that this was what had happened. Having created a myth, they would not remember that it was mythical. Their Mary Magdalene—no fiction, no composite, no betrayal of a once venerated woman—became the only Mary Magdalene that had ever existed.

This obliteration of the textual distinctions served to evoke an ideal of virtue that drew its heat from being a celibate's vision, conjured for celibates. Gregory the Great's overly particular interest in the fallen woman's past—what that oil had been used for, how that hair had been displayed, that mouth—brought into the center of church piety a vaguely prurient energy that would thrive under the licensing sponsorship of one of the church's most revered reforming popes. Eventually, Magdalene, as a denuded object of Renaissance and Baroque painterly preoccupation, became a figure of nothing less than holy pornography, guaranteeing the ever-lustful harlot—if lustful now for the ecstasy of holiness—a permanent place in the Catholic imagination.

Thus Mary of Magdala, who began as a powerful woman at Jesus' side, "became," in Haskins' summary, "the redeemed whore and Christianity's model of repentance, a manageable, controllable figure, and effective weapon and instrument of propaganda against her own sex." There were reasons of narrative form for which this happened. There was a harnessing of sexual restlessness to this image. There was the humane appeal of a story that emphasized the possibility of forgiveness and redemption. But what most drove the anti-sexual sexualizing of Mary Magdalene was the male need to dominate women. In the Catholic Church, as elsewhere, that need is still being met.

The Saintly Sinner
The Two-Thousand-Year Obsession with Mary Magdalene

BY JOAN ACOCELLA

If one needed more proof of Mary Magdalene's role as the "It" girl for the early twenty-first century—more, that is, than her role as the star of *The Da Vinci Code* novel and film, the bestselling book and movie of our time—then what better icing on the cake than to have her own lengthy profile in the hip, stylish *New Yorker* magazine?

That *New Yorker* piece, by Joan Acocella, published in early 2006, is one of the best introductions to the vast canvas of debate and discussion about Mary Magdalene that has yet been written, which is why we have included it here. Acocella's regular beat at the magazine is as dance critic—indeed, she is widely recognized as among the handful of people who have established dance criticism as a modern art form unto itself. Perhaps it is her exposure to dance and its powerful, primal, sometimes sacred, sometimes ecstatic, sometimes erotic, sometimes gender-bending role in human history that made her particularly sensitive to some of the nuances in the Mary Magdalene debate.

In any event, Acocella has written brilliantly about dance, but also about other subjects that have relevance to the Mary Magdalene debate. In her pathbreaking book about the early-twentieth-century American novelist Willa Cather, Acocella had to deal with a female figure to whom many varying and contrary roles had been ascribed—populist leftist, conservative defender of a romantic era gone by, classical Christian idealist, empowered, independent woman, and sex-obsessed lesbian, to name just a few. While perfectly capable of decoding the symbolism in Cather's work, Acocella also rejected overinterpretation of symbolic content, noting that for certain critics, "No tree can grow, no river flow, in Cather's landscapes without this being a penis or menstrual period." In the modern discussion of Mary Magdalene, she will encounter what may be a similar trend of overreaching in interpreting the symbolic content in texts and artworks.

Acocella has also written extensively about psychology, including a book-length work specifically on women and multiple personality disorder. Her critique of the ease with which complex psychological syndromes are labeled and misunderstood, especially in women, may also have given her a special insight into those biblical references to Jesus casting out the "seven demons" from Mary Magdalene.

Many of the experts we have called upon for *Secrets of Mary Magdalene* are also cited by Acocella in her essay. These include Bruce Chilton, Susan Haskins, Katherine Jansen, Marvin Meyer, Elaine Pagels, Jane Schaberg, and Margaret Starbird, among others. The views of each of the aforementioned experts are well represented elsewhere in *Secrets,* so our readers need only look at our Table of Contents to find a fuller elaboration of their views.

The Catholic Church presumably has enough on its hands right now without worrying about popular fiction, but the Holy See cannot have failed to notice that Dan Brown's "The Da Vinci Code," a novel claiming that Jesus was married, has been on the *Times* best-seller list for almost three years. (Its message will soon spread more widely: the paperback is due out next month, and the movie version will be released in May.) Brown is by no means the first to have suggested that Christ had a sex life—Martin Luther said it—but the most notorious recent statement of the theory was a 1982 book, "Holy Blood, Holy Grail," by Michael Baigent, Richard Leigh, and Henry Lincoln. "Holy Blood," which was one of the main sources for "The Da Vinci Code," proposes that after the Crucifixion Jesus' wife, with at least one of their children, escaped to France, where their descendants married into the Merovingian dynasty and are still around today. Nobody knows this, though, because, according to the authors' scenario, the truth has been kept under wraps for a thousand years by a secret society called the Priory of Sion. The book offers a fantastically elaborated conspiracy theory—involving Leonardo da Vinci, Isaac Newton, Victor Hugo, and Jean Cocteau (all "grand masters" of the Priory of Sion), plus Emma Calvé and various others—that cannot be briefly summarized, but the upshot is that the Priory may now be ready to go public with its story. The authors warn that the organization may intend to set up a theocratic United States of Europe, with a descendant of Jesus as its priest-king but with the actual business of government being handled by some other party—the Priory of Sion, for example.

And who is the woman who caused all this trouble? Who married Jesus and bore his offspring and thereby laid the foundation for the overthrow of post-Enlightenment culture? Mary Magdalene.

Mary Magdalene gets only fourteen mentions in the New Testament. Luke and Mark describe her as the subject of one of Jesus' exorcisms—he cast "seven devils" out of her—and as one of several women who followed him. In all four Gospels, she is present at the Crucifixion. Nevertheless, her role remains minuscule, until, all of a sudden, after Christ's death, it becomes hugely magnified. Each of the Gospels tells the story a little differently, but, basically, the Magdalene, either alone or with other women, goes to the tomb on the third day to anoint Jesus' body, and it is to her (or them) that an angel or Christ himself announces that he is risen from the dead, and instructs her to go tell this to his disciples. That command gave the Magdalene a completely new standing. The Resurrection is the proof of the truth of Christian faith. As the first person to announce it, Mary Magdalene became, as she was later designated, "the apostle to the apostles."

But there was a problem. Why her? Why a person who previously had been referred to only in passing? Above all, why a woman?

The fact that all four Gospels say that the Magdalene was the one strongly suggests that this indeed is what people said had happened. If so, however, she needed to be improved upon. That was easy enough. Today, with so many Biblical literalists around, we have to fuss about what Scripture actually says, but in the early centuries after Christ's death such questions were less important, because most people couldn't read. The four Gospels, for the most part, are collections of oral traditions. Once they were written down, they served as a guide for preaching, but only as a guide. Preachers embroidered upon them freely, and artists—indeed, everyone—made their own adjustments. The English scholar Marina Warner makes this point in her book on the Virgin Mary, "Alone of All Her Sex" (1976). As Warner shows, many of the details of the Nativity so familiar to us from paintings and hymns and school pageants—"the hay and the snow and the smell of animals' warm bodies"—are not in the New Testament. People made them up; they wanted a better story. Likewise, they made up a better Mary Magdalene.

Jesus, for his time and place, was notably unsexist. In Samaria, when he talked with the woman at the well—this is the longest personal exchange he has with anyone in the Bible—his disciples "marvelled"; a Jewish man did not, in public, speak to a woman unrelated to him. In another episode, in Luke, Jesus is dining with Simon the Pharisee when a "woman in the city," a "sinner"—presumably a prosti-

tute—enters the house, washes Jesus' feet with her tears, dries them
with her hair, kisses them, and then anoints them with balm from a
jar. Simon says to Christ that if he can accept that tribute from such a
person then he is surely not a prophet. Christ answers that the "sinner" has shown him more love than Simon has.

According to some scholars, Christ's equanimity regarding gender
was honored in some early Christian communities, where women
served as leaders. But by the second century, as the so-called "orthodox Church" consolidated itself, the women were being shunted
aside, along with the thing that they were increasingly seen to stand
for: sex. It was not until the twelfth century that all Roman Catholic
priests were absolutely required to be celibate, but the call for celibacy began sounding long before, and the writings of the Church fathers were very tough on sex. By the fourth century, Christ's mother
was declared a virgin. Chastity became the ideal; women, the incite-
ment to unchastity, were stigmatized.

How, then, could the Resurrection announcement have been made
to one of that party? In what seems, in retrospect, an ingenious solution, Luke's "sinner" was said to be the Magdalene. This made a kind
of sense. Luke first introduces the Magdalene by name only two
verses after the story of the "sinner." Then, there were the "seven devils" that Christ cast out of the Magdalene. What devils would a woman
have besides concupiscence? Finally, unlike many other females in the
Gospels—Mary the mother of James, Mary the wife of Cleophas,
etc.—Mary Magdalene, when she is named, is identified not by a relationship with a man but by her city, Magdala, a prosperous fishing
village on the Sea of Galilee. Thus the Magdalene was probably a
woman who lived on her own, a rare and suspect thing in Jewish society of the period. Add to that the fact that Magdala had a reputation as
a licentious city, and that the Magdalene apparently had money (Luke
says that she ministered to Jesus out of her "substance"), and we arrive
at the conclusion: Mary Magdalene was the sinner who washed
Christ's feet with her tears.

One wonders, at first, how it would help the Church's new chastity
campaign for the first witness of the Resurrection to be a prostitute.
But, as noted, the Church was pretty much stuck with the Magda-

lene. Furthermore, the keynote of Jesus' ministry was humility. A god who chose to be born in a stable might also decide to announce his Resurrection to a prostitute. And Luke's sinner was not just a prostitute; she was a repentant prostitute, shedding tears so copious that they sufficed to clean the feet of a man who had just walked the dusty road to the Pharisee's house. But the crucial gain of grafting this woman onto the Magdalene was that it gave the Magdalene some fullness as a character while also lowering her standing. The conflation was already being made by the third or fourth century, and in the sixth century it was ratified in a sermon by Pope Gregory the Great. Mary Magdalene, one of the few independent women in the New Testament, became a whore.

As such, she was a tremendous success. Europe, once it was converted to Christianity, was not content to have all those holy people in the Bible confine their activities—or, more important, their relics—to the Middle East. And so the Magdalene, among others, was sent west. After the Crucifixion, it was said, infidels placed her in a rudderless boat and pushed it out to sea, in full confidence that it would capsize. But, piloted by the hand of God, the Magdalene's bark arrived at Marseilles, whereupon she undertook a career of strenuous evangelism and converted southern Gaul. Eventually, however, she tired of preaching and retreated to a cave in a mountain near Marseilles, where she wept and repented her foul youth. She wore no clothes; she was covered only by her long hair (or, in some paintings, by an appalling sort of fur). Nor did she take any food. Once a day, angels would descend to carry her to Heaven, where she received "heavenly sustenance," and then fly her back to her grotto. This went on for thirty years. Then, one day, her friend Maximin, the bishop of Aix, found her in his church levitating two cubits above the floor and surrounded by a choir of angels. She promptly expired.

This is a summary of various stories, but most of them can be found in "The Golden Legend," a collection of saints' lives written by a thirteenth-century Dominican, Jacobus de Voragine, who later became the archbishop of Genoa. After the Bible, "The Golden Legend" is said to have been the most widely read text of the Middle Ages. On its basis, sermons were composed, plays written, altarpieces painted, stories told by the hearth fire. The Magdalene, according to some sources, became France's most popular saint after the Virgin Mary. In the eleventh century, an especially fervent Magdalene cult grew up in the Burgundian town of Vézelay, whose church claimed to have her relics—an assertion undoubtedly influenced by the fact that Vézelay was on one of the main routes to Santiago de Compostela, in Spain, Christendom's third most important pilgrimage site (after Jerusalem and Rome). Vézelay soon became another important pilgrimage site, substantially benefitting the local economy. In 1267, the monks of Vézelay had the Magdalene's relics dug up from beneath the church—an event attended by the king.

Some people, though, wondered how the Magdalene's body got to Burgundy, when the legend said that she had died in Provence. The Provençal Prince Charles of Salerno, a devout man, was especially pained by this relocation. And so in 1279, only twelve years after the Vézelay exhumation, a new set of Magdalene relics was discovered, in the crypt of St. Maximin, near Aix-en-Provence. St. Maximin became a competing pilgrimage site. As time passed, five whole bodies of the Magdalene, together with spare parts, were discovered in various lo-cales. Her saint's day, July 22nd, became a major holiday. In Viviers, it was said, a peasant who dared to plow his fields on that day was struck by lightning. Numerous professions—winegrowers, garden-ers, sailors, barrelmakers, weavers—took her as their patron saint. Church after church was named after her, as were many baby girls.

How did she become such a favorite? In recent years, there have been a number of so-called "reception studies" of the Magdalene, his-tories of how her image changed over time. Two good examples are Susan Haskins's "Mary Magdalene: Myth and Metaphor" (1993) and Katherine Jansen's "The Making of the Magdalen: Preaching and Pop-ular Devotion in the Later Middle Ages" (2001). According to these writers, it was partly because urbanization in the twelfth century caused a rise in prostitution that the Magdalene, that well-known whore, became so prominent at this time. Preachers stressed—indeed, invented—her wayward youth. She was beautiful, they said, with masses of red-gold hair, and she was an heiress; she lived in a cas-tle. But she had no male relative to arrange a suitable marriage for her, and so she abandoned herself to *luxuria,* or lust. Day by day, she

sat at her mirror, applying cosmetics and perfumes, the better to en-
snare innocent young men. Soon, according to the medieval preachers (who apparently regarded wealth as no deterrent to prostitution),
she began to sell her body—a lesson, they declared, to all young
women tempted by *luxuria*. Jansen quotes a thirteenth-century friar
who put himself in the mind of such a girl, sitting before her looking
glass: "She pulls her dress to one side to reveal bare skin, loosens her
sash to reveal her cleavage. Her body is still home, but in God's eyes
she is already in a brothel." Preaching was only part of the campaign.
All across Europe, institutions were set up, under the aegis of Mary
Magdalene, for prostitutes willing to repent their ways.

While she was being held up as a warning, however, the young
Magdalene was also an object of admiration. She was chosen as the
patron saint not just of barrelmakers and gardeners but also of glove-
makers, perfume manufacturers, and hairdressers—in other words,
the purveyors of all those fripperies which led her to her fall. (She
also became the patroness of prostitutes. In Beaucaire, on her saint's
day, the local whores ran a race in her honor.) Apart from her beauty,
what appealed to people was her reputed emotionalism. In medieval
representations of the Crucifixion and the Deposition, the Magdalene
typically appears mad with grief. Often, her mouth is open; she is
screaming. Her hair flies; her cloak flies. She kisses Christ's bleeding
feet. She knows that it is for her sins, too, that Christ has died. Compared with her, the Virgin is usually far more composed. The period
between the eleventh and thirteenth centuries was the high tide of the
worship of the Virgin Mary. According to Marina Warner, all the human failings that were removed from the Virgin were displaced onto
the Magdalene, and each cult grew thereby. But, when it came to guilt
over one's trespasses, the Magdalene, not the stainless Virgin, was the
saint people needed. As Haskins puts it, she was "a model for mere
mortals who could sin and sin again, and yet through repentance still
hope to reach heaven."

This shifting image of the Magdalene—sometimes a pinup, sometimes a sermon—stabilized in the Renaissance. As the great scholar
Mario Praz put it, she became a "Venus in sackcloth." In a painting by

Titian from 1530–35, we see her, in her grotto, gazing up to Heaven. At the same time, between the strands of her flowing hair, we see the pearly breasts that in her life—as in all lives, Titian is saying, complicitly—were the cause of sin. But the equipoise held only briefly. In the sixteenth century came the Protestants' challenge to the sacrament of penance, which, through the sale of indulgences, had been so abused by the Church. The Counter-Reformation therefore placed strong emphasis on penance, and as part of that cleanup campaign we get notably chaste images of the Magdalene, such as Georges de La Tour's famous series, with the pious saint now fully clothed and with a skull by her side—a reminder of how beauty ends up. The Magdalene also figured heavily in the devotional poetry of the English seventeenth century. Richard Crashaw's "Saint Mary Magdalene, or The Weeper" (1646) pictures Christ "followed by two faithful fountains"—the Magdalene's two eyes—"two walking baths; two weeping motions; / Portable, and compendious oceans." This poem, together with other, like-minded representations, was sufficient to establish the word "maudlin," a derivative of Magdalene, in the English language, with the meaning of "mawkishly lachrymose."

With the Enlightenment, Mary Magdalene, like other holy matters, suffered some neglect. But in nineteenth-century England she was again invoked by reformers, for prostitution was epidemic in Victorian London. More convents were established for rescued prostitutes in the Magdalene's name. (Actually, as Haskins explains, they were halfway houses, where the girls did needlework while awaiting a modest marriage or a job in a shop.) The very word "magdalen" was widely used to mean "fallen woman." At the end of the century, a great wave of prurience broke over European art; in that, too, the Magdalene had a place, and not in a devotional guise. In some paintings, she appears buck naked—full body, frontal—without even the pseudo cover of her hair. She appealed also to the "black Symbolism" of the time. In an 1888 engraving by the Belgian Symbolist Félicien Rops, she crumples over, without a stitch on, at the foot of the Cross, as she embraces Christ's feet.

In the twentieth century, the Magdalene received more exalted tributes. Rainer Maria Rilke, Marina Tsvetaeva, and Boris Pasternak all devoted beautiful poems to her. They are love poems, about her relationship with Christ, but they are grave and nuanced. Popular representations of the Magdalene in our time have been less subtle. Tim Rice and Andrew Lloyd Webber's 1971 musical "Jesus Christ Superstar" portrayed her frankly as a whore, in love with Jesus. In Franco Zeffirelli's 1977 TV movie "Jesus of Nazareth," we first see the Magdalene as she is finishing up with a client. In Martin Scorsese's "The Last Temptation of Christ" (1988), based on Nikos Kazantzákis's novel, the Magdalene becomes a prostitute only because Jesus, her childhood companion, rejected her sexually. Not that he wanted to. Later, on the Cross, he is assailed by a fantasy (vividly filmed) of bedding her and conceiving a child. Apparently, this is too much for her; she dies. So, after his fantasy, does Jesus. Mel Gibson's "The Passion of the Christ" uses the Magdalene only as a weeper at the Crucifixion, but it is a rare case.

In fact, Gibson's film is the only one in this catalogue that conforms to current Church doctrine. In the nineteen-sixties, the Church finally caught up with some of the more fantastic of the saints' lives, and in 1969 the liturgical calendar was revised. A number of long-honored saints' days were dropped, for lack of evidence that the saint in question had ever existed. (That included St. Christopher, to the grief of many people still wearing his medal.) Other saints had their entries rewritten, and the Magdalene's was one. She was no longer a prostitute, the Church said, and the Song of Songs, that sexy poem, was no longer to be read on her saint's day. As the film record demonstrates, some people wanted no part of this cleaned-up Magdalene. Others began asking how she got sullied in the first place.

The crucial development in Magdalene scholarship was the discovery of the Nag Hammadi library. Biblical scholars had understood for a long time that the orthodox Church was just the segment of the Church that won out over competing Christian sects, notably the so-called Gnostics. But, apart from what could be gathered from the Church fathers' denunciations of these supposed heretics, students of early Christianity knew little about them. Then, one day in December of 1945, an Arab peasant named Muhammad Ali al-Samman drove his camel to the foothills near the town of Nag Hammadi, in Upper Egypt, to collect fertilizer for his fields, and as he dug he unearthed a clay jar about three feet high. Hoping that it might contain treasure, he broke it open and, to his disappointment, found only a bunch of papyrus books, bound in leather. He took the books home and tossed them in a courtyard where he kept his animals. In the weeks that followed, his mother used some pages from the books to light her stove; other pages were bartered for cigarettes and fruit. But eventually, after a long journey through the hands of antiquities dealers, black marketers, smugglers, and scholars, Samman's find was recognized as a priceless library of Gnostic writings—thirteen codices, containing fifty-two texts—recorded in Coptic (an early form of Egyptian) in the fourth century but translated from Greek originals dating from between the second and fourth centuries. In time, the books were confiscated by the Egyptian government and moved to the Coptic Museum in Cairo, where they remain today. (They were published in 1972–77.) Actually, they were not the first Gnostic texts to be discovered. Others had come to light in the late eighteenth and nineteenth centuries, but most of them were not published until after the time of the Nag Hammadi discovery.

Anyone who wants to know the full, surprising contents of the Gnostic Gospels—with a Demiurge (not God) creating the universe, and the story of the Fall told from the point of view of the serpent, a friend to mankind—should consult Elaine Pagels's classic "The Gnostic Gospels" (1979) or Marvin Meyer's "The Gnostic Discoveries: The Impact of the Nag Hammadi Library" (HarperSanFrancisco; $21.95), which was published last fall. Meyer is more descriptive, Pagels more analytic. What is important for this story is that Mary Magdalene is a central figure in the Gnostic Gospels and, compared with her European legend, an utterly new character. Not only is she not a prostitute; she is an evangelical hero and Christ's favorite disciple.

The key text is the Gospel of Mary. As the treatise opens, the Risen Christ is preaching to his disciples. There is no such thing as sin, he says. Also, the disciples, in their quest for the divine, should follow no authorities, heed no rules, but simply look within themselves. Having delivered these lessons, Jesus departs, leaving his disciples quaking with fear. No sin? No rules? If they teach these doctrines, they may end up getting killed, like him. At that point, Mary Magdalene takes over. "Do not weep or grieve or be in doubt," she tells the others. (This and the following quotations from the Gnostic texts are Meyer's translations.) Peter then says to the Magdalene that they all know Jesus loved her more than any other woman, and he asks her if there is anything that she learned privately from the Saviour. The Magdalene responds by describing a vision she had of the soul's ascent to truth—a story she shared with Jesus. (She adds his comments.) Four pages are missing from this passage, and some readers may not regret their loss. Accounts of Gnostic visions are sometimes like people's descriptions of their dreams: bizarre yet boring—and long. The Magdalene's story seems to have struck her audience that way. "Did he [Jesus] really speak with a woman in private, without our knowledge?" Peter now asks his brothers. "Should we all turn and listen to her? Did he prefer her to us?" Mary bursts into tears and asks Peter if he thinks she's lying. Another disciple, Levi, interrupts: "Peter, you always are angry. . . . If the Savior made her worthy, who are you to reject her?"

This text exemplifies the principle for which Gnosticism was named. In Greek, *gnosis* means "knowledge." To the Gnostic communities, it meant a kind of spiritual understanding—the goal of all believers—that was achieved only through intense self-examination, typically accompanied by visions. The Gospel of Mary shows the Magdalene as an expert in this practice. It also presents her as a leader, full of confidence and zeal. Another of the Gnostic texts, Pistis Sophia ("Faith Wisdom"), takes the form of a dialogue between Jesus and the disciples. Of the forty-six questions put to Jesus, thirty-nine come from the Magdalene. Peter finally complains that no one else has a chance to speak. Another feature, then, of the Gnostic portrait of the Magdalene is the quarrel between her and Peter. Jesus repeatedly defends her, and that is the final, critical point about the Gnostic Magdalene: Jesus' preference for her. In another Gospel, she is referred to as his "companion," whom he often kissed. Some readers have taken this to mean that she was his mistress or wife, but kissing was common among people in the Middle East at that time, and the companionship seems to be based on Jesus' conviction of her superior understanding. When the disciples ask him, "Why do you love her more than all of us?," he answers, uncomfortably, "If a blind person and one who can see are both in darkness, they are the same. When the light comes, one who can see will see the light, and the blind person will stay in darkness."

So, while the orthodox Church was busy eliminating women from positions of power, the Gnostic sects seem to have been following a different route. One of their texts says that Jesus had seven women as well as twelve men among his disciples. The Gnostic pantheon includes female divinities. But Exhibit A is the Magdalene: her leadership and Christ's endorsement of it. This is not to say that the Gnostic Gospels portray a gender-blind community. In another passage in which Peter complains about the Magdalene—"Mary should leave us," he says, "for females are not worthy of life"—Jesus replies, "Look, I shall guide her to make her male, so that she too may become a living spirit resembling you males. For every female who makes herself male will enter heaven's kingdom." This statement, a disappointment to many admirers of Gnosticism, has been explained by scholars as a reflection of the ancient belief, accepted even by the forward-thinking Gnostics, that women stood for earthly matters, while men were more in touch with the divine. Jesus is saying that his female disciples, despite their sex, will become spiritual. Peter clearly does not agree. So the authority of women was a point of conflict among the Gnostics, too.

We know how the orthodox Church—which, not incidentally, claimed its apostolic mission from Peter—solved this problem, and the fact that the Gnostic communities seem to have been solving it otherwise was one of the reasons that they were regarded as heretics. In any case, it was in the fourth century, at the moment when the orthodox Church was finally, after centuries of persecution, achieving stability, that the leaders of a Gnostic community near Nag Hammadi, apparently feeling that they were now in serious danger, put their most precious books in a jar and buried it in the hillside.

Their problem wasn't just women, though. As Elaine Pagels explains, the Church's whole effort at this time was to create an institution, and certain Gnostic principles—above all, the rejection of rules and hierarchies —were utterly incompatible with institutionalization.

Pagels also points out that Gnosticism, for all its egalitarianism, was elitist. To qualify, you had to set yourself, over a long course of study, to discovering the divine within yourself. This was not for everyone, and the orthodox Church wanted everyone. Accordingly, the Church did not ask people to search for the divine—their priest would tell them what the divine was—and it assured them that as long as they confessed certain prescribed articles of faith and observed certain simple rituals, they, too, could enter the Kingdom of Heaven. Without these reasonable, followable rules, Pagels writes, "one can scarcely imagine how the Christian faith could have survived."

Other writers have been less understanding. Feminist Bible scholarship began in the early nineteenth century and carried on quietly until the nineteen-sixties, when it acquired new force in the wake of Vatican II. Soon afterward came the publication of the Nag Hammadi library. The feminists had long suspected that the New Testament, together with its commentators, had downplayed women's contributions to the founding of Christianity. Here was the proof. Writings on the Magdalene exploded after 1975. Conveniently, this happened at the same time as the rise of postmodern literary theory, which held that all texts were unstable and porous, marked by "gaps" that the reader had to fill. If anything ever had gaps, it was the revised Magdalene. She wasn't a prostitute anymore, but what was she? Young scholars tried to figure out what happened to her story. To mention only two recent books, Ann Graham Brock, in "Mary Magdalene, the First Apostle: The Struggle for Authority" (2003), and Holly E. Hearon, in "The Mary Magdalene Tradition: Witness and Counter-Witness in Early Christian Communities" (2004), took on the New Testament Gospels, claiming that they suppressed the oral traditions descending from the Magdalene in favor of traditions descending from Peter's ministry.

But the most searching and passionately argued of the books in this category is "The Resurrection of Mary Magdalene: Legends, Apocrypha, and the New Testament" (2002), by Jane Schaberg, a professor at the University of Detroit Mercy. With tweezers, as it were, Schaberg goes through the New Testament, the Gnostic Gospels, and later writings to pull out and expose the textual maneuvers by which, in her words, the Magdalene was "replaced, appropriated, and left behind" by the orthodox Church. Between the first and fourth centuries, she believes, Christianity coalesced into a few broad traditions. One was Magdalene Christianity, whose goal was to put an end to the oppression of the world's powerless. Magdalene Christianity was egalitarian in its organization, like the Jesus movement in which it originated. In that campaign, Schaberg says, Jesus was "not hero or leader or God" but just a brother to his fellow-reformers. It was only after his death and supposed Resurrection that the focus shifted from the group to him alone, and that he was deified. Clearly, however, Schaberg sees him as having had special authority within the movement, for she proposes that he chose the Magdalene as his successor. That, she says, is what the Resurrection announcement was about. The Resurrection, to Jesus, meant the ethical renewal of the world, and in making the Resurrection announcement to the Magdalene he was passing this mission on to her. But, while the Magdalene and the communities she inspired were fulfilling this assignment, other traditions, notably those descending from Peter and Paul, were branching off in less egalitarian directions. Those were the traditions that won, and, lest anyone recall the woman who wanted to create a different sort of Church, they "murdered" her memory, by turning her into a harlot.

Schaberg says that all this is guesswork. That's fine by her. Since the nineteen-seventies, there has been a true paradigm shift in Biblical scholarship. Before, people thought that Christianity was a truth; even the reformers sought only a modification of that truth. But, with the publication of the Gnostic Gospels, abetted by postmodern theory, a number of young scholars came to regard early Christianity entirely differently—as a *process,* a vast, centuries-long argument among competing sects, during which certain choices were made. And, as these writers saw it, choices were still being made, which meant that any new proposals, however conjectural, were not only useful but essential. People don't have to worry about contradicting the New Testament, Schaberg says. That document was just a draft: "a collage of fragments, aborted ideas, blackouts, white spaces, instructions, verbal experimentations, doodles, dots." Earlier writers had also said that Christians had to make their own Christianity—and that it should be political. In the words of the Harvard theologian Elisabeth Schüssler Fiorenza, feminist reinterpretations were a good thing, a way to "develop and adjudicate our own Christological meaning-making in the face of violence and killing today." Fiorenza's views, cousin to "liberation theology" (she calls the Magdalene one of "the disappeared"), were embraced by many young Bible scholars. Schaberg describes herself as a "guerrilla exegete."

Not all the reformers have bared their teeth. In November, Doubleday brought out "Mary Magdalene: A Biography" ($23.95), by Bruce Chilton, an Episcopal priest and a professor of religion at Bard College. According to Chilton, the Magdalene was one of the "shaping forces of Christianity." Especially important, as he sees it, was her visionary experience, both in the Gnostic Gospels and in the Resurrection announcement, which he takes to be a subjective, not an objective, event. Chilton, then, is one of those who believe that they can advance a more modern, acceptable Christianity by questioning the existence of miracles. Many of the Catholic reformers, like Fiorenza and Schaberg, seem to be past that stage. They belong to a Church that *really* believes in miracles, and whatever skepticism they felt regarding those fantastic events appears to have been exhausted years ago. Schaberg, when confronted with the question of whether Christ underwent a bodily resurrection, refuses to make the call. "Who knows?" she says. "Who cares?" Chilton cares. To him, apparently, as to many of the older liberal clergy, miracles are a mumbo-jumbo separating the faithful from the true meaning of Scripture. And so, in his view, Lazarus was not raised from the dead. He was probably buried alive by mistake—Jesus rescued him. Likewise, it is only "resuscitation literalists" who believe that Christ underwent a bodily resurrection. If the tomb was empty, maybe somebody stole the body. Christ was a man, with an idea about love and justice, and we should follow his lead without bothering about those old stories. By now, however, such an argument seems, itself, an old story, of limited usefulness. Many, probably most, of the world's two billion Christians do believe in miracles, and want to. This makes life more interesting and serious to them. To mount reform on a denial of miracles seems futile and also—however unwittingly—unkind.

The Catholic reformers, from what I can tell, are not just more radical. They also seem more likely to spawn fringe groups such as "goddess worship." In 1993, Margaret Starbird, a good Catholic who never publishes anything without letting her pastor read it first, came out with her book "The Woman with the Alabaster Jar: Mary Magdalene and the Holy Grail." Starbird says that when she read "Holy Blood, Holy Grail" she was "shattered" by its claim that Jesus was married. She didn't reject it out of hand, though. She did seven years of research, and concluded that "Holy Blood" was right: Jesus was married to the Magdalene. Not only that, but the suppression of this secret—and of the "forgotten feminine" in general—had caused terrible trouble in the world: environmental pollution, child abuse, war. But now the divine goddess was fed up. Statues of the Virgin Mary "have been seen to shed tears in churches worldwide. . . . Even the stones cry out!" So do Disney movies. In "The Little Mermaid," Ariel's true identity is the "Lost Bride," the Magdalene. The forgotten feminine is on its way back.

Starbird goes beyond analysis; she writes a love story. Jesus was a tall, handsome fellow; the Magdalene was a shy Jewish maiden, accustomed to sitting in her garden and gazing at little birds. One day, they were introduced. "His dark eyes caressed her." We are taken through their wedding night, alas. Soon afterward, Jesus tells the Magdalene, now pregnant, that he has to go on a dangerous mission and that she must stay behind. "She buried her tears in the warmth of his shoulder." The academic feminists have very little patience with the Jesus-married-the-Magdalene plot. As Schaberg sees it, these stories are not about the Magdalene. They are about Jesus; they are an effort to make him a "real man," and not just for humanistic, Christ-is-your-friend reasons. (In the sixties, there were some naughty suggestions that maybe Jesus was gay.) Insofar as the love plot concerns the Magdalene, Schaberg writes, it is again demeaning, an attempt to convert this independent woman into a "normal" female. Starbird's book bears out that theory.

She is not the only one who has resorted to fiction. There have been quite a few novels about the Magdalene in the past few decades, and many of them, according to Susan Haskins, are reluctant to part with the Magdalene's reputation as a prostitute. The trend is to celebrate her as a sexually liberated woman. Behind this, of course, is second-stage feminism, but I think there is another motive as well, an effort to smuggle a little liveliness back into the Magdalene's story.

A problem for the Magdalene revival, or at least for the theologians, is that it has had to draw its reconfigured heroine from the austere philosophy of the Gnostics. A religion, in order to succeed, must offer a little fun: stories, symbols, rituals. The Catholic saints, however ill-founded their biographies, are a vivid group, each with a certain kind of hair and a certain hat, and accompanied by a lion or a dragon or something else interesting. They are like a collection of dolls or superheroes, or like the Hindu pantheon—full of color and variety. The New Testament, for the most part, gives the Magdalene no concrete life. The medieval legend filled that void, equipped her with a boat, a grotto, some friends. Take these things away, and you are back to zero. The Gnostic Gospels don't provide much of a personality for her, and what they do come up with is not endearing. The Gnostic Magdalene is a showy visionary. At one point, she responds to something Jesus has said by staring into the air for an hour. She is also a swot, the best student in class, constantly raising her hand. If I had been Peter, I would have complained, too. The feminists are of course right to point to her Gnostic virtues—the visionary faculty, the zeal—as an answer to the Church's demotion of her, and of all women. Still, we miss the red-gold hair, the ointment jar.

At one moment, however, the faceless Magdalene is given not just a face but a great, flaming personal drama. This is not in the Gnostic Gospels but in the New Testament, in John's account of the Resurrection announcement. Here the Magdalene goes to the tomb in darkness, before dawn, and she goes alone. We feel her hurry, her sense of danger. To her astonishment, she finds the stone rolled away. She runs back to the disciples and tells them, "They have taken away the Lord out of the sepulchre, and we know not where they have laid him." Peter and another disciple take over. They rush to the tomb; indeed, they race to see who can get there first. (This exemplary male competition became a favorite scene in medieval morality plays. In John's Gospel, it adds a bright little note of comedy to the otherwise dark tale.) When they arrive, they see that the Magdalene was right: the body is gone. They go back home, presumably baffled, but the Magdalene stays behind, weeping. She looks again into the tomb, and now she sees two angels dressed in white. They ask her why she is crying, and she repeats her simple complaint: "They have taken away my Lord, and I know not where they have laid him." Even with angels, she's still looking for the body. But then she turns around and sees another figure, who says to her, "Why weepest thou? Whom seekest thou?" The tomb is in a garden, and the Magdalene thinks this man must be the gardener. A third time—it's like a song—she repeats her complaint: "Sir, if thou have borne him hence, tell me where thou hast laid him." Now comes the stab through the heart. "Mary," the "gardener" says to her, and instantly she knows. "Rabboni" (roughly, "My dear rabbi"), she replies, and apparently she reaches out to him, because he says, "Touch me not." (This is the Latin Bible's famous phrase "Noli me tangere.") "But," he tells her, "go to my brethren, and say unto them, I ascend unto my Father." He then vanishes, and she is left by herself.

This scene is the New Testament's most powerful statement about the confrontation with death, about losing forever the thing you love. The setting is beautiful: the green garden, the morning light, the angels. Then we hear the cruel words: "Don't touch me." He was there; he had called her name; she had reached out to embrace him. Now she must stand back, let him go, and make her way alone. The young Bible scholars should have all our support, and we should agree with them that the energetic, far-seeing Magdalene of the Gnostic texts is good evidence that the Church should ordain women. But that is not the evidence of the Magdalene's authority on matters of the soul. John's story is the evidence.

Changing Our Perceptions
of Mary Magdalene

AN INTERVIEW WITH BRUCE CHILTON

Bruce Chilton, ordained Episcopal priest, writer, and Bernard Iddings Bell Professor of Religion at Bard College, wants to set the record straight: Mary Magdalene is not the second-class person who most of us have learned about. She is instead one of Christianity's creators. She is "the disciple who best appreciated Jesus' visionary teaching of the Resurrection," Chilton believes. "Without her, Christianity would have been entirely different. It is not even clear that its core faith in Jesus' victory over the grave could have emerged at all without Mary."

In this interview, Chilton argues that to begin to understand Mary Magdalene's important role properly, we should see her in the context of the Jewish tradition at the time—one in which women *did* have a place. Mary, like women elsewhere in the Near Eastern world, was a visionary who practiced the sacred ceremony of anointment and, like Jesus, expelled evil spirits or malignant forces through exorcism rituals.

Chilton, whose most recent book is *Mary Magdalene: A Biography* (see page 96 for an excerpt), concludes by sharing his thoughts about the importance of Mary Magdalene's vision and how her wisdom informs the Christian tradition as well as his own practice of it.

Biography is reconstruction, an effort that becomes particularly difficult when, as in the case of Mary Magdalene, there is no contemporaneous record, and layers and layers of controversial "renovation" have to be taken into account. Yet in your book Mary Magdalene: A Biography, *you attempt to do just that. How did you go about it?*

I think that one can take the information that does exist about Mary Magdalene within the gospels, and relate that contextually to life within early Judaism in her period. The three activities associated with Mary Magdalene in the gospels are exorcism, anointing, and vision. Those stories are very tightly connected to her, so they amount to our best data available about Mary Magdalene. Then we have to take those practices and relate them to what was going on among other Jewish practitioners of the time.

I took each story of an exorcism, for example, and compared that to other stories of exorcism in Jewish literature, and elsewhere

in the Near Eastern world. I applied a similar method to the understanding of anointing, which was widespread within the practice of
the Near East, and also to vision. And what I found was that all
three of these practices were especially associated with women
within the early Judaism of this time. The idea put forward by some
modern scholars that women had no place in the religious life of
Judaism is simply untrue.

I was able to document cases of other women who engaged in
the world of vision, who practiced anointing, and who were involved in exorcism. And by comparing their practices with Mary's,
we can see what's unusual about hers, and how those practices contributed to the rise of Christianity.

*If it is a misconception that women generally had no place in the religious
life of the time, are there things about Mary Magdalene that we might
equally have ignored, or refashioned to suit our perceptions?*

Mary Magdalene has been described as the "it" girl of modern theology, and with being "it" there naturally come a whole series of pro-
jections that tend to distort her actual contribution to the New
Testament. She has typically been referred to as a prostitute or even
as having had a sexual relationship with Jesus. Or there's the reverse:
the claim that we have to see her as entirely celibate from the moment of her conversion. What is clearly evident in both cases is our
continuing obsession with the question of Mary Magdalene's sexuality. Since the Middle Ages we have been asking, in one form or another: did she do it, or did she not? Unfortunately, what this means
is that what she *actually* contributed has been entirely ignored.

What we can say on the basis of the gospel tradition, quite cate-
gorically, is that Mary Magdalene was the first person to have a vision of Jesus raised from the dead after he was crucified, that Mary
Magdalene pioneered a sacrament of anointing that Jesus himself
authorized, and also that Mary Magdalene had the best knowledge
of how it was that Jesus dealt with evil impulses within the human
heart and conveyed that knowledge to others. That means that
Mary practiced three sacraments: exorcism, anointing, and vision,
which were foundational to early Christianity. And yet these are

The Four Marys of the New Testament

Mary, the mother of Jesus. She is the most important Mary in the canonical scripture. Her virginity symbolizes her service to God and fulfills the ancient prediction that the future messiah would be born of a virgin. Her attendance at the Crucifixion arguably demonstrates her willingness to submit to her holy Father's will.

Mary Magdalene. Her image as the "repentant sinner" has served neatly as a counterpoint to the Virgin Mary, the holy Mother. From her earliest role as a primary force in the interpretation of Jesus' teachings and the "apostle to the apostles," she was soon degraded. By the end of the first century she was cast as a rival to Peter, then shunted aside as a woman who could not be imagined as a leader in the Roman world, and, finally, by the sixth century, harlotized. She would mistakenly carry that label until 1969, when the Vatican at last reinterpreted her role.

Mary of Bethany. The sister of Martha and Lazarus. After Jesus raised Lazarus from the dead, the Gospel of John says this Mary lavishly anointed Jesus' feet with an expensive ointment and dried them with her hair. Her identity was melded with those of Mary Magdalene and the unnamed "sinner" from the city by Pope Gregory "the Great" in 591 AD.

The "woman of the city." By implication a prostitute, she is the nameless person in Luke 7:36–50 who also anoints Jesus. It is not until the following chapter that Luke introduces Mary Magdalene by name. But Pope Gregory nevertheless concluded that the sinner and the Magdalene were one and the same person. Church fathers, theologians, artists, and the yearly reading from Luke's condemnation of the sinner on Mary Magdalene's feast day fostered the prostitute image of Mary Magdalene until the 20th century.

largely obscured today because of the way in which we obsess about what are, after all, incidental questions about her life.

Please tell us more about those three most important religious and symbolic acts starting with the ritual of anointment. She was said to have anointed Jesus twice, once when he was alive and once after he was no longer alive. Tell us about that process, both as act and as symbol.

Anointing within the ancient world was typically performed by women in households, or in the case of the movement of Jesus, within the group of associated disciples. Mary Magdalene is named as the principal anointer more than once, and for that reason it appears that among the women who followed Jesus as disciples, she was the one best known for the practice of anointing.

Anointing meant the application of olive oil onto a person's body or head. The anointing of Jesus' head is actually specified in one case, where Mary comes and takes oil that has been perfumed and pours it out over Jesus' body. It's a beautiful, evocative scene, because in the gospel according to Mark, the identity of this woman is at first not given. We don't understand who it is. But after she has put all of this expensive oil onto Jesus, and the disciples complain about the expense, Jesus says, "She has anointed my body beforehand for burial. And wherever this message is announced, what she has done will be spoken in memory of her." That gives us the key to the identity of this woman, because it is precisely Mary Magdalene who later in Mark's gospel goes to the tomb in order to anoint Jesus' body.

In your book, you point to the fact that exorcism was a fundamental part of Jesus' preaching. And, once Mary Magdalene becomes a disciple and apostle, she, too, you say, becomes known for her exorcism. Of course, the key link here is Jesus' casting out of Mary Magdalene's demons—demons which come to be widely interpreted as relating to her sex life.

Luke's gospel refers to there having been seven demons that went out from Mary Magdalene. It doesn't specify what those demons were. And I believe that attempts to do so now are even more implausible than trying to perform psychology at this kind of distance in time. The point that Luke is making in that particular section of the gospel is, first of all, that Mary Magdalene's affliction was deep. This was a serial possession that Jesus had to deal with by persistent exorcism. Luke also suggests that Mary Magdalene developed a very close relationship to Jesus because he needed to treat her in a serial fashion. Mary had been a recipient of Jesus' exorcism with an insider's knowledge of what was involved. And this helps to explain why it is that within the gospels we have some very detailed stories that relate not only how Jesus exorcised, but the way in which he thought of exorcism. These stories are best attributed to Mary Magdalene, the one disciple who understood his practice better than anyone else.

It is unquestionably the case that as the centuries went on and teachers within the church gave examples of what an unclean spirit or a demon could make you do, they often fastened upon sexual sins more than others. And so the fact that Mary Magdalene had had seven demons led by association to the idea that she was also a prostitute. But, in fact, within the time of Jesus, the understanding of unclean spirits was not limited to sexuality. An unclean spirit was understood as any of those impulses within us which, when they come to be in charge of us, can cause us to hurt ourselves, to hurt others, to act in a way that is deliberately malicious.

In other words, the science of exorcism in the ancient world, as practiced by Jesus and others, was targeted upon the issue of how to cope with evil within the human heart, which often results in violent and disturbing behavior. So when Luke refers to seven demons, what he means to say is that Mary Magdalene had a range of these afflictions, much as someone today might be described as having different kinds of compulsions or addictions that need to be dealt with as a whole if they're going to be treated at all.

Finally, please talk about the importance of Mary Magdalene's vision as it relates to her vision of the risen Jesus. Some have gone as far as to suggest that, rather than being symbolic and spiritual, it was actually part of her demonology—in a word, a hallucination.

Knowledge of biblical history and faith in God are two different things, and yet ultimately they are also related to one another. They can come together in understanding a particular kind of human experience—spiritual vision, which was a vivid and central aspect of religious experience in the ancient world, but muted and marginalized in the practice of religion today.

For example, in the instance where Mary Magdalene has her vision of the risen Jesus, we in the modern world may be inclined to equate that use of the word *vision* with some form of hysteria. But, as you become familiar with ancient literature, you can see that the practice of vision was designed to bring those who were devoted to God to that place where they could understand God as being the ground of reality. Vision can then also allow us to see the material world around us, not as the ultimate truth but only as something that leads us into that truth. The ancient world is filled with its own kinds of wisdom. History is our channel into that wisdom. Sometimes we discover forms of wisdom that appear so strong and so powerful to us that we also appropriate them for ourselves. I certainly have done that in the case of the sacraments of Mary Magdalene, and understanding her has deepened my awareness not only of how Christianity was formed, but also of how I could go about practicing it in the twenty-first century.

The Long Miscast Outcast

BY RICHARD COVINGTON

In retrospect, it is surely one of the most infamous sermons in the history of the Catholic Church. On September 14, 591, Pope Gregory conflated the Mary Magdalene of the seven demons with Mary of Bethany, who anoints Jesus, and the unnamed sinner who dried Jesus' feet with her hair. Suddenly Mary Magdalene was turned into a "sinful woman" who used unguent "to perfume her flesh in forbidden acts." In this famous case of guilt by association, she would become known as the penitent prostitute. Of course, Jesus forgave her for her sins and she became repentant—a model parishioners could well learn to emulate. It was a distortion that lasted nearly fourteen hundred years.

Some theologians and scholars believe it was an unfortunate simplification at a time of turmoil, when people wanted certainty. "Maybe it was for the ease of storytelling, for the ease of remembering ... [or] for the ease of tracing a broader understanding of the careers of these Marys as people who followed Jesus," says Father Jean-Pierre Ruiz of New York. Or maybe it was a conspiracy, "the legacy of a smear campaign launched by the early Church," as the fictional Leigh Teabing asserts in his discussions with Robert Langdon and Sophie Neveu in *The Da Vinci Code*.

Whatever the motivation, almost all scholars, theologians, and experts inside and outside the Catholic Church now generally agree that Mary Magdalene has been much maligned over the centuries. Richard Covington, writing in a special edition of *U.S. News & World Report,* "Women of the Bible," summarizes the wide-ranging impact this "mistake" had during the millennium and a half when it represented the official view of the Vatican.

Few characters in the New Testament have been so sorely miscast as Mary Magdalene, whose reputation as a fallen woman originated not in the Bible but in a sixth-century sermon by Pope Gregory the Great. Not only is she not the repentant prostitute of legend, meditating and levitating in a cave, but she was not necessarily even a notable sinner: Being possessed by "seven demons" that were exorcised by Jesus, she was arguably more victim than sinner. And the idea, popularized by *The Da Vinci Code,* that Mary was Jesus' wife and bore his child, while not totally disprovable, is the longest of long shots.

But arguments over whether Mary Magdalene was Jesus' wife, a reformed harlot, or the adulterous woman Jesus saved from stoning pale in comparison with the most rancorously disputed aspect of her legacy—what exactly she witnessed at Jesus' Resurrection. In a new biography of Mary Magdalene, Bruce Chilton contends that Mary witnessed not the Resurrection of a flesh-and-blood Jesus but a spiritual visitation. This is one of the principal reasons that she had been sidelined in the New Testament, says Chilton, . . . [who also argues that] Mary Magdalene's nonphysical interpretation of Resurrection was ultimately suppressed because it came uncomfortably close to the view of the Gnostics, a heretical sect of Christianity that flourished in the second and third centuries. But it came to light in 1896 when the second-century Gospel of Mary was acquired by a German scholar. In this fragmentary eight-page papyrus text in Coptic, Mary has a vision in which Jesus tells her she witnessed his reborn image with her "mind." . . . She then urges the apostles to follow Jesus' instructions to spread his teachings to nonbelievers.

When Peter angrily scoffs at the idea that Jesus would entrust such an important vision to a woman, another disciple, Levi, rebukes him as "hot-tempered." But now, after centuries of neglect, outlandish distortions, and outright male fantasies, Mary Magdalene is beginning to regain her place as . . . one of the prime catalysts and shaping forces of Christianity. Catholic groups around the country celebrate July 22, the anniversary of her death, as Mary Magdalene's feast day, using the occasion as a way to counter myths surrounding her and promote the ordination of women.

"We're trying to right a 2,000-year-old wrong," Christine Schenk, executive director of FutureChurch, a Cleveland-based organization behind the movement, told *U.S. Catholic* magazine.

Mary first appears in the Bible around A.D. 25 in Capernaum, a fishing town on the Sea of Galilee, where Jesus is rapidly gaining reputation as a healer. Afflicted with "seven demons," this single woman is probably 25 or 26. A few years older than Jesus and Jewish as well, she has made her way from Magdala (the origin of her name Magdalene), a cramped, smelly fish-processing town seething with angry, dispossessed farmers 7 miles to the southwest. It's not hard to picture Mary fleeing this hellhole in desperation, full of gratitude for finding someone who might save her from her demons. . . .

Although Luke speaks of Mary as one of the women who provide for Jesus "out of their means," the Gospel does not says she is rich, like Joanna, another follower, who is married to King Herod's steward. And it's not easy to imagine anyone wealthy coming from a place like Magdala.

Still, Renaissance painters like Caravaggio and others portrayed the wealthy, fallen Mary as a red-haired siren draped in ermine, silk, and pearls. In these fantasies, the idly rich woman turned to prostitution not for money but for vanity, making her repentance and forgiveness that much sweeter.

After Jesus cures her, Mary becomes the most influential woman in his movement, the oral source for the accounts of other exorcisms in the New Testament. . . . Mary also figures prominently in rituals of healing and anointing, practices intended to invoke the Holy Spirit. . . . [And she] is unquestionably one of Jesus' most faithful followers, witnessing the Crucifixion with his mother, Mary, while the male apostles flee to avoid arrest. In all four New Testament Gospels, Mary Magdalene is the first (either alone or with a group of women) to arrive at Jesus' tomb, where she encounters an angel (or a pair of angels) who instructs her to go tell the disciples that Jesus has risen. . . .

It is not by chance that Mary Magdalene is among the first to learn of Jesus' rebirth. Surely, the divine prophet who foresaw his own Crucifixion also foresaw the witnesses of his Resurrection; in a sense, Jesus chose Mary Magdalene as the herald of his return. For her pivotal role in the Resurrection, she became known as "the apostle of the apostles," a figure powerful enough to chide the apostles to follow Jesus' command to preach to nonbelievers, despite the risks.

In Eastern Orthodox tradition, Mary Magdalene travels to Rome, where she preaches to Tiberius, then settles in Ephesus in northwest Turkey with Mary, the mother of Jesus, and the apostle John. Other accounts place her in southern France or even in India with the apostle Thomas. According to Chilton, she returns to Magdala, where she continues preaching, healing, and anointing. In A.D. 67, she becomes one of thousands of victims massacred by the Romans in reprisal for an armed rebellion.

Soon after, the early leaders of the emergent church, including the authors of the New Testament Gospels, written around 70–95, continued the process of erasing Mary Magdalene and other female followers that had begun with Peter and the other male disciples. In one text, the heretical Gnostic Gospel of Thomas, Jesus himself makes the astonishing statement that Mary, and indeed all women, cannot enter the kingdom of heaven unless they become male.

In order to offer a moral alternative to the decadent Roman religion, the emergent church trumpeted male-dominated traditional family values. "This allowed Christianity to make great strides in the Greco-Roman world, but at the enormous price of forgetting about the movement's influential women," says Chilton.

In the sixth century, Pope Gregory the Great brought Mary firmly back into the picture—not the way she was but as the church wanted her to be. With breathtaking oversimplification, Gregory conflated Mary Magdalene of the seven demons with the unnamed "sinner" who washed Jesus' feet with her hair in Luke (a close reading of Luke 7 and 8 shows that they are not the same woman) and also Mary of Bethany, who anoints Jesus with nard in John.

Gregory reasoned that if a woman like Mary, who had fallen so low, could be forgiven through faith and the church, her carnality transformed into spirituality, the worst sinners could hope for salvation. Mary Magdalene wiped away Eve's original sin. "In paradise, a woman was the cause of death for a man; coming from the sepulcher, a woman proclaimed life to men," Gregory declared in his famous sermon in 591. The Eastern Orthodox Church, however, never accepted Gregory's melding of the three women.

In short order, Mary Magdalene soon became identified with the adulterous woman Jesus saved from stoning in John and with another woman who is not even mentioned in the New Testament—Mary of Egypt, a fourth-century prostitute who converted to Christianity and lived in a cave for the rest of her life.

Historian Jane Schaberg coined the term "Harlotization" to describe Mary's negative makeover, a process that disempowered a powerful leader of the faith.

Tales about the hermit Mary clawing her breasts and tearing out her hair in penance for her sins abounded, inspiring the creation of orders of flagellant monks. Churches claiming bodily relics proliferated, with nearly 200 boasting a piece of the saint by the end of the 13th century. At Saint-Maximin in southern France, Dominican friars still display her skull with a miraculously preserved scrap of skin where Jesus touched her forehead after the Resurrection.

Painters like the 13th-century Italian Master of the Magdalene, Hans Holbein, and William Blake focused on her role in the Resurrection, while artists like Titian portrayed the saint in ecstasy, barely covering her naked body with long reddish-brown hair.

Victorian photographers posed seminude adolescent girls, many living in charity schools named after her, as "Magdalenes," a prurient mixed message perpetuating the saint's image as the vixenish Lady Godiva of Christianity.

Finally, in 1969, 1,378 years after Gregory fused three New Testament women into Mary Magdalene—and more than 450 years since religious scholars rejected this fusion confusion—the church officially corrected the mistake. Even so, the legend of the repentant prostitute still exercises a tenacious hold on the public imagination.

Filmmakers like Martin Scorsese in 1998's *Last Temptation of Christ* and Mel Gibson in *The Passion of Christ* in 2004 keep the fiction alive.

The sexy, reformed Mary Magdalene is a symbol that's proven difficult to abandon. But the visionary Mary, full of faith at the foot of the cross and messenger of the Resurrection, a founding disciple entrusted by Jesus with a special mission to spread God's word, carries the greater ring of truth.

2 Embracing the Traditions of Women and the Sacred

I am Nature, the universal Mother, mistress of all elements, primordial child of time, sovereign of all things spiritual, queen of the dead, queen also of the immortals, the single manifestation of all gods and goddesses. My nod governs the shining heights of Heaven, the wholesome sea breezes, the lamentable silences of the world below. Though I am worshipped in many aspects, known by countless names, and propitiated with all manner of different rites, yet the whole round earth venerates me.

—APULEIUS, *The Golden Ass*

Myths of the Great Goddess teach compassion for all living beings. There you come to appreciate the real sanctity of the earth itself, because it is the body of the Goddess.

—JOSEPH CAMPBELL

Send her out of thy holy heaven, and from the throne of thy majesty, that she may be with me, and may labour with me, that I may know what is acceptable with thee. For she knoweth and understandeth all things, and shall lead me soberly in my works, and shall preserve me by her power.

—BOOK OF WISDOM OF SOLOMON

I believe that the earliest Christian heresy was the denial of the Bride.

—MARGARET STARBIRD

When God Was a Woman

BY MERLIN STONE

We may find ourselves wondering to what degree the suppression of women's rites has actually been the suppression of women's rights.

—MERLIN STONE

Merlin Stone's deep interest in the role of the Goddess in our earliest societies was sparked by her art: she is a widely exhibited sculptor and a professor of art and art history. A decade's worth of research resulted in her classic book, *When God Was a Woman,* first published in 1976.

The premise of the book is that societies as early as the Paleolithic worshipped women as the "creatresses" of life. Indeed, all ancient religions were female based, says Stone, and it was not until the Indo-European tribes with their male-centered beliefs conquered much of the biblical lands that the goddess tradition began to be suppressed. The final push to suppress the goddess tradition, Stone argues, was undertaken by the Levites, the dominant branch of Hebrew prophets and priests. Their drive toward a male-centered religion continued on into the era of Mary Magdalene and the earliest days of Christianity where, she says, it has stayed ever since.

Stone's theories don't lack for controversy as they are directly at odds with the prevailing scholarship showing that, whereas goddess figures were important to the religious rites of many ancient cultures, there is no evidence that any of them were the dominant figures, or that there was ever a clear dividing line between a goddess era and a god era. Nevertheless, Stone's views have gained considerable currency in recent years, and a wide range of thinkers and writers link her ideas about prehistory to themes about Mary Magdalene and the early Christian movement.

Though we live amid high-rise steel buildings, formica countertops, and electronic television screens, there is something in all of us, women and men alike, that makes us feel deeply connected with the past. . . . For people raised and programmed on the patriarchal religions of today, religions that affect us in even the most secular aspects of our society, perhaps there remains a lingering, almost innate memory of sacred shrines and temples tended by priestesses who served in the religion of the original supreme deity. In the beginning, people prayed to the Creatress of Life, the Mistress of Heaven. At the very dawn of religion, God was a woman. Do you remember? . . . .

The archaeological artifacts suggest that in all the Neolithic and early Chalcolithic societies the Divine Ancestress, generally referred to by most writers as the Mother Goddess, was revered as the supreme deity. She provided not only human life but a controllable food supply as well. . . . [The religion scholar] Werner Schmidt says of these early cultures, "Here it was the women who showed themselves supreme; they were not only the bearers of children but also the chief producers of food. By realizing that it was possible to cultivate, as well as to gather, they had made the earth valuable and they became, consequently, its possessors. Thus they won both economic and social power and prestige. . . ."

Though at first the Goddess appears to have reigned alone, at some yet unknown point in time She acquired a son or brother (depending upon the geographic location), who was also Her lover and consort. . . . Professor E. O. James writes, "Whether or not this reflects a primeval system of matriarchal social organization, as is by no means improbable, the fact remains that the Goddess at first had precedence over the Young-god with whom she was associated as her son or husband or lover."

It was this youth who was symbolized by the male role in the sacred annual sexual union with the Goddess. . . . Known in various languages as Damuzi, Tammuz, Attis, Adonis, Osiris, or Baal, this consort died in his youth, causing an annual period of grief and lamentation among those who paid homage to the Goddess. . . . This relationship of the Goddess to Her son, or in certain places to a handsome youth who symbolized the son, was known in Egypt by 3000 BC; it occurred in the earliest literature of Sumer, emerged in later Babylon, Anatolia, and Canaan, survived in the classical Greek legend of Aphrodite and Adonis, and was even known in pre-Christian Rome as the rituals of Cybele and Attis, possibly there influencing the symbolism and rituals of early Christianity. . . .

But just as the people of the early Neolithic cultures may have come down from Europe, so later waves of even more northern peoples descended into the Near East . . . and their arrival was not a gradual assimilation into the area, as the Goddess peoples' seems to have been, but rather a series of aggressive invasions, resulting in the conquest, area by area, of the Goddess people.

Indo-Europeans Come to Dominate Babylon, Asseria, and Other Regions

These northern invaders, generally known as Indo-Europeans, brought their own religion with them, the worship of a young warrior god and/or a supreme father god. Their arrival is archaeologically and historically attested by 2400 BC, . . . [and] the pattern that emerged after the invasions was an amalgamation of the two theologies, the strength of one or the other often noticeably different from city to city. As the invaders gained more territories and continued to grow more powerful over the next two thousand years, this synthesized religion often juxtaposed the female and male deities, not as equals, but with the male as the dominant husband or even as Her murderer. Yet myths, statues, and documentary evidence reveal the continual presence of the Goddess and the survival of the customs and rituals connected to the religion, despite the efforts of the conquerors to destroy or belittle the ancient worship. . . .

The arrival of the Indo-Aryan tribes [in a sixteenth-century BC wave, and then again in the third and second centuries BC], the presentation of their male deities as superior to the female deities of the indigenous populations of the lands they invaded, and the subsequent intricate interlacing of the two theological concepts are recorded mythologically in each culture. It is in these myths that we witness the attitudes that led to the suppression of Goddess worship.

As Sheila Collins writes, "Theology is ultimately political. The way human communities deify the transcendent and determine the categories of good and evil have more to do with the power dynamics of the social systems which create the theologies than with the spontaneous revelation of truth from another quarter."

. . . The Indo-European male deity, unlike the son/lover of the Goddess religion, was most often portrayed as a storm god, high on a mountain, blazing with the light of fire or lightning. This recurrent symbolism suggests that these northern people may once have worshiped volcanoes as the manifestations of their god. . . . In some areas, this god was annexed to the Goddess as a husband, such as the storm god Taru and the Sun Goddess of Arinna or Zeus and Hera. In some legends he emerged as a rebellious young man, who heroically destroyed the older female deity, at times upon the previously assured promise of supremacy in the divine hierarchy. In many of these myths the female deity is symbolized as a serpent or dragon, most often associated with darkness and evil.

. . . But it was upon the last assaults by the Hebrews and eventually by the Christians of the first centuries after Christ that the religion was finally suppressed and nearly forgotten. It is in these accounts of the Indo-European people that we may find the origins of many of the ideas of the early Hebrews. The concept of the god on the mountaintop, blazing with light, the duality between light and dark symbolized as good and evil, the myth of the male deity's defeat of the serpent as well as the leadership of a supreme ruling class, each so prevalent in Indo-European religion and society, are to be found in Hebrew religious and political concepts as well. This influence or possible connection with the Indo-European peoples may provide the explanation for the extreme patriarchal attitudes of the Hebrews. . . .

"Ye Shall Destroy Their Altars and Break Their Images"

So antagonistic were the Levite priests toward the religion of the Goddess in Canaan . . . that laws were written prohibiting the worship of these "other gods." The laws were so severe that they commanded the members of the Hebrew religion to murder even their own children if they did not worship Yahweh. The Levite laws of the Bible ordered: "If your brother or son or daughter or wife or friend suggest serving other gods, you must kill him, your hand must be the first raised in putting him to death and all the people shall follow you" (Deut. 13:6). . . .

The Levites . . . insisted that all women must be publicly designated as the private property of some man, father or husband. Thus they

developed and instituted the concept of sexual *morality*—for women.
. . . Thus premarital virginity and marital fidelity were proclaimed by
Levite law as divinely essential for all Hebrew women, the antithesis
of the attitudes toward female sexuality held in the religion of the
Goddess.

Yet the influence and prestige of the ancient religion were ever
present. As we have seen, there are continual biblical reports of
"paganism" in every era; it loomed as a constant problem, described
throughout the Old Testament. The prophet-priests of Yahweh threatened. They scolded. The Levite writers labeled any sexually autonomous women, including the sacred women of the temple, as whores
and harlots and demanded the enforcement of their own patriarchal
attitudes concerning the sexual ownership of women. Once having
invented this concept of "morality," they flung accusations of "im-
morality" at the women whose behavior and lives, in accordance with
their own most ancient beliefs, were of the highest and most sacred
nature.

Most revealing was the symbolic analogy they drew between any
women who refused to abide by the laws of the new morality—continually referred to as harlots and adulteresses—and the waywardness
and defection of the entire Hebrew people in their constant lack of
fidelity to Yahweh. The use of female sexual infidelity as the ultimate
sin—so serious that it was regarded as analogous to the betrayal of
Yahweh—affords us some insight into the Levite attitude toward the
sexually autonomous woman.

Conclusion

The orders for the destruction of the religion of the Goddess were
built into the very canons and laws of the male religions that replaced
it. It is clear that the ancient reverence for the female deity did not
simply cease to be but that its disappearance was gradually brought
about, initially by the Indo-European invaders, later by the Hebrews,
eventually by the Christians, and even further by the Mohammedans.
Along with the ultimate acceptance of the male religions throughout a
large part of the world, the precepts of sexual "morality," that is, pre-

marital virginity and marital fidelity for women, were incorporated into the attitudes and laws of the societies that embraced them. . . .

It is then, perhaps, not overly speculative to suggest that the myth of Adam and Eve . . . may have been intentionally written and included in the creation story of the Bible as yet another assault upon the Goddess religion.

Within the legend of the creation of all existence and life by Yahweh, the story that supposedly explained what happened at the very beginning of time, the image of woman as the dangerously seductive temptress, who brought about the fall of all humanity, may have been inserted. Knowing all that we do about the sacred sexual customs in the religion of the Goddess, the continual presence of these customs among the Hebrews even in Jerusalem, the use of dragon or serpent myths, often in conjunction with creation stories, by the Indo-Europeans, and the vestiges of the Leviathan myth in the Old Testament we may gain a most clarifying and enlightening insight into the symbolism and message contained in the biblical myth of Adam and Eve. We may find that the seemingly innocent myth of Paradise and how the world began was actually carefully constructed and propagated to "keep women in their place," the place assigned to them by the Levite tribe of biblical Canaan. . . .

It is time to bring the facts about the early female religions to light. They have been hidden away too long. . . . With these facts we will be able to clear away the centuries of confusion, misunderstanding and suppression of information, so that we may gain the vantage point necessary for examining the image, status and roles still assigned to women today. With these facts we will gain the historical and political perspective that will enable us to refute the ideas of "natural or divinely ordained roles," finally opening the way for a more realistic recognition of the capabilities and potential of children and adults, whether female or male, as individual human beings. When the ancient sources of the gender stereotyping of today are better understood, the myth of the Garden of Eden will no longer be able to haunt us.

Killing off a defiant consort was not the answer, any more than silencing and debilitating women economically has been. Perhaps when women and men bite that apple—or fig—at the same time, learn to consider each other's ideas and opinions with respect, and regard the world and its riches as a place that belongs to every living being on it, we can begin to say we have become a truly civilized species.

Sex in the Temple
The Tradition of the Sacred Prostitute

AN INTERVIEW WITH NANCY QUALLS-CORBETT

Feminine spirituality is derived from the pairing of the carnal with the sacred, argues Nancy Qualls-Corbett, a Jungian analyst and authority on the relationship between sexuality and spirituality. Our search for spiritual meaning, therefore, is not just a journey toward religion, but also toward psychology, she argues, invoking Carl Jung, the pioneering Swiss psychologist who emphasized that the psyche could best be understood by exploring the worlds of dreams, art, mythology, world religion, and philosophy.

Jung was a clinician, but was also steeped in the realms of Eastern philosophy, alchemy, astrology, art, literature, symbolism, and archetypes. He stressed that modern humans rely too heavily on science and logic and would benefit from integrating spirituality and appreciation of the unconscious realm in their daily lives. The Jungian influence on Dan Brown and his Harvard symbologist character, Robert Langdon, is arguably strong. So, too, is the Jungian influence on many of the New Age writers, who explore themes that include Gnosticism, neopaganism, and metaphoric interpretations of Mary Magdalene's experience.

Jung was also known for his emphasis on male and female archetypes, as well as the importance of balancing their respective roles in a dualist union.

For Nancy Qualls-Corbett, this balance is lost in a Christian dogma that has excluded "anything feminine from its picture of God, much to the psychic detriment of the faith." She continues, "Without a feminine base of any kind we have churches that developed as one-sided or neurotic structures," thanks to the way in which "Mary Magdalene was demeaned and marginalized by the men who took power in the early patriarchal church and fundamentally warped its foundation." Even today, she contends, we are disinclined to associate anything or anyone who is consecrated to God and made sacred with that which is considered sensuous and carnal. Yet when "our world was young . . . there was no conflict between one's human sexual nature and one's religious or spiritual nature. Each gave life and meaning to the other and provided an important balance in the world of antiquity: a union of the divine with the mortal."

We spoke with Nancy Qualls-Corbett about her book *The Sacred Prostitute* to gain a deeper understanding of how such themes were manifested in ancient times. Her answers, which many readers may find controversial to say the least, shed light on the ways in which these traditions continue to have an impact and also reveal some surprising commonalities between Mary Magdalene and Qualls-Corbett's vision of the "sacred prostitute."

Quite a few scholars and other experts have made many of us familiar with such terms as sacred union and sacred marriage. But sacred prostitution? Please help us understand that concept.

Excavated from the ruins of the earliest civilizations in Babylonia and Sumer, ancient clay tablets, vase paintings, and little statues dating from approximately 18,000 BCE describe or depict women who performed love's act in the Temple of Love. This was an act of worship and the priestess of the goddess of love was a sacred prostitute. She welcomed the world-weary stranger into the privacy of this sanctified place and offered herself to him under the aegis of the goddess. In the presence of the divine goddess, this ritual was transforming. The sacred prostitute, perhaps an initiate, could experience the fullness of womanhood, her feminine nature awakened to life. The element of divine love now resided in her. The stranger, too, experienced the mysteries of sex and religion that accompanied the regeneration of the soul. This sacred sexual act was considered a ritual of *hieros gamos* or the sacred marriage as it represented the spiritual union of the divine with the mortal.

In other ancient locales, the ritual of sacred marriage was experienced in slightly different ways. At the New Year's celebration, called the "Fixing of Destiny," people sang hymns to the goddess: "The king goes with lifted head to the holy lap; He goes with lifted head to the holy lap of Inanna." Inanna refers to the Sumerian goddess of love and fertility, who assured the fecundity of the land and human life with her blessing of love and the art of lovemaking. The king, representing the god, and a chosen sacred prostitute, representing the goddess, were led to the ziggurat whereby their mating insured fertility of the land. Her human emotions and creative, bodily energies united the personal and the suprapersonal. She touched basic regenerative powers and, thereby, as the goddess incarnate, assured the continuity of life and love. The sacred prostitute was the human vessel wherein earthly and spiritual forces united. An enactment of the sacred marriage, as portrayed recently in both *The Da Vinci Code* and the Kubrick film *Eyes Wide Shut,* reflects this sensibility.

In later civilizations Inanna, and other goddesses, became more differentiated; one goddess was identified with fertility or a Mother Goddess, while a distinct other was worshiped for feminine sexual beauty. The Greeks, for instance, knew the former as Demeter, while Aphrodite was venerated for her splendor in physical beauty, love, passion, and delight. The goddess of love and the goddess of fertility were revered as the divine feminine.

Why did the concept of the sacred prostitute originate? How did it translate into the reality of the time?

Women who performed the menial tasks in the temples were thought to be in close relationship with the goddess and thus empowered to grant blessings. It is thought also that this ritual may have been a vestige from earlier primitive ceremonies when the tribal chief deflowered the maiden prior to her marriage. Another hypothesis is that as the goddess and her consort bestowed fertility to the land, the act should be imitated by women who sought her blessing.

In different cultures at different time periods women became sacred prostitutes. This was no disgrace but rather an honor. They were considered "the wife of the god." In certain locales only women of noble birth could participate. In Thebes the wife of the high priest was entitled "chief concubine." The third-century BCE Greek historian Herodotus wrote, "Babylonian custom . . . compels every woman of the land once in her life to sit in the temple of love and have intercourse with some stranger." At the temples of Aphrodite in Eryx, Corinth, and Comanas, according to Strabo, a first-century Greek geographer, philosopher, and historian, sacred prostitutes numbered in the thousands. They were accorded social status and were educated. In some cases, they remained politically and legally equal to men by their right to inherit land. It was believed that as the goddess brought her gifts of love—the arts of lovemaking, passion, and joy—from her heavenly realm to mortals below, the sacred prostitute, as priestess of the goddess, imparted this blessing to humankind.

How does Mary Magdalene fit in?

Although clouded in confusion from biblical scripture, I think and feel that Mary Magdalene was endowed with the selfsame attributes as the sacred prostitute. In many ways she followed her heart, although the way must have been arduous. I can only imagine what courage and inward strength she possessed to counter the defining role of womanhood at that time. Luke describes her, and other women followers, as being of "substance," which is usually interpreted as financially supportive. Yet the word has additional meanings, like "consequential" and "necessary." Is this not more in keeping with her role?

You have based your analysis on Carl Jung's archetypes. What is an archetype? What role do they play in human thinking and behavior?

Dr. Jung referred to the deeper strata of the psyche as the collective unconscious, differentiating it from the personal unconscious that contains repressed material from an individual's personal experiences. The collective unconscious contains psychic components— the archetypes—which are omnipresent, unchanging, and common to all people. Like instincts, they are inherited. As psychic energy they have the ability to regulate, modify consciousness, and color one's experience of the world; therefore, they may be thought of as patterns of behavior. The hero or witch, for example, is an archetypal image that arises spontaneously from dreams and myths. These images are products of the unconscious manifesting in consciousness as symbols. Behind the symbol's visible and objective meaning is an invisible and more profound meaning: what is the hero or witch "energy" within me and how does it propel me to act?

We can say in effect that we don't "have" archetypes; the archetypes "have" us. When we speak of the goddess of love we speak of an archetypal image. When we fall in love, we feel ecstatically energized when that one particular archetype is activated. Homer's ode to Aphrodite describes her as beautiful, radiant, and a lover of laughter. We feel the same pattern. We send our beloved red roses, a symbol of love, because it is the flower of Aphrodite.

How does the concept of the archetype apply to goddess figures—and to Mary Magdalene?

In world mythologies we find two distinct aspects of the feminine archetype: static or motherly, and dynamic or erotic. The archetypal images of the mother and the sensuous woman are also prominent in Christian mythology, but these images are altered by conscious beliefs. The mother archetypal image, Mary, is revered as virginal, asexual—not a full-breasted, wide-hipped reflection of fecundity as the mother goddess in ancient days was perceived. The erotic feminine archetypal image, Mary Magdalene, is debased, called a prostitute, and condemned for her sexuality, which was identified as temptation and mortification of the flesh.

I see this attitude changing as indicated by the current intense interest in Mary Magdalene coupled with conscious challenging of outmoded beliefs that diminish or debase feminine nature. The archetypal image of the erotic feminine, symbolized by Mary Magdalene, the human woman, reconnects us to the aspect of the divine feminine in our innermost being, as did the sacred prostitute.

You have said that by losing the feminine form from its picture of God, the Christian church has become a "neurotic structure." How and when did the goddess become, as you have also put it, "disembodied"? And what are its implications?

Through the ages the prevailing matriarchal system evolved into one that was patriarchal. Once agriculture and religion were the primary nucleus of life; later the focus shifted to commerce, war, and control of more expansive lands. The acts of giving birth and sustaining life were no longer held in the same high esteem as that of heroic conquering deeds. Gradually, through millenniums to approximately 5000 BCE, women became subordinate because their roles were no longer important in the context of these new values. Through the passing centuries the pantheon of gods and goddesses crumbled as one Supreme God was recognized. The Temple of

Love gave way to the House of the Lord. Sexual pleasure and spiritual values could no longer coexist; life's joys on earth were repressed as man sought eternal life. The goddess and her advocacy of rekindling the soul through sexual expression was now debased and seen as evil.

There was, of course, little trace of the divine feminine in the newly founded Christian church's hierarchical structure of popes, bishops, and priests. To a small degree it was incorporated in Eastern Orthodoxy as Theotokos and Sophia, and later, the attributes of the sacred feminine were assimilated into the image of the Blessed Virgin Mother, especially in Catholic countries. The church declared Christendom to be the bride of God, Christ and Ecclesia as *sponsus* and *sponsa*. While a beautiful sentiment, this is a rather esoteric and abstract image, a vision that is difficult to connect with emotionally. A great dichotomy was experienced in the Middle Ages when Gothic cathedrals rose to heavenly heights in veneration of Mary, but human women were burned as witches. The "disembodiment" of the goddess meant regressive attitudes toward nature's fertility, feminine values of relatedness, and the spiritual component inherent in lovemaking.

What does repressing the feminine do to us, as individuals and within a society? How can we "regenerate" ourselves?

When the feminine principle of Eros is repressed, there is no connection to one's inner being, to humanity, and to nature. Without the mediating quality of relatedness, power raises a mighty hand. A sense of power creates hubris or an inflated ego, which in turn pollutes the heart and makes one hardened and cynical. These attitudes are reflected in society. Thinking is more valued than feeling; science more valued than the arts. There is no balance. Societal values become hard-edged as militarism, consumerism, and politics are held in high esteem. And human loving emotions and nature turn to dust.

Without the element of divine love mediating sexual experience, gratification is short lived. We lose reverence for the bountifulness of nature and all living things. The heart is not touched, the soul is not nourished, and the spiritual dimension is not realized. Men lose the experience of intimacy not only with the "external" woman, but also with their own unconscious feminine nature, the *anima*. Likewise, women, without beholding the blessed gifts of feminine nature, either despise or abuse their body, or use it in flagrant ways to satisfy ego needs. An ancient myth of Aphrodite tells of women who met her with disdain, ridiculed and mocked her. She turned them all into stone. By the same token, women today are not immune to becoming hardened and stony when no regard to the divine feminine is held.

I'm afraid there is no magic elixir for regeneration. Beginning steps for men and women alike may be as simple as making an effort to marvel at the goddess's moon or to admire a delicate red rose. We can act in ways to show genuine concern to humanity and our planet. We cannot reconstruct the Temple of Love in our external world, but we can build it from within. We can recall the blessing of the goddess and, like the sacred prostitute, bring her gifts into the world.

What is the true strength of the divine feminine? How is it reflected in women today?

The strength that women of all times possess is manifested in an inner connectedness with the feminine nature. Her being is not dependent on the reaction of others. She does what she does because it is congruent with inner explorations of her unique self—the absolute antithesis of enacting a role of a "sexy woman." When working and living within a patriarchal system, she may not be able to change the system, but neither does she allow it to change her. The woman who is in allegiance with her feminine nature may not be considered beautiful, sexy, or provocative by today's standards; she is more fully recognized by her countenance: a warm receptive glow that emanates from within. There is a definitive quality about her presence that all but defies definition. This woman holds the blessing of the divine feminine not for personal ego aggrandizement but with reverence, in order to carry it forward into the world.

Mary Magdalene and the Sacred Union

AN INTERVIEW WITH MARGARET STARBIRD

Margaret Starbird is a tireless and persuasive advocate for restoring the concept of the "sacred union" into the heart of Christianity—a heart she believes was lost in the rush to orthodoxy and the establishment of rigid patriarchal doctrine. A devout Catholic who set out years ago to debunk the "royal blood" thesis of *Holy Blood, Holy Grail* and ended up convinced of its veracity instead, she has written a half dozen books about the sacred feminine and its centrality to true Christianity. Among the best known are *The Woman with the Alabaster Jar: Mary Magdalen and the Holy Grail* and *The Goddess in the Gospels: Reclaiming the Sacred Feminine.*

Margaret Starbird makes the case that Mary Magdalene and Jesus had a "holy, dynastic marriage." Separating Mary from Jesus, as she says the church has done, represents "a distortion of the most basic model for life on our planet—the 'sacred union' of devoted partners."

Although considered overly speculative by many in the scholarly mainstream, many others agree with much of what Starbird has said. All are likely to acknowledge that her books are important for understanding the modern fascination with Mary Magdalene and her new mythology. Dan Brown specifically cites her work as having been a major influence informing the story told in *The Da Vinci Code.*

Margaret Starbird is in great demand as a speaker, and as a leader of workshops and retreats, the form of public appearance she most prefers. She was previously interviewed by us for *Secrets of the Code.*

Let's begin with a somewhat personal question: You have said that your journey over the last twenty years has changed you in numerous ways and given you a new sense of your own spirituality. Can you elaborate? Where has the journey taken you, and what does Mary Magdalene mean to you on a personal level?

I came to the quest for the Lost Bride as a devout Roman Catholic and member of a small charismatic prayer community. In the mid-1970s, we were shown that something crucial was missing from the foundations of Christianity, with devastating consequences. We gradually realized that this loss involved the desecration of the feminine. At the time, we renewed our devotions to the Virgin Mary, but after reading *Holy Blood, Holy Grail* in 1985, I sensed that the full-bodied revelation of the sacred feminine was incarnate in Mary Magdalene. Uncovering the truth about the status of Mary Magdalene has allowed me to create an image of the divine as an intimate partnership and to consciously integrate this understanding into my own faith and experience.

The concept of the sacred feminine, of course, shines throughout your writings. Please trace it back a bit more for us in the context of your religious education.

In the 1970s, many women went out seeking the lost Goddess traditions, but I was not one of them. I was a faithful daughter of my Roman Catholic Church and firmly rooted in her traditions. In 1988, I was researching Mark 14, the anointing of Jesus by the woman with the alabaster jar of precious nard, for a class at Vanderbilt Divinity School. In researching the gospel anointing passages, I came upon their connection with the "sacred marriage" liturgies indigenous to fertility cults of the ancient Near East, described in recently translated liturgical poetry from Sumer, Babylon, Canaan, and Egypt. Because my M.A. studies were in comparative literature, I don't consider ancient pagan rites taboo. They are literature. I discovered that the anointing of the Sacred King was the prerogative of the Bride, who later meets her sacrificed Bridegroom resurrected in the Garden. How can we fail to notice the similarities of these ancient rites with the Passion narratives of the Christian gospels where the "Bride" plays the same role? If "sacred partnership" was a cornerstone of early Christianity, shouldn't we make an attempt to restore it? I'm encouraged when I see amazing numbers of people embracing the "sacred union."

Including, of course, Dan Brown in his phenomenally successful The Da Vinci Code. *Many of the ideas he expresses there have their basis in your work; indeed, he puts your book* The Woman with the Alabaster Jar *in a prominent place on Leigh Teabing's bookshelf. From your ideal vantage point, what do you think Dan Brown got right, and what did he get wrong?*

Dan Brown managed to pour Mary Magdalene's story into the mainstream, ensuring that it reached every corner of the planet. He understood that the importance of the story was not an elitist

Mary Magdalene and the Goddess Image

Visual representations of Mary Magdalene frequently relate to the goddess figures of myth, folklore, and legend. We have no contemporaneous image of her; we can never point to just one image, at one particular time in history, and say, "That's really her, as she was." That is why, when talking about Mary Magdalene in art, we are really talking about layers of imbued meaning. Thus, the conflation of both named and anonymous biblical women whom St. Gregory the Great identifies as Mary Magdalene, I identify as the "Magdalene Mosaic."

Mary Magdalene as well as Mary of Nazareth are many times associated with the attributes and characteristics of previous goddesses, particularly by artists in parts of France, Germany, Italy, and Spain. According to certain ancient Egyptian texts, the goddess Isis is the wife of the god Osiris. When he is killed and his body is cut into pieces by his enemies, Isis and her sister Nephthys seek out all the parts, put him back together, anoint his body, and mourn by his side for three days. On the third day, he comes back from the dead. So this idea of anointing, of waiting for three days by the tomb, or of life coming back is not an uncommon connection between pre-Christian goddess traditions and Mary Magdalene.

Similarly, Mary Magdalene has connections with Inanna, Astarte, Aphrodite, Venus, and with other such goddesses. What do they all represent? Love, passion, and feminine sensuality as well as domestic skills and domestic arts with which the Magdalene becomes connected during certain periods of Christian history. Many times they have to do with being faithful to one person in the way that the Magdalene is faithful from the point of her conversion by Jesus to beyond his Resurrection.

—DIANE APOSTOLOS-CAPPADONA

claim to a special bloodline, but rather, the "sacred union" at the heart of the Christian gospel.

What has all this attention meant to you personally?

For me, the "sacred union" represents a move to radical gender equality and inclusiveness. It is the single most important cultural shift of our time. Dan Brown's novel has helped to promote the idea. My work is reaching an ever wider and more enthusiastic audience, and I'm receiving an escalating number of invitations to present retreats and seminars about the Lost Bride.

As a result of your discussions around the country in the past two years, have you heard things, or found things, that have changed your understanding of some concepts, or modified your views? If so, in what way?

I'm constantly receiving new insights and confirmations of the "sacred union" that underlies reality. I am processing a greater understanding of the archetype embodied in Mary Magdalene: the Sophia/Wisdom principle of the ancients as expressed also in the Hebrew Bible—"In the beginning" was not only the Logos, but also the Sophia.

Let's get back to fundamentals. For readers who may not be familiar with it, what is the sacred feminine? And what caused its loss?

The sacred feminine is a way of declaring that God is not exclusively masculine, as painted on the ceiling of the Sistine Chapel, but has feminine attributes as well. This is clear from beautiful passages in the Hebrew Bible and from the gospels that speak of God in feminine metaphors: "Can a mother forget her baby, or a woman the child within her womb?" (Isaiah 49:15). I am especially grateful for the writings of Peter Kingsley with regard to the loss of the "Sophia" in Western civilization. "She" who is called the "Mirror of God's Divinity" and "Delight" was apparently abandoned by Plato and later Greek thinkers who continued to call themselves "philosophers" ("lovers of Sophia") when, in fact, they had shifted the paradigm to become "lovers of Logos" (logic, rational, left-brained modes of thinking and being).

We know that there was worship and appreciation for the sacred feminine in Egyptian, Greek, and other traditions. Yet, generally speaking, these cultures didn't seem to treat women very well at the everyday level—at least not by modern-day standards. Could it not be argued that, although she may have represented wisdom, she only did so at the pleasure of the patriarchy?

In Egypt, pharaohs married their sisters, reflecting the life-giving relationship of their goddess-god couple, Isis and Osiris. And in the Hebrew Bible we find wonderful stories of very strong heroines— Deborah, Judith, and Esther, along with numerous prophetesses. The "platonic shift" to masculine modes came later, and then Greek civilization superseded the ancient ways following Alexander's global conquests. But the sacred feminine is not just about "women's rights." The feminine includes right-brain modes of thinking, being, and relating to reality through inner wisdom; that is, intuition, experiential body-centered—rather than brain-centered—wisdom. If the people in Southeast Asia who saw the tsunami wave had run to higher ground as the elephants and monkeys did, they would not have perished on the beaches. Western tourists were so far removed from their "roots" that they couldn't sense the danger. The "Sophia" not only represents that connection with our "earth" and "instinctual" body wisdom, but also with community relationships, including long-term concern for justice, mercy, and the welfare of the "little ones"—"unto the seventh generation," as Native American grandmothers express it. As we make these values conscious, we reconcile both masculine and feminine energies—helping to heal the desert.

Symbolism, gematria, sacred numbers—you have dedicated a great deal of your time and energy to researching these. The results are fascinating. But a question lingers: did the scribes of that time intend to convey them as such, or are we looking down a well only to see our own reflection? Some of these findings—we're thinking of the Bible Code, for example—don't stand up to historical scrutiny. In other words, what confidence can we have that these hidden meanings were put there intentionally?

There is nothing New Age about *gematria*. Gematria is an aspect of scripture long neglected by Bible scholars. It is an ancient literary device found in the works of Plato and other philosophers, as well as in the Hebrew Bible. Instead of setting key phrases to music, it sets them to number. Both Greek and Hebrew letters have numerical values and were used as numbers. Certain significant titles and phrases in the Bible produce numerical sums that reflect cosmic principles found in the geometry of sacred architecture—from the pyramids and Stonehenge to the "Holy City" described in the book of Revelation. Scholars have researched this subject, including John Michell (*The City of Revelation* and *The Dimensions of Paradise*) and David Fideler (*Jesus Christ, Sun of God*). The evidence that authors of the New Testament intentionally coined names, titles, and phrases to connect with sacred cosmic principles is, in my opinion, beyond all doubt.

Turning to the evolution of orthodox Christianity, can you give us your
perspective on why the church distorted the roles of both Mary Magdalene
and Jesus?

My personal view is that the early church lost Mary Magdalene because her friends and family were trying so hard to protect her
from perceived threats posed by Roman authorities and the heirs of
King Herod "the Butcher." Mary Magdalene literally disappears.
Paul's letters do not mention her, nor does the book of Acts. What
happened? From preeminent follower and devotee, she is stricken
from the record. The "orthodox" eventually marginalized those factions that supported the family connections of Jesus (Nazareans
and Ebionites) as well as the Gnostic teachings that elevated the
status of Magdalene. Apparently, by the end of the second century,
the church fathers, heavily influenced by Irenaeus and Tertullian,
were denigrating the important role of women and the egalitarian
nature of the earliest Christian communities.

In denying the role of the Sacred Bride, the church fathers in effect gave us a distorted view of Jesus. He became envisioned as a
celibate god, seated on a celestial throne—the celibate son of a Virgin Mother. The "mandala" of sacred partnership had been effectively scuttled.

What is the basis for thinking Mary Magdalene ever went to France? Didn't
this idea first appear in The Golden Legend, *written by a bishop who*
acknowledged his work had embellishments?

Bishop Jacobus de Voragine did not invent the story of Mary Magdalene and her siblings in France. He only wrote a fictionalized version of her life based on legends indigenous to the land. By the time
his *Golden Legend* was published [c. 1267] the Inquisition was already in full force. But earlier sources, including sermons and
prayers from old breviaries, attest to the presence of Mary, Martha,
and Lazarus in the Rhône valley. Legends indigenous to the region
were imbedded in a rich oral tradition attested by various medieval
chroniclers. Gervais de Tilbury wrote in 1212 regarding the seventy-two disciples of Jesus who were driven from Judea and exposed to the sea in a boat without oars. He names Lazarus, Martha,
Mary Magdalene, Maximin, and others of the early Christian com-

munity. The Sire de Joinville narrates how he and King Louis IX, on their journey home from the Crusade in 1254, stopped by to visit St. Maximin and St. Baume, "a deep cave in a rock, wherein it is said the Holy Magdalene resided."

The original of a manuscript called *The Life of Saint Mary Magdalene and of Her Sister Martha* probably dates to the late twelfth century and is a composite based on earlier sources, probably including sermons of Rabanus Maurus, a ninth-century bishop of Mainz. In 1040, Benedict IX stated that the relics of St. Lazarus were enshrined at St. Victor's Abbey in Marseilles. And in a history of the kingdom of Arles, we find reference to William Gerard, son of the king of Italy, who took a pilgrimage in 935 to St. Baume "where Magdalene lived and died." In addition, the Merovingian king Clovis is said to have taken a pilgrimage to the tomb of St. Martha at Tarascon, which would take belief in that site back to AD 500. Stories about the family of Bethany, including the Mary called "the Magdalene," are well attested throughout the region for centuries before Bishop de Voragine ever wrote his highly imaginative version of her legend.

Leaping from the Middle Ages to this one, do you believe that we are in the midst of a long-term resurgence of interest in the "sacred union" as represented by Mary Magdalene, who has been called the "It" girl of our times?

At other times in history, movements have attempted to reclaim the Bride: the troubadours in southern France praised the virtues of their "Dompna" and the Pre-Raphaelites in nineteenth-century England painted glorious images of Mary Magdalene and wrote poems in her honor. The modern movement has the advantage of the World Wide Web spreading information to all corners of the earth in nanoseconds. No Inquisition can squelch the rising enthusiasm for restoring the Bride; it's spreading by spontaneous combustion!

What would you recommend to women who are hoping to restore the lost Goddess in their lives?

Some people promote the misconception that I'm recommending Goddess worship. I'm actually advocating that we restore balance to Christianity by restoring the wife and beloved of Jesus to her proper role. Many scripture scholars and Christian clergy state publicly that a married Jesus would not contradict doctrine, since doctrine insists that Jesus was fully human. Christianity has long recognized Jesus as the Sacred Bridegroom. How can they have failed to recognize his Bride?

Is there anything else you've recently come upon in your research on Mary Magdalene that you'd like to discuss?

I'm convinced that Mary Magdalene was not "of Magdala." The town now called Magdala was called Taricheae in biblical times. Josephus, a Jew who wrote his first draft of *Jewish War* in Aramaic, calls the town Taricheae, as does every other written record of the period prior to AD 70. Taricheae was destroyed in AD 67, and the town that was rebuilt on the old site on the shores of the Sea of Galilee was named Magdala Nunnayah (Aramaic for "Tower of the Fishes"). But by that time, Mary Magdalene was long gone.

I think a prophetic passage from the Hebrew Bible, Micah 4:8–11, is the most likely source for the title of "the Magdalene": "To you, O Magdal-eder, Watchtower of the Flock, shall dominion be restored." The passage goes on to prophesy her exile and eventual rescue. "Nations will defile you" (Micah 4:11). The entire passage sums up the plight of the bereaved Bride, crying over the deceased king, sent into exile, defamed and defiled. I believe that many scripture scholars have failed to acknowledge this passage as the source of the title "h Magdalhnh" only because they refuse to consider the idea that she was the bereaved Bride sent into foreign exile. The "Daughter of Sion" in the passage from Micah finds specific application in the story of Mary Magdalene, just as the "Suffering Servant" in the prophecies of Isaiah found specific application to Jesus.

I also consider hugely significant the "fishes" medallion found recently on the mosaic floor of a third- to fourth-century Christian edifice in Megiddo, Israel. This discovery confirms that early Christians honored the zodiac symbol for Pisces long before they chose to identify themselves with the cross. Jesus, their *ICHTHYS*, was styled as the "Avatar" or "Lord" (*Kyrios*) of the dawning Age of Pisces. The symbol for that new age was not one fish alone, but two. I have long asserted that Mary Magdalene represented that "other fish" from the zodiac sign, which was perceived as a "partnership" sign, manifested in the egalitarian nature of the earliest Christian communities. She was eventually "deep-sixed" to Davy Jones's Locker, and the depths of our collective unconscious, her voice silenced when she was branded a prostitute. We need to reclaim the "sacred partnership" that was once at the heart of the Christian "Way."

The Women Around Jesus and Their Role in Forming Christianity

AN INTERVIEW WITH MARY ROSE D'ANGELO

Biblical and other ancient texts suggest but few details about the life of women in the time of Jesus. We do know that some women had leadership roles in various religions at the time, including ranking positions in the Jewish synagogue and in some of the "pagan" religions. And the Bible tells us it was women who provided Jesus and the disciples "from their means." When they and the other followers parted ways with the Jewish community, they did so in "house churches." But what were the cultural assumptions at the time? What may have attracted these women to Jesus and his teachings? Is it incorrect or unfounded to assume, as is often done, that women had few or no rights, nor the ability to be independent? To answer such questions, we spoke with Mary Rose D'Angelo, theology professor at Notre Dame and author of numerous articles on women and the origins of Christianity.

D'Angelo's argument, as stated in the introduction of her edited work, *Women & Christian Origins,* is essentially that although cultural norms and the political domination of the Romans must be considered when studying the role of women in early Christianity, we should not assume that female roles were always restricted and weak. Albeit greatly circumscribed by modern standards, women of the time, including Mary Magdalene, did wield some power. They also had religious and political female role models to whom they could look for inspiration and guidance.

Jesus is known for having female as well as male followers, which seems to
have flown in the face of the established patriarchy of the time. Who were the
women around Jesus, and what do we know about them?

We don't know much about the women, or men, around Jesus beyond the names of a few of them—and they are very common
names. The women's names are all Hebrew or Aramaic; some of
the men have Greek names, but the men are also likely to have
been Jews. Mark names three women: Mary Magdalene, Mary the
mother of James and Joses, and Salome as having "followed" Jesus
from Galilee and "ministered" to him there. The two Marys are represented as witnesses to Jesus' death and burial, and the three
named women are witnesses to the empty tomb and the vision of
an angel.

Matthew and Luke each give revised versions of Mark. In Luke,
the women seem to be demoted from active participants in the
movement to "ministering to/providing for them [Jesus and the
twelve] out of their goods." Matthew represents Mary and "the
other Mary" as witnesses to the tomb and as the first to see the
risen Jesus. The Gospel of John views Mary Magdalene not only as
witness to Jesus' death and the empty tomb, but also as the first visionary—the first to see the risen Jesus—and sends her with the
message that explains Jesus' fate. The only mention of Mary before
she appears at the cross in the canonical gospels is Luke 8:1–3,
which describes her as having had seven demons cast out of her by
Jesus. This may be the author's invention and may have been an attempt to diminish her. But it is not possible to determine this.

The Gospel of Thomas also depicts Mary and Salome as disciples
of Jesus, and the Gospel of Mary represents her as a visionary and
leader among the disciples.

What evidence is there to show whether or not Jesus treated the women
around him on the basis of gender equality?

I don't think there is much evidence for complete gender equality
in most first-century settings, and the gospels rarely raise the question of the status of women (Gospel of Thomas 114 and Gospel of
Mary are exceptions). What the texts do give us is evidence that
women were among the participants in the reign-of-God move-

ment in which Jesus preached, as well as in the early Christian mission that preached his death and Resurrection. As the texts stand, they may assume more participation by women than appears at first reading.

Why would Jesus and his teachings have appealed to women, or men, for that matter? What would have made them leave their homes and, we imagine, their "good reputations" to follow an itinerant preacher from town to town?

The people around Jesus were responding to the promise that God was about to act on their behalf. The terms by which they understood that would have been Jewish. We can deduct that they were energized by the idea that God was fulfilling the promises made to Israel: justice for the poor, an end to oppression, suffering, and foreign dominations—probably, that there would be a radical change, that God would somehow get rid of the Romans so that worship in Israel would no longer be under their supervision.

These followers or companions of Jesus went with him from one place to another preaching. Only a few are named and it is impossible to tell how many were involved. Most are men, but women are also named as having traveled to Galilee and Jerusalem with him.

Leaving house and home was a response to the call itself; a matter of joining something not understood to be permanent. It's hard to say what expectations they had or how others would have reacted to the movement; different people will react in different ways, as people react to different movements now. It's possible that some of their contemporaries saw the women who went on the road with the reign-of-God movement as disreputable, but if so the gospels don't give any clear evidence of their views.

There were other movements that went out to meet God's deed on behalf of Israel. For instance, Josephus tells of a new exodus, or new entry, movement about fifteen years after Jesus' death, led by a prophet named Theudas. They went out across the Jordan to wait for God to lead them back into possession of the land. Since they are said to have gone out with all their belongings, this movement probably included women, and perhaps whole families. They were slaughtered by the Romans.

How would women have been involved in Jesus' work? What roles might they have played?

If we look at the Gospel of Mark, the author says that women went on the road but pays little attention to that fact. And the author passes over the issue of why it mattered that these women were at the cross. In the Gospel of Luke, the author introduces the women early and suggests that some of them are of an elevated class—Johanna is the wife of Harod's steward, for example. And Luke also says that these women followed alongside and supported Jesus and the others from their goods. It may be that Luke is trying to defend the women of the movement by presenting them as respectable women with some income. In Luke, these women do something different than what the disciples do, providing for them out of their wealth, but in Mark there's no distinction. If women really were on the road with Jesus, it seems improbable that they had a separate role from the disciples. The distinction that Luke makes probably serves a specific purpose—there seems to be a concern about making sure they are seen as women of substance, respectable women. One of the things we should remember is that we know almost nothing individually about these people. We know historically that there were women who owned and controlled property and ran businesses. Widows would have had dowries—money the husband could use during the marriage but which went back to the woman and her family if the man died. Would married women be able to participate without their husbands' consent? Questions like that can never be answered by generalities. Even then, women said no to husbands and made choices their spouses did not like.

Both during and after Jesus' time, women are likely to have been active in the preaching of the reign-of-God in ways that were possible for Jewish and Roman women but probably not typical for them, or for Christian women. For instance, there were women prophets, like the unnamed woman of Mark and the women in 1 Cor 11:4–5 in early Christianity, as there were in Jewish and Roman contexts. Women had some financial independence and were able to travel, offer and accept hospitality, conduct business, and the like.

Who might these women have considered role models? Were there current or
historical women they could look to for spiritual inspiration?

There were such women. The book of Judith was written close to this time, for example, and Esther and Ruth were also important. There were stories about women warriors. There's the Deborah story in which Deborah appears as a judge and war hero, and also as a sage and prophet. Miriam and Huldah were also female prophets, and Rahab, who hid the spies in Joshua 2, appears as a model in ancient Jewish and Christian texts. Women at the time would have read these stories—those who could—and others would have heard them read or told.

Women's roles in ancient Judaism and early Christianity have long been ignored or forgotten, but there also has been some deliberate cover-up. In Romans 16, Paul greets a group of people in which women's names are included. One such name is "Junia"; she and a man are greeted together as "famous among the apostles." Acts 1:16–26 seems to limit "apostle" to twelve named men, and the gospels are usually read in light of this passage; however, here the term is used for a woman. Paul says that she had been a co-prisoner with him; she was before him in Christ. He calls her "kin." Her name is a Roman name, so she is likely to have been a freed woman or the client of a Roman citizen. Her male partner's name is Greek. This is basically all we know about her.

Her name was recognized as a woman's name up until the late Middle Ages. But during the Reformation and Renaissance, the idea that a woman couldn't be called an apostle took hold. With one accent mark, editors and copyists began to change the name Junia into a man's name, Junianos, despite the fact that that male name was not one known to have been in use in the first century. Now, in the light of recent research, the Greek text and scholarly translations like the New Revised Standard Version recognize it again as a woman's name.

Scholars like Wayne Meeks, Elisabeth Schüssler Fiorenza, and Peter Lampe have used Romans 16 as a source of sociological information about the early Christian mission. Lampe argues that women may have been more active in the early Christian community than men, pointing out that more of the "worker" or "labor" words are attached to women's names. I'm not certain as to whether you can truly deduce this, but I do believe that women as well as men were active originators of Christianity. In a way, that's why Mary Magdalene gets—and deserves—particular attention. She's the bearer and interpreter of the message that Jesus has risen, and that is the foundational message of Christianity.

3 Becoming the Apostle of Apostles

The companion of the [Savior] is Mary Magdalene. The [Savior loved] her more than [all] the disciples [and he] kissed her often on her [mouth]. The rest of the disciples were offended by it and expressed disapproval.

The other [disciples] . . . said to him, "Why do you love her more than all of us?" The Savior answered and said to them, "Why do I not love you like her? If a blind person and one who can see are both in darkness, they are the same. When the light comes, one who can see will see the light, and the blind person will stay in darkness."

      —THE GOSPEL OF PHILIP

Then Mary wept and said to Peter, "My brother Peter, what are you imagining? Do you think that I have thought up these things by myself in my heart or that I am telling lies about the Savior?"

Levi answered, speaking to Peter, "Peter, you have always been a wrathful person. Now I see you contending against the woman like the Adversaries. For if the Savior made her worthy, who are you then for your part to reject her? Assuredly the Savior's knowledge of her is completely reliable. That is why he loved her more than us."

      —THE GOSPEL OF MARY

Blessed Mary, you whom I shall complete with all the mysteries on high, speak openly, for you are one whose heart is set on heaven's kingdom more than all your brothers.

      —PISTIS SOPHIA

Biographical Glimpses of Mary from Magdala

BY BRUCE CHILTON

The barest scraps of information the New Testament tells us about Mary Magdalene have turned, over time, into a Brobdingnagian cornucopia of myths, legends, debates, imaginings, scholarly tomes, cultural revisionism, and fictional blockbusters.

There are only a dozen references to Mary Magdalene in the New Testament, and few offer more than the hints and implications about the facts and events of her life. And the four accepted gospel accounts can't seem to write about her with any consistency.

For example, Matthew, Mark, and John mention she is at the Crucifixion—but Luke is not explicit on the point. Her presence at the Resurrection is mentioned in Mark, Luke, and John, but not in Matthew. John mentions she "saw the stone already taken away from the tomb and then went to tell the disciples that "I have seen the Lord." Mark says, "He first appeared to Mary Magdalene," and leaves it at that. Luke gives the most detailed account of the Resurrection scene but says that when Mary and the other women "announced all these things to the eleven and to all the others . . . their story seemed like nonsense and [the disciples] did not believe them."

As several experts writing in *Secrets of Mary Magdalene* make clear, the Gnostic Gospels tell us a great deal more about Mary's understanding of Jesus's teachings, and her status as a companion to Jesus, but not much more about Mary Magdalene the person.

Scholars have worked carefully to tease out Mary Magdalene's background from the snippets of information that appear in the accepted as well as the alternate scriptures: her place of birth, the political and social milieu of the time, her first encounters with the radical rabbi named Jesus. The challenge has been to try and respect that fine line separating informed scholarship and sensible inference from mere speculation and the imagination of storytellers, artists, religious leaders, and novelists.

Bruce Chilton, the scholar introduced in the first chapter, succeeds as well as anyone in making the most of the relevant information without crossing that line, especially in his well-received *Mary Magdalene: A Biography,* the source of this excerpt. In that book, Chilton puts forward the case that the classical sources of religious experience portray God as influencing the lives of people by removing evil (exorcism), curing disease (healing), and offering signs of the divine (visions). He says, "Mary Magdalene took up these practices with Jesus and refined them."

Mary appears for the first time in the chronology of Jesus' life in this brief passage from Luke's Gospel:

> And there were some women who had been healed from evil spirits and ailments—Mary who was called Magdalene, from whom seven demons had gone out, and Joanna, Khuza's wife [Herod's commissioner], and Susanna and many others who provided for them from their belongings. (8:2–3)

Luke indicates when she entered Jesus' life and why she sought him out. Jesus' reputation must have drawn her the ten hard miles from her home in Magdala to Capernaum, which is where he lived from 24 C.E. until the early part of 27 C.E. She probably came to him alone, on foot, over rock roads and rough paths, possessed by demons, her clothing in tatters. By my estimate, she sought him out in 25 C.E., after Jesus had become known in Galilee as a rabbi who opened his arms to people considered sinful and did battle with the demons that afflicted them. . . .

Luke does not present Mary as the wealthy, elegant seductress of medieval legend and modern fantasy. . . . Luke [also] does not indicate how old Mary was when she met Jesus, but she was most likely in her twenties, slightly older than he, mature enough to have developed a complicated case of possession (intimated by the reference to "seven demons"). The Gospels say nothing about her family. She was evidently unmarried at an age when one would expect a woman to have settled and produced children.

Given Mary's demonic possession, there is little mystery about her being single. Possession carried the stigma of impurity, not the natural impurity of childbirth (for example), but the contagion of an unclean spirit. She had no doubt been ostracized in Magdala in view of her many demons. The Jews of Galilee defined themselves, in contrast to the Gentiles around them, by their devotion to stringent laws of purity that were commanded by the Torah, the Law of Moses that was written in Hebrew and passed on in oral form in the Aramaic language. What they ate, whom they could eat and associate with, how they farmed, whom they could touch or not touch, the people they could marry, the kind of sex they had and when they had it—all this and more was determined by this Torah. The Galileans' purity was their identity, more precious and delightful in their minds than prosperity under the Romans or even survival. They resorted to violent resistance sporadically during the first century to expunge the impurity the Romans had brought to their land, even when that resistance proved suicidal.

"Unclean spirits," as Jesus and his followers often called demons, inhabited Mary. These demons were considered contagious, moving from person to person and place to place, transmitted by people like Mary who were known to be possessed. In the Hellenistic world, an invisible contagion of this kind was called a *daimon,* the origin of the word *demon.* But a *daimon* needn't be harmful in the sources of Greco-Roman thought. *Daimones* hovered in the space between the terrestrial world and the realm of the gods. When Socrates was asked how he knew how to act when he faced an ethical dilemma, he said that he listened to his *daimonion ti,* a nameless "little *daimon*" that guided him. . . .

However Mary came by her *daimonia,* they rendered her unclean within the society of Jewish Galilee. She was probably very much alone when she arrived in Capernaum . . . [since] unmarried women past the age of being virgins had a liminal, uncontrolled status, as troublesome to the families that had failed to marry them off as to the women themselves. . . .

Had Mary turned to prostitution before she met Jesus? Had she been raped or exploited during her journey from Magdala? Those are good questions, although no text or reasonable inference from a text answers them. To affirm or deny these possibilities takes us beyond the available evidence. But we can say that in Mary Magdalene's time and place—as in ours—likely victims of sin were often portrayed as being sinners themselves. . . .

Mary Magdalene approached the right rabbi when she sought out Jesus. He reveled in his reputation for consorting with allegedly loose women (the word *loose* being applicable to any woman who did not bear her husband's or her father's name, or some other token of male protection). There were many unattached women among Jesus' disciples; when people called him "the friend of customs-agents and sinners" (Matthew 11:19), that was not a compliment, and Jesus' critics ranked these female disciples among the "sinners." . . .

Mary Magdalene's persistent reputation for promiscuity in medieval legend and in many modern novels rests on the mistake of presuming that women with demons were necessarily promiscuous. Exorcism in the ancient world was not only about sex, although scholars sometimes assume that describing a person as possessed denigrates that person, even after the cure. This was not the case: Ancient thinkers knew how to distinguish a person from his or her afflictions in a way their modern counterparts might learn from. . . .

People loved to hear Jesus' vision of a new age, a complete transformation of the world as they knew it. They felt themselves transformed by the many parables he wove to take them into the world where divine justice and mercy would reign supreme and transform all humanity. In his exorcisms and healings, Jesus put this vision of the transformative Kingdom into action.

Mary joined these gatherings and participated in festive meals in houses in and around Capernaum, where Jesus talked about God's extraordinary secret *malkhuta*. Rabbi Jesus must have been especially voluble while he drank wine and ate sheep or goat and fresh vegetables provided by accommodating hosts, tracing visions of how God would change everything someday soon and the Israelites who were eating together would banquet with Abraham, Isaac, and Jacob, risen from the dead. If you knew the Kingdom was at hand, you could celebrate its arrival, lying back on a couch of straw (or a real couch, if your host was wealthy), even while Caesar still ruled.

It is easy to imagine how Mary, an outsider who herself had been marginalized and ostracized, without a place in the social web of Galilee, might have responded to these parables of vindication and the vanquishing of Israel's oppressors. She may have had to push her way through crowds to see Jesus, but once she got his attention, he attended to her, as is clear from Luke's Gospel. We don't know what that first meeting would have been like, but it proved auspicious, for both the rabbi and the possessed woman in rags, very much alone, who was destined to become one of his most important disciples.

The fact that Mary bore the name "Magdalene" among Jesus' followers supports the impression that she became part of his inner circle in Capernaum. He gave such names to his closest disciples, after he had known them for an extended period of time. . . . The designation "Magdalene" distinguishes Mary from the other Marys who were associated with Jesus. Several women named Miriam, the Semitic name anglicized as Mary, were close to Jesus, including his mother and the mother of the disciples James and Joses (Mark 15:40). Moses' sister was called Miriam, and Jews in Galilee and elsewhere proudly embraced that name for their own daughters. But only one of the Miriams in Jesus' group was identified as coming from a town called Magdala in the Aramaic spoken there.

Magdala was important both practically and symbolically for Jesus and his disciples. The name Magdala derives from the term *migdal,* a low stone tower for keeping fish. . . . The Galilean sprat was one of Rabbi Jesus' favorite foods, as it was for many of his countrymen. Dried fish was also popular among his followers long after his death and far from Galilee, because Jews and non-Jews in Jesus' movement could eat fish together without raising the question of whether it was kosher, always an issue in cases where meat was involved. In fact, the fish became a symbol for Christians during the second century: The letters of the word *fish* in Greek were an acronym for "Jesus Christ, God's Son, Savior" and stood for Christ.

Fish meant currency, trade and prosperity for Magdala's Jews. Their dried and salted fish was sold inland in Galilee and across the water in the self-governing Gentile region of Decapolis. . . . But most significantly, Magdala supplied Tiberias, a vast, [nearby] city that . . . proved central to Mary Magdalene's identity all her life. . . .

The city was built in the Roman style, with aqueducts, temples, baths, theaters, and a stadium. Pious Jews reacted negatively, to say the least, to this monument to Roman values arising in their midst. Temples for idols like Mars, Apollo, and Diana were bad enough. Statues of Venus in the baths made them trysting places for lovers and aspiring lovers of all kinds of tastes, a flagrant example of exactly the kind of behavior that the Torah abhorred. . . . The first-century Jewish historian Josephus says that the Jews who moved to the city were the flotsam of Galilee, trash washed up on the shore . . . [and] from the point of view of the standard practice of Judaism these settlers became the vehicles of the uncleanness . . . throughout the Galilean region.

Tiberias's proximity to and economic domination of Magdala subjected Mary's town to the forces of impurity. Tiberias produced contagion, and this contagion is what Mary carried in her body. Beyond its obvious association with fish, *this* is what the cognomen "Magdalene" meant to Mary's contemporaries.

Mary's nickname, "Magdalene," also resonates with a name applied to Jesus, linking the two of them in key Gospel texts with a verbal echo. Jesus "the Nazarene" (*Nazarenos* in Greek) is the grammatical equivalent of "Magdalene" (which also represents the Greek usage), allowing for a change of gender. . . . English pronunciation conceals a rhyme that would have caught the ear of any Greek or Aramaic speaker who heard these names spoken aloud: The texts reverberate with an implicit connection between Jesus and Mary.

To call Jesus "the Nazarene" naturally evokes Nazareth as his native village, just as the designation "Magdalene" evokes Magdala on the Sea of Galilee. The verbal echo between the names reflects the geographical proximity between the two villages and their contacts with each other. . . . The use of "Nazarene" also resonates with the traditional word usage "Nazarite" (*Nazir* in Hebrew), which means "consecrated." The name Nazarene, paired with the designation "the holy one of God," evokes Jesus' consecration and reinforces his spiritual threat to the world of the demons in the dramatic opening exorcism in Mark's Gospel (1:23–27):

> And at once there was in their synagogue a person with an unclean spirit. He cried out and said, We have nothing for you, Nazarene Jesus! Have you come to destroy us? I know who you are—the holy one of God! Jesus scolded it and said: Shut up, and get out from him! The unclean spirit convulsed him, sounded with a big sound, and got out from him. And all were astonished.

The epithet "Nazarene," repeated in Mark's Gospel and echoed in the name "Magdalene," is a constant reminder of the disconcerting sanctity that challenges the whole realm of unclean spirits and at the same time reveals Jesus' identity.

Just as Jesus' contemporaries are "astonished" when the demons in Capernaum shudder in the presence of his purity, the Magdalene and her companions are "completely astonished" by a vision of a young man who tells them Jesus "the Nazarene" has risen from the dead (Mark 16:1–8). Here, too, revelation perplexes those it comes to, and that disturbance echoes through the names Nazarene and Magdalene.

To Jesus' mind, Mary was the Magdalene, the woman who had embodied the impurity to which Herod had subjected Magdala. To Mary, Jesus was the Nazarene, the force of Galilean rural purity that could vanquish her demons. Together, these names invoke the way Jesus and Mary became joined, the enduring link between them, and the disturbing thought that the force of the holy cannot be contained by the ordinary conventions of this world.

The Gospel of Mary

BY KAREN L. KING

"Few people today are acquainted with the Gospel of Mary," says Karen King, "yet these scant pages provide an intriguing glimpse into a kind of Christianity lost for almost fifteen hundred years." King, who is Winn Professor of Ecclesiastical History at Harvard University's Divinity School and one of the world's leading scholars of early Christianity, authored the seminal *The Gospel of Mary of Magdala: Jesus and the First Woman Apostle* in 2003.

A single, fragmentary copy of the Gospel of Mary in Coptic was discovered in 1896—fifty years before the famous Nag Hammadi find that gave scholars a whole treasure trove of additional alternate gospels to study. (See Plate 1.) Two additional fragments in Greek have come to light since, but that still adds up to only about half of the complete text. The eight pages that do exist offer a radically different view of early Christianity—so radical that is not surprising that "orthodox" Christianity labeled it as a heresy and attempted to marginalize its believers.

Specifically, says King, this "astonishingly brief narrative" presents the case that Jesus taught that the path to eternal life lay not in suffering and death—as presented in the canonical gospels—but through the path of inner spiritual knowledge. Most radical of all is its revelation about the role of Mary Magdalene and other women in early Christianity. Argues King, the Gospel of Mary "exposes the erroneous view that Mary of Magdala was a prostitute for what it is—a piece of theological fiction, presents the most straightforward and convincing argument in any early Christian writing for the legitimacy of women's leadership, offers a sharp critique of illegitimate power and a utopian vision of spiritual perfection, challenges our rather romantic views about the harmony and unanimity of the first Christians, and asks us to rethink the basis for church authority. All in the name of a woman."

Here we present a summary of King's findings, showing the reader why the old master story of Christian origins—that Jesus passed down a singular "true" teaching to his male "club" of disciples—is giving way to a set of new interpretations of the original Christian message, at once richer in their meaning, more true to what we know now about the early Christian movement (i.e., the likely diversity of beliefs), and certainly more resonant with the modern experience.

When Jesus died, he did not leave behind him an established church with a clear organizational structure. The patriarchal and hierarchical leadership of the church developed only slowly over time and out of a wide variety of possibilities. Early Christians experimented with a variety of formal arrangements, from relatively unstructured charismatic organizations to more fixed hierarchical orders. In some congregations, leadership was shared among men and women according to the movement of the Spirit in inspiring gifts of prophecy, teaching, healing, administrations, and service. Others were headed by elders, bishops, deacons, and widows. Some had formal offices; others meted out duties according to capacity and inclination in a discipleship of equals. In many, women and slaves were important leaders; others resisted this reversal of the dominant social order and worked to exclude them. The Gospel of Mary was written at a time when it was not yet clear which direction church organization would take.

From at least the time of Paul, Christian churches had stressed the presence of the Spirit within the churches, and the manifestation of spiritual gifts among all believers. They assumed that Jesus intended to generate a movement that would spread his teaching into all nations. The Gospel of Mary traces its own spiritual legacy to the early Christian tradition that Jesus had commissioned his disciples to preach the gospel. The dialogues among the disciples are framed in order to explore the meaning of Jesus' admonition to preach the gospel. What is the content of that gospel? Who has understood it and who has the authority to preach it? What insures that the true path to salvation is being taught? The Gospel of Mary takes very clear positions on each of these issues, but the controversy that erupts among the disciples also shows that the author of the Gospel of Mary was fully aware that not all Christians agreed with its views.

Increasingly the tide would turn toward favoring a patriarchal, hierarchical authority. It was the predominant form by which power was exercised in the Roman world, and it afforded at once more stability and more respectability than charismatically organized groups, which stern Roman sensibilities apparently found radical and disorderly. In the early fourth century when the Roman emperor Constantine first legalized Christianity by issuing an edict of toleration, he recognized a group of male bishops as the established leadership of the church, and in doing so sanctioned a power structure that would govern Christianity for centuries to come. But Constantine only gave systematic order and imperial approval to what was largely already in place. For by the second century, bishops had begun to base their claim to be the legitimate leaders of the church on apostolic succession, claiming to trace their authority through a direct line to Jesus' immediate male followers, who were styled as the great apostolic founders of Christianity. This succession of past witnesses, it was argued, ensured the truth of the Church's teaching and guaranteed the salvation of believers.

The Gospel of Mary directly challenges the validity of such claims, and offers instead a vision of Christian community in which authority is based not solely or even primarily upon a succession of past witnesses, but upon understanding and appropriating the gospel. Authority is vested not in a male hierarchy, but in the leadership of men and women who have attained strength of character and spiritual maturity. Prophetic speech and visions are given a place of primacy as the manifestation of spiritual understanding and the source of sound teaching. Christian community constituted a new humanity, in the image of the true Human within, in which the superficial distinctions of the flesh lacked any spiritual significance. Women as well as men could assume leadership roles on the basis of their spiritual development. The Gospel of Mary rejects any view of God as divine ruler and judge and, hence, repudiates those as proper roles for Christian leadership. The true model for leadership is the Savior, the teacher and mediator of divine wisdom and salvation who cautions his disciples against laying down fixed laws and rules that will come to enslave them.

According to the master story of Christian origins, Jesus passed down the true teaching to his male disciples during his lifetime. They, as witnesses to the Resurrection, were commissioned to go out and spread this teaching to the ends of the earth; and only later was that true apostolic teaching corrupted by Satan, who sowed the weeds of heresy in the apostolic fields. According to the Gospel of Mary, however, the weeds were sown by the apostles themselves. Men like Peter and Andrew misunderstood the Savior's teaching and sowed discord within the community. According to the master story, the full doctrine of Christianity was fixed by Jesus and passed on in the doctrines of the Church. The Gospel of Mary instead suggests that the story of the gospel is unfinished. Christian doctrine and practice are not fixed dogmas that one can only accept or reject; rather Christians are required to step into the story and work together to shape the meaning of the gospel in their own time. Because human passions and love of the world incline people to error, discerning the truth requires effort, and it insists that communities of faith take responsibility for how they appropriate tradition in a world too often ruled by powers of injustice and domination.

For centuries, the master story has shaped people's imagination of the first Christian centuries; it has provided a myth of origins which casts the early Church as a place where true, uniform, and unadulterated Christianity triumphed. This story has again and again fueled the fires of reformers who appeal to it to legitimize changes in Christianity as it encountered very different conditions and cultural settings around the world. Historians, however, have come more and more to understand the Gospel of Mary's portrait—despite its imaginary elaborations—as in a number of respects more historically accurate than that of the master story. The earliest Christian texts we have don't portray a harmonious and unified Church of spiritual perfection, but communities working through the issues of conflict and difference. The Gospel of Mary also makes it quite clear that the appeal to particular kinds of apostolic authority is a theological stance, not an historical judgment. It is unlikely that twelve male disciples, each with the identical understanding of Jesus' teaching, went out and started the movements that would eventually become the religion of Christianity. We know too much about the influential activities of other figures, not least of whom are Paul, Jesus' brother James, and Mary Magdalene, to think that. The ancient texts from Egypt show that early Christians were not of one mind—even about so crucial an issue as whether the cross and physical resurrection of Jesus were important for salvation or not. The Gospel of Mary and other works argue energetically that the appropriation of Jesus' teachings points the way to true discipleship and salvation.

The historical importance of the Gospel of Mary lies in letting us see the contours of some crucial debates over the authority of apostolic tradition, prophetic experience, and women's leadership. We are in a better position to judge what was at stake in the road Christianity followed by walking a way down one of the paths that has been little trodden.

The Alternative Gospel Tradition

AN INTERVIEW WITH MARVIN MEYER

The discovery of the Nag Hammadi manuscripts in 1945 is one of the most important finds in the history of religion. Unearthed by an Egyptian peasant, these fragmentary leather-bound books were found in a large jar which apparently had been stored in the desert since about 400 CE. Collectively, these documents have come to be known as the Gnostic Gospels, a term alluding to the special inner knowledge sought by a series of religious movements whose philosophy was influential in Judaism, Greco-Roman religions, and what we have now come to learn were different varieties of Christianity. Taken together, these documents, also known as the Nag Hammadi Library, have provided a fascinating alternative perspective on Jesus—as well as on Mary Magdalene and many of his other early followers—and the philosophical ideas that were debated in the ancient world.

Since the find, scholars have explored the many ways these alternative gospels differ from those in the New Testament, as well as the methods by which some forces in the early Christian movement suppressed them as heresy. Such differences include the way Mary Magdalene is portrayed in several of them and the emphasis on a salvation that comes from inner knowledge, as opposed to the worship of God through his son Jesus that we read in the New Testament. Also, in these alternative gospels, Jesus does not rise from the tomb, or die for people's sins. Widely divergent views of sin, truth, morality, self-knowledge, and other subjects are presented.

However, as scholar Marvin Meyer explains in the interview that follows, the popular notion of these schools of thought as running on completely separate and opposing tracks—one a master narrative, the other a heresy—is simplistic. Meyer, professor of Bible and Christian Studies at Chapman University, points to some fundamental similarities between Gnostic and traditional gospel accounts. Both are monotheistic and adhere to the notion that humanity was created in the image and likeness of God, he says, and they both see Jesus as the figure who reveals God to mankind. This leads Meyer, along with other scholars, to caution against putting either the canonical gospels or these alternative gospels into a mold. They represent a diversity of views on a common subject, Meyer says. "It lets us see the Christian movement as defined by a wide variety of people and different groups who are all on their own quest for what it means to be following Jesus."

Nevertheless, a major difference among the orthodox gospels and these non-canonical texts is the way they portray the role of Mary Magdalene, as we saw in the previous selection by Karen King. While in general it may be said that these alternative gospels treat men and women with greater equality than the traditional gospel vision, and spiritual development is seen as more important than gender, the Gospel of Thomas seems to be a major exception. Here, talking about Mary, Jesus tells us "women are not worthy of life" and "I myself will lead her in order to make her male." As one might imagine, no other passage in the Gospels has generated as much heat as this one, and Meyer spends some time in this interview explaining the puzzling passage. He concludes by citing some of his favorite passages about Mary Magdalene found in the Gnostic Gospels.

Meyer is the author of *The Gnostic Discoveries, The Gnostic Gospels of Jesus, The Unknown Sayings of Jesus,* and *The Gospels of Mary.* His book *The Gospel of Thomas: The Hidden Sayings of Jesus* has been listed as one of the hundred best spiritual books of the twentieth century. Most recently, Dr. Meyer edited and translated the most important alternative gospel–type document to come to light since the Nag Hammadi finds, the Gospel of Judas.

The discovery of the Gnostic Gospels in 1945 and subsequent detailed studies of them have led scholars and theologians to reconstruct the platform of early Christianity. It is almost part of our religious DNA that early Christianity evolved in a straight progression: Jesus spread the message, Peter built the church, the Council of Nicea consolidated the doctrine, and that's

that. Now, suddenly, we are becoming aware that there were a multitude of
Christianities, and that various movements vied for doctrinal orthodoxy.
How do you look at all this?

My way of reconstructing the history of the church begins with this principle: in the beginning there was diversity. Now, that doesn't mean that people were fighting like cats and dogs all the time, but it does mean that there were different ways of understanding what the good news of Jesus really entailed and what it meant to follow Jesus. Some of these differences turned into polemics—it was not always kind and gentle stuff.

This sort of argumentation appears in accounts of Mary where there are hard words between Mary and Peter. The "Peter people" and the "Mary people" just don't get along all that well, and finally Peter's people carry the day: *TU ES PETRUS ET SUPER HANC PET-RAM AEDIFICABO ECCLESIAM MEAM* is inscribed in St. Peter's Basilica in the Vatican. "You are Peter, and upon this rock I will build my church."

This is the linear view of church history, and it's bad history. It suggests there is only one way to think about how God works when, in the beginning, there was diversity, and the diversity was not specifically right-thinking or wrong-thinking, orthodox or heretical. There was no orthodoxy or heresy per se. These are po-litical terms. And who talked more loudly, who had the votes, who finally carried the day, who got to call themselves orthodox? The heretics were the ones who just didn't have the numbers; they got labeled godless people and wicked men and women, probably mo-tivated by the devil. They became "outsiders" and not a legitimate part of the movement—in league with their father, the devil.

Which leads us directly to the Gnostic movement.

Yes. By the second century the increasing amount of diversity yielded thinkers who searched for *gnosis* (inner knowledge), which flowered into what we now call Gnostic religion. Many people at the time began to gravitate to the inner knowledge concept instead of what had come to be the prevailing notion that salvation lay in worshipping something outside one's self.

This seems to be a way of thinking that modern men and women can identify with, this concept that the truth lies within. And it was popular then. So why did it not prevail?

The issue with the Gnostics was they never got their act together to get organized and to get political. While the Gnostics were meditating and looking for the God within, the followers of Peter's way had their feet on the ground. They mowed their lawns and painted their churches—and assembled a canon and got into bed with Constantine.

What makes the Gnostic way so different from the New Testament way?

There are three key differences as reflected in the New Testament and the alternate gospels.

First, the Resurrection. All of modern Christianity is built on this New Testament concept. Yet the Gospel of Mary and the Gospel of Philip, and the others we now know about and call either Gnostic Gospels or mystical gospels, don't have a crucifixion, blood atonement, or a resurrection, at least in the literal sense.

But if you believe the most valuable lesson of the Resurrection story is the emergence of life and light as being triumphant in the human experience, then you have plenty of that in these gospels— including in the recently uncovered Gospel of Judas. In fact, the Gospel of Judas is a good example of my point. There is a huge amount of life and light at the end of the text, but it's not understood as an empty tomb, or angels or a youth in a tomb. It's understood as being the spiritual person that comes to expression, the *inner* person that finally comes to life. So it's a very different vision to be sure, but not altogether a foreign one.

Second—and what we have become so familiar with in the wake of *The Da Vinci Code* phenomenon, as well as the popularization of feminist scholarship based on these alternate gospels—is the treatment of Mary Magdalene. As I see it, the story of Mary Magdalene in the New Testament is a story reduced to a subplot. That doesn't mean that it's insignificant. In fact, of all the women who are mentioned, with the possible exception of Mary the mother of Jesus, she has more prominence than most, and she is usually listed first in any order of women. She's the one mentioned by name who has been cleansed of demons and whose resources helped support the movement. And of course she is central to the Resurrection story. Still, Mary Magdalene's story is a subplot.

It is obvious that in these other gospels we see a Mary Magdalene who is a much more independent person, and her story is not a subplot at all. In some cases she can be seen to have a very dynamic role. She is the one who is appreciated by Jesus and who really understands him.

So from the point of view of a storyteller, the difference is between being a minor character in a subplot or a protagonist in the main story.

And the third?

The third is the role of sin. I believe that among the Gnostics, sin was not the basic human problem; ignorance was. If we just come to knowledge—if we can eradicate darkness, ignorance, lack of insight—we'll do the right thing. We'll realize what we're all about. Faith in atonement, faith that Jesus died for your sins is not the answer; rather, it is coming to knowledge—realizing that if you're a Christian, Jesus can help you wake up. He can tell you things that will bring you to a knowledge of who he is and who you are. And then you'll find that spark of the divine, that light of God, that spirit of God within—and you will be saved.

The way out of the human problem is not going to be faith, belief in someone, or the sacrifice of someone to placate an angry God. You can begin to see that wouldn't have made any sense to Gnostics. Even now, I think there are some real issues here. I mean, do polite Christians who have just gone through Holy Week really think that God is an angry, furious God? And that the only way to get rid of that anger is to make some kind of sacrifice? That somebody's blood has to be shed, and not just an animal's but a human's? And not just a human's, but that of God's own son?

In other words, according to the Gnostic Gospels, you may call something sin, but really, in the scheme of things, there isn't any ultimate thing out there called sin. However, if you get mixed up with something that leads to ignorance and distraction, then you call that sin. The real issue is not that somehow God is angry with you because you've sinned. The real issue is get your act together: realize that you belong to the side of light. Know who you are, come to knowledge, and you will find your salvation in that. So sin is not high on the list of concerns that these Gnostic texts deal with.

How about the concept of evil? How did the Gnostics tackle that?

There was a lot of interest in evil within the Gnostic movement. Indeed, St. Augustine (354–430) and others thought that the Gnostics were *too* preoccupied with evil—acting as if evil was something real and tangible. The Gnostics believed that the creator or demiurge was a fairly nasty fellow, and they gave him harsh names like Yaldabaoth (Child of Chaos), Samael (Blind God), and Sakla (Fool) in order to demonstrate how he was responsible for much of the ignorance, evil, and death in the world. This was in contrast to the more Platonic idea (adopted by St. Augustine) which suggests that whatever exists is good, and to the extent that something does not exist it is evil—thus evil is the ultimate absence of good. This position flew in the face of the Gnostic conviction that we must be aware of the evil around us and the supernatural powers that oppress us if we are to be liberated from them.

In other words, the Gnostics responded to the Platonists by saying, "Well, you know the problem here is that there are some strong supernatural powers around, and whether you call them satanic figures or not, they are a mean-spirited lot. And part of the reality of life is that you have to learn to cope with various evils. You can't just wish them away in a philosophical fashion, pretending they don't exist, and still participate fully in being." Their view was that you feel evil in your flesh as sickness, or see it in the tyranny of power. These are the realities of life you have to deal with. It is through meditation and self-knowledge that you can finally encounter the reality of evil and transcend it, and learn how to live in bliss through it all, in spite of it all.

Then there is the whole issue of the role of women. My impression is that in the canonical gospels the role of women is important, yet still circumscribed.

But not in the Gnostic texts, where women seem generally to have a higher status—which was part of the debate between Mary Magdalene and Simon Peter.

In the Gnostic texts, Mary Magdalene is the one who always says, "Forget about gender. We are talking about being made truly human. We're not talking about whether the guys or the women are going to be triumphant in the battle of the sexes." Peter is for the battle of the sexes while Mary rises above that kind of thing and talks about what it means to be truly human. I find that very liberating and quite delightful.

This is so different from what comes to mind when we think of mainstream Christianity that I wonder whether Gnostics really should be considered Christian.

Your point is interesting. Some scholars would say, for instance, that the Gospel of Judas is not a Christian gospel because in it, as in many of the Gnostic Gospels, Jesus doesn't die for anyone's sins. Nor does he physically rise and leave an empty tomb. In my opinion, that simply indicates a different approach to who Jesus was and what his value was. The Christian movement was defined by a wide variety of different people and groups who were all on their own quest for what it meant to follow Jesus, walk with Jesus, believe in Jesus, and believe in God. In a way I'm putting that diversity in the context of a single movement. The Gospel of Judas is a Christian gospel. The Gospel of Mary is a Christian gospel. The Gospel of Philip is a Christian gospel. It is all part of Christianity—as opposed to, I think, what happens in the orthodox way of looking at things, which suggests that "those people" cannot be part of the inner circle. To exclude these believers is to keep them on the outside. Then they are the "other."

You have stressed the diversity of early Christian thought, even among the various Gnostic Gospels. Many people like to quote from the Gospel of Philip, where it says Jesus "loved her more than [all] the disciples, [and used to] kiss her [often] on her [. . .]". Most scholars infer the last word to be "mouth," therefore hinting at an erotic relationship of some sort. But there is a second implication, perhaps even more important. It is that Jesus seems to make no distinction between a woman's ability to achieve deep spiritual insight and a man's.

But then there is the Gospel of Thomas. Here, too, Jesus seems to be endorsing an equal, integrated balance between male and female. In saying 22, Jesus says that to enter the kingdom of heaven "make the inside like the outside, and the above like the below, and when you make the male and the female one and the same, so that male be not male nor the female female . . ." But the gospel ends with a shock. Saying 114 begins with Simon Peter's suggestion that Mary leave their circle "for women are not worthy of life." To which Jesus responds in what we today would consider strong anti-feminist rhetoric: "I myself shall lead her in order to make her male, so that she too may become a living spirit resembling you males. For every woman who makes herself male will enter the kingdom of heaven."

You have done a great deal of study on this gospel. Can you give us your interpretation of what appears to be Jesus' anti-female stance?

Well, I think that as the years pass I'm getting a little better handle on the Gospel of Thomas and I feel pretty good about the text right now. I don't quite know how to classify it; I've had no comfort at all classifying it as a Gnostic gospel. Nevertheless, I think that in the end the Gospel of Thomas reflects an epistemology that has to do with a particular wisdom approach.

I really see it as a wisdom gospel, where Jesus is using the technique—also seen in the canonical gospels—of not defining everything but rather leaving stories unfinished or with a question hanging in the air. This approach makes Thomas an interactive gospel, a dialogue meant to provoke thought, and open to wide interpretation.

So was there a specific message built into the last saying of the Gospel of Thomas? Or are we to assume that this is a polemical piece that reiterates much of what we find in the literature regarding Peter being very keen on gender categories, and Mary often being the one who was critiqued? My guess is that it is the latter, interpreted in different ways as different people have encountered it. And I imagine that if in fact it was a monastic group that copied the Gospel of Thomas, and if a monk in a cell picked it up and read the last saying, he may not have had an enlightened mystical view of it, or a symbolic view. I'm sure he thought of that beautiful woman who walked by—in fact who tempted him and made him think evil sexual thoughts—well, she can be saved, too, but she'll have to discard her femaleness and her sexuality, and become male and God-like.

When you take a look at the issue of gender modification, of the female becoming male, there is a huge literature. In much of the literature, this type of gender change tends to be symbolic and the categories tend to be metaphorical. In fact, in a fair amount of the literature, it is implied that regardless of the person's actual physical sex, there is both a male and a female side to all humans. And it is the male side that needs to be nurtured.

If you buy into this symbolic way of thinking, the male side has to do with heaven and mind, and the female side with mother earth and the manifest world—the cycle of life and death, sense perception, everything that is part of the physical world. And so from this point of view, if the female is to become male, the female has to transcend this world and become a part of the world above.

Let's go back to the contrast between sayings 22 and 114, where one can see this concept being applied.

Saying 22 has a vision of androgyny, of male and female becoming one. And then we have this provocative saying at the end, so provocative that some people think it was probably added by a monk who hated women. But in actuality these were two sides of the same coin in the ancient world. There are stories which relate that in the beginning there was the androgyne, and the androgyne was cut in half. Plato in *The Symposium* has a view of humanity that suggests you can have males, females, and androgynes.

So we can say the male and female once were in paradise, and in the beginning we were one, and now we're two. And someday we'll be one again in a beatific existence. That's one way to look at it. But there is also another view of gender, and that is the single-gender approach. This view suggests that there really is only one gender and that is the male gender. It is the complete gender: if you simply take away the male sex organs, the penis from a man, you have a female. Or if you have a female who completes herself or is completed by the gods and goddesses, then she may sprout male sexual organs.

In some mythological literature, women are trying to escape the limitations of marriage or the limitations of being female, so they pray to the gods to be transformed into a male, and all of a sudden they feel pressure in their abdomen, and out come male sexual organs. They sprout themselves a phallus. Looking at it that way, they may be called androgynous because they are women who have grown a penis. And so they have become complete. They have realized the completeness of the one gender.

What I think is going on in the Gospel of Thomas, in sayings 22 and 114, is that two different images of androgyny are being presented. The view we find attractive today is that oneness is obtained through union. The other we reject as being inappropriate—that the female can become male.

But I think saying 114 is treated more symbolically in Gnostic and mystical literature. The tendency there is not to play these games with sprouting phalluses, but rather to speak metaphorically about life in this world as being female, and life in the world above—life with God, life of the mind—as being male.

Now having said that, it doesn't mean that either is going to be very palatable. I still think we feel as if we have a seed lodged in our teeth when we look at saying 114. It still irritates us, and perhaps it should. Such gender symbolism as we find in saying 114 may fit into the ancient world, but it feels quite out of place in ours.

Which parts of the Gnostic Gospels have helped your personal understanding of Mary Magdalene? Are there anecdotes that have a particular appeal to you?

I think my favorite passage would probably come out of the Gospel of Mary when, after the Crucifixion, the disciples are beside themselves. Mary soothes them, saying, "Do not weep or grieve or be in doubt, for his grace will be with you all and will protect you. Rather, let us praise his greatness, for he has prepared us and made us truly human."This is such a powerful way of thinking. In this way of understanding the good news of Jesus, to follow Jesus is to realize our true place as human beings, and to discover that the most profound experience of salvation occurs as we attain true humanity. That is a wonderful humanistic message.

Another favorite passage is out of the Pistis Sophia. Jesus is instructing the disciples, including Mary Magdalene, and ends by saying, "Whoever has ears to hear should hear." There follows a vivid image: "Now it happened when Mary heard these words as the Savior was speaking, she gazed into the air for an hour and said, 'Master, command me to speak openly.'" The compassionate Jesus answers, "Blessed Mary, you whom I shall complete with all the mysteries on high, speak openly, for you are one whose heart is set on heaven's kingdom more than all your brothers." You could not ask for a better endorsement of her spiritual strength than that.

Are you concerned that this kind of spiritual vision is being lost amid all the hoopla? That all the controversies—whether or not Mary Magdalene and Jesus had sex, whether she ended up in France and established a bloodline, etc.—will make us miss the point of her story, just as Pope Gregory's remarks about her or the French medieval Magdalene legends distract us?

Yes, I feel that very strongly. There is mixed evidence to support these controversies, and no way to resolve them. Arguments from silence, which often are the ones people resort to and shout the loudest about, are notoriously speculative. Arguing about the possibility that Jesus and Mary Magdalene were sexual partners, or married, may be another way to marginalize her, and we may fall into the same trap. Luke said she was hysterical. Pope Gregory the Great said she was a whore. We might say, "Oh, she was just the sexual partner of the really important guy." And then we miss what the texts are trying to emphasize—namely, that she was an intelligent, independent woman and a spiritual leader.

The Greatest Exaggerations Ever Told

A Critique of the "New" Interpretations
of the Gnostic Gospels

AN INTERVIEW WITH PHILIP JENKINS

The discovery of the Nag Hammadi Library—popularly known as the Gnostic Gospels—has introduced a revolution in our understanding of early Christianity. Introduced and popularized by a new group of feminist and other scholars, spurred on by a media eager to advance discussion and debate in an era of religious revival, and catapulted into the popular imagination by *The Da Vinci Code,* these texts have become the new accepted wisdom about Mary Magdalene's role among Jesus' disciples.

Philip Jenkins believes this new conventional wisdom is due not so much to what the gospels actually say than to our penchant for seeing what we wish to see. He argues that many of these so-called new discoveries have been known about for at least two hundred years. Moreover, these alternative gospels were written much later than the canonical gospels, putting them as far away from the time of Jesus as we in the United States are from the time of the French and Indian Wars. As no written contemporary records of the time of Jesus exist, asks Jenkins rhetorically, can an oral history two to three hundred years old really be trusted? Hopefully, he says, when the next set of biblical texts surface, they can be "evaluated on their merits, and not solely for their value in cultural battles."

Jenkins is a professor of history and religious study at Pennsylvania State University and has detailed these views in his book *Hidden Gospels: How the Search for Jesus Lost Its Way.*

The subtitle of your book Hidden Gospels *is a provocative one:* How the Search for Jesus Lost Its Way. *Can you summarize what you mean by it? And has the search for Mary Magdalene similarly "lost its way"?*

My title has a deliberate pun with the word "Way," which is the term that the earliest followers of Jesus used to describe the new faith, even before it became "Christianity." They were followers of the Way (Greek, *hodos*). Once you know that, you can find the word dotted throughout the New Testament and especially the gospels and the book of Acts. I suggested that a lot of modern scholars presented a misleading picture of Jesus and had lost their "way." The Jesus they were presenting was chiefly based on a particular interpretation of two reconstructed documents, the lost gospel Q and the earliest layers of the Gospel of Thomas. From these sources, they claimed that the "original Jesus," as far as we can see, was a wisdom teacher, and that supernatural stories grew around him later. My argument instead is that miracles, healing, and the supernatural were at the very heart of the earliest Jesus movement, and that the reconstructed "Wisdom Jesus" was based on a misunderstanding of those early texts.

In the same way, I think that Mary Magdalene is a fascinating character, but that much modern writing about her has lost its way in the sense of reading her through modern eyes, as a representative of feminist spirituality, of a lost era of women's leadership in the church, and so on. Albert Schweitzer described the quest for Jesus as looking down a well and describing the face that you see down there as the face of Jesus, when of course it is only your own reflection. That is what has been happening with some recent views of Mary Magdalene. As the saying has it, we see things not as they are, we see things as we are.

It used to be, you write, that the phrase "the gospel truth" symbolized an absolute standard of truth—but now, in part because of the Nag Hammadi find, in part because of the whole Da Vinci Code phenomenon, scholars and the general public seem to have come to the opposite conclusion: that there is more than one truth, that instead of one Christianity, there are many. And these alternate views should get equal billing, if not greater weight.

One frustrating point about the "new" scholarship on early Christianity is that it keeps on reinventing the wheel. If you look at biblical scholarship a century or more ago, those are exactly the ideas that people were discussing freely way back then. In 1934, Walter Bauer wrote a devastating book called *Orthodoxy and Heresy in Early Christianity*, which argued that in the second and third centuries, different kinds of Christianity were orthodox in different parts of the world, and each had its own gospel. Only gradually did one particular school win out, declare itself orthodox, and retroactively proclaim its own documents the "true gospels." These ideas are nothing like new.

The problem with all this is that Bauer exaggerated vastly. Gospels are not created equal. Some are much earlier than others, either in terms of when they were written or the sources to which they had access. Unquestionably, the four canonical gospels are more ancient in both senses than any competitors, though a couple of gospel fragments from Egypt might contain the remnants of other early texts. The reason church leaders are not paying attention to other so-called gospels is that the great majority of those texts were only starting to be written at that stage, and many would not even be written until well into the third century. The mainstream church does not exclude the "hidden gospels" because it thinks they are unorthodox, but rather because they know these are recent productions not deserving of respect as historical documents.

Dating is critical in determining authority. And that is why a text like the Gospel of Mary can tell us a great deal about the early third century, when it was written, but nothing at all about the historical Mary Magdalene, who had probably died two hundred years earlier.

You believe that the Nag Hammadi find has enriched our understanding of the early Christian movement—but that we are reading too much into it. Why? Have these gospels not forced us to reconsider our understanding of Mary Magdalene in a positive way—as an apostle and even as role model?

The Nag Hammadi texts are a vastly informative source, and they teach us much about the early Christian world. They tell us next to nothing, though, that is new about Mary Magdalene, either as a real historical figure or a legendary leader of early Christianity. Already in the late nineteenth century, anyone interested in religion—in Christianity, in New Age religion, in feminist spirituality—would have turned straight to the pages of the famous Pistis Sophia, a lengthy dialogue in which the main characters are Jesus and Mary Magdalene, and she is depicted as a leading disciple and a great spiritual figure. This shows us something about the veneration that some Gnostics had for Mary, probably in the third century—but as I said, nothing whatever about the actual woman of that name.

And the Pistis Sophia is only one source we had long before Nag Hammadi. Even the Gospel of Mary was not found at Nag Hammadi, but was rediscovered in 1896. We also have lots of snippets of dialogue between Jesus and Mary in gospel fragments we have known since the earliest Christian writers. In other words, most of what people claim as an explosive new discovery is nothing of the kind.

Some scholars have found a receptive audience for the notion that these "hidden gospels" reveal to the world "a glorious might-have-been," to use your words, if only they had not been declared heresy and then willfully concealed by the Petrine church. What's wrong with that view?

The events described in your question assume a chronology, that the Gnostics were around very early, and then the sneaky church concealed the truth about them. The second- and third-century church doesn't conceal the gospels, it just knows they are recent, and therefore not worth much. Moreover, if the church did conceal the Gnostic Gospels, they did a lousy job of it, since early Fathers preserve so much of their texts.

But yes, I do think that the main appeal of the "hidden gospels" is that they allow modern people to think about the roads not taken. To take an example, in 1900, like today, people looked at the great religions of Asia, and felt deep regret that Christianity seemed to condemn Buddhism or Hinduism. Could we not learn from the great spiritual teachings of Asia? The Gnostic Gospels, however, portray a Jesus who is much more in tune with the world of the Asian guru, which appeals to our sensibilities. One of the early blockbusters of modern Jesus fiction was George Moore's *The Brook Kerith,* published in 1916, and that portrays Jesus exactly in the mode of the Buddhist sage, who survives the Crucifixion, and ends up joining a party of Buddhist monks going back to India. As I said, *The Da Vinci Code* is not the first book to make radical arguments like that—it's not even the hundredth. D. H. Lawrence played with the idea of a married Jesus, so did Frank Harris, so did Robert Graves. Many writers also explored the idea of Jesus surviving the Crucifixion.

Oh, and the idea of Jesus marrying Mary Magdalene is another very old chestnut. I'm actually surprised that nobody has yet picked up Christopher Marlowe's idea that Jesus used to have sex with the evangelist John. Maybe someone is working on that novel right now.

Every generation needs to reconstruct early Christianity in its own image, and it does. Not surprisingly, the "discovery" of the married Jesus coincides neatly with the furor within the Catholic Church over issues of celibacy and women's claims to leadership, and charges of plots and concealment follow neatly on from the clergy abuse scandals.

You seem to point your finger and say: without you, mass media, being a willing accomplice—because you are slave to political correctness and the "feel good" social environment of the day—this revisionism would not have become as popular as it has, because it certainly doesn't deserve it. Can you explain?

I would not be foolish enough to criticize the media for trying to do their primary job, which is to attract the largest possible audience. But by definition, news is always about the *new*. Religion scholars get weary when they get the normal phone call around Easter—"So, anything new about the Resurrection?"—and if there isn't, journalists have a natural tendency to publicize theories that might be fringe or actively loopy. They also tend to frame stories in terms of exciting narrative, of amazing discoveries, courageous rogue scholars tackling entrenched establishments, new documents rocking the world of scholarship, and so on. The problem in all this is that we lose the perspective of memory, and that in fact so little of what is allegedly new and revolutionary is anything like new, and has been well known to scholars for literally centuries. The narrative of lost mysteries and sudden rediscovery has built into it a pattern of recurrent amnesia.

If, as you say, the "new scholarship" and the media have created an over-the-top view of the Nag Hammadi finds and other newly discovered gospels, what is the proper way for us to understand Mary Magdalene as a person, as an apostle, as a spiritual leader? And has the whole Da Vinci Code phenomenon helped or hindered our understanding of early Christianity and the role of Mary Magdalene?

For me, the post-resurrection encounters between Jesus and Mary Magdalene are not just superb as literature, they are among the most moving passages in religious scripture of any kind. Literally, my hair stands on end when I read them. It is not surprising that so many artists and authors have used and cited the scenes. Let me take this opportunity to cite Rudyard Kipling's gorgeous story "The Gardener," a use of the Jesus and Magdalene encounter in a modern setting (in fairness, he merges that Mary with the mother of Jesus).

Having gone on at length about why I do not believe the Gnostic Gospels tell us anything worthwhile about the real Magdalene, let me go on to say that the canonical gospels themselves make her a fascinating figure. Personally, I have no doubt that she was a critical figure in the earliest Christian community, and I have no trouble whatever in believing that she bore the title of apostle.

We also need to confront the real mystery of how the gospels treat Jesus' appearance to Mary, and what happened to that idea in the early church. In the earliest account of the Resurrection, written by Paul in the 50s, Mary is not mentioned, and Peter receives the first Resurrection appearance. Yet all the gospels make Mary the star of the narrative. Mark as we have it is unfinished, but there's no doubt that he meant to end with an appearance to the women. So, does Paul (a) not know the Mary Magdalene tradition? (b) not believe it? or (c) regard it as unworthy of inclusion because Mary is a woman? If (a), when and how does such an apparently early tradition get going?

It would be easy to believe that the first story told of a Resurrection appearance to Mary, who was doubly questionable in being a woman who had a record of personality disorder—our modern terminology for having seven demons cast out of her. In that case, shortly afterwards, the church would try to clean up its act by having a first appearance to Peter, and try to bury the Mary story altogether. The pagan critic Celsus certainly regarded Mary as a shoddy witness. But in reality, it's the other way around! The Mary stories evolve separately from the Petrine accounts, though who can say at this stage whether they grew earlier, later, or in parallel? Nineteenth-century scholars like Renan and Strauss found the origin of the Resurrection idea in the "subjective visions first of the women at the tomb, and then of other disciples, influenced by their intense love for Christ, and their excited mental state."

In short, why is Mary Magdalene there at all, unless there was an early and quite insurmountable tradition that gave her priority in the whole Easter story? But if there was, why isn't she in Paul? One issue here might concern the conflict—or at least, the lack of it—between Galilee and Jerusalem traditions, or to put it another way: Peter versus Mary. Here's a suggestion—maybe the Galilean disciples had their own set of ideas and traditions, with Peter as hero, and that's what Paul picked up when he visited Palestine. But the church in the Jerusalem area remembered Mary Magdalene as its heroine, and ensured that their story ended up in the gospels. And who knows, but that she might also have been a prominent figure in the church around there?

Finally, I think that recent fantasies about Mary Magdalene have really distracted attention from the radicalism of early Christianity, which affected gender issues as much as anything. This is something we Westerners miss, but which readers in Africa or Asia pick up, because they are more familiar with traditional social arrangements. For me, one of the most powerful parts of the New Testament is the scene where Jesus talks to the Samaritan woman at the well, and in so doing tramples countless taboos and restrictions. Now think of that from a modern Asian perspective. It was not just in ancient Palestine that Jesus' interaction with the Samaritan woman at the well would have crossed accepted boundaries, or that the woman's active participation in dialogue seemed daring. We need to look beyond Mary Magdalene to Jesus' other interactions with women, and to do so on the basis of reliable historical materials, not fantasies from a couple of centuries later.

*Where do you come down on all the controversy surrounding Dan Brown and the people whose point of view he holds up as inspiration for his book— people such as Lynn Picknett (*Templar Revelation*) and Henry Baigent and his colleagues (*Holy Blood, Holy Grail*)?*

People like Baigent, Brown, and Picknett are popular writers who have nothing whatever to do with serious scholarship, and should not be discussed in the same breath as the scholars Elaine Pagels or Karen King. Dan Brown, in particular, is a novelist and as such has no obligation whatever to historical truth. While I personally don't like his writing style, he clearly has thrilled millions, and to that extent I wish him good luck—as if he needs my good wishes. My concern with his work is that he presents a view of Christianity that is absolutely at variance with any vaguely orthodox view of the faith, and his view of the grand church conspiracy feeds into quite radical anti-Catholic sentiment.

So my answer would be a plea for consistency. If works of art are going to offend people, let everyone be equally liable to offense. Let's not single out one group—such as the Catholic Church—for attack, while everyone else gets off free. I honestly don't believe in banning books, since I am close to being a First Amendment absolutist. But let's have equal opportunity offense.

So rather than getting those speculative ideas about Jesus, Mary Magdalene, and "revisionist" Christianity from The Da Vinci Code, *where should people turn instead?*

I would love to see modern publishers reprint the classic works of speculation about Jesus and the early church written a hundred years ago by George Moore, Frank Harris, Robert Graves, and others. The books and stories are fine in their own right, and people would be amazed to see how few new things there really were under the sun. And I would be delighted if people who read this interview rushed out to read Kipling's short story "The Gardener."

Mary Magdalene
An Heretical Portrait

by John Lamb Lash

There is an unobserved irony at play in all modern scholarship on Gnosticism, writes John Lash in this thought-provoking essay. In their own time and setting, Gnostic teachings and practices were condemned as heretical by church fathers such as Irenaeus and Augustine. Indeed, Lash believes Gnosticism posed such a fundamental threat to Roman Christianity that the early church fathers insisted on the banishment of Gnostic writings so that they could impose their system of doctrine without question, criticism, or opposition—and they very nearly succeeded.

But the basic question of whether or not Gnosticism was indeed a heresy in the sense of being a negative, dangerous belief system is little addressed in our own time. Ironically, says Lash, scholars today tend to consider Gnosticism to be valuable only for what it reveals about early Christianity, not for what it says in its own right. Most of what we learn about this ancient heresy goes toward explaining and, in some respects, enhancing the belief system that suppressed it.

Lash, who is the author of four books and co-founder and principal writer for www.Metahistory.org, describes himself as an "independent eclectic scholar." He sees in the figure of Mary Magdalene an opportunity to recover the genuine heretical features of Gnosticism. He says his forthcoming book, *Not in His Image: Gnostic Vision, Sacred Ecology, and the Future of Belief* will bring back "the Sophianic vision of the Mysteries." In what may be one of the most radical views in *Secrets of Mary Magdalene,* Lash profiles Mary as a pagan *gnostikos,* a teacher of anti-salvationist views, a striking contrast to her frequent portrayal as simply a devout follower of Jesus. In this essay, the companion of Jesus emerges as a heretic true to her Gnostic origins rather than a female accomplice in the Christian message of salvation.

Dan Brown's novel *The Da Vinci Code* has triggered intense interest in the formerly marginal, and possibly heretical, figure of Mary Magdalene. Appearing through a rift in the collective psyche, a revelation is taking shape, with Magdalene at its trembling focus. But a revelation of what? To whom? For what purpose? Whatever else it may do, this widespread recognition of Magdalene promises to change the way Jesus is viewed, and perhaps even the way salvation is attained. Once

This article is a condensed version of a three-part essay written for www.Metahistory.org, a site dedicated to the critique of belief systems. It features a wide range of writings on Mary Magdalene, Sophia, and *gnosis.*

she is included in the story of the Savior, Magdalene alters that story. The presence of the notorious harlot registers in the collective imagination at three, ever-deepening levels of impact:

Level one, where an alternative story of the life of Jesus emerges.
Level two, where the hitherto unknown background of Jesus' life, including Pagan and non-Christian factors, emerges.
Level three, where the Passion of Christ mutates into the passion of the Lovers, and archetypes clash like tectonic plates.

Level One: The Alternative Life of Jesus

At the first level of impact, Mary Magdalene introduces an alternative story about the life of Jesus. The key incident is the meeting in the garden on Easter morning, when Magdalene encounters Jesus in his "resurrected" form. Scholars debate the several passages in the Gospels that may or may not refer to her, but they are unanimous that this episode does. The meeting hints at a profound complicity between Jesus (or the "Christ" in his divine, superhuman aspect) and the woman who, we are told, mistakes him for the gardener. Gnostic texts do not describe this meeting, but they clearly state that Mary Magdalene, though a mortal woman, was the equal and counterpart to the Risen Lord. In the Pistis Sophia where Magdalene converses with the Lord after his ascension, she is called "the woman who knew All." The fragmentary Gospel of Mary is said to record in her own words a teaching on human nature.

In Gnostic terms (that is, in heretical terms), Magdalene represents the divine element in humanity as much as Jesus does. And she speaks about humanity from divine inspiration that holds an authority equal to his.

The Da Vinci Code has little to say about the message of Magdalene. Instead, it plays on the controversial claim that she is Jesus' wife and, more importantly, the mother of his children. Those who reject this tale argue that it is a distortion, or a downright lie, or it does not accord with the historical facts (as if the New Testament can be taken for fact!), it blasphemes the divinity of Jesus, etc. Those who endorse the story argue that it presents a more human view of Jesus, includes women in the founding events of Christianity, and presents a gender-balanced model of spirituality. Whatever the arguments pro and con, putting Magdalene in the picture changes what *we are willing to believe* about the main character of the story, who may arguably be regarded as the central figure in human history.

The core beliefs that drive human behavior are rarely transmitted in a direct manner, in plain and open language. Rather, they are encoded in stories, scripts, narratives. The effect that beliefs exert upon us can best be fathomed when we recognize how they are encoded in story-form, for it is *through identification with a story* that we take on beliefs and meld them to our identity. Encoded in the conventional story of Jesus is the belief that sex is a down-and-dirty business of the flesh, in which no Son of a Christian God would sully himself. In Christian belief, sexuality both causes and characterizes our separation from the Divine. This belief was initially scripted in the story of the Fall in the Old Testament: Upon discovering their sexuality, Adam and Eve are rejected from Paradise (i.e., the blissful state produced by the direct presence of God, the Divine). The New Testament encodes the belief that Jesus, being divine, could not and did not indulge in sexual acts.

At the first level of impact, the alternative story raises the sexuality of the man Jesus into high relief. On this touchy issue, the alternative story about Jesus splits into two distinct plot-lines. Along one line runs the sacred bloodline scenario introduced by Baigent, Lincoln, and Leigh in *Holy Blood, Holy Grail,* and fictionalized by Dan Brown. All parties to this plot assume that the sexuality of Jesus had a biological result: children born to him by Mary Magdalene. This plot-line encodes the belief that Jesus was of a special nature, being more than human, or perhaps a fully divine incarnation, and so his genetic lineage must be considered sacred, holy, divine. The *Sangreal* scenario restates the ancient belief in the descent of humans from divine stock. This is the basis of theocracy; i.e., rulership by the gods or their descendents. Coded into the alternative story of Jesus, this belief provides the basis for a grandiose conspiracy theory about a secret society whose members intend to restore theocracy in Europe by revealing the lost bloodline of Jesus and Magdalene.

All this is pretty sensational stuff, it seems. But something more sensational has yet to be revealed, for the *Sangraal / Sangreal* tale is not the only plot-line that can be derived from the Gnostic Magdalene material. It is not even the most probable plot-line. Asserting that Jesus had sex with a woman may seem outrageous to many people, but there is a further outrage in store: the assertion that he did so, not to procreate, but merely for the pleasure of it. This proposition brings us to the second level of impact, where we encounter the Pagan background of the Jesus story, which has been written out of the New Testament, and largely ignored by Baigent, Brown, and others.

Level Two: The Story of Pagan Spirituality

Procreation belongs to the declared plan of the Father God. In the Old Testament, Jehovah encourages the Hebrews to breed and spread over the earth. To this day, the Catholic Church condemns contraception on two counts: because sexual intercourse for pleasure is a sin, and because humans have no right to meddle with the procreative function given to us by the Creator. Long before the Church defined and enforced these doctrines, Pagans (i.e., non-Christians) in the classical world had quite a good time with lavish, guiltless sexuality. Gnostics (*gnostokoi,* "those who know about divine things"), in particular, held strong views on sexual liberation.

Here the second plot-line, the tale less told, veers sharply away from the holy bloodline scenario uncritically adopted by Dan Brown, and currently bedazzling the entire world. Linking Jesus to a theocratic conspiracy may work sensationally well in fiction, but in fact the textual materials *of Gnostic derivation* on Magdalene and Jesus do not support this plot-line, for Gnostics opposed the Christian view of human divinity that informs the theocratic program. In other words, in rejecting human divinity (the Incarnation, theologically speaking), Gnostics opposed the very notion of theocracy. How can the sacred bloodline scenario rely on Gnostic sources when Gnostics rejected all pretensions of theocratic descent?

Some Nag Hammadi texts squarely reject the Incarnation and the Resurrection, the two primary marks of Jesus' divinity. The Gospel of

Philip, which contains the famous cameo of Jesus kissing Magdalene, says that "those who say they will die first and then rise are in error," and *The Second Treatise of the Great Seth* condemns the Incarnation as a sham, "an imitation of the true enlightened ones" that leads people to embrace "the doctrine of a dead man." To Gnostics, what is divine in humanity is not blood or even disembodied spirit but *nous,* the god-like intelligence that connects us to the Goddess Sophia, whose name means "wisdom." According to the Gnostic creation-myth taught in the Mysteries, Sophia first produced humanity (the *Anthropos*) as a feat of her own imagination (*Ennoia*), and then she morphed into the planet earth (*Gaia*), so that she herself became the setting for human-ity to unfold its god-like faculty, *nous.* Humanity is divine *by endowment of this faculty,* and Jesus is no exception, although he might have been regarded as a notable teacher of the Anthropos, i.e., authentic human-ity, in Gnostic terms. (Even if this were so, the Gnostic Jesus cannot be identified with the quasi-historical Jesus of the New Testament, be-cause the words attributed to *that* Jesus contain precious little of the Anthropos message.)

The Anthropic theology of the Gnostics was the summit of Pagan spirituality, the highpoint of an ancient legacy that long predated Christianity. (James Robinson, head of the Nag Hammadi translation team, asserts that Gnosticism was a rich and widespread movement in the Pagan world, not merely a marginal development within early Christianity, and more ancient than the date of the surviving materials suggests.) Regarded as Pagans and heretics, Jesus and Magdalene would have been a pair of initiated teachers from the Mysteries, the spiritual universities of the classical world. As such, they would have taught the divine potential of humanity, but not claimed divinity for themselves, or anyone. Early Church ideologues who hated the Gnos-tics falsely accused them of claiming divine status, but careful analysis of Gnostic writings side by side with the patristic arguments against them show this to be malicious disinformation. As I explain in my book, *Not in His Image,* the main requirement of initiation in the Mys-teries was ego death and transcendence of single-self identity—a far cry, indeed, from self-aggrandizement to a divine level. The aim of *gnosis* was to know as the Gods know, not to become God in human form, nor even to find God in one's innermost self.

Against the background of Pagan spirituality, Magdalene looks far more outrageous than she does as the faithful wife of Jesus and devoted mother of his children. Almost all we know about her comes from Gnostic sources, texts that portray her as an accomplished seer, an initiated teacher or *telestes*. She would have been an enlightened woman facing a world in spiritual crisis. At the dawn of the Piscean Age (around 120 BCE), some Pagan teachers emerged from the anonymity of the Mystery cults and undertook a public mission to address the dominant controversy of that time. Sparked by the public disclosure of the precession of the equinoxes by Hipparchus around 150 BCE, this controversy centered on a single, crucial question: Is human fate predetermined, or can we each be guided to a path in life of our own choosing? In that period of tremendous upheaval, a kind of New Age fever raged across the Roman Empire. Many people expected a messiah to come and bring social justice; others, like the Zaddikim of the Dead Sea, awaited the end of the world and rapture-like salvation by extraterrestrials in shining chariots. Pictured as Gnostic initiates (Jewish or not), Jesus and Magdalene would have been committed to the task of spiritual guidance, helping people in all classes of society to find their way against the dictates of fate.

It was a moment of tremendous promise, when a great shift for humanity might have transpired. What happened instead was that Roman Christianity took control of the social and spiritual life of the classical world, and the opportunity to fulfill the genuine potential of the *Anthropos,* modeled in the Sophianic vision of the Gnostics, was denied, turned into heresy, and violently repressed. The murder of the Gnostic teacher Hypatia in 415 AD marks the plunge of the Western world into the Dark Ages.

The Pagan profile of Jesus and Magdalene, which is strongly supported by historical and textual evidence, totally undercuts the sacred bloodline scenario. Even if Jesus and Magdalene did have sex, they would not have had children. Few points are unanimous in Gnostic scholarship, but on this one issue all scholars agree: Gnostics rejected procreation as collusion with the Demiurge, a demented pseudo-deity whom they identified with Jehovah; but they embraced joyous, uninhibited sexuality as both a celebration of human innocence and a form of spiritual yoga. The Gospel of Philip describes how initiates

unite sexually in the *nymphion* ("bridal chamber") to perform a sacramental rite that encases them in a luminous protective cocoon. For
Gnostics, as for their Asian counterparts, the adepts of Tantra, sexual
rapture was a divine flush that induced enlightenment and immunized
them against negative thought-forms or intrusive psychic entities.
Orgiastic sex was a key spiritual practice in some Gnostic groups,
such as the Ophites or "snake-worshippers." Ophis, the divine serpent, was identical with the Kundalini of Asian tradition. Had Jesus
and Magdalene been Pagan initiates, as the Gnostic evidence indicates, they would not have had children but they would have practiced
Tantric sex. Epiphanius of Salamis, a Christian convert who infiltrated
a Gnostic sect around 335 AD, left an X-rated account of such practices in his Panarion. There seems to have been quite a lot of foreplay
and cavorting in Pagan sacramental sex. Epiphanius cites a lost passage from The Questions of Mary (Panarion 26.8.2-3) where Jesus
meets Magdalene for a frolic on a mountainside and instructs her in
the fine points of oral intercourse.

The high-end spiritual hedonism of the Gnostics was, and still is,
far more threatening to conventional beliefs about Jesus than the
homey profile of Magdalene as wife and mother. But so far this dicey
aspect of the holy harlot's career remains relatively unknown, and the
bloodline scenario holds a monopoly on Magdalene's role.

Level Three: The Story of the Lovers

The secret dossier of Epiphanius has considerable shock value, of
course, but we are still not at the deepest point of impact generated
by the figure of Mary Magdalene. Taken to the third level, the scenario of the Gnostic teachers mutates toward one of the most potent
archetypes known to humanity: the Lovers.

Baigent, Brown, and others overlook the fact that Gnostic texts call
Magdalene the companion (*koinonos*) of Jesus, never his wife. Thus,
the Gnostic sources primary to the alternative story cannot be used to
support the claim of marriage. Magdalene is the consort (*paredros*) of
Jesus, comparable to the *maithuna* or sexual-spiritual partner in Asian
Tantra. Originally, the *paredros* was a high priestess who mated with

an aspiring king in order to test his eligibility to rule with tenderness and strength (the two key traits of a good lover). She literally anointed the candidate with her sexual juices. The Greek term *christos* is a translation of the Hebrew *mashias,* "messiah, the anointed one." In the New Testament Apocrypha (a collection of non-Nag Hammadi texts), the Acts of John describes a mystic dance performed by Jesus at the Last Supper. Traditionally, Magdalene is the woman with the alabaster jar who anointed the feet of Jesus—not so he can die on the cross, but so he can dance and celebrate the miracle of being alive. The "round dance of Jesus" presents a vivid contrast to the brutal melodrama of the Crucifixion, which John, the intimate witness, dismisses as a sado-masochistic hallucination. This is radical Gnosticism, featuring Magdalene as an heretical figure equal to Jesus. The Acts of John was so threatening to the Roman Church that for centuries after the Mysteries were suppressed, copies of it were sought out and burned, along with those who owned them.

A medieval legend says that Mary Magdalene went to Provence in Southern France. This legend is not of Gnostic derivation, but neither does it support the sacred bloodline scenario. Considering the heretical profile of the holy harlot, Magdalene's exile may be imagined quite differently than has been assumed in the Baigent-Brown scenario. Her intent could have been to perpetuate, not a bloodline connection, but *the ideal of spiritual union in carnal love,* following the Gnostic practices described in the Gospel of Philip and celebrated in the anointed dance of the Acts of John. The bond of passionate love, when it includes a genuine spiritual dimension, enshrines the beloved person in the heart of the lover, and unites them both by a power that transcends death. Their immortality dwells in their passion for each other, and insures that they will be united after death.

This language may sound extravagant, but it is totally consistent with the archetype of the Divine Lovers, the potent imaginal complex we encounter at the third level of Magdalene's impact. Within the frame of traditional belief, Jesus Christ conforms to the archetype of the Savior, the divine instrument of redemption, both the model and the guarantor of eternal life. The Savior is a scapegoat, an innocent victim who dies for the sins of others. Hence, Jesus embodies the archetype of the Divine Victim. Belief in Jesus and credence in his mission depends on accepting him as the human reflection of the Victim archetype, but the inclusion of Magdalene in the Jesus story presents a breathtaking option: to imagine Jesus Christ as Lover rather than Victim.

Granted, the Savior-Victim archetype holds tremendous power over human imagination, but the Lovers have equal, or surpassing, power. In the human psyche, these two archetypes collide like tectonic plates, one of which is sure to ride over the other, sooner or later. With the world-wide introduction of Mary Magdalene as a key figure in the life of Jesus, the archetype of the Lovers has been tectonically lifted. If it continues to rise, it will eventually override the other plate.

In fact, historically speaking, it has already begun to so do. In the 12th century, the region of Southern France where Magdalene is said to have landed after the death of Jesus saw the blossoming of a rich spiritual, cultural, and literary movement, the Cult of Amor. Central to this movement was the troubadour poetry that celebrated a mysterious woman, the Lady addressed as Domna, a shortening of the Latin *domina,* feminine form of "lord, master." By an astonishing inversion, the troubadours saw the "Lord," not in the sacrificed Savior, but in an alluring woman whose beauty inspired some of the greatest literature the world has known. In *Tristan,* written by Gottfried von Strasbourg around 1210 AD, the poet compares the passion of Tristan and Isolde to the sacrament of bread and wine. Their spiritual love is as a strong *in the flesh* as the Presence of Christ in the eucharist (a dogma asserted by the Fourth Lateran Council of 1215). This momentous shift from religious to romantic faith happened because the archetype of the Lovers had overridden the Savior, altering forever the role of Jesus Christ in human imagination.

The deep psycho-spiritual impact that produced the cult of romantic love came not from Jesus, but from his consort and counterpart, Mary Magdalene. Her message is about the divinity of human passion and its power to transcend death. This message, which might be considered the ultimate heresy, has not survived in written words, but in the figure and mystique of a harlot and heretic. To paraphrase a much-cited line from the sixties, the Magdalene *is* the message.

4 Mary Magdalene

Marginalized, Harlotized, and "Put in Her Place"

Across time, Mary went from being an important disciple whose superior status depended on the confidence Jesus himself had invested in her, to a repentant whore whose status depended on the erotic charge of her history and the misery of her stricken conscience. . . . from one that challenged men's misogynist assumptions to one that confirmed them.

—James Carroll

Only one form of Christianity . . . emerged as victorious from the conflicts of the second and third centuries. This one form of Christianity decided what was the "correct" Christian perspective; it decided who could exercise authority over Christian belief and practice; and it determined what forms of Christianity would be marginalized, set aside, destroyed. It also decided which books to canonize into scripture and which books to set aside as "heretical," teaching false ideas. . . .

—Bart Ehrman

Man enjoys the great advantage of having a god endorse the code he writes; and since man exercises a sovereign authority over women it is especially fortunate that this authority has been vested in him by the Supreme Being.

—Simone de Beauvoir, *The Second Sex*

An Apostle Diminished
The Challenge to Mary Magdalene's Authority

AN INTERVIEW WITH ANN GRAHAM BROCK

Christianity seems to have been born not only in struggle against the status quo of two thousand years ago, but with rivalry and contention for power and control within the movement, almost from its first days. This contentiousness seems to have had less to do with the words of Jesus than with a struggle for authority. After Jesus ascended, who among his closest followers would be able to call themselves disciples? Who would be designated as worthy of spreading Jesus' message as an apostle?

By all rights, it would seem Mary Magdalene would have been a leading candidate: after all, she was chosen to be the messenger—the "apostle"—of the most important message of all: the Resurrection of Jesus.

So what happened? Why was she not given the title of Apostle in the New Testament? It was a political decision, argues the scholar Ann Graham Brock, made by the writers of the canonical gospels to bolster Peter's role and diminish that of Mary Magdalene. Brock, author of *Mary Magdalene, the First Apostle: The Struggle for Authority,* explains it this way: "The criteria by which various early Christian authors attributed apostolic authority to certain followers of Jesus and not to others in early Christian documents provide insights into the politics of various factions of the early church."

In this interview, Brock summarizes her findings. It seems that even before Mary Magdalene was officially harlotized in the sixth century, she was marginalized, in spite of what many scholars today believe to be her close and intimate connections to Jesus and her central role as witness to his Resurrection.

Very little actually appears in the Bible to tell us who Mary Magdalene was, and the only information we do have appears in the four canonical gospels of the New Testament. Can you talk a bit about how she is depicted in each of the gospels? Why do you believe there are differences between them?

With respect to Mary Magdalene, the gospels of the New Testament provide us with some important similarities but also some interesting differences. All four mention Mary Magdalene (which is more than we can say about some of the male disciples) and, with only one exception, whenever the texts refer to a group of women, they always name her first. Most importantly, all four gospels portray Mary Magdalene (along with the other women in some cases) as chosen to be the first witness of the Resurrection.

Despite all the similarities, however, there are also some significant differences. The gospel portrayals of Mary Magdalene differ
for a number of reasons, in part because the various gospel writers
had somewhat different traditions handed down to them, but even
more importantly, because they had different interests or purposes
for writing. Church politics also had some significant influence. For
instance, three out of the four gospels portray Mary Magdalene
alone or with all the women receiving the commissioning to go and
tell the others the good news, but Luke does not. Instead, only
Luke mentions an individual Resurrection appearance of Jesus to
Simon (Peter), the disciple whom the Gospel of Luke raises to even
greater prominence than all the other gospels.

*Out of these varied depictions, is there one portrayal that you feel is most
accurate? Or most important?*

The two best portrayals of Mary Magdalene are those in Matthew
and John. What I appreciate about the Gospel of Matthew is the way
it provides us with one of the most complete and inclusive reports:
whenever there are multiple traditions concerning Mary, it provides
both narratives rather than choosing one tradition over another. For
example, one ancient tradition that circulated tells us that a heavenly apparition(s) appeared to Mary Magdalene and the women
(recorded in Mark 16:1–8, Matt 28:1–8, and Luke 24:1–12), while
another one tells us that Jesus himself appeared to Mary Magdalene
(recorded in Matt 28:9–10 and John 20:14–18), but Matthew provides us a balance by recording both of these traditions—first the
angel and then Jesus.

The text that is perhaps most valuable for Magdalene studies,
however, is the one in John because it begins to accord her the
recognition and prominence that her figure seems to have achieved
historically. This gospel focuses more exclusively upon her at the
tomb (not even mentioning the other women) and does so with the
most detailed descriptions of the Resurrection appearances. John
provides a long description of her Resurrection encounter with Jesus, in which he calls Mary by name, she recognizes him, and he
then gives her instructions. Moreover, this gospel is the only one

that subsequently provides us with the dialogue in which she finds the other disciples and tells them, "I have seen the Lord."

In your book, Mary Magdalene, The First Apostle, *you make the argument that the church has denied Mary of her rightful title. What qualified someone to be an apostle? Did Mary Magdalene not meet the criteria? Were there other reasons she may have been "disqualified"?*

Several definitions of "apostle" circulated in the early Christian churches, but despite the differences in these definitions, they all had a common thread; that is, the correlation between being an apostle and receiving a Resurrection appearance. In fact, Paul's epistles make this correlation clear as he claims his apostleship by arguing that he received a Resurrection appearance from Christ. Paul writes, for example, "Am I not an apostle? Have I not seen the risen Lord?" (1 Cor 9:1).

The only Gospel that does not portray Mary Magdalene as having the grounds to be an apostle is the Gospel of Luke. I explain in my book why it seems more than coincidental that the portrayal of Mary in this gospel appears significantly different from her portrayals in most of the other accounts. Only this gospel introduces her as someone possessed by seven demons who therefore needed healing from Jesus. Only this gospel further diminishes her role, and that of the other women at the cross, by adding additional acquaintances into the Crucifixion scene and even mentioning them first. And when the women, named at last, recount this miracle to the disciples, the male disciples evaluate their witness as "foolish, idle talk." Most importantly, the Gospel of Luke makes no reference to Jesus' Resurrection appearance to Mary Magdalene and portrays no commissioning from either an angel or Jesus. If we look at the text carefully, we can find in Luke a discernible relationship between the ways in which the author shapes the traditions to heighten the prominence of Peter while at the same time diminishing Mary Magdalene's position.

In many of the writings about Mary Magdalene today we frequently see her referred to as "the apostle of the apostles." Isn't there a contradiction here? How did she come by that title if it isn't mentioned in these Bible stories?

Although we do not know the exact origin, Hippolytus, bishop and martyr of Rome, may have been the one to set the precedent for this title with the following quotation concerning Mary Magdalene and the other women: "Lest the female apostles doubt the angels, Christ himself came to them so that the women would be apostles of Christ and by their obedience rectify the sin of the ancient Eve. . . . Christ showed himself to the (male) apostles and said to them: '. . . It is I who appeared to these women and I who wanted to send them to you as apostles'" (*De Cantico* 24–26, CSCO 264, 43–49). Thus, Hippolytus here affirms the role of women as apostles of Christ, and since Mary Magdalene was the one who received this honor first (and exclusively in John), she eventually comes to be the one known as the *apostola apostolorum.*

Is it fair to say, then, that gender is an issue at the heart of these conflicts? What does the rivalry between Peter and Mary mean in a political and social context? And where else do we see women being "attacked" in this way?

We surely would not want to oversimplify the situation to say that gender is the only issue, but some of the content of the dialogues certainly suggests that it was a significant factor. However, we need to be careful about what conclusions we can draw from these confrontations. We cannot assume, for instance, that these controversies necessarily took place historically between Peter and Mary, but there is a good possibility that those early Christians who looked toward Peter and those who looked toward Mary Magdalene as an authority may well have come into conflict with one another. These stories depict such tensions, and even though we do not know the exact cause of these tensions, they may have had something to do with women's leadership and their rightful place in the movement, especially since the issue of gender crops up in almost every controversy dialogue.

For example:

(1) You find such references in the Gospel of Thomas, a first- or second-century text with 114 sayings of Jesus that rarely singles out the disciples individually by name (only seven contemporaries of Jesus and only five of them possess an individual speaking part in the text: Thomas, Simon Peter, Matthew, Mary, and Salome). In one of those instances, Peter complains specifically about Mary and

includes women in the process, saying, "Let Mary leave us for women are not worthy of life" (GTh 114). Notice that he does not directly challenge only Mary, saying, "Let Mary leave us for *she* is not worthy of life." Rather, his challenge claims that *women* are not worthy of life.

(2) In the Gospel of Mary Peter objects to Mary's vision and again his portrayal includes a reference to gender: "Did he [Jesus] really speak with a *woman* without our knowledge (and) not openly? Are we to turn about and all listen to her?" (GMary 16–20). (It is interesting that by contrast, Andrew's objection in the text does not revolve around the person of Mary but is based, instead, on theological arguments. He says, "For certainly these teachings are strange ideas.")

Also, (3) in Pistis Sophia I, Peter complains about Mary with the words, "My Lord we are not able to suffer this woman who takes the opportunity from us, and does not allow anyone of us to speak, but she speaks many times" (PS, Book 1, chap. 36), and (4) in Pistis Sophia IV Peter again complains: "My Lord, let the women cease to question, that we also may question" (PS, Book 4, chap. 146).

Although these narratives indicate challenges to Mary's authority, these explicit controversy stories also depict that Mary had some support among the other disciples. For example, Levi defends Mary after the figure of Peter attacks her with the words "Surely he [Jesus] did not want to show that she is *more worthy* than we are" (PRyl 463, recto 15–16). Levi responds to Peter's challenge: "If the Savior deemed her worthy, who are you indeed to reject her? For surely, knowing her, he loved her very well" (PRyl 463, verso 5–8). The Coptic version of this text similarly reflects this kind of support: "If the Savior deemed her worthy, who are you to scorn her? Surely the Savior knows her very well. That is why he loved her more than us" (GMary 18,10–15).

This kind of controversy over women's leadership continued for centuries to come and remains a hot topic even in congregations today.

What were the implications of the struggle for authority between Peter and Mary? How did it come about that women were seen as full participants at

the time of Jesus and then, within a few centuries, were pretty much under
the thumb of the patriarchal church?

There is no doubt that a competition for authority developed in the early church. Even Paul had to defend his rightful place. It appears that in the beginning stages of Christianity women enjoyed a greater role as leaders, especially since the early churches often met in their homes. The women naturally helped to serve the *agape* meal—the common meal for fellowship and charity—and the accompanying communion because it was taking place within their household and domain. Such female participation is consistent with the portrayal of Jesus empowering female figures throughout the gospel narratives (see, for example, his treatment of the Samaritan woman at the well in John 4). It is extremely interesting to me that when you consider all the narratives and all the sayings in the New Testament that we have received concerning Jesus, we have not one in which he tells women to be silent. His ability to empower women as well as men may have been part of what made early Christianity such a threat to the status quo and the patriarchal society that the Romans cherished.

With time Christianity's powerful message continued to reach more and more people, so much so that the gatherings eventually became so large that they had to move into governmental buildings called basilicas. It was at this point that women were often moved to the margins of authority and even silenced. Losing the memories or traditions of strong female role models in early Christianity benefited no one except those who were in competition for the same kind of authority or status. To characterize this struggle for authority as a full-scale "organized conspiracy" against Mary Magdalene and women is, in my opinion, a gross overgeneralization. I am sure it was not all that well organized, even though it was effective. The diminishment of Mary Magdalene's status definitely worked in favor of those who wished women to be less visible in their leadership because it was in part through her example that other women had been claiming a precedent for the authority to preach or spread the good news. With her disparagement as a prostitute, her leadership position obviously became undermined and devalued.

*In your book, you go into some detail about the ways you have found Mary
Magdalene to have been diminished: as witness, as apostle, and as role
model. Can you give us some examples?*

There are numerous examples of ways in which Mary Magdalene's
role has suffered over the years. We have already touched upon
ways in which misidentifications of her as a prostitute diminished
Mary Magdalene's reputation as an authority and leadership figure.
Another way in which her position is diminished appears in certain
translations of the Resurrection story in Syriac or Coptic that replace Mary Magdalene with Mary the Mother in the final garden
scene with the resurrected Jesus. Such a substitution should not be
taken lightly because being the first Resurrection witness carried
with it a great deal of authority. The Coptic version of the Greek
Acts of Philip also presents a substitution, this time of Peter for
Mary as the person who accompanies Philip on his missionary journey. These are only some of the examples of the numerous ways in
which her role has undergone misrepresentations, substitutions, or
even complete omissions. Recovering her role as a witness, leader,
and apostle is essential to gaining greater gender justice within
Christianity.

*Where do you stand in the continuing discussion about whether or not Mary
Magdalene was married to Jesus? And, as interesting as it may be, does this
debate obscure something of Mary Magdalene that is more important to
focus on?*

If we had incontrovertible evidence that Jesus had been married,
then Mary Magdalene would be the most likely candidate by a long
shot. However, we have no such evidence. There are those who
have argued for some time now that because Jesus was a devout
Jew, by all rights people would have expected him to marry. Such a
statement, however, is heavily overgeneralized because although
expectations were high that Jewish men Jesus' age would marry,
we do not have to go very far to find exceptions to that rule, including one of his own kinsmen, John the Baptist, as well as Paul of
Tarsus, and numerous other early Christian leaders at the time.

Although in many ways Jesus may well have been a devout Jew,
on the other hand, he also apparently found instances in which he

needed to reinterpret the rules (such as his healing on the Sabbath) or if he needed to call certain practices into question (such as his cleansing of the temple).

My initial response to the question of his marriage to Mary Magdalene is to wonder why it is so hard for people to imagine that she may have simply been an outstanding and important figure in her own right, alongside Peter, James, and the other early disciples. What I find most problematic about the pairing of Mary Magdalene with Jesus in this way is that their relationship is so often sexualized. In the past Mary Magdalene has been wrongly depicted as a repentant whore and now, even though at least they have made an "honest woman" of her, she is still a sexual being rather than a spiritual leader. Is it not possible that Mary Magdalene was an outstanding disciple who truly comprehended what Jesus was teaching without necessarily having had an actual physical union with him?

What might it mean for Christian history and Christianity today if Mary's interpretation of Jesus' teaching had prevailed instead of Peter's?
It is indeed difficult to say how much of Mary's interpretation of Jesus' teachings still remains with us today since we do not actually know what Mary's interpretation was. I think we can at the very minimum surmise that there would be less controversy today concerning women's rightful leadership and contribution to the church had Mary Magdalene's role gained more recognition. The result may have been a more egalitarian church and one that uniformly ordained women for service, but beyond that, I think it is difficult to say.

But one of the most important questions we could be asking is why we do not find more universal recognition among Christians of Mary Magdalene's status as an early apostle. It is important that we examine the reasons for resistance even today to the evidence we have that women often took the lead in forging the beginnings of Christianity.

The Battle for Scripture and the Faiths We Didn't Get a Chance to Know

AN INTERVIEW WITH BART D. EHRMAN

When I went to graduate school, I had this fantasy of early Christianity as the Golden Age, unified, simple and pure. A kind of play Bibleland.

—ELAINE PAGELS

The common belief regarding the development of Christianity is that there was an unbroken chain of wisdom that started with Jesus, was passed on to the apostles, and in turn was received by the apostles' successors in the organized church— elders, ministers, priests, and bishops. There was one organization, one faith, one practice, all combined to "guarantee the unity and uniformity of Christian belief and practice," as Karen King puts it. This orthodoxy was ratified by the New Testament canon, by the Council of Nicea, and by the carefully proscribed rituals of the church.

In the past few decades, however, a wide range of scholarship has shown us that early Christianity, while monotheistic, was anything but monolithic. There is no single, master narrative. In point of fact, Christianity's first few centuries can better be described as a great religious stew, with various oral traditions, alternate scriptures, lost gospels, mystery cults, and other teachings all vying for acceptance and primacy.

Among the leaders doing the pioneering work of studying the crosscurrents of that era is Bart D. Ehrman, chair of the Department of Religious Studies at the University of North Carolina at Chapel Hill. Ehrman is an authority on the life of Jesus and the propagation of his teachings in the first centuries after his death. This is the subject of one of Ehrman's earlier books, *Lost Christianities: the Battle for Scripture and the Faiths We Never Knew,* and his current *Peter, Paul, and Mary Magdalene.*

In this interview, Ehrman talks about the most important alternative threads of what we now call Christianity (a term that didn't come into existence until the second century). Over time, these alternate sects came to be seen as a threat to the spreading orthodoxy. Competing ideas were, in effect, systematically declared to be heresy and then suppressed or marginalized by the church triumphant.

Ehrman welcomes the popular interest in the early days of Christianity, propelled by *The Da Vinci Code,* which he calls "unusually intelligent for this genre." Still, he would like to set the record straight, and point out that the actual history of early Christianity is as replete with struggles, personalities, perfidy, and surprising revelations as any current thriller.

You have brought to light ways in which Christian belief underwent change as this new theology and its body of documents moved from the Holy Land in the time of Jesus to become the de facto state religion of the Roman Empire several centuries later.What, in fact, are some of those changes? How drastic or trivial are these differences?

Christianity shifted from being an other-worldly Jewish religion, in which the end of all time is at hand and people should not live for the values of their society but should deny themselves in preparation for the coming Kingdom, to being a this-worldly Gentile religion. The latter did not stress the imminent end of all things and taught instead that it is important to work with the world in order to convert the world, so that people could have life after they died. Some people would argue that the Christianity that ended up triumphing was a completely different religion from the one that started in Jerusalem after the death of Jesus—that it is, in fact, a different religion from that of Jesus himself! In this view of things, Christianity is less the religion that Jesus taught (the religion *of* Jesus) than the religion that proclaims Jesus (the religion *about* Jesus). I'd say these are fairly enormous differences.

The so-called Gnostic Gospels, found near the Egyptian town of Nag Hammadi, have rightly gained a great deal of attention.What has been the most important implication of this find from your perspective?

The most important "discovery" of modern times has been that early Christianity was extremely diverse—far more diverse than previous scholars ever could have imagined. What we have learned from the Gnostic Gospels is that there were groups of Christians who believed an enormous range of things that most people today would not even call Christian. For example, some believed that the world is a cosmic mistake, created by an inferior, lesser deity rather than by the Lord God Almighty; that Christ did not really suffer on the cross; that the way to eternal life is not through belief in Jesus' death but through understanding his secret teachings. These, and many many other beliefs, were held by people who considered themselves Christian, who claimed to be following the teachings of Jesus and his apostles, and who had books to *prove* it—books allegedly written by the apostles themselves. If nothing else, the discoveries of Nag Hammadi have opened our eyes to just how diverse the early Christians really were.

People who read the Gnostic Gospels in English translation frequently come away very confused. The gospels are filled with ideas that are very foreign to mainstream Western religious thinking. Given that many different groups have been lumped under one rubric, that of "Gnostics," is there a single consistent body of thought expressed in these documents?

The books are confusing not only in English translation, but also in the Coptic originals! The authors of these books did not think like most of us. Many of them were very metaphysically and mythically oriented. They were not interested in setting out straightforward propositional truths, but were intrigued with the poetics of existence and the mysteries of this world and how we came to inhabit it.

Having said that, I think it does help to have a conceptual understanding of what the Gnostic systems involved, as I try to lay out in another of my books called *Lost Christianities.* In a nutshell, Gnostics believed that this world was not a good place, but was the result of a cosmic disaster. Some of us do not belong here, they said, but are spirits from the world above who have been trapped or imprisoned in these material bodies. The goal of the Gnostic religions is to teach us how to escape. We can escape the material trappings of this world by learning the secret knowledge (Greek: *gnosis*) of who we really are, where we came from, how we got here, and how we can return. Salvation then comes to those who learn the truth about themselves, and these Gnostic books—many of them very confusing, to be sure—are attempts to help us come to fuller self-knowledge. When we understand it, then we can be set free.

The attempt at fuller self-knowledge is surely a timeless aspiration. It existed before the time of Jesus, and it continues to exist in New Age spiritualists. So what would have made what the Gnostics believed in irrelevant? Why would they—and all the other early Christian sects—have died out?

Although there were a variety of historical and cultural reasons, most of these groups probably died out because they were attacked—successfully attacked, on theological grounds—and they weren't nearly as effective in their own propaganda campaigns. They failed to recruit new converts even while the orthodox groups created a strong structure, used letter campaigns and other means to propagate their views—and their rhetoric convinced people.

But what really secured the victory was that the Roman emperor Constantine converted to Christianity. Naturally, he converted to the kind of Christianity that was dominant at that time. Once Constantine converts to an orthodox form of Christianity, and once the state has power, and the state is Christian, then the state starts asserting its influence over Christianity. So by the end of the fourth century, there's actually legislation against heretics. So the empire that used to be completely anti-Christian becomes Christian. And it doesn't just become Christian, but also tries to dictate what shape Christianity ought to be.

The ramifications of this change of events are enormous, of course. It changed the entire way the Western world understands itself, and how people understand something. Think of the concept of guilt alone: if some other groups had won, things might have been completely different.

Is Dan Brown right when he suggests that the real "heretics" may be the Romans who turned a religion of the oppressed—in which women were given prominent roles and certain deeply antimaterialistic beliefs can be traced—into the state religion of the Roman Empire, which was characterized by hierarchy, patriarchy, and politics?

It is not true to say that it was Constantine who once and for all altered the religion, turning it from a women-friendly to a patriarchal religion, who decided that Jesus would be God, who chose which books to include in the New Testament. None of these things was done by Constantine. They had already been done (or were later to be done, in the case of the formation of the canon) decades—well over a century, in fact—before Constantine ever came on the scene. But these shifts certainly did happen. Christianity started out giving a high role and authority to women, who were eventually oppressed and silenced. It started out as an other-worldly religion, and it became a religion that embraced the values and norms of the world. It started out in opposition to the state and all it stood for, and it came both to embrace and to be embraced by the state.

Christianity at the end of the fourth century would have been virtually unrecognizable to Christians at the beginning of the first.

It is thought by some prominent religious scholars that women in general, and Mary Magdalene in particular, had an important and very visible role in among these sects. Is there evidence of this in the alternative gospels? Is there a discernible trend there about how women in the church were treated?

Orthodox Christians weren't the only ones who oppressed women, insisting on their silence and submissiveness. You can find similar trends in other forms of Christianity as well. That being said, it is striking that some Gnostic groups were known for their emphasis on women and their view that the secret revelations that bring salvation could come to women as well as men. Witness the Gospel of Mary, the only gospel named for a woman to have survived antiquity, where the entire point is that Jesus revealed the truth to Mary Magdalene, and explicitly *not* to the male disciples!

Penitent Sinner, Apostolic Saint
The Mary Magdalene Cult Emerges

BY KATHERINE LUDWIG JANSEN

It seems to me that every period creates a Mary Magdalen that fulfills its needs and desires. The medieval period created a Mary Magdalen who was a sinner, whose life was a lesson in hope and repentance. But she was also a saint, one who was a powerful apostle and preacher. These aspects of the saint reflected and refracted societal needs of the medieval period. Our own period's interest in Mary Magdalen is fueled by very different needs and desires. The women's movement, which gave birth to women's history, has allowed us to rediscover our historical foremothers, Mary Magdalen among them. Studies of spiri-

Katherine Ludwig Jansen, a associate professor of history at Catholic University, is the author of *The Making of the Magdalen: Preaching and Popular Devotion in the Later Middle Ages.*

tuality—historical and otherwise—have allowed us to formulate questions that have led us to a better understanding of the function of the cult of the saints in different historical contexts. Studies focused tightly on Mary Magdalen have helped us to see how spirituality is expressed differently across time and space. Gender studies have led us to ask if it is possible to delineate female spirituality and religious expression from its male counterpart. And finally, religious politics should not be forgotten. The contemporary question of women's ordination in the Catholic Church has certainly invigorated new investigations into Mary Magdalen's role in the early church.

Pope Gregory's New Magdalen

It is important to bear in mind that representations of Mary Magdalen developed over time, a very long time, from the early Christian period to our own day. These representations are products of their age and to understand them fully we must understand the context that produced them. In the late antique period (the fourth and fifth centuries), the age of the church fathers, there was certainly interest in Mary Magdalen, but arguably no more so than in any scriptural figure—the interest was there only so far as it pertained to the scriptural commentary that patristic authors such as Augustine of Hippo and Ambrose of Milan were engaged in. There was no clear consensus on Mary Magdalen's identity, and there was even confusion as the church fathers struggled to harmonize the discordant gospel accounts of her life.

Our first written testimony in which the figure of Mary Magdalen has become the sinner-saint, or more accurately, the successful graft of Luke's nameless female sinner (Luke 7:37–50) onto the scriptural figure of Mary of Magdala, comes from the early Middle Ages, a period historians generally demarcate as running from 500–1000. In 591, Pope Gregory I, also known as Gregory the Great, preached a homily in Rome that established a definitive Magdalen-figure for the ages, one who was both sinner and saint.

Now, we must remember that the period in which Gregory lived was one of great uncertainty. The Roman empire had crumbled in the previous century, and with it, so had effective political leadership, administration, and social services. The Rome of Gregory's day was reeling from the devastation wreaked by the Gothic Wars and the plague; moreover, the Longobardi or Lombards, a fierce Germanic tribe who had conquered most of Northern Italy, continued to threaten the gates of the eternal city. In a time of great uncertainty and dislocation, Gregory the Great, always the good pastor, was trying to create a bit of certainty for his devastated flock. Through scriptural exegesis, he was attempting to impose a type of order and stability in one small part of this chaotic and disintegrating world. The "new Magdalen" created by the bishop of Rome was the work of a beleaguered pastor attending the needs of his beleaguered flock, who had probably raised questions about Magdalenian identity. Thus was born the figure of the sinner-saint whom the early medieval period bequeathed to the Christian world. Gregory's authority was so great in the Middle Ages and well beyond that his composite saint was largely accepted in the West. It is always worth mentioning, however, that the Byzantine church never accepted this conflation.

From Pious Fiction to Golden Legend: Mary Magdalen in Provence

The image of the Magdalen preaching in Provence can be traced to an eleventh-century legend from Vézelay that tried to account for the saint's presence in southern France. This legend, known now to scholars as the *vita apostolica* (The Apostolic Life), began circulating in the West. As the legend narrated, when the first wave of Christian persecutions began, Mary Magdalen and her cohort—including Martha and Lazarus, among others—were expelled from Jerusalem. They were put into a rudderless boat and cast adrift at sea. By divine providence they washed ashore in Provence, where they disbursed to preach the new Christian faith. Mary Magdalen evangelized first in Marseilles, then in Aix-en-Provence, where she eventually retired to live out her life as a solitary hermit in the surrounding wilderness. By the twelfth century these pious fictions, which first emerged to add authenticity to the new pilgrimage sanctuary at Vézelay, named in her honor, were now considered the biographical facts of Mary Magdalen's life. By the mid-thirteenth century, this legend had become part of her "official biography," so much so that it was included in the most popular book on the saints, Jacobus de Voragine's *The Golden Legend*, a medieval "best seller" second only to the Bible. Medieval people believed they now had all the evidence that they needed to believe that Mary Magdalen had evangelized Provence and had lived there for the last thirty years of her life. That is, it was all around them: in the sermons that they heard preached, in the art that they saw on church walls, in the hymns that they heard sung, and in the devotional readings on the saints that they read or heard. We cannot fault medieval people for believing these pious fictions, but we moderns would do well to remember that the evidence for Mary Magdalen's apostolic career in Provence does not pre-date the eleventh century.

"Magdalenian Fermentation" or, Sowing the Seeds of Devotion

Although Provence and Burgundy had the most important pilgrimage sites dedicated to Mary Magdalen in the Middle Ages, we mustn't think that devotion to the saint was restricted to France. We have evidence that her cult began as early as the eighth century in Britain: The monk and church historian Bede recorded her feast-day in his liturgical calendar written circa 720 A.D. There are other tantalizing but scattered witnesses of devotion to the saint elsewhere in the early medieval period, but it was the eleventh century that was truly the age of "Magdalenian fermentation," as the late French historian of Mary Magdalen, Victor Saxer, has so memorably termed it. As we have seen, this was the period that produced the cult at Vézelay and its associated legendary texts that circulated in relation to the devotion centered there. Nonetheless, I would argue that it was not until the thirteenth century, the age of the mendicant friars (the Franciscan and the Dominican Orders) that devotion to St. Mary Magdalen was truly internationalized. Both Orders were very much devoted to the saint. St. Francis modeled his devotion to the suffering Christ on Mary Magdalen's fidelity to the Lord, which can be seen in the many visual representations of Francis from the period in which he replaces Mary

Magdalen at the foot of the cross. The Dominican Order, on the other hand, was so devoted to the saint, especially her apostolic aspect, that they named her patron of their Order. The friars disseminated their devotion to the saint through their preaching campaigns, and because the Orders were founded in Italy, these were first directed at the great urban centers of central and northern Italy. Of course their Mary Magdalen was not merely the scriptural Mary of Magdala, she was the penitent saint that Pope Gregory the Great had created in the sixth century now combined with the legendary saint—the "apostle of Provence"—that Vézelay had constructed in the eleventh century. In addition to being the stock-in-trade of the friars, sermons were the mass media of the day. And it was through preaching that knowledge of Mary Magdalen reached ordinary people across Europe.

The friars had great success in sowing the seeds of the Magdalen cult in Italy: Throughout the peninsula churches, convents, and monasteries were dedicated in honor of the saint. By the fourteenth century the name "Maddalena" had become a popular female name for both religious and lay women, particularly in Tuscany. And donors—both religious and lay—commissioned chapels, panel paintings, and altarpieces to commemorate their devotion to different aspects of the saint. But the situation in the south of Italy was quite different. The southern part of the peninsula had been ruled since 1266 by foreigners: the French House of Anjou. Significantly, it was that same dynasty that ruled Provence and whose heir, Charles II, had rediscovered Mary Magdalen's relics in 1279. And as the people of southern Italy chafed under the rule of their foreign French rulers, so they remained indifferent to Mary Magdalen, whom they considered too much allied to the Angevin dynasty. So although we find many institutions, convents, churches, and chapels named for Mary Magdalen in southern Italy, particularly in Naples, the capital of the Angevin realm, they were not monuments commissioned by the citizens of the kingdom. They were for the most part founded by members of the Angevin family or their close associates. Thus in the south of Italy, I think we can identify a politics of sanctity in which the Magdalen cult was regarded with suspicion as a foreign import and too tinged with Angevin politics to take root while that family ruled the southern part of the Italian peninsula known as the Kingdom of Naples.

Her Legacy: *Apostolorum Apostola*

The title "apostle of the apostles" (*apostolorum apostola*) is an honorific title that seems to have entered into common usage in reference to St. Mary Magdalen in the twelfth century. Many of the greatest theologians of the period—Hugh of Cluny, Peter Abelard, and Bernard of Clairvaux, among them—each use the title when referring to Mary Magdalen. The appellation of course refers to Mary Magdalen's privileged position as having first witnessed the risen Christ (in three of the four Gospels) and her mandate from him to bear the good news of his Resurrection to the other disciples. Significantly, the title was not only textual but visual. Images, especially manuscript miniatures, emerged in this period and depict Mary Magdalen preaching to the other disciples. As we have already seen, by the twelfth century the legends associating the saint with an apostolic ministry in Provence were already in circulation, constituting the saint as apostle of Provence. It is possible that the circulation of these legends inspired the creation of the title "apostle of the apostles." The origins of the title will probably always remain obscured in the mists of time; what we do know is that writers and artists continued to depict Mary Magdalen as "apostle of the apostles" throughout the medieval period. And even if theologians and canonists forbade women from preaching publicly, Mary Magdalen was for the most part exempt from this dictate. She was represented preaching in sermons, pious literature, sacred plays, and in the visual material where she was more than once represented preaching in a pulpit.

The title and the image endured throughout the medieval period but fell victim to the reforms carried out in the wake of the Council of Trent, the sixteenth-century council convened in order to respond to the critiques leveled by Protestant reformers at the Catholic Church. One of those critiques was aimed at the cult of the saints, many of whose biographies the Protestant reformers ridiculed for having been embellished by legend. As such, the Catholic reformers responded by decreeing that the literary lives of the saints henceforth should be as historically accurate as possible and all legendary accretions should be stripped away. As we have seen earlier, the scriptural facts of Mary Magdalen's life had been embellished by legend and when the legend was stripped away, so unfortunately was the title "apostle of the apostles." Even if the title drew its inspiration from scripture, neither the Protestantism nor the Catholicism of the period was hospitable to the idea of religious women preaching to men.

It seems to me the title of "apostle of the apostles" is one of the most important legacies that the medieval world has bequeathed to us regarding the saint. It encapsulates the tremendous importance of the fact that Mary Magdalen, a woman, was chosen to witness Christ's Resurrection and moreover, that it was on her that Christ bestowed the privilege of preaching the Resurrection, the central tenet of the Christian faith. That, in my view, constitutes strong evidence, based on scripture and tradition, that supports the case for women's ordination in the Catholic Church. It is this last point where contemporary concerns overlap with medieval representations of the saint: Then as now the figure of Mary Magdalen, apostle of the apostles, is a symbol of tremendous import, power, and inspiration.

The Mary Magdalene Controversies

BY ARNE J. DE KEIJZER

Was She the "Sinful Woman"?

Many contributors to *Secrets of Mary Magdalene* refer to the now infamous sermon by Pope Gregory the Great (540–604), in which he conflated two other women—Mary of Bethany and the anonymous "woman in the city, who was a sinner"—with Mary Magdalene. In one fell swoop in 591, he delivered what is considered by many modern scholars to be the final blow in a series that saw women increasingly marginalized because of their perceived threat to the "one true faith." His sermon cut off an ongoing discussion about Mary Magdalene's identity at the time and put her good name in a box labeled "penitent sinner." The box would not be opened again for 1,378 years.

Many possible explanations exist for Gregory's actions. Perhaps, as some scholars believe, the unfortunate melding was done in good faith in order to simplify complex biblical elements in an era of theological and political uncertainty. For example, some of the bishops of the church felt that the various gospels, along with a wide debate among teachers on what to teach, created too much disarray. Or, as others say, it was part of a conspiracy by church fathers to stamp out the last vestiges of female power. Whatever the motivation, this judgment of Mary Magdalene as prostitute and penitent quickly became a reference point for Catholic theology. Pope Gregory accomplished this in two steps. First, by declaring that the reading from the pulpit on Mary Magdalene's feast day, July 22, henceforth would be from Luke 7:

> . . . behold, a woman in the city, which was a sinner, when she knew that Jesus sat at meat in the Pharisee's house, brought an alabaster box of ointment, and stood at his feet behind him weeping, and began to wash his feet with tears, and did wipe them with the hairs of her head, and kissed his feet, and anointed them with the ointment. Now when the Pharisee which had bidden him [to eat in his house] saw it, he spake with himself, saying, this man, if he were a prophet, would have known who and what manner of woman this is that toucheth him: for she is a sinner (7:36–9).

Secondly, he delivered a Homily in which he charged the faithful to follow this interpretation of the verse:

> She whom Luke calls the sinful woman, whom John calls Mary, we believe to be the Mary from whom seven devils were ejected according to Mark. And what did the seven devils signify, if not all vices? . . . It is clear, brothers, that the woman previously used the unguent to perfume her flesh in forbidden acts. What she therefore displayed more scandalously, she was now offering to God in a more praiseworthy manner. She had coveted with earthly eyes, but now through

penitence these are consumed with tears. She displayed her hair to set off her face, but now her hair dries her tears. She had spoken proud things with her mouth, but in kissing the Lord's feet, she now planted her mouth on the Redeemer's feet. For every delight, therefore, she had had in herself, she now immolated herself. She turned the mass of her crimes to virtues, in order to serve God entirely in penance, for as much as she had wrongly held God in contempt.

In great part because of pressure from within, the Vatican finally overruled this interpretation about Mary Magdalene in 1969, with neither an apology nor even an official statement. The Second Vatican Council simply altered the reading for the feast day as part of a general reform of the church calendar regarding the way many saints were to be remembered. The Roman missal and the Roman calendar now directed the reading be changed from Luke 7 to the Gospel of John, Chapter 20, verses 1–2 and 11–18:

1 The first day of the week cometh Mary Magdalene early, when it was yet dark, unto the sepulchre, and seeth the stone taken away from the sepulchre.

2 Then she runneth, and cometh to Simon Peter, and to the other disciple, whom Jesus loved, and saith unto them, They have taken away the LORD out of the sepulchre, and we know not where they have laid him.

11 But Mary stood without at the sepulchre weeping: and as she wept, she stooped down, and looked into the sepulchre,

12 And seeth two angels in white sitting, the one at the head, and the other at the feet, where the body of Jesus had lain.

13 And they say unto her, Woman, why weepest thou? She saith unto them, Because they have taken away my LORD, and I know not where they have laid him.

14 And when she had thus said, she turned herself back, and saw Jesus standing, and knew not that it was Jesus.

15 Jesus saith unto her, Woman, why weepest thou? whom seekest thou? She, supposing him to be the gardener, saith unto him, Sir, if thou have borne him hence, tell me where thou hast laid him, and I will take him away.

16 Jesus saith unto her, Mary. She turned herself, and saith unto
him, Rabboni; which is to say, Master.

17 Jesus saith unto her, Touch me not; for I am not yet ascended
to my Father: but go to my brethren, and say unto them, I
ascend unto my Father, and your Father; and to my God, and
your God.

18 Mary Magdalene came and told the disciples that she had seen
the LORD, and that he had spoken these things unto her.

Thereby Pope John Paul II reversed his predecessor and changed
Mary Magdalene back from a repentant sinner to the person who
emerges from the gospel as central to the Resurrection story—as
well as in her own right.

Was She Married to Jesus?

*Behold . . . the greatest cover-up in human history. Not only was Jesus
Christ married, but He was a father. My dear, Mary Magdalene was the
Holy Vessel. She was the chalice that bore the royal bloodline of Jesus
Christ. She was the womb that bore the lineage, and the vine from which
the sacred fruit sprang forth!*

—DAN BROWN, *The Da Vinci Code*

*I think the recent interest in making Mary Magdalene Mrs. Jesus or the
lover of Jesus in part has more to do with Jesus than with Mary
Magdalene. If he's going to be a real guy he has to have a woman. It's
another way of using a woman to think about a man.*

—JANE SCHABERG

While The Da Vinci Code *has prompted fascination with Mary
Magdalene's conjugal status, this much misunderstood woman of the New
Testament did far more than stay at home and bake date-palm cookies.*

—DENISE FLAM

The question of whether Mary and Jesus were married has inspired many a spirited (and intriguing) debate, certainly. But it tends to obscure a much more profound issue, one that goes to the heart of the Christian message: the divinity of Jesus.

As the son of God conveyed in the canonical gospels, he is divine, and though he is tempted, he rises above the sins and foibles of mankind. In the New Testament book of the Epistle of the Hebrews (4:15), he is "like us in all things except sin." This seems to include sex.

But if Jesus is married, he returns to being a human, a "mere" prophet—if a radical and unique one. Or, as in the words of a *Da Vinci Code* character, "a great and powerful man, but a man nevertheless. A mortal." (Arguably, the positive side of such a transformation from Jesus as divine to simply a mortal would also end forever the deep ambivalence about sexuality held by those within a monastic culture.)

The range of expert opinion on this question is broad, to say the least. Some believe the question is heresy itself; that there is no evidence whatsoever of this union in the New Testament or the alternate gospels. Some don't rule it out. Others think it unlikely—but possible. And for still others, it's an "of course." As for the "man on the street," a survey undertaken by the religious website www.Beliefnet. com found that when asked whether Jesus was married, 41 percent of respondents answered "Of course not," 23 percent said "Yes, he was, to Mary Magdalene," 5 percent said "Yes, but we don't know to whom," and 31 percent said "It doesn't matter."

Our own survey, presented as a "thought provocation," samples opinions from a wide range of scholars, theologians, and experts—a good jumping off point for further intellectual inquiry.

No, Jesus and Mary were not married

As might be expected, the strongest voices in support of this position are from Catholics. Greg Jones, a Catholic scholar and rector, puts the case in a nutshell: "There is no basis in fact, history, or scripture to claim that Mary Magdalene and Jesus ever married, conceived children, kissed, or even held hands."

Richard P. McBrien, professor of theology at the University of Notre Dame, agrees with Jones, citing three reasons: First, the gospels make no mention of a marriage. Second, there was an anti-erotic bias present in early Christianity. Third, "when St. Paul invoked his own right to marry, why did he not appeal to Jesus' marriage to support his argument?" Nevertheless, McBrien says, "It would not have compromised the divinity of Jesus for him to have been married." And it's only a "short putt" that *if* he married, it would have been to Mary Magdalene.

Are you kidding? asks Kenneth Woodward, a contributing editor at *Newsweek* and frequent writer on religion. Woodward believes Mary Magdalene is the victim of a "cultural makeover," a "project for a certain kind of ideologically committed feminist scholarship."

Darrell Bock, a Bible scholar at Dallas Theological Seminary, believes the thought of a marriage is not only dead wrong, but is a position that reeks of conspiracy. The whole debate, Bock says, reflects "an attempt to—and I'm going to use this term on purpose—relegate Christianity to a level that is like other religions." Marriage would reduce Jesus to "a great religious figure, one among many, rather than being a unique figure who is uniquely divine."

Surprisingly, perhaps, scholars and theologians who have been known to launch sharp critiques of what they call the new "ideologically committed, revisionist feminist scholarship" actually agree with their theological adversaries on this controversial topic. For example, they would clearly agree with the feminist scholar Katherine Ludwig Jansen of the Catholic University of America, who has written, "the only evidence we have to document her existence is that which is contained in the New Testament." And, like many of her colleagues, Jansen maintains there is not a word in the New Testament about such a union.

Susan Haskins, in her book *Mary Magdalen: Myth and Metaphor,* says, yes, she was the companion of Jesus and also "chief female disciple, first apostle, and beloved friend of Christ." But Haskins also believes the sexual imagery conveyed in the Bible and Gnostic Gospels is but "a metaphor for the reunion of Christ and the Church which takes place in the bridal chamber," and is "symbolic of the love of Christ for the Church." So were they actually married? Haskins dismisses that proposition as "bizarre."

Esther de Boer, who, like many of her colleagues is otherwise highly critical of the patriarchy of the Catholic Church, also discounts the theory that the "close companion" phrase from the Gospel of Philip suggests that Jesus and Mary Magdalene were married, or even lovers. "We must not understand this 'kissing' in a sexual sense but in a spiritual sense," she says. "The grace which those who kiss exchange makes them born again."

No, but . . .

Bruce Chilton, who recently wrote a biography of Mary Magdalene (see excerpts, p. 96), says there is no indication they were married and no reason to concern ourselves theologically with it even if that was the case. "I think it's perfectly plausible to say that they might have had a sexual relationship with one another. However, in making that assertion, it's also wise to distinguish that from saying therefore they were married. Neither of them was a very good candidate for marriage [given the Jewish family tradition at the time]."

Possibly, perhaps even likely, but certainly not definite

John Spong, a retired Episcopal bishop and author of *Born of a Woman*, says a marriage between Mary Magdalene and Jesus is "likely," a conclusion he comes to based on Christianity's historic maltreatment of women. "The negativity that surrounds the idea that Jesus might have been married is increasingly strange in our age. It reflects the residue of that deep Christian negativity toward women that still infects the church." Spong concludes that while there is no proof, the Bible presents a "cumulative argument that suggests that Jesus might well have been married, that Mary Magdalene, as the primary woman in the Gospel story itself, was Jesus' wife, and this record was suppressed but not annihilated by the Christian church before the Gospels came to be written."

Lynn Picknett and Clive Prince, in their book *The Templar Revelation,* among the primary sources for Dan Brown's *The Da Vinci Code,* write, "There is evidence that the Magdalene was Jesus' wife—or at least, his lover." She considers silence on the subject "very odd" since Jews thought celibacy "was improper" and Jesus and his disciples might have "caused a stir among the authorities . . . for fear of homosexuality." But the gospel's silence on the subject, thinks Picknett, could have another interpretation. "He could have had a sexual partner who was not his wife, or had been through a form of marriage that was not recognized by the Jews."

Maybe, maybe not, but it's unimportant

Jane Schaberg, author of *The Resurrection of Mary Magdalene,* believes that the way the Gospel of Philip portrays the relationship between Mary Magdalene and Jesus, while ambiguous and enigmatic, is extremely important and profound. Such ambiguity avoids two alternatives that both buy into patriarchal notions of the female body: (1) that any male-female relationship must involve sexual relations; and (2) that "'sacred' or 'spiritual' male-female relations must not." The marriage issue is a fixation, Schaberg believes, and not a helpful one.

Gerald O'Collins, professor of theology at the Pontifical Gregorian University in Rome, says these theories have been put forward because "they sell well." He adds, "It's good stuff for novels, and it's spicy, but it degrades the real Mary Magdalene . . ."

Elizabeth Clare Prophet, author of *Mary Magdalene and the Divine Feminine,* describes herself as a pioneer "in practical spirituality, including the use of the creative power of sound for personal growth and world transformation." She agrees that the debate over their marriage misses the point. "Whatever happened between them may not be written in the history books, and I don't profess to know myself, but it wouldn't matter to me. It wouldn't in any way detract from the Saviour if he had married Mary Magdalene and had children, because his power and magnitude is not based on how he chose to have his relationship with her."

Of course they were married!

Mary Magdalene experts whom Dan Brown relied upon to advance his theory of the holy bloodline are, of course, in favor of this proposition. Margaret Starbird, one such source, believes the scriptures support her theory that Jesus was the husband of Mary Magdalene, a theory she first published in her 1993 book, *The Woman with the Alabaster Jar.*

Timothy Freke and Peter Gandy, in *Jesus and the Lost Gospels,* write: "In the Gospel of Luke Mary wipes her hair on Jesus' feet. According to Jewish law, only a husband was allowed to see a woman's hair unbound and if a woman let down her hair in front of another man, this was a sign of impropriety and grounds for mandatory divorce . . ." This incident, then, can be seen as portraying Jesus and Mary either as man and wife or as libertine lovers with scant regard for moral niceties."

To Laurence Gardner, author, musician, historian, and Knight Templar, the question has already been settled in the canonical gospels. In *The Magdalene Legacy* he writes: "The Gospels (all four of them) certainly do state that Jesus was married."

The most vigorous proponent of the "yes, they were married" theory may be Barbara Thiering, an Australian scholar whose specialty is the Dead Sea Scrolls. Thiering has written that, per the traditional custom of the Essenes, "early in Jesus' ministry, he and Mary Magdalene underwent the first ceremony beginning the trial marriage." At 6:00 p.m. on Tuesday, June 6, 30 AD, no less. Moreover, Thiering argues that "at the season of the crucifixion Mary was three months pregnant, and the final, binding marriage was performed."

Not only married, but with offspring who passed on the royal bloodline

Interestingly, the authors of *Holy Blood, Holy Grail,* who sued Dan Brown in a London court for "plagiarizing" their bloodline thesis (they lost), believe there is plenty of argument in favor of the pair having sexual relations and offspring, but they do not go as far as to say they were definitely married.

Margaret Starbird believes Mary Magdalene was pregnant at the time of the Crucifixion but, having to flee persecution, she gave birth to a daughter in Egypt before both mother and daughter went on to France. It was this daughter who, according to those who believe in the legend, became the first in a bloodline of French kings, a lineage that *The Da Vinci Code* and like-minded tales insist continues to this day.

Barbara Thiering extends her "yes, they were married" theory to the "fact" that they had three children altogether: a daughter (Tamar), born in AD 33 (after the Crucifixion), and two sons, one born in AD 37 (Jesus Justus) and one born in AD 44 (James). Thiering bases this analysis on what she calls the *pesher* of the Dead Sea Scrolls—*pesher* meaning "interpretation" in the sense of "solution" in Hebrew. The reason Jesus could have had two more children after the Crucifixion, she maintains, is because he survived the ordeal and subsequently took an active part in establishing the Christian church. But there's more: Thiering has "discovered" that upon the schism of the early church in AD 44, "Mary left the marriage, believing that Jesus had departed from true religious ideas." Jesus went on to marry a woman named Lydia in AD 50, with whom he had two more children.

Laurence Gardner has basically the same thesis as Thiering with respect to the number of children, but adds a daughter and sees a different outcome for the family. "In AD 53 Jesus junior was officially proclaimed Crown Prince at the synagogue in Corinth." Both brothers end up in Provence with their mother, where Jesus Justus becomes a father who names his son Jesus III. Daughter Tamar appears to have married St. Paul in Athens in AD 53, Gardner believes.

Two British authors, Tom Kenyon and Judi Sion, report that while it is certain that Mary Magdalene went to France, she is likely to have gone to Britain as well. Extending this thesis, Ani Williams, a New Age singer who supplies "sound medicine" and leads pilgrimages along the Mary Magdalene trail, claims that on her journey to Britain she was accompanied by Joseph of Arimathea, who brought over the Holy Grail and buried it at Glastonbury Abbey. This is also the thesis of Graham Phillips, an "investigator of historical mysteries," in his book *The Chalice of Magdalene*.

What to conclude? With no written record from the time Jesus and Mary actually lived, there cannot be a definite answer. Perhaps, like so many other aspects of the Mary Magdalene story, she acted according to however we wanted her to act.

Was She Both the "Beloved Disciple" and the Real Author of the Gospel of John?

The Gospel of John has two mysteries about it that have vexed scholars since the earliest days of Christianity. One is the name of the person to whom John refers only as the "Beloved Disciple" (more literally, "the disciple whom Jesus loved"). Second is the question of who actually wrote this text; unlike Mathew, Mark, and Luke, no author or authors have been identified. Who might John be? Some have put forward the theory that the answer to both questions is one person: Mary Magdalene.

Guesses about authorship have ranged from the disciple John of Zebedee to John the Baptist to Lazarus of Bethany. None of these are the right candidates, says Ramon K. Jusino, a Catholic scholar, school teacher, and author of the widely circulated essay "Mary Magdalene: Author of the Fourth Gospel?" He is largely convinced that the Fourth Gospel was actually written by Mary, and that it was she who was the Beloved Disciple. He is not alone. The respected scholar Esther De Boer has called Mary Magdalene "a serious candidate" for the disciple loved in the Gospel of John and, in a highly nuanced argument, so does biblical scholar Sandra Schneider.

Jusino bases some of his case on inferences from the Gnostic gospels of Mary and Philip. Both portray Mary Magdalene as (a) a disciple and (b) the disciple "Jesus loved more than the others." It's not a stretch, therefore, to infer John was talking about the Magdalene, Jusino argues. He believes she was actually the founder of the early Christian community and began to accumulate the teachings of Jesus, which were later to be subsumed into a second, heavily redacted version of John. No leader of the early Christian community could countenance the fact that Jesus may have had a woman as a disciple, Jusino believes, so the solution was to expunge her name, replacing it with the anonymous—and male—Beloved Disciple.

As for the Beloved Disciple being Mary, Jusino bases his belief on a textual analysis of two scenes: Mary Magdalene's presence at the foot of the cross and at the empty tomb. These two scenes, he says, were too well established to simply be erased. Yet the redactor wished to claim the (male) Beloved Disciple as an eyewitness to these events. He solved this dilemma by including both figures, thus reinforcing the idea that they were two separate people. But Jusino notes structural inconsistencies in the text, which have been corroborated by other scholars, that he says point to the redactor's insertion of an extra person in the scenes. It was this edited version that became the canonical Fourth Gospel, known as the Gospel of John.

Ann Graham Brock, an expert on the evolution of the early Christian movement, is doubtful. "Even though I am open to many possibilities," Brock says, "and I have spent years searching for vestiges of Mary Magdalene's legacy, I must confess that so far I have not been persuaded that Mary Magdalene is the author of John. To be sure, this gospel exhibits more interest in the contributions of women than any of the other three canonical gospels. . . . Mary Magdalene is indeed very important to the Gospel of John; nevertheless, such interest is not enough evidence to be able to claim Mary Magdalene as the author. I would have to see more."

In the conclusion to his controversial yet thoroughly researched article, Jusino concedes that the quest for the Fourth Gospel's true author remains a good detective story. But there are clues everywhere, he says, and is certain there are documents waiting to be discovered that will confirm what he firmly believes: that the identity of the Beloved Disciple as well as the Fourth Gospel's author is Mary from Magdala.

Mormonism and Mary Magdalene

BY MAXINE HANKS

Mormonism may be the only Christian religion that embraced, from its origins, a belief that Jesus was married and had children. The idea is not new to Mormons, who believe that marriage is necessary for godhood, or highest "exaltation" in heaven.

This idea was taught by Joseph Smith, Mormonism's founder, according to his closest associates (called "apostles"), who related Smith's private teachings after his death. Apparently, Smith never publicly taught or published any specifics about Jesus' wife or children. And the Church of Jesus Christ of Latter-day Saints (LDS) has never officially confirmed a belief in Jesus' marriage. Indeed, it has publicly denied it was ever a part of church doctrine. Still, the idea of a married Jesus is known in Mormonism, as a long-held, sacred, discreet, folk doctrine.

The Mormon belief in Jesus' marriage actually says little about Mary Magdalene, and more about the lineage of Jesus. Smith identified at least two individuals as being "direct descendant[s] of Jesus Christ." Smith also implied the same about himself. Six months after Smith's death, Brigham Young suggested that Smith's cryptic claim that "no man knows my history" alluded to his sacred bloodline. "You have heard Joseph say that the people did not know him . . . Some have supposed that he meant Spirit, but it was the blood relation."*

Notions of a chosen bloodline or lineage run strong in Mormonism. Smith wrote in 1835: "The order of this priesthood was confirmed to be handed down from father to son, and rightly belongs to the literal descendants of the chosen seed, to whom the promises were made." (Doctrine and Covenants 107:40). In 1858 Brigham Young said, "Hidden in the blood of many LDS runs the blood of Israel from numerous directions, including that of the Savior. But it is

Maxine Hanks is a writer, lecturer, and feminist theologian whose book, *Women and Authority*, reclaimed feminist theology and history in Mormonism. A former Mormon and Church of Jesus Christ of Latter-day Saints missionary, she became a Gnostic in 1996.

*All Brigham Young quotes are from *Dynasty of the Holy Grail: Mormonism's Sacred Bloodline* by Vern Swanson, 2006.

specifically through the divine blood-right of Jesus Christ through Joseph Smith Jr. that all members of the Church are lawful heirs of the promise."

Early Mormons believed Jesus married in order to preserve his lineage and priesthood. Apostle Orson Hyde said, "Jesus was the bridegroom at the marriage of Cana of Galilee. . . . We say it was Jesus Christ who was married, to be brought into relation whereby he could see his seed before he was crucified." Smith's nephew, church president Joseph F. Smith said Jesus married to fulfill "the entire law of god."

Yet Mormons also took the idea one step further, suggesting that Jesus was married to more than one woman. Smith's nephew also said that "Mary and Martha manifested a much closer relationship than merely a believer [in Jesus]." Smith's apostles often cited the Bethany sisters as Jesus' wives, along with Mary Magdalene. Orson Hyde said, "Mary, Martha, and others were his wives, and . . . he begat children."

Given a messiah with multiple wives, Smith himself married thirty-four women. The early Mormon doctrine of polygamy seemed wedded to the idea that Jesus was married. Smith's revelation on polygamy reads as coming from Jesus Christ:

> "I, the Lord, justified . . . the principle and doctrine of their having many wives and concubines. . . . I reveal unto you a new and an everlasting covenant . . . except ye abide my law ye cannot attain to this glory . . . that where I am ye shall be also. . . . Receive ye . . . the law of my Holy Priesthood. (1843, Doctrine and Covenants 132)

It appears that early Mormons believed (1) Jesus was married and his wives were likely Magdalene, Martha, and Mary of Bethany; (2) Jesus' descendants preserved his royal bloodline and priesthood; and (3) Joseph Smith was a descendant of Jesus, inheriting his bloodline and priesthood, along with other Mormons. As a Mormon, I heard these teachings many times; the faith's focus on genealogy produced lineage charts like the one showing my family line "going all the way back to Christ."

Where did Joseph Smith learn all this? Most of his teachings were attributed to his prophetic calling. He also explored a variety of spiritual traditions, including Jewish, Christian, Gnostic, Hermetic, mystic, magic, and Masonic ideas. Mormonism married Christian and esoteric traditions, creating a new vision wherein orthodoxy and heresy were reunited within one faith.

Yet Smith and his apostles didn't use esoteric terms like grail; they used biblical language. Thus the Mormon view of Jesus is more biblical than borrowed from esoteric lore. Mormons had a need to understand polygamy—as a chosen people called to restore the priestly lineage of Jesus the Messiah.

Smith envisioned Jesus as a resurrected male God, and polygamy as a law of God. Smith also envisioned Mormonism as the restoration of "original Christianity" as lived by Jesus; thus Mormonism would restore Jesus' practices, including marriage.

Mormonism did repeat a curious pattern from early Christianity: Joseph Smith was a religious martyr, and his wife Emma held high leadership. Yet the chief apostle Brigham Young prevailed in taking the majority of believers with him. A similar pattern is attributed to Jesus, Mary Magdalene, and Peter—an archetypal pattern of the wounded or dying king, survived by a grieving or displaced female companion and an assertive male successor who is hostile to her.

Early Mormon views revere Magdalene as both a witness and wife of Christ, yet formal Latter-day Saints teachings say little about her or her importance as a witness, or apostle. The implications of her role are unexplored. Still, Mormonism has an open canon of "continuing revelation" inviting new insights, inspiration, and interpretation. This allows past beliefs to change, recognizing the human need to evolve and the divine responsibility to improve.

After 1890 the Mormon practice of polygamy ended, and even doctrine was changed by Latter-day Saints leaders. However, the esoteric teaching by some about Jesus being married has never been refuted. What *has* been denied is that it was ever doctrine. In 2006 LDS released this statement: "The belief that Christ was married has never been official Church doctrine. It is neither sanctioned nor taught by the Church. While it is true that a few Church leaders in the mid-1800s expressed their opinions on the matter, it was not then, and is not now, Church doctrine."

5 The Mary Magdalene Roundtable

Mary Magdalene is a role model for women's apostleship, leadership, courage, fidelity, and power.

  —SUSAN HASKINS

Mary Magdalene to me is a woman prophet. It's continuing that prophetic voice that makes her stand in but slightly outside the Christian tradition that makes her a fascinating and enigmatic figure.

  —DEIRDRE GOOD

She's a connector between all the parts of our lives, . . . and maybe in her absence she's more present than when she is physically in front of us.

  —DIANE APOSTOLOS-CAPPADONA

To me, Mary Magdalene isn't a goddess. She's not a figure of such profound holiness that she's unapproachable. She's more like a sister. She had good times and bad times and she found what she was looking for. That's my Mary Magdalene.

  —LESA BELLEVIE

I think you can regard Mary Magdalene as saintly, you can regard her image as refurbished, you can regard her as not a whore, or you can regard her as apostle to the apostles. But you will still shut her in a box if you ignore her implication for the roles of women in contemporary religious practices or in the wider social movements.

  —JANE SCHABERG

The Mary Magdalene Roundtable

It was an extraordinary event. In early 2006, as we were bringing together all the various strands of the editorial work for *Secrets of Mary Magdalene,* we invited six of the world's leading experts on Mary Magdalene to a roundtable-style discussion of the major issues, themes, debates, and controversies in the twenty-first-century context of Mary Magdalene studies.

Each of the six experts has written, spoken, and published extensively on Mary Magdalene and related subjects: the historical Jesus, the early Christian movement, Gnosticism and other alternative strains within Christianity, alternative scriptures, the role of women in the early church, art, archaeology, culture from the biblical era to the present day, and many other topics in the nexus of gender/spirituality/religion/myth/archetype. There was a unique spirit in the room as these experts, all women, all brilliant, all deeply knowledgeable about ancient and modern subjects, all passionate about their ideas and viewpoints, engaged in an absorbing, free-flowing discussion with each other.

In different ways, each of the roundtable participants evoked a compelling emotional power and intellectual complexity reflecting years of pathbreaking work to understand Mary Magdalene, and to develop new ideas about the events of two thousand years ago and what they imply for our image of her.

Those who gathered for this intriguing roundtable discussion were:

Katherine Kurs, moderator, a member of the faculty of religious studies at Eugene Lang College of the New School University. Her book *Searching for Your Soul* was named one of the best religion/spirituality books of 1999.

Elaine Pagels, Harrington Spear Paine Professor of Religion at Princeton University and author of the award-winning and bestselling book *The Gnostic Gospels,* as well as *Beyond Belief.*

Susan Haskins, art and culture historian; author of the bestselling *Mary Magdalen: Myth and Metaphor,* now in its second edition.

Lesa Bellevie, founder and webmaster of www.Magdalene.org, and author of *The Complete Idiot's Guide to Mary Magdalene.*

Deirdre Good, professor of the New Testament at the General Theological Seminary in New York, and editor of *Mariam, the Magdalen, and the Mother.*

Diane Apostolos-Cappadona, adjunct professor in art and culture at Georgetown University, author of *A Dictionary of Christian Art,* and curator for the exhibition "In Search of Mary Magdalene: Images and Traditions."

Jane Schaberg, professor of religious studies and women's studies at the

---

We would like to acknowledge the support and cooperation of Hidden Treasures Productions, Inc., which filmed the event and has brought it to life in a DVD version, also called *Secrets of Mary Magdalene.*

University of Detroit Mercy, and author of *The Resurrection of Mary Magdalene: Legends, Apocrypha, and the Christian Testament.*

KURS: *Welcome to all. We have a wonderful opportunity today to share ideas and to exchange our thoughts on a subject of passionate interest to so many: Mary Magdalene. At times, it seems that her power is self-contained and at other times that it is generated through the company she's kept over the centuries. And certainly she has meant different things to different people, depending on their perspective. But let me start off by asking a somewhat personal question. Who is Mary Magdalene to you?*

PAGELS: As a historian, I'm assuming that she was a follower of Jesus in the early period, that she was probably prominent and well known to be close to Jesus, that she was an independent woman, not associated with a male companion other than Jesus, perhaps, and that she then became the symbolic focus of an enormous amount of controversy about the participation of women, the exclusion of women, the inclusion of sexuality, the exclusion of sexuality, and the very peculiar constellation of imaginations surrounding those topics for the last two thousand years.

BELLEVIE: I tend to see Mary Magdalene as she was identified by Gnostics in the third century; that is, as the symbolic bride of Christ, who represents the human desire to know God. Also, I find it inspiring that she's such a complex figure. Real people have complex lives; she felt real human emotions and she had a real human life, so I identify her as one of us. That's Mary Magdalene to me.

GOOD: Mary Magdalene for me embodies a tenacious presence in the face of complete and utter despair, when there seems to be no hope, no life, no future. Mary Magdalene's silent witness is important today. We live in a post-9/11 world in which sometimes we can't bury the bodies because they're not there. Mary Magdalene reminds us that, in the absence of the bodies of those we love, our presence is crucial, and it's the only presence from which hope springs.

SCHABERG: My spiritual life and my scholarly life are entangled, so I like to think of the Magdalene figure as a historian would, as an actual person who lived and who, I think, has a better claim than Paul to being the founder of Christianity, in terms of being a primary witness to the Resurrection. But I don't like to think of her as silent. I think of her as an early prophet. She had been silenced but is silent no longer.

APOSTOLOS-CAPPADONA: In a certain way, my answer parallels yours, Jane, but the language is a little different in the sense that we all live or operate in an esoteric or a philosophic or a scholarly way, and also in an everyday way. And somehow Mary Magdalene connects the boundaries or the parts of those two spheres. One finds in her a source of intellectual inquiry, historical concern, and academic interest, and at the same time she's always popping up in my life—I'm on a holiday and suddenly there she is in some piece of art that I didn't know was there, or I find her in another book, so that she operates between the spheres in my life all the time. In a way, I think that's very similar to what Jane is saying about herself and Mary Magdalene, but I think there is also a sense that we need to think of her in many ways. She's a connector between all the parts of our lives, between all aspects of our beings, and maybe in her absence she's more present than when she is physically in front of us.

HASKINS: For me, Mary Magdalene is the figure in the gospels who seems to embody all the elements of the feminine that were lost for so long. She is strong, she's courageous, she's fearless, and she's independent. I think those characteristics are what should embody the feminine, or what the feminine should embody, and that's how I see her: as a very powerful message or symbol for women. In the late-twentieth and into the twenty-first century, Mary Magdalene has become a dynamic figure of womanhood who's exciting, beautiful, passionate. She's not the woman we knew who was beautiful but always weeping for her sins; now she's standing up for herself. In the gospels, she meets the risen Christ and in a certain sense she represents the strength and courage and fidelity of womanhood and its relationship to the divine. She has united herself with that divine figure, and this is possibly something that most women would like to be able to do, to experience a sense of wholeness, created out of that union of herself with Jesus or the divine.

BELLEVIE: She is indeed a potent symbol for the individual in search of union with the divine, as the symbolic bride of Christ. And the bride-bridegroom language has applied to both the individual and to Christianity as a collective, to a group of people in search of communion with God. So it's incredibly powerful, sensual language that's reminiscent of the woman in the Song of Songs who is searching for her beloved.

SCHABERG: Mary Magdalene, for our time, is an action figure—one who stands for getting involved, for voting correctly, for informing yourself, and for getting off your butt. She represents a fusion of the erotic and the spiritual and the intellectual. She's like a Tina Turner or a Dixie Chick—she stands for making a difference in the time that you live.

The "It" Girl of Our Times

KURS: *Scholars, theologians, parishioners, and others have been debating the role of Mary Magdalene for centuries. And radical interpretations of her as the bride of Jesus have been around for at least a hundred years. The discovery and translation of the alternate, Gnostic Gospels found in 1945 created a stir among experts, but, on the whole, the public didn't enter the debate. Now, suddenly, Mary Magdalene is daily in the news, and in sermons of all faiths, and in documentaries on television. Why? What accounts for this sudden surge of interest? Surely it isn't simply* The Da Vinci Code, *is it?*

PAGELS: What strikes me is that we have new information about Mary Magdalene from very ancient texts like the Gospel of Mary and Pistis Sophia and the gospels of Philip and Thomas. We've never had this before. Some of the material has been available for a while, but only now are many people hearing about it.

HASKINS: Yes, the role of women in the mainstream New Testament gospels has traditionally been seen as negligible and unimportant, in part because of the translations of the texts by mostly male scholars. Recent feminine scholarship has been extraordinary in finding new roles based on Mary Magdalene, or based not on Mary Magdalene but on a conflation of her with other women in the gospels, which show a dynamic place for women both inside and outside the church today. She is a model for women's apostleship, leadership, courage, fidelity, power—twenty-five years ago, you would never have thought of Mary Magdalene in terms of these extraordinarily important roles. It's very exciting that this dynamic creature has come to stand for these new feminine roles, as opposed to the position she'd been relegated to for about two thousand years.

BELLEVIE: This new perspective of seeing Mary Magdalene as "dynamic creature"—as you just aptly described her, Susan—also reminds us of why we did not see her like that until comparatively recently. I'm talking about the patriarchy of traditional Christianity, and the concomitant loss of the "pagan" belief in the sacred feminine. Christianity certainly didn't invent patriarchy, but around the Middle Ages there was a great deal of mythology that grew up around the idea of a lost feminine principle. Carl Jung wrote about this, his students wrote about it, Joseph Campbell observed it in mythology—there were a lot of stories circulating during that early period. Maybe the Grail romances, as well as some of the lost feminine folklore like Cinderella and its many, many variants, are all talking about the lost feminine principle. What's happening today is that people are interpreting these medieval stories of a lost feminine principle as an expression of Mary Magdalene's loss, specifically as Jesus' bride. I think what is occurring in the modern mythology about Mary Magdalene's loss may be yet another expression of this general loss we're feeling about feminine principles being devalued.

SCHABERG: I agree there are many reasons for the so-called Magdalene mania, one of which owes a lot to the fact that we're in the midst of a new phase of the women's movement, and feminist scholarship has done a lot to create revisionist views of history. Religious studies is one important aspect of this line of scholarship.

Another reason is the scholarly information that tells us the image of Mary Magdalene as a whore has been a distortion—that idea has already come into the popular imagination, and it feeds into these other readings of her figure. Dissatisfaction with church politics and church hanky-panky, such as the pedophilia crisis, leads many people to be wary of any kind of church cover-ups, and that feeds into Dan Brown's ideas about mysterious codes and secret business. I think also the popular imagination is very dissatisfied with the fact that religion and sexuality, in Christian terms at any rate, have not had a good partnership; we need new thinking along those lines. The churches, and one might say religion in general, have suppressed the leadership abilities of women, the history of women in leadership roles, and feminine metaphors for the sacred and the divine. That's a snowball that's rolling, and it's not going to be stopped.

And then, unfortunately, there is another reason as well: the figure has become commercial. You can make money off Mary Magdalene. She's like a little playtoy, like a Barbie.

GOOD: But let us not lose sight of the positive perspective. Mary Magdalene has been a role model for many women all through the Christian tradition. Unfortunately, we have very few records of the thoughts and prayers of such women, but we do have prayer books and liturgical texts that tell us something about Mary Magdalene in the prayer life of individuals. I think today Mary Magdalene also plays a very important role as proclaimer of the good news. In fact, for many women who are going to be ordained as priests in the Episcopal tradition of which I am a part, Mary Magdalene is an important model.

BELLEVIE: Yes, this is all happening at a time when we are in a social climate where people can float ideas that once were considered heretical, and women are empowered to challenge the status quo. A lot of people are recognizing that there is a gender imbalance that's built into the structure of Christianity, and Mary Magdalene has become a focus for this controversy. As follower of Jesus, Mary Magdalene may have had as much authority to teach as Jesus' male followers, and people are asking, "Why is it that women have been excluded from a lot of the leadership positions in Christianity?"

APOSTOLOS-CAPPADONA: The public fascination with Mary Magdalene is not new, of course. Among the interesting phenomena about the Magdalene—and I use the plural "phenomena" intentionally—

are these explosions of interest in her. It's as if she goes dormant for certain periods of time, and then suddenly everywhere you look are new legends and new imagery and everyone is talking about her. We had this kind of explosion in the thirteenth century in France; we had this kind of explosion in Italian art during the Renaissance. There are different time periods when this happens, and it usually can be connected to some sort of cultural or theological phenomenon.

One recent such explosion actually preceded the publication of Dan Brown's novel *The Da Vinci Code*. If you've been looking for Magdalene material, or Magdalenia, as I sometimes to refer to it, you find a lot of it appearing somewhere around the year 2000. Although I know people who do, I don't think it had any connection to the millennium fervor, because it comes instead from feminist scholars' interest in the ordination of women. In looking for support for a ministry by women, they asked the enduring question, "Who was Mary Magdalene?"

However, the Mary Magdalene movement gains extraordinary attention, in my opinion, because of 9/11, though the connection is based not on the terrorist act itself but rather on its aftermath. For those who lost family or friends in one of the buildings or in the plane crashes, the horrible reality was that there may not have been a body to mourn. You may not have a body to bury—you had, rather, an empty tomb. And when faced with an empty tomb, we turn always to Mary Magdalene. She is the one who stands at the foot of the cross, she is the one who stands by the empty tomb. She is the one who waits and who is then gifted, not simply with the grace of tears, not simply with her conversion, but with the first vision of the resurrected Christ, with the affirmation of new life. This affirmation is what faith is about.

Mary Magdalene, According to the Gospels

KURS: *Let's take a step back. You have described how Mary Magdalene's status has undergone an extraordinary transformation, but as a basis for comparison, let's look back at the "original" texts. There's the Mary*

Magdalene as described in the New Testament. But even there, the authors
of Matthew, Mark, Luke, and John tell us slightly different stories. And with
the recent discovery of what have become popularly known as the Gnostic
Gospels, the differences are even more pronounced. Help us make sense of
these various perspectives handed down to us from the first, second, and third
centuries, and tell us how they have shaped our modern view.

GOOD: Note that in the New Testament each of the gospels is introduced as the "gospel according to." It's according to Matthew,
Mark, Luke, or John. In other words, there is one gospel, but presented here are four different versions of it. The way I look at it is
that multiplicity is at the heart of the gospel message; it's not a ho-
mogeneity of message. Once people have decided that diversity is
enshrined in the principle of gospel, even as the canon limits the
gospels to four, you can say that outside the canon, from a historical
point of view, we have many more than four gospels. The Gospel of
Mary is one of those gospels outside the canon; the Gospel of
Philip is another. In the fourth century there's the Pistis Sophia; this
is another text that is full of material about Mary Magdalene. When
you take all the materials into account, from a historical point of
view, you have such an exciting range of texts beyond the four
gospels of the New Testament.

PAGELS: To give an example of the differences within the canonical
gospels, some of the texts say that she was a woman healed by Jesus, that she traveled and apparently was part of the circle of Jesus'
followers. As I read the Gospel of Luke, the women and the disciples were separate. So Mary was clearly not a disciple. But there's
an ambiguity about her, because she's described in all the New Testament gospels as the first, or one of the first, to have seen Jesus
resurrected from the dead, and that's very significant. That might
mean in another context that she would have been an apostle had
she been a man.

SCHABERG: In the Gospel of Mark, whose original end is at 16:8,
though there are other endings that have been tacked on over the
centuries, Mary doesn't get a vision and she and the other women
flee from the tomb and say nothing to anyone because they're
afraid. The end. In all of the gospels Mary Magdalene is at the cross.

There are no appearances to her in Luke, and there's no commission either. In some of the gospels, Mark and John and Matthew, she's told to go tell of her vision, while in Luke she is not. And in Luke, when she does tell, her words are regarded as raving, frantic, in a fever, but the reader knows that's not so.

KURS: *We know that the mainstream church, in its struggle to define orthodoxy, considered the Gnostic texts heresy and tried to destroy them. Introduce us to these gospels, which include the gospels of Mary, of Philip, of Thomas, and many more.*

PAGELS: The texts we call the Gnostic Gospels were discovered in upper Egypt in 1945, when an Arab villager was digging for fertilizer in a cliffside. He found a huge jar, and inside it were twelve or thirteen ancient books containing gospels, many of which we had never known. We knew that in the ancient world there had been many gospels, but some were buried, destroyed, or burned by leaders of the church who regarded them as abominable heresy. We never knew before what the heretics had said, we just knew they were terrible. And then we finally hear them speak in their own words.

GOOD: One of these gospels, the Gospel of Mary, is the account of her vision of the resurrected Jesus. When she reports her vision to the disciples, some of them are alarmed that these things could've been said to her and not to them, while others are supportive and want to hear more about the vision. This Gnostic text is unfortunately missing six pages, but what we can tell from the beginning and the end is that Mary consoles the disciples in their grief and encourages them by the words of the vision. At the end of the text she encourages the disciples to go out and, as the text literally says, "put on the perfect human" and proclaim the good news. This is how the commission ends, with the whole gospel of proclamations.

PAGELS: There are people today who call themselves Gnostic Christians, partly because they love the teachings of these texts, which remind one of Jewish or Buddhist mystical teachings. They encompass the idea that you can discover the divine source if you look for it inside yourself. I met a Gnostic bishop, a beautiful Cuban woman, who said she was initiated into the mysteries of Mary Magdalene in

France, where that tradition goes back for many centuries. She leads a Gnostic church in California. The Christian movement these days is much wider than what we call the orthodox tradition. We thought we knew about Jesus and the disciples, and everything we formerly believed comes from that knowledge. But now we see a much wider perspective. We have texts like the Dialogue of the Savior, where Mary Magdalene, together with Matthew and Thomas, is a major disciple. She's spoken of as the woman who understands all things. This understanding is not an intellectual process, it's a wisdom of the heart, and that's what these so-called Gnostics are seeking. It's not an abstraction, it's about spiritual depth and divine wisdom. This other range of sources opens up many questions that the church fathers did not want to have asked.

KURS: *Church fathers did ask questions about how to properly interpret the texts they did adopt; that is, the gospels of Matthew, Mark, Luke, and John. As all of us who study religion still do, because they still hold many puzzles. But let's start with what we might consider the heart of the matter in a discussion about Mary Magdalene: her role at the Resurrection, which reveals a lot about her status—or lack of it—among the disciples and the consequent development of early Christianity.*

PAGELS: There are only two figures in the New Testament who are said to have seen Jesus by themselves after the Resurrection. One is Peter and the other is Mary. Now, had she been a man, it would have been assumed that she was a disciple or an apostle, one of Jesus' representatives. Her vision would have qualified her. It's important to note that having the Resurrection appearance is a basis on which to claim authority, and it's her authority that's really in question.

But we find a lot in the New Testament that attempts to disqualify Mary Magdalene and makes sure that you know that even though she saw Jesus and was one of these enormously privileged figures—she and Peter alone—she's not a disciple. Her experience doesn't count; she's a woman, so she cannot testify in court under Jewish law at the time, and therefore she has to go to the disciples, and they authorize whether Jesus is actually risen, because her testimony is regarded as insignificant.

BELLEVIE: There's some fancy footwork going on related to the question of Mary Magdalene's testimony of the Resurrection. I think if we put a man in that role the picture would be very different; if a man had been the first witness of the Resurrection and had gone to tell the disciples, he would be probably held up as the primary apostle. I think that the fact that she's female is still influencing the way she's viewed.

PAGELS: What's striking is the contrast between treatment of women in canonical and noncanonical texts, because in Luke and the other gospels, there are the women and there are the disciples. And the women aren't the disciples and the disciples aren't the women. But when you look at the Gospel of Thomas, the Gospel of Mary, the Gospel of Philip, and the Dialogue of the Savior, Mary appears not only as one of the disciples but as one of the most significant disciples. The traditions that maintain that Peter is the most important disciple typically denigrate Mary, and the traditions that value Mary usually see Peter as a rather negative character. So there seems to be this rivalry articulated or expressed between Peter and Mary about which one is Jesus' favorite or closest disciple and to whom he's entrusted his revelation. In one of the writings, called Wisdom of Faith, Peter complains to Jesus that Mary is talking all the time; he thinks she should keep silent and say nothing, but in that text Jesus encourages her to talk. You can see why this is not part of the canon. This is not part of Catholic tradition. If you have a church that claims that only men are chosen by Jesus to be priests and teachers, you certainly don't want a gospel that says Mary Magdalene not only wasn't a prostitute but was a great disciple especially loved by Jesus.

SCHABERG: We also have that scene in the garden, as told in John 20, with its erotic elements. The erotica almost overpowers the idea that this is a witness to the resurrected Jesus.

PAGELS: What do you think of that scene? Because I'm puzzled by it.

SCHABERG: I started noticing that the Magdalene is usually positioned lower in the art. The risen Jesus is standing, and sometimes Mary Magdalene is actually reaching toward his groin. As you know,

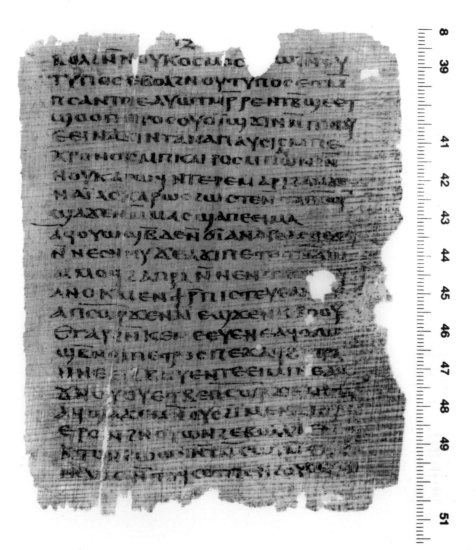

PLATE 1: An original manuscript page, in Coptic, of the *Gospel of Mary*. Here, the Magdalene finishes her recounting of the words Jesus had spoken only to her. Andrew expresses disbelief, and Peter asks, upset, "Did he speak with a woman in private without our knowing it? Are we to turn around and listen to her? Did he choose her over us?" Mary asks Peter directly if he thinks she is "telling lies," and the page ends with Levi asking Peter, ". . . if the Savior made her worthy, who are you then for your part to reject her?" See Chapters 1 and 3 for further discussion of this alternate Gospel.

The Gospel of Mary (Papyrus Berolinensis), fifth century CE, Coptic script. Byzantine papyrus, 13.5 x 10.5 cm. Inv. P 8502, fragment 17. (Bildarchiv Preussischer Kulturbesitz/Art Resource, NY. Photo: Joerg P. Anders)

PLATE 2:
Carlo Crivelli (1435/40–1493),
Saint Mary Magdalene, polyptych, detail,
Collegiata di S. Lucia,
Montefiore dell'Aso, Italy.
(Photo: Scala/Art Resource, NY)

PLATE 3: *Crucifixion* and *The Women at the Tomb*, c. 586 CE, from the Rabula Gospels, Zagba on the Euphrates, Syria. MS. Plut.1,56, f.13r., Biblioteca Laurenziana, Florence. (Photo: Scala/Art Resource, NY)

PLATE 4 ABOVE: Jean Fouquet, *Mary Magdalen at the Feast of Simon*, c. 1445, from *Les Heures d'Étienne Chavalier*, Mss. fr.71, Musée Condé, Chantilly, France. (Photo: Erich Lessing/Art Resource, NY)

PLATE 5 OPPOSITE: *Mary Magdalen*, n.d., S. Domenico, Pistoia, Italy. (Photo: Scala/Art Resource, NY)

PLATE 6: Fra Angelico, *Noli Me Tangere*, c. 1440–45, Museo di S. Marco, Florence.
(Photo: Scala/Art Resource, NY)

PLATE 7: Lucas Moser, *Altar of Magdalene,* wings closed, 1423, Parish Church, Tiefenbronn, Germany. (Photo: Erich Lessing/Art Resource, NY)

PLATE 8: Masaccio, *Crucifixion,* early fifteenth century, Museo Nazionale di Capodimonte, Naples, Italy. (Photo: Scala/Art Resource, NY)

PLATE 9: Lucas Cranach the Elder, *Christ and the Adulteress,* mid-1540s, The Metropolitan Museum of Art, New York, The Jack and Belle Linsky Collection. (1982.6-.0.35)

PLATE 10: El Greco, *Penitent Magdalen,* n.d., Museum of Fine Arts (Szépmûvészeti Muzeum), Budapest, Hungary. (Photo: Erich Lessing/Art Resource, NY)

PLATE 11: Arnold Böecklin, *Maria Magdalena Beweint den Toten Christus* (Mary Magdalen Deplores the Dead Christ), 1867, Kunstmuseum, Basel, Switzerland. (Photo: Erich Lessing/Art Resource, NY)

PLATE 12: William Etty, *Nude Female Contemplating a Skull and Crucifix* (Study of the Magdalen), mid-nineteenth century, Victoria and Albert Museum, London. (Photo: Art Resource, NY)

PLATE 13: Max Beckmann, *Christ and the Woman Taken in Adultery*, 1917, The Saint Louis Art Museum, St. Louis, Bequest of Curt Valentin.

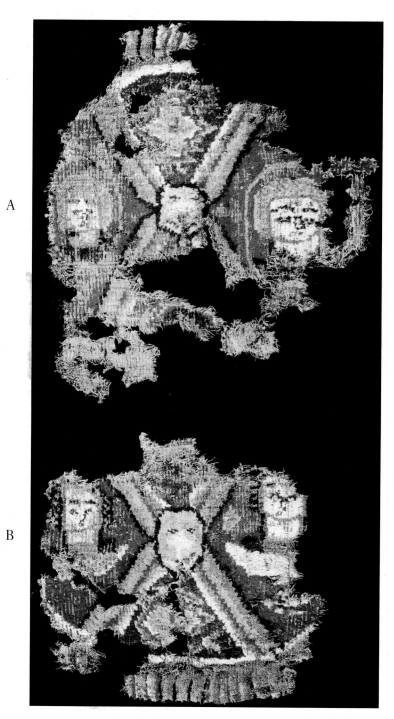

A

B

PLATE 14: Two fragments from the Exile Carpet, c. 150–180 CE, Mediterannean region. (Photo: Jeremy Pine)

PLATE 15: Reproduction of the Exile Carpet as it would have looked when complete. (Rendering and photo: Jeremy Pine)

PLATE 16: *The Bible of the Poor* (Biblia Pauperum), fifteenth century, facsimile edition of the British Library Blockbook, with translation and commentary by Albert C. Labriola and John W. Smeltz. (By permission of The British Library (C.9.d.2). Photo: British Library, London)

there's the idea that she wanted to hold on to the body, and that, I think, is a very serious misreading visually. Not that there aren't erotic elements in it, but it's been reduced to those erotic elements.

PAGELS: Many people have claimed that this scene suggests that Mary was some kind of witness or an apostle, and I actually think that John is making the opposite point. In the Gospel of John, Jesus speaks to Mary and suddenly she recognizes him and says "Rabboni," which means "my teacher." And in that moment of recognition, there's a very tender moment. He says, "Don't embrace me, as I haven't yet ascended to my Father." It's a beautiful scene, and a quite unforgettable one. And many feminists love this story; they say, "Look, John has shown us that Jesus favors Mary Magdalene and places her in very high regard."

I think John is doing something much trickier, though I wish they were right. What he's actually saying is: I know that Mary Magdalene was the first witness of the Resurrection; why, then, do I not think she's a disciple? She naturally would be if she were a man. The answer to that is what Jesus says to Mary in the garden; this is what John invents. When Mary sees Jesus, he says, "Don't touch me. I haven't yet ascended to heaven," and that means he hasn't received the power to bestow upon her. The very next scene he goes up to heaven, receives divine power from his Father, and breathes the Holy Spirit upon his disciples. Mary Magdalene is not included.

So this story demonstrates the opposite of what some of us wish it did. It demonstrates that Mary, although she was the first to see the risen Jesus, is not a disciple. Because she is not present when he conveys the power of the Holy Spirit to the disciples and makes them disciples. I think it's quite a misreading that Mary is there glorified. In fact, I think John is pointing out why orthodox tradition adamantly refuses to allow Mary to be regarded as a disciple.

SCHABERG: I read that scene very differently. I started noticing some connections between that scene, where she's supposed to go and say that Jesus said "I am ascending," and the Elijah and Elisha account, where Elijah is about to depart and Elisha, his disciple, is holding him back. Then Elijah says to Elisha, "If you see me ascending you'll have a double share of my spirit." So I'm reading it in that way. But I think you're right, as John 20 is written I suspect there's a source that has been played with—not lost, but tampered with. Mary has been made very ignorant, in contrast to the so-called Gnostic Mary Magdalene. In John, Mary doesn't know where the body is, she doesn't know who Jesus is, she doesn't know anything.

GOOD: In John's gospel, though, Mary Magdalene is said to be a preacher, particularly because she's given the commission by Jesus to go and tell the brothers, "I am ascending."These are the words of Jesus—"I am ascending to my Father and your Father, to my God and your God"—and so this becomes her apostolic commission. Now, in illustrated versions of this she preaches to the puzzled disciples, who are off-stage somewhere looking mystified and even in great distress. She has an outstretched finger, and she's emphatically proclaiming the good news of the Resurrection as they are looking incredulous. There are other noncanonical texts in which Jesus tells Mary Magdalene to go to Peter and remind Peter of what Jesus has said to him because Peter is in danger of forgetting it. So it's very interesting that Mary's role is never in doubt as a preacher and as an apostle from the first century onward, at least in the texts.

APOSTOLOS-CAPPADONA: The irony to me is Eastern Orthodox Christianity never sees, at least canonically, Mary Magdalene as anyone other than the "holy-equal-unto-the-apostles"—not the apostola, not apostle to the apostles, but the holy equal unto the apostles. She is the witness, she is the myrrophore—the myth bearer—the one who brings the ointment. She's not really a fallen woman, she's not the great sinner, she's not any of these conflations so critical to Western Christianity. Instead, she goes and preaches in Rome before Peter and preaches to the emperor, according to Eastern Orthodox tradition. She does all of this, yet do we have women holding positions of ecclesiastical authority in Orthodoxy? Do we see women having an authoritative voice in Eastern Orthodoxy? If she was a trailblazer, no woman followed. So my concern is that by trying to retrieve whoever Mary is in the Western Christian traditions in the hope that she will then give women a significant ecclesiastical voice does not necessarily follow given the history of Eastern Orthodox Christianity.

BELLEVIE: The biggest lesson I think we can learn from Mary Magdalene is indirect; it's about how we think about early Christianity and how it came to be what it is today. It turns out that early Christianity was very diverse, there were many ideas circulating about the Christian story and about Mary Magdalene. A lot of people are now hearing these different views of Mary Magdalene and asking, Why haven't I heard about this? Why didn't I know there were all these Gnostic Gospels floating around? Why didn't I know these other versions of the story? So people are really becoming involved in their religion and in their spirituality, whereas before they may have been somewhat complacent. That's a big benefit of the current popularity of Mary Magdalene.

Mary Magdalene as the Repentant Sinner

KURS: *Let's talk about the association of Mary Magdalene with prostitution. Is there historical evidence for it? Where did that idea come from? It's a very charged image that has endured. And certainly it's one that appears often in visual representation as well as in the oral tradition.*

PAGELS: I think it's important to say clearly what is evident from the sources. We know that there is nothing in the New Testament that identifies her as a prostitute. It's only later, centuries later, that some people within the church traditions associate Mary Magdalene with a story of a prostitute who repents and wipes Jesus' feet with her hair. And that association is now almost automatic for many people who grew up with Christian tradition, but it's simply not present in the New Testament.

HASKINS: This distortion is based on the story in Luke that Mary Magdalene had seven devils driven from her. We don't know what those seven devils were, but if you look at the gospels the demons cast out of men are not their sexuality—they are depravity, mental illness, and so on, not sexuality. But in the case of Mary Magdalene, her demons are the seven vices, and the church harps on this. These devils, these sins, are her luxury, her vanity, her lust.

From about the seventh century on, Mary Magdalene had been seen as a repentant sinner in a church that from the second and third centuries onward was becoming a male ecclesiastical hierarchy. Developing ideas about Jesus' divinity, and about his birth to a virgin, began to reflect on the figure of Mary Magdalene, who until this point was just a disciple of Jesus. By the end of the sixth century, Pope Gregory the Great decided that her sin, as she had to be a repentant woman, was her sexuality. This is in counterpart to the Virgin's virginity. In order to have a woman redeemed she had to reject her sexuality.

The sermons you read are always about Mary Magdalene's beauty, her hair, which lured men, her eyes, which lured men, her body, which lured men. And now at the feet of Christ she was this person who dried Christ's feet with her hair, she kissed his feet with her lips, she was prostrate on the ground. She became a symbol of repentant femininity. It was an utterly negative attitude toward women, and that's what Mary Magdalene represented. She was propaganda for the church against women. In one fourteenth-century Italian fresco Mary is standing wearing this wonderful garment, but it's slit up the sides; and a Dominican preacher railed that Christ opened his side for the redemption of humanity whereas Mary Magdalene opened her side for men's eyes. This voyeuristic, misogynistic way of looking at the figure of Mary Magdalene was a very powerful message to women. She's used in sermons as the model of repentance for all sinners, but particularly for women.

Good: There are some people, perhaps Christians today even, who think that paying attention to a woman prostitute in Christian tradition is a waste of time, and that many of the texts that give us information about Mary Magdalene are late, derivative, secondary, not canonical. So why bother? To those people I would simply say, it's important to ask oneself about 50 percent of the human race. Half of the human race are women, and we need to look at the way women are recognized in Christian tradition, at how they play significant, even complementary, roles. Mary Magdalene offers one possibility of understanding this in a way that is physical, corporeal, real, and tangible.

The connection of Mary Magdalene with prostitution and with the dejected and despised elements of society—particularly women in hostels in the Middle Ages and even in the nineteenth century and in places in Europe today—has played a most important role in raising the level of care and hospitality that must be offered as a mandate for Christians. So when we think of Mary Magdalene as a prostitute, we shouldn't be so quick to dismiss this aspect of the tradition. It's much too facile to say, okay, the New Testament doesn't give evidence of prostitution, and therefore it doesn't belong to Mary Magdalene. In fact many women, many despised people, have found access to the Christian tradition through Mary Magdalene's association with "fallen" women, so we must remember not to disparage that image so quickly.

SCHABERG: Feminist understandings of prostitution are varied. There are some feminist scholars who would look very positively on women's use of their own sexuality and their profit from their own sexuality, while other people would regard it as a tragic choice, hardly even a choice. But the fact that Mary Magdalene was associated with it is something that we shouldn't forget as feminists, because it's of interest to the welfare of women, the positive aspects of women's sexuality, and the profit that's made from women, from abusing women.

The Mary Magdalene Mosaic

KURS: *Over the centuries, people's ideas about Mary Magdalene and who she was changed greatly, in part because of confusion about her identity. This is reflected in the history of art. Diane, tell us about the various representations of her, and what they tell us about the religious attitudes of the day.*

APOSTOLOS-CAPPADONA: At varied points in Christian history, we have different ways of understanding Mary Magdalene—as the fallen woman, as the apostle to the apostles, as the first witness to the Resurrection, in the different ways she is depicted in liturgical dramas—with her hair covered, with her hair uncovered, as the sinner at the feet of Jesus, at the foot of the cross. There is an embellishing and enlarging of her story as we travel through history. A Magdalene mosaic is created for us by Pope Gregory when he pulls together several named and unnamed women from scripture—women with certain similar actions such as the anointing of the feet, carrying of oil, sinning—and makes them one. Contemporary feminists may say that we have to get rid of these negative attributes, we have to get back to the clarity of the text, we have to separate out all of these other roles and get to the heart of what scripture says she is. When that attempt has been made in the past, the congregations, the community, have rebelled.

We have already talked about the many ways her image has been denigrated, and it's reflected in hundreds of well-known artworks through the centuries. Yet in some ways that is the easy answer. There is also a more complex way to look at the way she has been portrayed more generally. If we were carefully surveying the history of images and stories about Mary Magdalene, we would see the many ways she embodies the fullness of human experience: our aging process, our weaknesses, our goodness and our strengths, our existence as sinners, as saints, as penitents. She was clearly a person who had passions and emotions, and who obviously loved. The mystery about her is why she isn't married. In our way of looking at the world, being married and having a child is probably the most passionate and romantic thing human beings do. So here we have this figure who in some way embodies female sensuality, passions, and feelings about spirituality and devotion, and yet we have this conundrum. Where is the husband? Where is the child?

We have to stop and ask, What are the different characteristics of love, what are the different passions, how are they defined at different times in history, and who is this woman who so loves but doesn't touch? Who is this woman who so embodies femininity that she is the patroness of perfume, of glove makers, of jewelers, of couturiers, of all these things that make a woman, in a sense, feminine. We have to pull back for a moment and ask ourselves about the different concepts of love. Our modern sense of passion is something very distinct from what it was in the early centuries of

Christianity or in the medieval period. *Paseo,* the root word of passion, means "to suffer." In our concept of love, the lowest level is the erotic. The next level of love involves caring about another person. The highest level of love is when you enter into some kind of union with God.

Which level of love does Mary Magdalene embody? Probably all of them, if we look at the many Magdalenes that exist. Where is the child? Well, I don't think there was a child; I don't think that kind of relationship existed with the person we know as the historical Jesus of Nazareth. The issue has always been that Mary Magdalene was an independent woman, and as an independent woman, she didn't need a child, she didn't need a husband. She needed her passion, her love, to be fulfilled in other ways. And she fulfills these passions in the legends and stories and images where she becomes the preacher, the missionary, the evangelist, the healer, the miracle worker. She is the woman who provides for other women to have their children. These are the things that attract people to her.

HASKINS: Let me add a political timeline to the negative changes in her image. Mary Magdalene started being changed into a repentant prostitute from a very early period in Christianity. You have all these early Christian fathers trying to figure out the roles of these various Marys in the gospels until, in 591 AD, Pope Gregory the Great decided that Mary Magdalene, this courageous and faithful witness of the Resurrection, was also two other women, now conflated into one repentant sinner.

The history gets even more complicated when Mary Magdalene gets tied in to the growing emphasis on celibacy in the church, which in 1100 becomes the doctrine that priests are not allowed to marry, and at the same time you have the growing idea of the Virgin's virginity, the importance of penance, and the divinity of Christ being created by the idea of his mother's virginity. So Mary Magdalene becomes this eremitical figure and the symbol of penitence. In 1215 the sacrament of penance was established, and all Christians had to go to church and make their confession and take Communion. Mary Magdalene was the symbol of both penance and Communion, but then she takes off with a completely new persona and becomes the symbol of lust, which is what woman embodied. Sermons about her were about her lust, her vanity, her worldly life.

Mary Magdalene: Prostitute or Mrs. Jesus?

KURS: *The subject of lust sure continues to swirl around Mary Magdalene. But, arguably, it has been "elevated" to the sphere of the sacred goddess tradition. Thanks to* The Da Vinci Code *as well as the popular works of writers like Margaret Starbird, Merlin Stone, and Lynn Picknett, and the influence of popular culture and New Age thinking, we have been offered a perspective that says that instead of Mary Magdalene being a "simple" prostitute she is a symbol of the sacred feminine—a tradition that includes the sacred prostitute, sacred sex rites, and sacred marriage. Why don't we sort out some of this, starting with the pre-Christian notion of sacred marriage, or* hieros gamos *in the Greek, and then tracing it through the gospel stories.*

BELLEVIE: In some of the pre-Christian religions of the Mesopotamian region there were fertility cults with a spirituality that revolved around the health and welfare of the land, as well as a concept of the community soul. So, *hieros gamos,* or the sacred marriage ritual, was one in which a woman took on the identity of a goddess and the man was perhaps a sacred king or had a symbolic role of kingship; they would be married, symbolically or literally, and their union would directly benefit the land and the people they represented. There's this notion now, in works by Margaret Starbird and some other authors, that the anointing scenes in the gospels, all four gospels, are reminiscent of *hieros gamos* rituals that took place in the Mesopotamian region, even though there is no clear evidence that such rituals occurred at all in the Roman Empire of the first century. These authors contend that the people were familiar enough with this concept that when they read the anointing scene of Jesus, they would have read *hieros gamos* symbolism into it.

SCHABERG: The idea behind *hieros gamos* is that sex between a man and a woman mirrors sex between a heavenly king and a heavenly queen in the divine kingdom. So in *The Da Vinci Code,* where you have the grandfather's butt pumping up in the air as he is having sex with someone, and the granddaughter sees that, what they're doing is a reenactment of the pagan ritual. They are performing sacred sex in the sense that it supposedly mirrors divine sex. Wouldn't that be nice.

APOSTOLOS-CAPPADONA: Those who believe that the anointing is some form of a *hieros gamos* are looking at Luke 7:36–50, which has the woman who knelt at the feet of the higher figure, the figure of authority. It looks like some action that a wife might perform for a husband. This is the scene portrayed in the Zeffirelli film *Jesus of Nazareth*—Anne Bancroft plays it with a lot of whimpering, groveling, tears, and gentility. It's a scene of gratitude: the sinner is forgiven, she's grateful and much loved. That's the moment everyone remembers.

PAGELS: There's an irony in this as it relates to Christianity, then and now. Traditional church images of Mary Magdalene often depicted her as a prostitute, while contemporary fantasies of Mary portray her as the wife and lover of Jesus. They're both eroticized images, but in different ways. There's either the bad one or the good one. What you find in ancient stories is quite different. Instead of being eroticized in male fantasy, she is seen as a disciple of Jesus, one who takes a very important role. She is very close to Jesus, and she receives visions and special teaching that he gives to her alone. Not only is she loved more than other women, she is loved more than the other disciples. The idea that she was entrusted with especially close and deep teaching is something that is even more objectionable to the churches, I think, than the idea that she was either a prostitute or a lover.

SCHABERG: I think that the recent interest in making Mary Magdalene Mrs. Jesus or the lover of Jesus has to do more with Jesus than with Mary Magdalene. She exists to say something about the sexuality of Jesus in those forms of interpretation, many of which are in novels. If he's gonna be a real guy—that is, not gay—he's going to have to have a woman. And that's another way of using a woman to think about a man.

KURS: *Speaking of Mr. and Mrs. Jesus, if we look back at some of the ancient texts, the texts that were not included in the New Testament—the Gospel of Philip, the Gospel of Thomas, the Pista Sophia—those images of ecstatic union are there. They seem to have been with us for thousands of years, embodying that quest to unite with God.*

PAGELS: Sometimes that desire is expressed in sexual forms. I'm thinking of a passage in the Gospel of Thomas in which another of the women speaks to Jesus and asks him, in rather sexual language, "Who are you, man, that you've come up on my couch and eaten from my table?" And he seems to rebuke her and says, "I'm not going to answer that question in the way that you place it. I'm the one who comes from what is the same." I think he's referring to the primordial creation, which is prior to male and female, and that he is saying, I come from what is prior to gender, my identity is not that of a man, any more than yours is that of a woman on a spiritual level. It goes beyond that to an identity that is found in God beyond gender. So that's another way of imagining a kind of union.

KURS: *And those rather provocative statements about how Mary received kisses on the mouth from Jesus? How are we to understand that?*

PAGELS: That's in the Gospel of Philip, actually, and of course it set off wild fictional treatments. It reads: "The companion of the Lord was Mary Magdalene and he loved her more than the other apostles and kissed her on the . . ." and then the text breaks, and people have filled in "mouth" because the Coptic word would fit into that blank, but we don't know. And, in fact, further into the text it seems to be less sexually sensational and more the kind of mystical language that you find in Jewish and Buddhist tradition. Using sexual imagery speaks of the kiss as the way that those who were initiated Christians conceive and give birth, and this is the so-called kiss of peace; after being baptized and receiving the Eucharist people kiss each other, and they give birth to new Christians this way. This is a transformation of the sexual procreative act into a spiritual procreative act, which happens in baptism.

APOSTOLOS-CAPPADONA: We also have to put this kiss into a cultural context, and ask what these terms or actions mean within the social attitudes of the time. As you're saying, it can be the kiss of peace or may represent the exchange of ideas, bringing the initiates into community, or rebirth.

KURS: *You're suggesting that the kiss is not as eroticized as we're making it out to be?*

PAGELS: In the context of the Gospel of Philip, the erotic is frequently used as a metaphor: sexual imagery is understood to be manifesting a spiritual connection. When you read Philip you have a sense that Jesus and Mary's love for one another has erotic qualities to it—erotic love as an expression of divine love is an important part of these texts. Sexual imagery has always been part of mystical tradition. When people speak about divine love they often speak about the bride and the bridegroom. The mystics of the Catholic Church, too, like St. John of the Cross, speak about being in love with God. The Song of Songs is about sexual love, but it's taken as an image of how God loves humans. Erotic and divine love are joined in a way that we don't find in orthodox tradition, which usually separates them quite sharply.

KURS: *The interplay between erotic and divine love certainly keeps showing up in the imagery of Mary Magdalene. In fact, Susan, I think you coined the rather neat phrase "pious pornography." Can you tell us what that means?*

HASKINS: Pious pornography basically refers to the images you get of Mary Magdalene from about the sixteenth century onward; from that point she is painted or sculpted as a naked woman. That convention derives from the legend that she went to the south of France and lived in a cavern, where she divested herself of her clothes and grew her hair down over her body. She prayed and fasted, and every day the angels came down and took her up to heaven for her heavenly meal. The image through the Renaissance became more about her nudity than anything else, and some of these images are very explicitly pornographic. She is flesh personified, or woman's flesh personified, even when she's reading, even when she's praying.

APOSTOLOS-CAPPADONA: Whether she's portrayed reading, whether she's in the garden, whether she's laying across a rock, we have to put these images within the cultural context of the historical periods in which they were created. Often, though not always, she's represented in a voyeuristic way. We have to look at the representations and talk about what's going on at that time. What are people thinking about, not simply with regard to Mary Magdalene, but in terms of the body, of humanity? What are they thinking about sexuality? What are they thinking about the basis of Christianity? Is it the Incarnation as the enfleshing of the spirit?

SCHABERG: The question is, what are they thinking about the female body? Actually, it's what are *men* thinking about the female body?

KURS: *So what role did Mary Magdalene's body play at different time periods?*

APOSTOLOS-CAPPADONA: I think when she starts to be shown undressed and reading, it's at the same time that Jerome is represented as undressed and reading. This is probably first found in the work of Adrien Isenbrant (d. 1551). There are parallels if you look at the history of the iconography of Jerome and of the Magdalene. When you first have Jerome reading in the wilderness, he's dressed; and the first images of the Magdalene reading in the wilderness show her dressed. Then Isenbrandt slowly starts taking her clothes off. A breast is exposed, while Jerome, in Isenbrandt, has part of his chest exposed. Eventually Jerome gets down to a loincloth.

KURS: *I'm hearing you say that even with the range of different visual images we have of Mary throughout time, they still have erotic overtones and they're still given to us by men.*

HASKINS: Yes, but you have to put them in their context. The sixteenth-century paintings were being done when the female body was an ideal body. Mary Magdalene would be described as an ideal beauty. She was a Venus in sackcloth, which is the way one art historian described her. So while she was portrayed as the image of the ideal woman, she also had this other persona put on her by the church.

After the rupture with the Protestants, Mary Magdalene became a propaganda weapon for the Catholic Church, which had a new focus on the sacrament of penance. By this point she had become the naked repentant person; earlier, she had not been naked, but now she was naked and repentant. And that transformation has to do with the legend of her going to the south of France and the correlation between vanity and clothes and naked truth. By converting and turning to God she now had a pure soul and a pure body, and her nakedness was a symbol of the truth that she had turned to.

Mary Magdalene had converted to Christ, she was newborn, she was naked, but there's also a question about the motives of the patrons, who were mostly aristocratic men. She was a pinup, to use that rather cheap language. You have people commissioning paintings of her entirely nude, with only a bit of hair to cover herself. There was one painter whose picture of Mary Magdalene would today appear on page three of a British newspaper—page three is where you put all the images of naked women. She's got not a stitch on her, just a lock of hair lying across her breast. And the following year that painter became a priest. The distinction between sacred and profane, well, there's not much of a distinction really.

The Mary Magdalene of *The Da Vinci Code*

KURS: *It's inevitable, I suppose, that no conversation about Mary Magdalene these days can escape* The Da Vinci Code. *People want to know: did Dan Brown get it right? Is the alternate accounting of history more accurate than what has been passed down to us from pulpits and classrooms?*

GOOD: On one hand, we're very grateful to Dan Brown for placing Mary Magdalene in the traditions of early Christianity, and we're grateful because he encourages people to read noncanonical texts in which Mary Magdalene plays an important role. However, the use he himself makes of these texts is very limited. Brown allows Mary Magdalene to appear only in connection with Jesus. She never has her own voice, we never hear her own prophetic witness to Jesus.

SCHABERG: Dan Brown's Mary Magdalene makes me really angry. She's not only Mrs. Jesus, she's a reduced wife, and there are lots of places where she's referred to as the vessel. How much more reducing can you do?

GOOD: In *The Da Vinci Code,* Dan Brown makes an extraordinary statement that inverts what we know of texts outside the canon: he makes texts like the Gospel of Mary and the Gospel of Philip into historical documents. Why? Because they contain evidence of a marriage between Jesus and Mary Magdalene. Now that sets every piece of scholarly work for two thousand years on its head. What we have hitherto thought to be the case is that the gospels of the New Testament—Matthew, Mark, Luke, and John—are likely to be closely connected to historical traditions, and in those gospels we find not a marriage between Jesus and Mary Magdalene but Mary Magdalene alongside other disciples as a follower of Jesus. She has a particular insight and knowledge and tenacity in that role as disciple and follower and then subsequently apostle. Now why does Dan Brown invert what we know of noncanonical texts? Because it suits his argument from a fictional point of view. He only highlights texts in which you might be able to see a marriage between Jesus and Mary Magdalene and he ignores the others. If you want to look at two texts to make a specific case, you can do it, but why not look at all texts and ask, "What is the cumulative evidence?"

Mary Magdalene as an Independent Woman

KURS: *Dan Brown and all others interested in the discussion about Mary Magdalene owe a great debt to the feminist scholars such as yourselves who have done so much work over the last twenty to thirty years to search, in text and in visual evidence, for what's come to be called a "usable past." What's the lesson we should take from the story about Mary Magdalene in that context? I'm listening to this notion of pious pornography we discussed a few minutes ago on the one hand, and of a strong, independent, spiritual woman on the other. Is Mary Magdalene a model for feminism as well as for the church?*

HASKINS: I think of her as a propaganda weapon against women, particularly with regard to these images of the repentant so-called prostitute. In order to become a holy woman she has to give away her sexuality and become asexual, which is what the church created her image to be.

SCHABERG: But I think a lot of feminist thought about prostitution is hesitant to ignore the fact that some prostitutes do claim that they are exercising options to use their sexuality, while other feminists think of prostitutes as victims. It's interesting, too—I've been told that many prostitutes groups are very attracted to this legend of Mary Magdalene the prostitute.

APOSTOLOS-CAPPADONA: In their eyes, she's an independent woman who is making her own way in the world, a world in which the possibilities are limited.

BELLEVIE: Even though the prostitute identity is a fiction, and it's acknowledged today that there's no scriptural basis for it, if we take away this potent tradition about Mary Magdalene, are we taking away a woman some people are able to identify with in other valuable ways? It's rather interesting that we are still willing to see her that way in some circumstances; a lot of rescue organizations are still recognized under Mary Magdalene's patronage. The Catholic Church changing her designation on a calendar isn't going to change fourteen hundred years of thinking that quickly. It's with us, and I think in some ways it can be healthy, because some people still have this notion of trying to live up to the standard that the Virgin Mary has been set up as, and no one can live up to that ideal. Mary Magdalene traditionally has been a figure that women can look to and think, "Well, if Jesus loved her, he can love me," and that's still occurring. People are still identifying with her in that way.

HASKINS: My idea of an unreconstructed Mary Magdalene is the gospel figure as we know it, without all the accretions and the other blended figures such as Luke's sinner and Mary of Bethany. The unreconstructed Mary is a dynamic figure who is the leader of the disciples in the gospels.

SCHABERG: I agree that she should be seen as a dynamic figure, but from my perspective I don't see a lot of use in this idea of apostle to the apostles. It goes nowhere. Eastern Orthodox or Vatican statements may say that she's an important apostle to the apostles, yes, but she's still kept in her compartment. Her significance as apostle to the apostles means nothing in terms of leadership opportunities for contemporary women.

APOSTOLOS-CAPPADONA: As I reconstruct the historical figure of Mary Magdalene, she is as a prophetic mystic, a very important person in the earliest moments of Christianity, or what would become Christianity. What I like to think I'm doing as a feminist scholar is what feminist scholars in other fields are doing; I am interested in reconstructing and reunderstanding history, in looking again at the past and emending the lacunae of the past so that we can participate in a worldwide movement for social change that moves us toward societies that are just for all women and children, who make up the bulk of the poor, and for non-elite men.

HASKINS: In the twentieth century, people, mainly women, have seen Mary Magdalene as a model because she was strong and independent. Mary Magdalene did what she wanted to do, she wasn't forced to do anything. According to the gospels, she followed her ideas right through to the end and was repaid for her fidelity by meeting the risen Christ. And now you can see her as a sort of sacred feminine that's within all women, and many women want to have that goddess figure or that sacred feminine as an empowering force that guides them to do what they think is right.

SCHABERG: Feminists' interpretations of Mary Magdalene are much more than interpretations that would pull the rug out from those who would resist women's ordination or women's leadership in religious circles. What feminist reconstruction of history is trying to do is work for the reform of social structures worldwide. This is a much more dangerous thing than just ordination.

PAGELS: What we see is a Mary Magdalene that feminists in the present are trying to invent. This is a person—a representative and symbolic person—who has been part of the tradition since the very beginning. It's like having a photograph in which one of the major images has been airbrushed out, and now we're seeing that

that image has been there from the beginning. And we see that it belongs as part of the tradition we know.

KURS: *Clearly, the church has not been able to contain Mary Magdalene. Her presence endures. Thank you for coming here today, to talk about her, to ponder her, and to have her among us.*

6 The Mary Magdalene Mosaic

*The individual had flowing red hair, delicate folded hands, and the hint of
a bosom. It was, without doubt . . . female . . . Sophie could not take her
eyes from the woman beside Christ. The Last Supper is supposed to be
thirteen men. Who is this woman? . . . "Everyone misses it," Teabing said.
"Our preconceived notions of this scene are so powerful that our mind
blocks out the incongruity and overrides our eyes."*

  —DAN BROWN, *The DaVinci Code*

*There is something about Mary Magdalene as a repentant prostitute which
allows painters and artists to keep the voluptuousness and sensuality
within the Christian tradition by making it repentant.*

  —KAREN L. KING, *The Gospel of Mary of Magdala*

*The deep ambivalence about sexuality held by those within monastic culture
did not . . . quite allow them to give up thinking about how desirable this
former prostitute must have been after her conversion. She is often depicted
as nude in the craggy rocks of La Sainte-Baume. Her long and lustrous hair,
covering the parts of her body that modesty conventionally requires to be
covered, is a staple of iconography in the West to this day, making Mary
Magdalene the Lady Godiva of Christian spirituality.*

  —BRUCE CHILTON, *Mary Magdalene: A Biography*

Revisiting "The Scarlet Lily"
Mary Magdalene in Western Art and Culture

BY DIANE APOSTOLOS-CAPPADONA

The point of her story is that she so loved Christ that she repented of her past and came to accept the mortality of flesh and immortality of the soul. Yet the way the pictures are painted contradicts the essence of this story. It is as though the transformation of her life brought about by her repentance has not taken place. The method of painting is incapable of making the renunciation she is meant to have made. She is painted as being, before she is anything else, a takeable and desirable woman. She is still the compliant object of the painting-method's seduction.

—JOHN BERGER, *Ways of Seeing*

No female figure in the history of Christian art has experienced as many visual and interpretive transformations as Mary Magdalene. Her image in Christian art, like her portrayal in Christianity, has been shaped and reshaped continually by cultural and theological shifts through two thousand years of Christian history. Through an exploration of her multiple metamorphoses as saint and sinner in Christian art—from its earliest days through the Medieval, Renaissance, Reformation, Counter-Reformation, Enlightenment, and Romantic eras and into the Ages of "Angst" and Aquarius—we can see a reflection of our own contemporary understanding of religion and spirituality.

The fundamental iconography of Mary Magdalene is that of a beautiful young woman with long flowing hair who holds a jar filled with unguent with which she is prepared to anoint the feet of Jesus in the

---

Diane Apostolos-Cappadona is a cultural historian who specializes in religious art and teaches at Georgetown University. Her original research into the iconology of Mary Magdalene began during her undergraduate study at George Washington University where Dr. Laurence Pereira Leite, Emeritus Professor of the History of Art, became her mentor in Christian art and culture. Her first published text on this intriguing biblical woman was "Images, Interpretations, and Traditions: A Study of the Magdalene" in *Interpreting Tradition: The Art of Theological Reflection,* ed. Jane Kopas (Chico: Scholar's Press, 1984): 109–23. This present essay, informed by the subsequent research of Susan Haskins, Katherine Ludwig Jansen, and other scholars, is a revisiting of that original manuscript. The description of Mary Magdalene as "the Scarlet Lily" references one of the more inventive biblical novels about her.

House of the Pharisees or his crucified body (Plate 3). Many popular representations depict her as one who is deep in contemplative penance, often with a skull, crucifix, or scourge, symbols of her conversion from sinner to saint. Whenever she is pictured in silent meditation and gazing into a mirror, it is not a reversion to her previous narcissism, but rather a spiritual introspection, a look into her own soul and its transformation. Oftentimes in Christian art, she is represented in a variety of physical and emotional conditions such as a disheveled and wan desert mother or as a distraught older woman in preparation for her death. Regardless of the theme of the art, Mary Magdalene is typically dressed in garments whose color symbolism is distinctive—shades of orange connote her previous worldly existence, whereas violet signifies her penitence and mourning. Her red mantle denotes love in all its varying degrees, from eros to agape, from familial to personal, from egocentric to communal.

Long, flowing, beautiful hair is a major attribute of Mary Magdalene, representing her dual role as the anointer of Jesus of Nazareth as well as the repentant and converted sinner. Hair has a variety of symbolic qualities in Christian art. In Classical, pre-Christian Mediterranean culture, copper-colored or red hair implied a venereal character—thereby visually affirming her as the unnamed adulteress who later becomes identified as a prostitute. However ambiguous it may seem, hair represents energy and fertility as well. A full head of hair represents élan vital, joie de vivre, and spiritual energy. In those days, abundant, beautiful hair signified individual spiritual development. Representations of Mary Magdalene with long, flowing tresses confirmed her spiritual development, especially following her conversion experience.

Throughout the classical Mediterranean world, young unmarried women wore their hair long and unbound, a style that became synonymous with visualizations of sacred love, whereas courtesans braided or piled their hair high on their heads, signifying profane love. Mary Magdalene's long, loose, flowing hair denoted simultaneously these cultural customs and the writings of the early church fathers, and the *Litany of the Saints* in which she is invoked as a virgin.

Early Christian artists did not examine the questions related to the identity of Mary Magdalene, or how by papal pronouncement a group of scriptural women became collapsed into one woman thereafter known as Mary Magdalene, sinner and saint. The preeminent idea for these artists was to express that the saint was not important as an *individual* but rather as the witness of the miracle or other episodes in the life of Jesus of Nazareth. Early Christian art was concerned with expressions and confessions of faith including the artist's own desire for salvation, but not with artistic creativity or theological innovations.

It is difficult, if not impossible, to find identifiable representations of Mary Magdalene in what became the next phase of religious art: Early Christian or Byzantine.[1] Rather, artists turned to depictions of those miracles in which she herself played a role, the Resurrection most especially, or those scriptural stories involving the unnamed women, such as the *Anointing at Bethany,* and the *Woman Taken in Adultery.* From the fourth century, sarcophagi from Milan and Servanne, ivory tableaux from Milan and Munich, the wooden doors of Santa Sabina in Rome, and mosaics at San Apollinare Nuovo in Ravenna all attest to some of the early artistic interest in a female figure we might identify as Mary Magdalene. The sixth-century Rabula Codex includes some unmistakable representations of her in the company of Mary of Nazareth in the Crucifixion, Empty Tomb, and Apparition of the Risen Christ (Plate 3).

Following the late sixth-century homily by Pope Gregory I that turned Mary Magdalene into a penitent sinner, early medieval art begins the visual history of the composite Mary Magdalene, or what I refer to as the "Magdalene mosaic." Visual evidence found in varied media ranging from mosaics and frescoes to manuscript illuminations and carvings confirm the then common artistic identification of Mary Magdalene with the unnamed and converted sinner. Representations of the varied anointing scenes are blended together as Mary Magdalene becomes identified with the other anonymous anointers. This visual acceptance of Mary Magdalene with the repentant sinner and Mary of Bethany, sister of Lazarus and Martha, solidified the composite scriptural image fostered by Gregory. This confusion of scriptural

1. See my essay "On the Visual and the Vision: The Magdalene in Early Christian and Byzantine Art and Culture" in *Mariam, The Magdalen, and the Mother,* ed. Deirdre Good (Bloomington: Indiana University Press, 2005): 123–49.

stories and Christian images resulted in a folk understanding of who Mary Magdalene was and what she represented to the Christian collective.

The Middle Ages

During the Middle Ages, Mary Magdalene begins her visual journey from "bit player" in the Christian drama of saintly female figures in Romanesque and Gothic art to become a major independent individual—a female hero in her own right. Depictions of Mary Magdalene become prevalent within the narrative and liturgical cycles in medieval cathedrals, from carved or painted arches to wall frescoes and portal sculptures. Contemporary with this artistic transformation, Mary Magdalene began to receive veneration as a penitential saint and became fused with that other reformed prostitute-turned-saint, Mary of Egypt, who lived a life of penance in the Egyptian desert (Plate 4).

The Middle Ages were a period of great individual and communal faith that recognized the power of sin, and enforced penance. The great plague of the fourteenth century, for example, underlined with daily expediency suffering, misery, and the fragility of human life. As the "great sinner" who received forgiveness, love, and the first "vision" of the Resurrection, Mary Magdalene came to symbolize on a daily basis encouragement and solace to her fellow sinners (Plate 5).

The Middle Ages witnessed an explosion of Christianity as well, signified by the Crusades, pilgrimages, liturgical dramas or Passion plays, and Franciscan spirituality. Mary Magdalene loomed large in the traveling plays, particularly as a central actor in the Lamentation and Resurrection scenes (Plate 6). One immediate artistic result of these plays was the change in her hair—no longer covered by a mantle or veil, her beautiful tresses now flowed loosely around her shoulders. This theatrical ploy to humanize the previous iconography of the saintly and matronly Mary Magdalene made her visually appealing to the audience.

Legendary and theological texts prove to be significant sources for these medieval metamorphoses of the image of Mary Magdalene. For example, she becomes the symbol of love, humility, and penitence for the emerging Franciscan spiritual tradition. Pseudo-Bonaventura's *Meditations on the Life of Christ* contained many important references to Mary Magdalene. Several medieval commentators affirmed the legend which revealed the true identity of the bridal couple at the Marriage at Cana: Mary Magdalene and John the Evangelist. Simultaneously, other medieval authors including Jacobus de Voragine sought to deny this unmasking of the bride's identity or any relating of it to Mary Magdalene in *The Golden Legend*. Bernard of Clairvaux's sermons on the Song of Songs, especially Sermon 57, followed the tradition established by Origen in his *Commentary on the Canticle of Canticles* linking the bride from the Cana narrative with Mary Magdalene as the anointer of Jesus of Nazareth. Quickly the matronly Magdalene figure disappeared from Christian consciousness as she became the symbolic merging of earthly love with spiritual love, of *eros* with *agape*. Thus, medieval Christianity brought forth a Mary Magdalene transformed from saintly matron into beautiful female hero of Christian virtue.

Perhaps the most important medieval devotions to Mary Magdalene, however, were those developed in medieval France. Mary Magdalene, or Marie-Madeleine as she is known, became France's Christian missionary and penitential saint extraordinaire.[2] Elaborate legends of her preaching and miracle-working throughout the south of France result in special veneration (Plate 7). In the thirteenth century, a chapel dedicated to Marie-Madeleine was built upon the site of a ruined Temple to Diana of Ephesus in Marseilles. Her legendary journey from Jerusalem to Provence is dated between 34 and 40 CE. According to tradition, she boarded a boat without sails or oars and journeyed across the Mediterranean with her sister Martha, her brother Lazarus, Mary Salome, Mary Jacob, Bishop Maximin, Sarah the Egyptian, and eighty-two disciples. They landed at Stes.-Maries-de-la-Mer where the other Marys and Sarah remained while Martha traveled to Tarascon, Lazarus to Marseilles, and Mary Magdalene to *le Sainte Baume* (the Holy Grotto) after evangelizing the region. She

---

2. The traditional historical sources such as Victor Saxer's two-volume study of Mary Magdalene in French history, *The Digby Magdalene,* and Jacobus de Voragine's *The Golden Legend* were supplemented by my on-site research in the Camargue and Provence in October 2005.

stayed there for thirty or thirty-three years, depending upon the legendary source, and led an ascetic life—in prayer and daily elevations to Mount St. Pilon where the angels serenaded her with celestial music and brought her the Eucharist. Although there arose a dispute whether her "authentic" relics were in Vézelay or St. Maximin-la-Sainte-Baume, her cathedrals and her grotto became pilgrimage sites for French kings and their courts.

Mary Magdalene began to assimilate—and not only in France—the characteristics of the classical virgin goddesses, like Diana of Ephesus, who were protectors of women, especially of fertility, pregnancy, and childbirth, and also of young children. Perhaps the more significant French legend that strengthened Marie-Madeleine's supplanting of Diana of Ephesus is that of the miraculous conception and birth of a son to a previously barren French queen. This miracle was soon followed by the restoration of the queen's life after she died either in childbirth or by drowning, depending upon which version of this pious legend you read or hear, such as the *Digby Magdalene* or *The Golden Legend*. Medieval altarpieces and liturgical plays coalesced with popular legends to confirm that Mary Magdalene was no longer merely an actor in the drama of salvation—she had become the female hero.

Dramatic evidence of her new status in the late Middle Ages could be found, literally, on the steps of cathedrals. Those images of Mary Magdalene seen within the mysteries of salvation which had been located previously on the front portals were removed, and moved inside the same cathedrals to decorate the windows, walls, and altar tableaux. With this change, those who prayed within the confines of the ecclesial structure found a new proximity to Mary Magdalene.

The Renaissance

The Renaissance, with its cultural affirmations of the human, saw the artistic representations of Mary Magdalene come into their own. Her popularity was now in full prominence. No longer constrained by narrative ties, Mary Magdalene's iconography expanded to include the visual motifs of sinner, witness, penitent, mourner, anointer, and patron saint. For example, from the late Middle Ages into the early

Renaissance, Mary Magdalene was represented under the cross and within the context of those scriptural sequences related to the "fallen woman" who anointed the head and the feet of Jesus of Nazareth. There can be little doubt that artists understood both of these women—Mary of Magdala and the anonymous anointer—to be one and the same woman. Thereby, this artistic direction reflected and nurtured legendary associations of Mary Magdalene for the Christian faithful. From artistic and spiritual perspectives, such an identification had practical, if not profound, motives—visual expression of the power and meaning of the expiatory death of Jesus of Nazareth for fallen humanity. Thereby, the crouching posture of this distraught and "fallen" woman at the foot of the cross provided a visual association to Christians of the promise of redemption (Plate 8).

Such representations visualize two scriptural images that had come to signify Mary Magdalene: first as the woman kneeling at the feet of Jesus of Nazareth, the very same feet that she had earlier anointed and wiped dry with her long, flowing hair, is simultaneously a visual pun on her "fallen" nature; and secondly, as she who stands like a sentry or watchtower, a legendary linguistic pun for the *migdol,* by the body of Jesus of Nazareth as he hung from the cross. This image of her kneeling at Jesus' feet became a major artistic convention for Mary Magdalene, an association begun as early as the fifth century in Western art.

During the late Middle Ages, the theme of the *Noli me tangere*—representations of the Risen Christ's appearance to Mary Magdalene after the Resurrection in John 20:17—began to appear in art and then flowered in the Renaissance.[3] This artistic motif would advance the growing importance of Mary Magdalene (Plates 4 and 6). Further, the Christian spirituality influenced by Francis of Assisi firmly established both medieval and theological symbolism of Mary Magdalene as *the* female symbol of penitence, humility, and love. Her popularity waxed with the desires of individual Christians to understand and experience forgiveness. Mary Magdalene was the great sinner who repented and was forgiven by Jesus of Nazareth, who then became his devoted disciple, and ultimately was the first person to

---

3. For an introduction to the history and symbolism of this iconographic motif, see my essay "Mary Magdalene: First Witness" in *Sacred History Magazine* 2.3 (May/June 2006): 30–33.

whom he appeared after the Resurrection.[4] Just as the liturgical dramas emphasized this image of Mary Magdalene, artists like Duccio, Giotto, and Fra Angelico (Plate 6) gave artistic expression to the *Noli me tangere* in their frescoes and altarpieces.

Given the Renaissance interest in the human, her connection with "the reformed prostitute" permitted presentation of the female body, oftentimes partially or totally nude. Artistic renderings of beautiful Magdalenes abounded within the contexts of Christian pedagogy, or the teachings on penance, and oftentimes as the "motif" for female portraiture.

Post-Renaissance

The historical epoch traditionally identified as the Reformation and Counter-Reformation was a time of intense emotional spirituality, especially in the south where allegiance to Roman Catholicism renewed the appeal and popularity of Mary Magdalene. The arts of this historical period are identified by the stylistic description of "baroque," from the Portuguese *barroco* for "irregularly shaped pearl," and given the religious divisions within Europe, were further categorized regionally, i.e., Northern Baroque and Southern Baroque. By its nature, Northern Baroque art turned away from traditional Christian art which it identified as "Roman Catholic"; nonetheless, pedagogical images of such biblical plates as Mary Magdalene fell into the obvious category of moral vs. immoral women (Plate 9). However, Southern Baroque painters exalted Mary Magdalene, who, along with Peter, became a symbolic defender of the Sacrament of Penance. This sacrament was denounced as heartily by the Reformers as it was defended by Roman Catholic theologians.

Southern Baroque artists popularized the motifs of the penitent Magdalene in the desert, the Last Communion of Mary Magdalene, and the contemplative Magdalene. They highlighted the sensual and

---

4. See my essay "'Pray with tears and your request will find a hearing': On the iconology of the Magdalene's Tears" in *Holy Tears: Weeping in the Religious Imagination,* ed. Kimberley C. Patton and John Stratton Hawley (Princeton: Princeton University Press, 2005): 201–28.

voluptuous nature of the Magdalene through the use of color, natural lighting, flowing drapery, and provocative poses. However, for the Catholic mind, these images retained their religious impact and spiritual motivation, which had in effect brought them into being in the first place. Many Southern Baroque artists represent Mary Magdalene as a beautiful young woman with long flowing hair who wears a revealing, perhaps diaphanous, garment and who tearfully contemplates her fate (Plate 10). Her nakedness symbolized not wantonness but the innocence and purity of the human spirit once it had experienced repentance and forgiveness. Mary Magdalene's popularity was due in part to her position as a defender of the faith, a symbolic crusader for the Roman Catholic tradition, which promised salvation through the sacramental mysteries of the church.

Eighteenth-century Europe saw the rise of science and the decline of religion in what would become known as the age of Enlightenment. The so-called secularization of Western culture touched all aspects of life, including the arts. Representations of Mary Magdalene evidence this growing division as she begins to live as a major personality in Christian spirituality on the one hand, and as a secular symbol for a reformed prostitute in art, literature, and common parlance on the other. In the seventeenth and eighteenth centuries, her artistic descendants often replace her former image in literature and the arts, now depicting her as "the whore (with a heart of gold)"—honest or wicked, good or evil, pathetic or comic.

Several nineteenth-century art movements initiated a revival of visual interest in Mary Magdalene. An initial revival of her iconography began in France with the restoration of the Bourbon monarchy and the reestablishment of her cult at Sainte Baume in 1822. Simultaneously, the Romantic Movement found the fictionalized image of Mary Magdalene as the great heroine of the Christian story to be of particular attraction. Crypto-religious art movements like the Pre-Raphaelite Brotherhood and the Nazarenes have a special affinity for dramatic representations of the composite image of Mary Magdalene (Plate 11). While painters such as Paul Baudry, William Etty, and Jean-Jacques Henner reconfigured the iconography of the "Penitent Magdalene" into an alibi for the female nude, the Symbolists' images of her highlight an important artistic metamorphosis in her image: she is now depicted as the femme fatale. She is transformed in a fashion similar to other great female figures like Judith, Salome, and Cleopatra. The emphasis on the abundantly flowing hair, androgynous body, and blatant sexuality characterize the basic iconography of the femme fatale image that develops in the nineteenth century (Plate 12).

By the end of the nineteenth century, her image became a lightning rod for sensuality and eroticism as the word *Magdalene* evolved into a synonym for prostitute in Victorian England, and her story became highly sexualized as witnessed by the popular French play *L'Amante du Christ* (1888). Artistic depictions such as those by Jean Béraud, Alfred Stevens, and James Ensor presented the pseudo-innocence of "salon paintings" while later nineteenth- and early twentieth-century painters like Félicien Rops, Auguste Rodin, Lovis Corinth, and Eric Gill created images of "ambiguous nude" Magdalenes in postures of such blatant physicality that they verged upon blasphemous eroticism.

Twentieth-century artists continued to render depictions of Mary Magdalene in abstraction, fragmentation, and nostalgic figurative modes as she became the model for "everywoman" in the age of angst and anxiety. Like their Early Christian counterparts, modern artists like Paul Cézanne, Otto Beckmann, Rico Lebrun, and Pablo Picasso were not interested in discerning this woman's true identity from scriptural sources; rather they sought to depict the cultural values and emotive meaning resident within her role as reformed-prostitute-turned-saint (Plate 13). More recent feminist artists like Kiki Smith and Marlene Dumas have, however, returned to the Magdalene's long-flowing hair as a visual connector between her historical personae and meaning for contemporary women. Dumas' series represent a fusion of the sacred (traditional Christian art) with the secular (commercial beauty in the late twentieth century), while Smith's work is a visual argument for the female instinct for survival even in the face of degradation and imprisonment.

Final Thoughts

Mary Magdalene's popularity throughout the last twenty centuries is grounded in the successful transformations of her image formed by and reflecting changes in Christian and secular spirituality. These reinterpretations were based on her archetypal meaning and artistic attempts to represent that meaning in a language that speaks with immediacy to each new generation. No one image of Mary Magdalene reveals or expresses the fullness of who she was for Christian believers, while the many Magdalene motifs are independent of but interdependent upon each other.

Her appeal has endured on a personal and devotional level throughout the Christian era, sometimes with great intensity. As enigmatic as her image may be or as interested as scholars are, it is her continuing popularity among the Christian collective that confirms her religious significance. She became a classic image of the redemptive and transformative nature of Christian love. The average Christian finds him or herself closer to accepting the reality of the otherwise abstract concepts of sin and forgiveness as concrete human experiences when images through Mary Magdalene come to represent the fullness of human experience in her journey from sinner to saint.

Further, in her journey through the centuries, Mary Magdalene took on a mosaic of meanings: she was variously prostitute, goddess, preacher, mystic, contemplative, miracle-worker, and muse inspiring artists and writers as well as the Christian faithful. Several of these images, especially that of prostitute and muse, might initially appear as inappropriate references for the saintly Mary Magdalene. Her fusion with the unnamed adulteress of John 7:53–8:11 and the anonymous anointer of Luke 7:36–50 led to her eventual evolution into *the* repentant prostitute. She symbolizes human frailty as her sinfulness is acknowledged and she is redeemed by the freely given love of Jesus of Nazareth. In this way, what otherwise might appear to be profane becomes a metaphor for spiritual transformation. Similarly, the Magdalene as muse inspiring artists and writers might appear as a rather curious expression of spirituality—especially in the context of some of the more sensual representations. Yet such inspiration even when it produces a secular artwork—or such controversial novels as *The Last Temptation of Christ* or *The DaVinci Code*—ultimately results in the continued visibility and recognition of religion.

In her own unique fashion, Mary Magdalene incorporates several of the paradoxical images and characteristics of "woman" within the framework of the Christian traditions. For example, she has been characterized as promiscuous, virginal, destructive, creative, maidenly, and maternal. Further studies of her "femaleness" would illuminate our understanding of the role of woman in the Christian traditions and in Western culture as each major reinterpretation of Mary Magdalene explicates that particular cultural understanding of woman and her societal role.

Mary Magdalene has withstood the tests of time and history to emerge as a central figure in the twenty-first century as artistic reinterpretations affirm that she symbolized identifiable and fallible humanity which continues to undeservingly receive God's grace. It is Mary Magdalene who makes the possibility of *that* grace intelligible and the reality of *that* grace approachable for the average believer.

Interpreting the Exile Carpet
An Artwork Speaks Through Eighteen Centuries of Time

by Jeremy Pine

One of the obvious challenges in trying to understand Mary Magdalene as a historical character is that there is so little genuine information about her and her life that comes from her historical time period or anything close to it. A very significant amount of legend and lore about Mary Magdalene appears to be a creative writing project from medieval times. And while the Middle Ages were a long time ago, they were only a thousand years ago, not two thousand. While there are many stories, particularly in French folklore, about Mary Magdalene escaping in a small, rudderless boat without sail from the Holy Land to the south of France after the Crucifixion, most of these stories can be shown to have only one millennium of provenance rather than two.

Shortly after our *Secrets of the Code* book was published in 2004, we received an email from an intriguing fellow who claimed he had come across a carpet fragment that depicted Mary Magdalene escaping to France in a boat. He told us that this carpet fragment had been tested and was authenticated as being about eighteen hundred years old. If this fragment really was eighteen hundred years old, and if it really depicted Mary Magdalene escaping in a boat, it would be the oldest known account of that story by a margin of over a millennium.

The story seemed more than a bit improbable. It sounded like it had been made up by someone who had spent too much time reading *The Da Vinci Code*. But we were intrigued. We did some checking. We discovered that this interesting man with these fascinating carpet fragments was known to some very sophisticated museum directors as the "world's leading expert on Himalayan textiles." We discovered that key people at the Metropolitan Museum of Art in New York thought very highly of him. And then we met him in person and heard even more fascinating stories about relics and artifacts he had found. The information about the carpet fragment that he shared with us, if true, if authenticatable, if his interpretation was correct, was as significant in some ways as the finding of the Gnostic Gospels or other documents from antiquity that have altered the course of modern scholarship. For what he was telling us was not only that the carpet fragment provided an ancient account of Mary Magdalene's escape to France, but that it also provided the earliest known depiction of Jesus in an artwork.

In preparing the books in the *Secrets* series, we generally don't do primary research. We don't do lab tests, we don't sponsor field work or research projects. We do seek to find the people with the most interesting, innovative, and important perspectives, and encourage them to share their ideas with our readers. With that in mind, we introduce you to Jeremy Pine and the amazing experience of what he calls the "Exile Carpet."

Pine is an American antiquarian who has been based in Kathmandu, Nepal, for thirty-five years. Specializing in antique textiles, he has had the opportunity to examine and research thousands of old pieces, including woolens, silks, and carpets. From 1993 to 1995, Pine was expedition director for the Institute of Science in Moscow and the State Institute of the History of Material Culture in St. Petersburg. In that capacity he led three expeditions to Tuva to excavate ancient tombs for the benefit of the Hermitage Museum. The last two years were spent in the little known and remote Valley of the Silver Mountain, or Mongün Taiga, just north of the Mongolian border. Married, with two children, Pine has recently retired from business to become the full-time curator of the Exile Carpet and its related treasures.

See what is in front of you, and what is hidden will be revealed.

—GOSPEL OF THOMAS

The Exile Carpet is an oval-shaped, pile-woven carpet. Now in two fragments, it would have originally measured approximately forty-eight inches from top to bottom.[1] Two rainbow-striped X's form the

---

1. It is not possible to tell, from what remains of the carpet, whether the Jesus figure in the center compartment was also in a boat or in some other position. In weaving the reproduction (see Plate 15), we have put him in a boat for the sake of symmetry. The implications of the various possible positions are a ripe topic for another discussion.

seven compartments of the piece. In the top right compartment is a haloed, redheaded figure in a blue boat (all known boats or depictions of boats in this period have this shape), with a mark on the forehead. In the top left compartment is a similar figure, but of about half the size, also with the mark on the forehead. The bottom left compartment contains a dark-haired figure that is not divine (no halo), but who carries some "extra baggage" in the boat. There is a similar figure in the bottom right compartment, except a pair of ducks is swimming next to the boat. The bottom left and bottom right figures also have the mark.

Four lion masks adorn the four points of the diamond-shaped central compartment in which we can see the hair and double halo of the main figure.[2] Above and below are blossoms. A rainbow outer border would have encircled the entire carpet.

To interpret the design of this carpet, it is first necessary to determine its time period. That has been accomplished by carbon-14 dating. Having been twice tested, we can be positive that it is authentic. The tests also give us a reasonable certainty that it was produced in the second half of the second century, or perhaps the beginning of the third.

The red-haired figures effectively rule out an Eastern origin, and the style of art is so Greco-Egyptian that the Mediterranean area comes easily to mind as a place of manufacture. To understand the carpet then, we must examine what was happening in the Mediterranean world in the second century.

At that time, the cross was not yet adopted as a symbol for Christ. The X, however, was such a symbol, as X is the first letter of the word *Christ* in Greek. An X in a circle was called "the Monogram of Christ." The foundation of the design of the carpet is the two X's within an oval. This, plus the four lion masks at the points of the diamond they form suggest that the central figure in the Exile Carpet is Jesus Christ, the Lion of Judah (Revelation 5). Although only the hair and haloes remain, this is the earliest surviving image of Jesus Christ.

If the central figure is Jesus, then who are the divine redheads above? A large portion of the paintings of the Madonna and Child por-

---

2. The upper and lower lion masks are evident. However, the ears and eyes of the two masks on the left and right remain at the bottom of fragment A (see Plate 14).

tray one or both of them with red hair. But it is not likely that the smaller redheaded figure is Jesus as a child if he is shown in the center compartment with brown hair. The only other prominent redhead in the story of Jesus Christ is, of course, Mary Magdalene. There is also the story of her exile to Gaul, in a leaky, oarless, rudderless, and sailless boat. In many sculptures and paintings, which still exist in churches in Europe, Mary Magdalene is shown arriving on the shore in a blue boat. The carpet doesn't tell us if the boat leaked, but as for the rest, it fits the pattern of the legend.

At this time slaves were marked upon their foreheads, much as cattle are branded. There was a custom among early Christians to put a mark on their foreheads, or on their ear, to show themselves as slaves of Christ. This "mark of Christ" is evident on the forehead of the Mary Magdalene figure as well as the others. Meanwhile, the golden halo around her and the boat shows her to be divine.

There is another divine redheaded figure in the top left compartment. This figure appears to purposely be about half the size of the other. Could it be that this figure is meant to be a child?

There exist churches dedicated to Mary Magdalene's arrival in France, and several shrines in France lay claim to hosting everything from her relics to important incidents in her exiled years. The legend of her exile in France has many variations and in some of these she is accompanied by a child or children, whose father, presumably, is Jesus. This is the basis of the story of the "royal bloodline" of Jesus and Mary Magdalene. Nobody seems to deny the fact that she did go into exile there. The controversy has always been "who went with her?"

The group of Christians who used this carpet must have felt themselves to be very close to the holy family. The exile of Mary Magdalene as a main theme tells us that, by their own lights, they had some legitimate connection to the story.

In the middle of the second century, history offers us at least two possibilities. There were the Desposyni (belonging to the Lord), who were the descendants of Christ. This is now primarily interpreted to mean Jesus' cousins, half-brothers and -sisters, and their descendants. The carpet dates from over a hundred years after the Crucifixion, so there would be many branches of Desposyni around the Mediterranean by this time, each individual standing as the head of his or her own sect. If there were those who believed themselves to be descendants of Jesus and Mary Magdalene, they would have included themselves in this group.

The Exile Carpet was probably woven as an altar. Gnostic Christians were not known to have built or worshipped in churches. They would meet at different locations. Presumably the carpet, having been rolled out, would consecrate the place. If the worshippers were Desposyni, then the smaller figure at the top left might very well be Sarah (whose name means "princess" in Hebrew). In some versions of the Mary Magdalene legend she arrives in Gaul together with a daughter called Sarah. In that case the pair of ducks at the bottom of the piece would take on a greater significance, as in those times the ducks could be a symbol of the sacred union, the "wedding ring" in the piece.

At that time there was another interesting sect of Christians in the Mediterranean, the Carpocratians. Critics called Carpocrates the "father of Gnosticism." Notorious in the second century, Carpocrates and his followers drew the ire of the Orthodox Church. Irenaeus (c. 115–202), the Bishop of Lyons, and Clement of Alexandria (160–215) complained that Carpocrates, among other misdeeds, enslaved a presbyter of Alexandria to obtain from him a copy of the secret Gospel of Mark. Carpocrates is said to have preached the heresy that Jesus was born of Joseph, and was a man. He consecrated female priests. At the same time, the Carpocratians were said to have made images of Christ and others, "some of them painted, and others formed from different kinds of material." Indeed, the Carpocratians are the only Christians we know of for certain who did make images at that time, as doing so was still prohibited by the Second Commandment (Exodus 20:4). Carpocrates even claimed to have in his possession a portrait of Jesus Christ painted by Pontius Pilate himself. Furthermore, he claimed to have his particular teachings in an unbroken line from Mary Magdalene, Martha, and Salome.

There is then a strong possibility that Carpocrates had something to do with the design of the carpet, given the historical evidence. If that were the case, then the top left figure may very well be the daughter, Sarah. However, then there is the small chance that it can also be Salome or Martha [women said to have accompanied Mary

Magdalene to France in some accounts—ed.], she having by then been sainted by the Carpocratians. The fact that there are two X's in the piece might also suggest some of the dualism apparent in Gnostic philosophies of the time. Equality was a main tenet of Carpocrates, equality between man and woman, rich and poor, and so on. This could be another reason for the oval shape of the carpet, as then no one standing or sitting around it would be "at the head," very much the same intention as Arthur's Round Table.

Who are the dark-haired, nondivine people in the bottom boats, with the mark of Christ on their foreheads? Legends tell us that some relatives accompanied Mary Magdalene in the leaky boat. Perhaps these two are Lazarus and Joseph of Arimathea, carrying the Grail and other "baggage," according to legend. In any later works of art, these figures, too, would probably be sainted.

The blossoms at the top and bottom are probably roses. These could be symbols for subrosa, or "secret," for the top flower, and possibly superrosa, or "not secret," for the bottom one. A possible meaning is that their teachings were of two types: secret and public. Indeed, many contemporary scholars interpret the New Testament as the public teachings of Christianity, and many of the alternative or Gnostic Gospels as the secret teachings. The meanings of the rose are many. Finally, the rainbow stripes of the X's and the rainbow outer border surrounding the carpet can only be symbols for heaven, or the Kingdom of Heaven.

Whether the Exile Carpet is Desposyni, Carpocratian, or of another Gnostic sect, it tells the story of the exile of Mary Magdalene. As a work of art, it has not been edited, translated from one language to another, or rewoven to suit, as can happen with the written word. The appearance of this piece of documentary evidence raises questions on many levels—historical, philosophical, and theological. What we learn from interpreting the design of the carpet is that it is the earliest image of Jesus Christ. It is also the earliest image of Mary Magdalene. As one of the first whispers of Christianity, the Exile Carpet offers us proof of one thing. The "legend" of Mary Magdalene's flight and exile to Gaul is not a romantic medieval myth. The story was very much in existence at least a thousand years earlier, very close to the time that it would have happened.

Mary Magdalene's Secret History Encoded in a Seventeenth-Century Epic Poem

BY JOHN M. SAUL

If you think that the encoding and decoding of secret messages about Mary Magdalene as the Holy Grail is only the province of contemporary writers, the following
essay by John M. Saul shows why you should think again. In this essay, Saul initiates readers into an incredibly esoteric club—the handful of modern scholars
aware of the work of Pierre de Saint-Louis, an obscure French poet. Pierre de
Saint-Louis' seventeenth-century epic poem about Mary Magdalene contains
acrostics, double entendres, and convoluted allusions that Saul suggests may point
to a sense on the poet's part that Mary Magdalene was the bride of Jesus and the
mother of a royal bloodline.

John Saul holds a Ph.D. in geology from MIT More than thirty years ago, he
was among those doing the earliest research studies on the stories and legends
about Mary Magdalene in the French town of Rennes-le-Château. He recalls it as a
time when many people thought great "secrets" would be found in one or another
of the limestone caves in the region. "Mary Magdalene was little discussed in 1974
and everyone hoped, and some even expected, that the treasure of the Temple of
Jerusalem or the Templar treasure would be discovered in one of the caves." Saul
subsequently contributed to the research for the seminal book *Holy Blood, Holy
Grail,* first published in 1982, which kicked off much of modern international interest in French legends about Mary Magdalene being the bride of Jesus and mother
of his child, about the Merovingian kings, the Knights Templar, the Priory of Sion,
etc. Many of these themes attracted much subsequent attention after the publication of Dan Brown's novel *The Da Vinci Code* in 2003. Although Saul contributed
to the research for *Holy Blood, Holy Grail,* he did not agree with its authors about
a number of things, including whether information dispensed by Pierre Plantard,
the alleged grand master of the twentieth-century version of the Priory of Sion,
should be relied upon.

In the essay that follows, Saul provides his personal overview of the arguments
in *Holy Blood, Holy Grail* and *The Da Vinci Code* as they relate to Mary Magdalene and Jesus, and then goes on to discuss the very odd *Poem of the Magdalene*
written by Pierre de Saint-Louis more than three centuries ago.

As children and perhaps as adults, many people have dreamed of discovering something that nobody else knew about, a great secret of

some sort. In the seventeenth century a Discalced Carmelite friar did just that. He discovered, or thought he discovered, a truly great secret. There are indications, however, that things did not go well for him thereafter.

When *Holy Blood, Holy Grail* was published in 1982, it touched on this same centuries-old secret, a supposed marriage between Jesus and Mary Magdalene. According to its authors, a child or children may have been born of this marriage, with the subsequent bloodline protected by a secret group of "Grail keepers." Then, twenty years later, the hero of Dan Brown's novel *The Da Vinci Code* found himself on the track of present-day descendants of just such a marriage.

But why should these modern authors have fixed on Mary Magdalene, the supposedly fallen woman who had changed her ways in the presence of Jesus? Why evoke this saint whose icon is a covered pot or other vessel—commonly said to be a "Grail cup"—held by her midriff? What were the sources of information or inspiration for these modern writers?

Odd as it seems, it was only in the year 591, half a millennium after the death of Mary Magdalene, that she was definitively identified as a reformed prostitute. It was only with Pope Gregory the Great's *Homily* 33 that her reputation was transformed. Mary Magdalene and her reputation thus suffered a fate perhaps unique in history. Who, today, even a pope, could convincingly soil the reputation of a woman who had lived five hundred years ago, declaring her a prostitute, reformed or not? Who would have had reason to? True or false, to whom would it have made a difference at such a late date?

In recent years, the possible significance of this curious piece of history has come to light: its purpose may have been to delegitimize the Magdalene's children. For Mary Magdalene was Jewish (as was Jesus) and, according to Jewish law, the children of prostitutes are considered to be fatherless. Such children and their descendants could never pretend to be "King of the Jews," nor legitimate king of anyone else.

This legal circumstance might have solved a great potential problem for kings and popes in the very Christian Europe of the Middle Ages. For if someone, somewhere, *whether known or not,* was a legitimate descendant of Jesus—of the true blood of Christ—what would stop them from claiming the right to power? And could the church of Saint Peter then retain legitimacy?

According to *The Da Vinci Code,* in which the central female personage is addressed as "Princess," there is a secret group called the Priory of Sion that watches over and keeps the bloodline of Mary Magdalene, the *royal and legitimate* bloodline of Mary Magdalene. Dan Brown presented this group as "a real organization." Twenty years earlier, the authors of *Holy Blood, Holy Grail* had also investigated the Priory of Sion and had reached the same conclusions.

The starting point in investigating the Priory of Sion was a near-incoherent text registered by the French National Library (the *Bibliothèque Nationale*) in 1967 under the title *Dossiers Secrets d'Henri Lobineau* (shelfmark 4°Lm^1.249). Its contents include several long genealogies with a multitude of names, both familiar and obscure; short references to long-ago migrations of little-known peoples; coats of arms, some of which had quite obviously been concocted for the occasion; and the names of the grand masters of secret societies. Cited by the authors of *Holy Blood, Holy Grail,* the *Dossiers Secrets* does not actually refer to Jesus or Mary Magdalene. Nevertheless, it strongly indicates that the first kings of France, the Merovingians, described as "our first race of kings," were of biblical descent. According to the *Dossiers* themselves, this is the secret that the Priory of Sion has guarded over the last centuries.

The Da Vinci Code, which is a novel, cannot be treated as a reliable source for a historical study. Neither can the *Dossiers Secrets,* which sets an agenda for a hoped-for day when France will restore its sacred monarchy. Yet the *Dossiers* do contain much valid information, some of which would be extremely difficult to dig out, even by a talented researcher with access to a great library. This presents an enormous problem for anyone interested in the Priory of Sion and other related subjects. For Pierre Plantard (1920–2000), who, according to a multitude of indications, *must* be the person behind the modern Priory of Sion, and the *Dossiers Secrets* as well, was not a talented researcher. He was simply a pretender to a nonexistent throne, a nonintellectual school dropout who was systematically careless with facts and whose overall incompetence had on occasion landed him in jail for short terms. In short, he was a bumbler. But Plantard, who from 1989 called himself Pierre Plantard de Saint-Clair, had somehow obtained historical information denied to the rest of us.

Holy Blood, Holy Grail differs from both *The DaVinci Code* and *Dossiers Secrets.* It is not a novel, nor was it intended to further a private or secret agenda. Its purpose is to suggest the historical possibilities that arise on reading Plantard's fabrications in conjunction with the realization that the term "Holy Grail" comes from "Sangreal," a word of unknown origin which, if broken after the *g,* gives *sang réal,* meaning "holy blood." But who belonged to the Holy Bloodline in question? Pierre Plantard? The Saint-Clairs? Lost kings of Merovingian origin? Descendants of the biblical tribe of Benjamin, as suggested in the *Dossiers?* A supposed line descended from a marriage at Cana of Mary Magdalene and Jesus? In the end, the authors of *Holy Blood, Holy Grail* attempt to combine all these bloodlines, rejecting only that of the bumbling Monsieur Plantard. Their efforts result in a view of Western history in which almost any event of substantial interest can be tentatively linked to struggles involving supposed descendants of Jesus and Mary Magdalene.

Dan Brown, the authors of *Holy Blood, Holy Grail,* and even Pierre Plantard (despite his claims) were not tracing an actual genealogy. Instead, each was investigating an ancient royal tradition which, they all agree, has long had and still retains the ability to influence the making of history.

Ideas from this stream of tradition were in circulation well before our own times, and were expressed in the seventeenth century by the obscure poet Pierre de Saint-Louis in his *La Magdeleine au Desert de la Sainte-Baume en Provence* (Lyon, 1668, 1694, 1700; The Hague, 1714; and an undated edition with no place of publication). Near the beginning of this carefully composed poetic extravagance of over two hundred pages, we are given a "history lesson" and "a grammar lesson" in which the author's muse, who had been identified as Mary Magdalene, "CONJUGATES" with "the VERB"; that is, with Jesus. Théophile Gauthier (1811–1872), prolific French critic, author, and editor, described the poem as "in its own way as complete as the *Iliad* or the *Odyssey.* . . . It seems impossible for anyone to voluntarily compose such strange verses . . . and [the author's] literary wretchedness is not a commonplace wretchedness but studied, exquisite and conscientious. This poem with its *abracadabrant* verses is the most eccentric that has ever appeared in any of the world's languages." Simone de Reyff, a contemporary specialist on seventeenth-century French literature, adds that its author had a reputation as a perfectionist. *"Abracadabrant"* or not, Pierre de Saint-Louis evidently wrote exactly what he intended.

Pierre de Saint-Louis seems to have been born April 5, 1626, in Valréas, one of at least two sons of Jacques Barthélemy and Anne Canal. He abandoned his secular name of Jean-Louis ("Ludovic") Barthélemy on becoming a Discalced Carmelite in 1651. According to a catalogue entry in the library of Viollet le Duc, Pierre de Saint-Louis had lived at Aygalades near Marseilles until named regent of the College de Saint-Marcelin in Dauphiné. The catalogue also reports a story in which the author joined the Carmelites and wrote his poem following the death of a fiancée named Madeleine.

Writings by Pierre de Saint-Louis circulated in manuscript form during long periods, perhaps decades, and at least one of his surviving manuscripts has apparently never been carefully examined. (Voltaire mentions Pierre de Saint-Louis in his *Lettre à Thiriot,* 7 February 1738.)

For whatever reason, the year of death of Pierre de Saint-Louis is variously reported: "around 1670," 1672, 1673, "1677?" or, as may be more likely, 1683 or 1684. He is indicated to have died "in disgrace" in "Pinet in Switzerland," though a better bet concerning the place in question may be the Carmelite establishment at Eyzin-Pinet, south of Lyon. One gets a strong impression that something about his death was covered up and that some of the biographical details I have given might not stand up to scrutiny, the matter of Madeleine the fiancée, for example. Did she actually exist?

Much of what we know, or think we know, about Pierre de Saint-Louis comes from an article by "Follard" in the July 1750 issue of the *Mercure de France.* Yet as a frustrated historian, Jean de Servières, wrote in the review *Provincia* (Marseille, 1925): "We are not about to learn why the editors of the *Mercure de France* waited so long— twenty-three years!—before publishing Follard's biographical letter [on Pierre de Saint-Louis], nor the motives for finally publishing it."

And who, exactly, was "Follard"? Nicolas-Joseph Folard (1664–c.1736), an ecclesiastic in Nimes whose name comes down to us spelled with a single *l,* seems to be the only candidate author, but neither the style nor the choice of subject matter appear to be his.

Discussing *La Magdeleine au Desert de la Sainte-Baume en Provence* in his massive two-volume compendium, *Monuments inédits sur Sainte-Marie Madeleine en Provence . . .* (Paris, 1848), E. M. Faillon tells that "this work, for which the author paid with five years of vigils, stayed on the bookseller's shelf for a decade, totally ignored. Following the author's death, the stock was retrieved from the dust by a Jesuit named 'P. Berthet' (or 'Nicole') and immediately sold out. The book then had to be reprinted . . ."

Writing of the decision to reissue an edition in 1714, Servières reported that "an infinite number of people had written to Lyon from all over requesting copies, but in vain. It had been a long time since there had been any."

From its outset, the poem is odd, commencing with a dedication to "Madame de la Blache, Gabrielle de Levi," whose name seems to be Jewish but who is said by Pierre de Saint-Louis to come from a family descended from the Holy Virgin.

The author warns readers that they will encounter various types of wordplay and, in forming anagrams, he uses both "Magdelaine" and "Madeleine." Among his easier anagrams is one that gives *Je mets ici la grande Amante* ("Here I place *la grande Amante*"), with the word *Amante* usually translated as "Lover." Then, Freudian before his time, he presents the cave at Sainte Baume near Toulon, in which Mary Magdalene is said in legendary accounts to have lived, as a "terrifying cavern" (Book XI).

In addition to history and grammar lessons, readers of *La Magdeleine au Desert de la Sainte-Baume en Provence* learn of an echo which, when asked how posterity would remember the weeping "Mary," replies *"marrie,"* a word meaning "sorrowful" but which simultaneously evokes "married." Then in Book IV, a line compares the mourning Mary to *"une mer,"* and similarly in death she is called *"La Mer morte"* (Book X), the words themselves meaning "sea" and "the Dead Sea," but pronounced identically to "mother" and "deceased mother."

Individually, many of these curious matters might be explained away, albeit with increasing difficulty as more and more of them become apparent and explanations pile upon earlier explanations. Yet one passage in Book X was contrived with such very great care that it seems impossible to find any explanation that does not call upon traditions of a royal bloodline descended from Mary Magdalene. After providing diverse references to kings of France, the author evokes the standard iconographic depiction of the Magdalene holding a "Grail cup," the mysterious object traditionally said to preserve the blood of Jesus. The poet then instructs:

> Touchez cette Urne icy, la morte [Mary Magdalene] vous l'aprête,
> Que ce beau pot en main, soit vôtre pot-en-tête.

In English this would read:

> Touch this Urn the Departed Woman has prepared for you,
> May this lovely pot in the hand become your pot-in-the-head (*sic*).

Then, likening Mary Magdalene to a phoenix that rises from its ashes (Book X) and calling her "*excellente Princesse*" (Book XI), and passing through references to the seventeenth-century kings of France, designated "potentates" (Book X), Mary—as the "faithful Lover . . . of an obscure house [*maison obscure*]" (Book XI)—is described as a recipient who has [dynastically?] served and reserved (Book XI). At about this point, it may occur to the reader—who will have probably derived no immediate sense from "*pot-en-tête*," whether in French or as translated—that the resemblance between "*pot-en-tête*" and "*potentat*" (potentate) is not unintentional.

La Magdeleine au desert de la Sainte Baume en Provence, Poëme spirituel &. Chrêtien—whose exact title varies slightly from one edition to another—is a book that demands more than one reading. A first reading of "Spiritual caprice" in the unnumbered introductory pages, for example, had seemed neither capricious, nor spiritual, nor inspiring, nor interesting. (One commentator called these pages "rather insipid.") Yet here and there in this sixteen-line "caprice" we find four words that have been italicized, though not for any evident reason:

". . . *Marriage* . . . *Not* . . . *Clandestine* . . . *Fruit* . . ." So in common with twentieth-century authors, but with the "deniability" required by his circumstances, Pierre de Saint-Louis referred to the "fruit" of a once-known legitimate marriage.

At the end of his work, Pierre de Saint-Louis takes leave of Mary Magdalene, his "Vessel" about whom so much could still be said in a story that has "neither end nor beginning," and informs his readers that he has at least "exposed" its "Extract" (*l'Extrait*). "Extract" here might be read as "summary," but the author was far too talented to have awkwardly and pointlessly written of "exposing the summary of a Vessel." Instead, it seems that he has cautiously evoked the progeny of Mary Magdalene, the *"excellente Princesse"* who had spent the previous two hundred pages in the company of Jesus.

Pierre de Saint-Louis wrote another book-length manuscript whose publication was not authorized by the church authorities. The reason given was that with two books from this same author, "the world would be too rich".

A Painting of Mary Magdalene, Now Attributed to Leonardo da Vinci

BY DAN BURSTEIN

Of the many new insights about Mary Magdalene this book has un-covered, one of the more interesting concerns a Renaissance-era painting of Mary Magdalene, which was recently shown in public in Italy for the first time in more than fifty years. Previously, art historians had always attributed this painting to a minor Renaissance master, Gianpietrino, who was known to have been a student of Leonardo da Vinci. It had always been supposed that Leonardo might have supervised the painting.

But then Carlo Pedretti, perhaps the greatest living Leonardo scholar, announced, after considerable deliberation, "I am inclined to believe it is much more than a supervision of the student by the master." Eventually, this stunning, voluptuous portrait of Mary Magdalene would be displayed in an exhibition in Ancona, Italy, in October 2005, with the new presumption that it was, indeed, a Leonardo.

If this Mary Magdalene is a Leonardo, it would be the only time that Leonardo painted Mary Magdalene—unless one accepts the *Da Vinci Code* thesis that Mary Magdalene is depicted at the right hand of Jesus in Leonardo's *Last Supper*. Most professional art historians and Leonardo scholars reject the idea of a didactic, coded message by Leonardo in the *Last Supper* about Mary Magdalene as the bride of Christ and as the metaphoric Holy Grail. When asked about the feminine-looking character next to Jesus, traditional scholars are usually quick to point out that Italian Renaissance painters frequently depicted John, the Beloved, as the only one of the apostles without a beard and as looking very feminine and even sometimes asleep, leaning on Jesus. This was supposedly done in order to accentuate his youthfulness.

Carlo Pedretti is one of the very few art historians who gives any credence at all to how feminine the *Last Supper* character looks. During the initial worldwide curiosity about *The Da Vinci Code* in 2003–4, Pedretti gave interviews where he left the door farther ajar than other serious art historians as to the possibility that the figure in the *Last Supper* could be a woman. He never said or suggested it was Mary Magdalene. But in reflecting a certain amount of ambiguity about the gender of the person seated at the right hand of Jesus, he spoke volumes.

If the portrait of Mary is indeed a Leonardo, then, not surprisingly, this great creative genius has painted a Mary Magdalene like no other. His Mary Magdalene is earthy and sensual, but without shame, without repentance, without guilt. She is as beautifully painted and as mysterious as the *Mona Lisa,* but unlike the *Mona Lisa,* she communicates directly, openly, without mystery.

If I wanted to write a novel of the imagination about this painting, I would start with the presumption that, since Leonardo knew and understood so much about the future (after all, he designed flying machines, submarines, and motor cars and had early insights into complexity and chaos theory), he also knew something about the ancient past. And what this quintessential Renaissance humanist guessed about the past was that human beings were mortal, not divine, and that Jesus and Mary Magdalene were ordinary human beings, perhaps man and wife. Further, he might have guessed that emphasizing an attractive woman's sensuality—without the strictures of biblical morality, sin, guilt, and penitence—might be the right way to paint the beautiful female half of an archetypal male and female holistic union. This Mary Magdalene is stunning for her humanity and humanism, which is not at all surprising considering that Leonardo is probably the greatest humanist of the last millennium.

Is there a "mystery" about Leonardo? Did he know a great "secret"? Was he part of a grand "conspiracy"? Yes, to all those questions—but the positive answer has nothing to do with the so-called Priory of Sion or any such nonsense. Instead, Leonardo's great secret—his heresy— might have been as simple as understanding that to be human is to be holy, that to give, live, and celebrate life is humanity's highest calling, and that in that process, women have a very special and therefore very sacred role to play.

7 The Mary Magdalene of Legend & Lore

No other biblical figure—including Judas and perhaps even Jesus—has had such a vivid and bizarre post-biblical life in the human imagination, in legend, and in art.

—JANE SCHABERG, *The Resurrection of Mary Magdalene*

[After landing in Marseilles,] When blessed Mary Magdalene saw the people gathering at the shrine to offer sacrifice to the idols, she came forward, her manner calm and her face serene, and with well-chosen words called them away from the cult of idols and preached Christ fervidly to them. All who heard her were in admiration at her beauty, her eloquence, and the sweetness of her message . . . and no wonder, that the mouth which had pressed such pious and beautiful kisses on the Savior's feet should breathe forth the perfume of the word of God more profusely than others could.

—JACOBUS DE VORAGINE, "Readings on the Saints," 13th century

Mythologizing Mary Magdalene
The Golden Legend

JACOBUS DE VORAGINE

The Golden Legend is one of the central texts of the Middle Ages. It depicts the lives of the saints in a range of stories designed to have mass appeal—some seemingly factual, some obviously fictional, and some downright sensational. After the Bible, *The Golden Legend* is considered one of the most widely read and copied books of the time. By the end of the Middle Ages, it had been translated into most European languages. In his introduction to his translation, Richard Hamer, tutor in medieval English language and literature at Christ Church, Oxford, writes that "the huge success of the book, as evidenced by its widespread dissemination and use, and its 'defeat' in these terms of any possible rivals, is probable largely because it supplied just the right sort and amount of required information."

There are 182 stories in *The Golden Legend,* all written by the Dominican friar Jacobus de Voragine between 1259 and 1266. Arguably, none have had a greater impact on how the reputation of a saint has been carried forward into modern times than his colorful account of the life of Mary Magdalene. As could be expected, Pope Gregory's conflation of Mary Magdalene with Mary of Bethany—sister of Lazarus and Martha—and the unnamed sinner from the Gospel of Luke is in the story, but also portrayed is her voyage to France and her background as wealthy, wellborn, and even "owning" the town of Magdalum. There is prominent mention as well of her succumbing to "the pleasures of the flesh." Still, in the end, Jesus loves, accepts, and defends her.

The Golden Legend is not the basis for the Holy Grail story, nor the later-to-emerge theory of Jesus and Mary Magdalene as married. Instead, it shows her as a chaste, reformed sex offender whose turn to the sacred life made her one of the most holy and powerful of Christ's followers after his death.

Saint Mary Magdalene

Mary's cognomen "Magdalene" comes from Magdalum, the name of one of her ancestral properties. She was wellborn, descended of royal stock. Her father's name was Syrus, her mother was called Eucharia. With her brother Lazarus and her sister Martha she owned Magda-

Jacobus de Voragine, *The Golden Legend.* © 1993 Princeton University Press, 1995 paperback edition. Reprinted by permission of Princeton University Press.

lum, a walled town two miles from Genezareth, along with Bethany, not far from Jerusalem, and a considerable part of Jerusalem itself. They had, however, divided their holdings among themselves in such a way that Magdalum belonged to Mary (whence the name Magdalene), Lazarus kept the property in Jerusalem, and Bethany was Martha's. Magdalene gave herself totally to the pleasures of the flesh and Lazarus was devoted to the military, while prudent Martha kept close watch over her brother's and sister's estates and took care of the needs of her armed men, her servants, and the poor. After Christ's ascension, however, they all sold their possessions and laid the proceeds at the feet of the apostles.

Magdalene, then, was very rich, and sensuous pleasure keeps company with great wealth. Renowned as she was for her beauty and her riches, she was no less known for the way she gave her body to pleasure—so much so that her proper name was forgotten and she was commonly called "the sinner." Meanwhile, Christ was preaching here and there, and she, guided by the divine will, hastened to the house of Simon the leper, where, she had learned, he was at table. Being a sinner she did not dare mingle with the righteous, but stayed back and washed the Lord's feet with her tears, dried them with her hair, and anointed them with precious ointment. Because of the extreme heat of the sun the people of that region bathed and anointed themselves regularly.

Now Simon the Pharisee thought to himself that if this man were a prophet, he would never allow a sinful woman to touch him; but the Lord rebuked him for his proud righteousness and told the woman that all her sins were forgiven. This is the Magdalene upon whom Jesus conferred such great graces and to whom he showed so many marks of love. He cast seven devils out of her, set her totally afire with love of him, counted her among his closest familiars, was her guest, had her do the housekeeping on his travels, and kindly took her side at all times. He defended her when the Pharisee said she was unclean, when her sister implied that she was lazy, when Judas called her wasteful. Seeing her weep he could not contain his tears. For love of her he raised her brother, four days dead, to life, for love of her he freed her sister Martha from the issue of blood she had suffered for seven years, and in view of her merits he gave Martilla, her sister's handmaid, the privilege of calling out those memorable words: "Blessed is the womb that bore you."

———

In this next excerpt, Mary travels to Provence with her brother and sister and other Christians, including Maximin, who will go on to become the bishop of Aix. We see them landing in France and Mary's conversion of the land.

———

Some fourteen years after the Lord's passion and ascension into heaven, when the Jews had long since killed Stephen and expelled the other disciples from the confines of Judea, the disciples went off into the lands of the various nations and there sowed the word of the Lord. With the apostles at the time was one of Christ's seventy-two disciples, blessed Maximin, to whose care blessed Peter had entrusted Mary Magdalene. In the dispersion Maximin, Mary Magdalene, her brother Lazarus, her sister Martha, Martha's maid Martilla, blessed Cedonius, who was born blind and had been cured by the Lord, and many other Christians were herded by the unbelievers into a ship without pilot or rudder and sent out to sea so that they might all be drowned, but by God's will they eventually landed at Marseilles. There they found no one willing to give them shelter, so they took refuge under the portico of a shrine belonging to the people of that area. When blessed Mary Magdalene saw the people gathering at the shrine to offer sacrifice to the idols, she came forward, her manner calm and her face serene, and with well-chosen words called them away from the cult of idols and preached Christ fervidly to them. All who heard her were in admiration at her beauty, her eloquence, and the sweetness of her message . . . and no wonder, that the mouth which had pressed such pious and beautiful kisses on the Savior's feet should breathe forth the perfume of the word of God more profusely than others could.

———

After Mary Magdalene evangelizes France, she secludes herself in the wilderness to focus on heavenly contemplation. She lives there for thirty years without food or water, surviving on a holy repast provided by angels. In this excerpt, we see her last days on earth and her heavenly ascension.

———

There was a priest who wanted to live a solitary life and built himself a cell a few miles from the Magdalene's habitat. One day the Lord opened this priest's eyes, and with his own eyes he saw how the angels descended to the already-mentioned place where blessed Mary Magdalene dwelt, and how they lifted her into the upper air and an hour later brought her back to her place with divine praises. Wanting to learn the truth about this wondrous vision and commending himself prayerfully to his Creator, he hurried with daring and devotion toward the aforesaid place . . .

He called out: "I adjure you by the Lord, that if you are a human being or any rational creature living in that cave, you answer me and tell me the truth about yourself!" When he had repeated this three times, blessed Mary Magdalene answered him: "Come closer, and you can learn the truth about whatever your soul desires." Trembling, he had gone halfway across the intervening space when she said to him: "Do you remember what the Gospel says about Mary the notorious sinner, who washed the Savior's feet with her tears and dried them with her hair, and earned forgiveness for all her misdeeds?" "I do remember," the priest replied, "and more than thirty years have gone by since then. Holy Church also believes and confesses what you have said about her." "I am that woman," she said. "For the space of thirty years I have lived here unknown to everyone, and as you were allowed to see yesterday, every day I am borne aloft seven times by angelic hands, and have been found worthy to hear with the ears of my body the joyful jubilation of the heavenly hosts. Now, because it has been revealed to me by the Lord that I am soon to depart from this world, please go to blessed Maximin and take care to inform him that next year, on the day of the Lord's Resurrection, at the time when he regularly rises for matins, he is to go alone to his church, and there he will find me present and waited upon by angels." To the priest the voice sounded like the voice of an angel, but he saw no one.

The good man hurried to blessed Maximin and carried out his

errand. Saint Maximin, overjoyed, gave fulsome thanks to the Savior, and on the appointed day, at the appointed hour, went alone into the church and saw blessed Mary Magdalene amidst the choir of angels who had brought her there. She was raised up a distance of two cubits above the floor, standing among the angels and lifting her hands in prayer to God. When blessed Maximin hesitated about approaching her, she turned to him and said: "Come closer, father, and do not back away from your daughter." When he drew near to her, as we read in blessed Maximin's own books, the lady's countenance was so radiant, due to her continuous and daily vision of the angels, that one would more easily look straight into the sun than gaze upon her face.

All the clergy, including the priest already mentioned, were now called together, and blessed Mary Magdalene, shedding tears of joy, received the Lord's Body and Blood from the bishop. Then she lay down full length before the steps of the altar, and her most holy soul migrated to the Lord. After she expired, so powerful an odor of sweetness pervaded the church that for seven days all those who entered there noticed it.

Sacred Theft
The Restless Bones of Mary Magdalene

BY KATHERINE LUDWIG JANSEN

The Mary Magdalene cult that was to sweep France and the rest of Europe in the eleventh, twelfth, and thirteenth centuries first appeared in the ninth, when records begin to show the invocation of special prayers to celebrate her feast day, held annually on July 22. Physical signs of a Mary Magdalene cult can be seen in the tenth century, when a church in England claimed a relic of the saint, and an altar was dedicated in her honor in Germany. By the eleventh century, complete masses were dedicated to Mary Magdalene and signs of devotion to her could be seen everywhere.

Nowhere was this more evident than in southern France, where her cult came into full flower in the mid-eleventh century when Geoffrey, abbot of the great Romanesque church at Vézelay in Burgundy, claimed possession of Mary Magdalene relics. Until the monastery church at St. Maximin in Provence claimed that *it* had

the body of Mary Magdalene in a crypt in 1279, Vézelay was an important pilgrimage site—especially after 1050, when Pope Stephen issued a papal bull recognizing
the church's claims. The legend that Mary Magdalene personally brought Christianity to Gaul in the first century had such deep patriotic appeal that it remained stub-
bornly ledged in French popular belief until the nineteenth century, despite the best
efforts of historians to debunk it.

What made relics so important to worshippers in the Middle Ages? Why were
they in such great demand that one church stole from another, thereby breaking the
seventh commandment? What did this have to do with Mary Magdalene, and what
aspect of the Mary Magdalene legend did people want to "touch"? How does this
period fit into the ever-expanding mosaic of Magdalene imagery?

We asked these questions of Katherine Ludwig Jansen, who has devoted much of
her career to the study of the treatment of Mary Magdalene in the medieval period.
Jansen is an associate professor at the Catholic University of America and author of
*The Making of the Magdalen: Preaching and Popular Devotion in the Later Middle
Ages.* "Relics can be seen as transmitters between the supernatural and the natural
worlds," Jansen writes, "representing the concrete, tangible extension of sanctity in
this world." To this day, Mary Magdalene relics are said to exist, and are still venerated for providing a connection between the spiritual realm and the material world.

Since the early days of Christianity, the devout have venerated holy
relics as a way to gain the attention and favor of the saints, seeking intercession on behalf of infirmity, poverty, imminent peril, and the
challenges of daily life. Relics can be seen as the transmitters between
the supernatural and the natural worlds, representing the concrete,
tangible extension of sanctity in this world.

The earliest written record of relic veneration is described in the
Acts of Polycarp of Smyrna, who was martyred around the year 156. By
the fifth century, the bones of holy people other than martyrs also began to be venerated widely. By the eighth century a church council
had decreed that no church could be dedicated without a relic. Four
centuries after that, canon law decreed that every altar must contain a
relic.

Due to their holy lives, the saints were believed to be glorified in
heaven while their physical remains provided access to their patronage. To venerate a saint's relics meant calling on the protection or patronage—spiritual or temporal—of that saint. And that patronage
manifested itself most spectacularly in miracles such as the cure of
disease, the rescue from physical peril, and the settlement of disputes.

People believed these miracles to be the manifestation of God's power, working through the relics of the saints.

The logic of saintly patronage in the medieval period was based on the economy of gift exchange. The living earned the patronage of the holy dead by supplicating them with service or gifts; reciprocally, the saints had duties to their supplicants. I would point out that this network of patrons and clients was not at all dissimilar to the patron-client relationship of the Roman world, or the vassal-lord relationship of the feudal world. The use of relics, then, reflects a vision of the supernatural world as a social network of intercessors that linked living Christians to God. As part of the deep-seated social structure of the late antique and medieval worlds, legal oaths were more frequently sworn over relics than over the Bible.

Relics were so important to the medieval world that an active if somewhat irregular relic trade grew up to meet the needs of this economy of the sacred. This phenomenon is wonderfully explained in Patrick Geary's *Furta Sacra: Thefts of Relics in the Middle Ages,* in which he explains the logic of how this economy of relics stolen for pious purposes (*furta sacra*) operated. Interestingly, most of Western Christendom believed that Mary Magdalen's relics had once been the objects of a sacred theft. In the eleventh century, in order to account for the arrival of Saint Mary Magdalen's relics at the great Romanesque abbey church of Vézelay, a pious fiction that we will call "the Vézelay legend," began to circulate. This legend narrated that in the year 749, during the reign of Louis the Pious, Count Girart, founder of the monastery at Vézelay together with Abbot Heudo, dispatched a monk to Aix-en-Provence to rescue the imperiled remains of Jesus' beloved disciple from Saracen invaders. When the monk called Badilo arrived in Provence he found death and devastation everywhere—except, miraculously, at the mausoleum of Saint Mary Magdalen. Recognizing the sepulcher by the sculptural reliefs that depicted the events of her life as narrated in the gospels, Badilo opened the tomb to find the body of the saint lying intact and uncorrupted, her hands folded across her chest. As if that were not enough to convince him, a further sign authenticated his quarry: an otherworldly sweet perfume—a smell that could only have issued from one who had died in the odor of sanctity—emanated from the tomb as it was opened.

Anxious about the task before him, the next night Badilo received yet another portent: a vision of a woman attired in incandescent white who reassured him that his mission had been sanctioned by God. Fortified by this mystical encounter, Badilo spirited the bones of Mary Magdalen off to Burgundy the very next day where upon their arrival they were met with great joy, prayers, and ceremony befitting the advent of a saint. On March 19 the precious relics were installed in the abbey church at Vézelay and from that day forth great signs and wonders occurred at the sanctuary proving to all that the Lord favored the saint and her new cult site in Burgundy. Ultimately, then, it was believed to have been a *furtum sacrum*—a holy theft—that brought Mary Magdalen, the penitent saint, to rest at the abbey church of Vézelay.

Modern scholars have noted that the Vézelay legend is riddled with historical anachronisms, not least of which is the confusion and dating of Carolingian rulers, to say nothing of the foundation date of Vézelay itself. But historical accuracy was hardly the point. The legend was written to commemorate no less than to justify Vézelay's claim of possessing Mary Magdalen's earthly remains, claims that it had been propounding since at least the year 1037, a date that marks the installation of Geoffrey, a great devotee of the Magdalen, as abbot of Vézelay. By 1050 Pope Leo IX had issued a papal bull nominating Mary Magdalen as one of Vézelay's titular saints, placing her at the head of an already lengthy list that included the Virgin Mary, Peter, and Paul, among others. Significantly, this was only the first in a long sequence of papal bulls confirming Mary Magdalen's association with Vézelay; the next one came in 1058 when she was confirmed as Vézelay's sole patron. More important, the bull also confirmed Vézelay's venerable claim of possessing her relics.

Soon Vézelay became a pilgrimage shrine dedicated to the saint. Throughout the Middle Ages, embarkation on a pilgrimage was one of the most popular expressions of religious devotion in Christendom. The desire to visit and worship at holy places is intimately bound up with the veneration of holy relics, which, if venerated properly, had the power, it was believed, to perform miracles. Mary Magdalen's relics quickly developed a reputation for miracle-working. Her first recorded miracles at Vézelay were those performed on behalf of prisoners who had invoked the saint to free them from bondage.

Those who believed they had benefited from these intercessions eventually came on pilgrimages to her shrine at Vézelay to give thanks for grace received. They brought with them the iron fetters that bound them during their imprisonment and left them at the sanctuary as *ex votos,* the silent witnesses of miracles received. One chronicler reports that the shackles became so numerous that Abbot Geoffrey had a railing made of them, which encircled the high altar.

Miraculous prison escapes aside, Mary Magdalen's other early mir-ácles at Vézelay consisted mostly of healings. Vézelay's pinnacle of glory may well have come in 1146 when Bernard of Clairvaux preached the Second Crusade there at Easter in the presence of King Louis VII and Queen Eleanor of Aquitaine. The crowds were so great and so fervent that a reviewing stand collapsed as Saint Bernard was handing out crusader insignia to all who were vying to take up the cross. Chroniclers of the event credited the intercession of the pa-troness of Vézelay that no one was injured.

Vézelay, it should be noted, also became an international pilgrim-age destination, partly because it was well positioned along one of the main pilgrimage routes that conveyed the Christian faithful from Ger-many and the East down to the shrine of St. James at Santiago de Compostela in northern Spain. After stopping at Vézelay to venerate the relics of Saint Mary Magdalen, one could proceed farther south and worship at the shrine of Saint Leonard before continuing on to Santiago. The popular sanctuaries of Saint Martin at Tours and Saint Foy at Conques would not have been difficult side-trips off the road leading from Vézelay to Compostela. Indeed, by the middle of the eleventh century, pilgrims to Conques instituted a devotion to Mary Magdalen that they had learned at Vézelay. The presence of the relics of celebrated saints endowed the pilgrimage shrines, towns, and re-gions in which they were located with power and prestige. And not unlike today's tourist trade, the pilgrimage trade also served to infuse economic activity into the area that claimed miraculous relics.

Vézelay's heyday was relatively short-lived, for in 1279 Mary Mag-dalen's uncorrupted body was "found" in the crypt of St. Maximin in

Aix-en-Provence. It was "discovered" by Charles II of Anjou, Count of Provence and Prince of Salerno, who had a vested interest in grounding the saint's relics within his own jurisdiction. To make his case, he and his circle argued that the holy theft carried out by the monk Badilo two hundred years previously had, in fact, never transpired. They suggested that Badilo had misidentified the body. He had not carried off the body of Saint Mary Magdalen, as the monks of Vézelay claimed, but instead had stolen the remains of one Saint Sidonius. Mary Magdalen's relics, they said, remained undisturbed in the crypt. They also produced artifacts as material evidence: an ancient piece of parchment had been found with the mortal remains of the saint inscribed with the words HERE LIES THE BODY OF BLESSED MARY MAGDALEN.

All this was a great blow to the reputation of Vézelay, a coup de grâce from which it never recovered. Henceforth pilgrims transferred their allegiance (and their money) to the new shrine at St. Maximin, where the saint soon began performing miracles, memorialized by Jean Gobi the Elder in his *Miracle Collection,* compiled circa 1315. From the late thirteenth century onward, under the patronage of the Angevin counts of Provence and the Dominican Order, Mary Magdalen's cult now flourished in Aix-en-Provence.

Over the centuries, the fortunes of Mary Magdalen's sanctuary in the south of France have waxed and waned; nonetheless, on July 22 each year pilgrims, now accompanied by tourists and New Age seekers, make their way to the unfinished basilica in Aix-en-Provence in order to venerate the saint whose presence for well over nine hundred years has brought power, prestige, and not a little sex appeal to the region.

"I Don't Know If She *Was* Here,
but She *Is* Here"

A Mary Magdalene Pilgrimage to Southern France

BY ELIZABETH BARD

The legend of Mary Magdalene's life in France took root in the sixth century through the writings of Gregory of Tours (c. 538–594), the Gallo-Roman historian and powerful bishop of Tours. Buffs of *The Da Vinci Code* will take delight in knowing that Gregory's major work was his ten-volume *Historia Francorum* (*History of the Franks*), the chief contemporary source for Merovingian history—the same Merovingians whose kings, according to Brown's novel, carried the royal bloodline resulting from the marriage of Mary and Jesus.

There are many variations on the story of how Mary Magdalene ended up spending her last days in Provence, but they generally revolve around her fleeing Jerusalem for fear of prosecution and setting out from Palestine (or Egypt) in a boat without rudder, sails, or oars, accompanied by her daughter and anywhere from three to a half dozen companions. Favorable winds, tides, and, presumably, the intervention of the divine let the boat drift past Crete, Greece, Sicily, Italy, Malta, Sardinia, Corsica, Morocco, and everywhere else along the coast of the Mediterranean until it landed near Marseilles, in southern France. There she would live out her days preaching and meditating in a few select villages. Later came the relics, the feast days, the tourist shops, the bakeries selling *navattes* and *madeleines,* and the inns and cafes where weary pilgrims might tarry.

In the preceding essay, Katherine Jansen provided fascinating background on the relics trade and the town of Vézelay. To get an expert personally guided tour of what remains of Mary Magdalene's France, we dispatched Elizabeth Bard, journalist, art historian, and private guide to retrace the route's highlights and report on the layers of legend, myth, artwork, relics, and commerce that a twenty-first-century pilgrim might encounter.

Any journey following the footsteps of Mary Magdalene in France begins at the crossroads of history and legend. Mary Magdalene's prominent role in the bestselling *The Da Vinci Code* is hardly her first brush with controversy. The competition between Vézelay and Provence for her relics is one of the great capers of ecclesiastical history, full of scheming abbots, decaying body parts, and "holy thefts." The journey also reveals sites of exceptional beauty and tranquility—

an appropriate spiritual link to the saint who, even today, remains a model of the contemplative life.

Vézelay

The town of Vézelay is nestled in the gentle green hills of Burgundy. Today, walking up the narrow main street to the basilica dedicated to Mary Magdalene, past boutiques and gourmet restaurants serving the region's famed local wine, it is hard to imagine that nine hundred years ago this was a buzzing metropolis of ten thousand people, and one of the most important sites in Christendom. At the height of its fame in the eleventh and twelfth centuries, Vézelay attracted tens of thousands of pilgrims each year to see Mary Magdalene's relics.

Her association with the basilica, as well as her association with the south of France, is largely a product of the medieval period—legends that cast their shadows and suppositions back to the earliest days of Christianity. There are both spiritual and cynical reasons for this medieval enthusiasm for Mary Magdalene. To have your church linked with a saint who knew Jesus during his lifetime was a powerful good luck charm. Health, wealth, victory in battle, and pardon from sins could all be obtained if you had the proper intercessor with the divine. If France could not boast of the remains of one of the twelve apostles, as Santiago de Campostela claimed the body of St. James, Mary Magdalene, his most important female follower, came a close second. For some, she trumped them all; as the first person to see the Risen Christ, she was often called "apostle to the apostles."

There were also more worldly considerations. During the twelfth and thirteen centuries, when many of the most enduring versions of the Mary Magdalene legends were written, relics and the pilgrimages they inspired were big business. A pope-certified skull or finger could attract crowds equivalent to a medieval Euro Disney. The faithful would travel from town to town to see the bodies (or bits and pieces) of various saints; they all needed to be fed, lodged, and entertained during their stay. The basilica at Vézelay is conveniently located on Europe's most important pilgrimage route, from northern and eastern Europe to Santiago de Campostela in Spain. Walking up the hill toward the basilica, you can still see seashells, the symbol of St. James, embedded in the pavement to mark the way. As a sort of modern, if secular, pilgrim, I approached the basilica with equal parts skepticism and excitement.

The original basilica, dedicated to the Virgin Mary, began as a monastery and a convent on the estate of le Comte de Rousillion and his wife, Berthe. The couple had lost their only son and heir, and decided to give their fortune to the church. In 863, the property was donated to Rome for papal protection and a tax break. No longer under local authority, the church was to be in continuous conflict with local lords and the French crown. In 1120, the original church burnt to the ground, killing more than a thousand members of the congregation who were caught under its wooden roof.

The basilica that rose (c.1145) out of the ruins of that fire is one of the wonders of Romanesque architecture—a building that speaks across the centuries. The monks and sisters who now live at Vézelay like to say the building is constructed of stone and light. Walking through the abbey is a journey, both literal and spiritual, from darkness to light.

When you first enter the abbey, you find yourself in a somber, square room called a narthex. In the language of medieval architecture, the four corners of the square each stand for earthly, and thus imperfect, things: the four elements, the four points of the compass, the four humours (blood, phlegm, and yellow and black bile). This is where pilgrims would have dusted off from their voyage, then slept and eaten in the gallery upstairs. At the height of the basilica's fame, some eight hundred monks taught the catechism here, using the sculpture of the triumphant Christ in the central tympanum to instruct their students. Below the tympanum, a figure of St. John the Baptist welcomes the pilgrims.

The enormous interior doors of the abbey open into a different world. We are now in the world of the circle, which represents the spiritual, the perfect—the life without end that is the central promise of Christianity. Sunlight floods the nave of the church, with its rounded arches and candy-striped bands of black and white stone. In a happy accident of the building process, the chancel at the end of the church is a later Gothic construction (c.1160); the larger windows and pointed arches of the Gothic style lead us strategically toward the light.

Architects of the Romanesque and Gothic periods were extremely fond of arithmetic symbolism, which is in evidence throughout the basilica. On the second level of the chancel you will see fourteen niches, separated with round columns, representing Christ and his disciples at the Last Supper. (Jesus, in the center, gets a double niche topped with a cross, symbolizing his dual nature as God and man.) If you look at the second niche on your left, you will see a single square column representing Judas, the earthly and imperfect, among the rounded columns representing his more enlightened friends.

In addition to Christian pilgrims and curious tourists, there are also many "esoteric" pilgrims at Vézelay. The medieval period saw the flowering of many secret or initiate orders, and perhaps their rituals remain. Among the visitors I saw at Vézelay were two young women standing on either side of the nave hissing or blowing breath back and forth at each other. While the official bookstore of the basilica sells only Christian and tourist materials, the store next door offers titles on auras, shamanism, Kabbalah, and the ever-present Knights Templar.

The grand architectural and spiritual projects undertaken at Vézelay would have been neither possible nor necessary without the object of the pilgrims' devotion: the relics of Mary Magdalene. To justify their claim, Vézelay performed a sleight of hand that was to have a major impact on the fortunes of the basilica and the legends surrounding Mary Magdalene. After a period of decline in the early eleventh century, Vézelay underwent a financial and spiritual renaissance under a certain Abbot Geoffrey—and his chosen patron saint, Mary Magdalene.

Before Geoffrey's arrival in 1037, there is no particular mention of Mary Magdalene in association with Vézelay. Yet in 1058, Pope Stephen IX declared Mary Magdalene as Vézelay's sole protector, and put the official stamp on the abbey's claim to her relics. It seems that Geoffrey may have done some political lobbying with His Holiness in order to secure this honor.

To bolster the claim, the story of a *furta sacra,* or "holy theft," which had brought her body to Vézelay was circulated. According to the story, in the eighth century a monk named Badilon had been sent to Provence by the Comte de Rousillion to save Mary's bones from the invading Saracens.

The story seemed to do the trick. The pilgrimage business was booming, and the fire was fueled with tales of miracles performed by Mary Magdalene through the veneration of her relics. The saint was said to break the chains of prisoners, heal the sick, and even raise the dead. The site became so important that St. Bernard preached the Second Crusade from a wooden platform on the hillside (the church was not big enough to hold the crowds).

All this was done without a bone in sight. The faithful came to see a tomb, but a body was never produced. To answer skeptics who wondered how her body came to be in Burgundy, Vézelay offered this tautological reply: "All is possible to God who does what he pleases." The pilgrims, it seems, would have to rely on faith alone.

By the thirteenth century, faith in this answer was clearly wavering. Pilgrimages were in decline and Vézelay decided to come up with a definitive solution. On the night of October 4, 1265, the body of Mary Magdalene was "rediscovered" in the tomb where it had supposedly lain since Badilon's "holy theft." The medieval term for the discovery of relics is *invention,* which in this case may be more than appropriate. A bronze coffer was produced, containing relics carefully wrapped in silk and, to seal the deal, a great quantity of flowing hair.

For further confirmation of the relics' authenticity, the basilica enlisted the help of "St. Louis," the particularly pious king Louis IX. Louis was an enthusiast of both Mary Magdalene and Vézelay, and also owned an exceptional private collection of relics. In 1267, in the presence of Louis and honored guests, the relics were "translated," or moved, from the bronze coffer to a silver one. The king took a generous share for his own collection, and in his enthusiasm gave some to the crowd. Vézelay was left with an arm, jawbone, and three teeth.

These theatrical events were meant to seal Vézelay's claim on the relics once and for all, but the story did not hold up for long. In 1279, the monks at St. Maximin would claim their own "rediscovery" of Mary Magdalene relics in Provence, eventually beating Vézelay at its own game.

Unfortunately, not much evidence of this intrigue remains for the modern visitor. In 1567, during the religious wars, the basilica was sacked and the relics burned by Protestant armies. Today, in the crypt of Vézelay a reliquary held aloft by three golden figures—a monk, an angel and a king—holds a single rib. This rib, part of the body distributed by Louis in 1267, was given back to Vézelay in the nineteenth century by the cathedral at Sens.

Without the attraction of the "true" relics, the abbey's fame declined, and by the nineteenth century it had been all but abandoned, trees growing out of the floor and stones falling from the ceiling. The church was in danger of being razed to the ground when a young architect, Eugène Viollet-le-Duc, was given the task of restoring it in 1835. After his success at Vézelay he would go on to restore Notre Dame in Paris. The basilica and surrounding hill were declared a UNESCO World Heritage Site in 1979.

Marseille

For all Mary Magdalene's success at Vézelay, her legendary association with France actually begins in the city of Marseille. It is here that she is said to have landed after she was forced to flee Jerusalem and was set adrift in a rudderless boat. Depending on whom you read, this rather crowded boat also contained a number of other New Testament characters—Mary of Bethany (whose identity is often folded into that of Mary Magdalene), Martha, Lazarus, Mary Jacob, Mary Salome, the servant girl Sara, and St. Maximin—all of whom would be credited in some way with the conversion of pagan Gaul to Christianity.

When you arrive in modern Marseille, the first thing you notice is its reliance on the water. The city's monuments and commerce follow the contours of the harbor like barnacles clinging to the bottom of a ship. The sea figures highly in almost all the French Mary Magdalene legends, and the locals who live by and make their livelihoods from the sea have a special affinity for the saint who floated to their shores. Marseilles' most famous bakery, La Four des Navettes, founded in 1781, specializes in a long, thin breadstick-like pastry with a groove in the center, called a *navatte,* made to resemble the small fishing boats you still see in the harbor today.

The Grotto of St. Baume

Legend tells us that after preaching the "good news" in Marseille and the surrounding communities, Mary Magdalene retired to a remote cave in the nearby mountains where she lived as a hermit for thirty years. She survived with no food, no water, and no clothing—just a choir of heavenly angels to give her spiritual sustenance. This model of the contemplative life was to be very influential for the monastic orders of the medieval period, and many of the images of Mary Magdalene in Western art depict this chapter in her story. Often dressed only in her hair, like a biblical Lady Godiva, she is shown deep in thought, sometimes with a candle or contemplating a skull, symbols of mortality.

Driving up the stomach-churning mountain road in a four-by-four today, you can't help but wonder how a lone woman with donkey would have gotten herself up here. The grotto is high up on the cliff face; to reach it we took a wooded path: le Chemin des Roys (the Way of Kings). Louis XIII walked this way in 1622 to pray for a son to carry on the royal line. The wish was fulfilled, and the son, Louis XIV, came, in turn, with his mother, Anne of Austria, in 1660.

The church itself is nothing more than a natural cave, now closed in with a stone facade. Entering the grotto, you feel the immediate chill of the stone and hear the water dripping from the ceiling. Tradition says that there may have been a Christian shrine here as early as the fifth century, when pilgrims were sent by Jean Cassien, who founded the basilica of St. Victor in Marseille.

Like all of the French sites associated with Mary Magdalene, there are at least several centuries between the "events" of her life and the first historical traces of Christian activity. The exact location of Mary Magdalene's hermitage seems to have been identified during the medieval period. The site was dedicated to the Virgin Mary until around 1170. All this seems to bother no one.

The French Revolution and the following "Terror" were unkind to

My Pilgrimage to St. Baume

. . . .The path is steep and rocky but well tended; the forest dense and silent. We can see the site way above us, looming, dizzying, perched in the grey sheer rock. . . .The monk on duty lets us in; he tells us there are only six monks living here, and takes us into the cave.

It is chilling. Beneath a rough stone altar lies a stone female statue, covered from the waist down with a clear plastic sheet. Around it kneel statues that are headless, armless, some also swathed. It is like I imagine the morgue, or the scene of a crime. Against the jagged, dripping, rough walls other nineteenth-century statues are arranged or not arranged; . . . there are electrical wires about, and, strangely, lit tapers. Three garish, stained-glass windows from 1978 and the 80s (the converted sinner; Jesus' meal at Martha's house; *noli me tangere)* are not illuminated.

I know this place. It is my nightmare, women's fear, of utter isolation. It *is* the morgue, and the scene of a crime. . . .

—JANE SCHABERG, from *The Resurrection of Mary Magdalene*
(Continuum Books, 2002)

traditional pilgrimage sites like this one, particularly considering their royal patronage. Little remains inside the grotto church that dates from before the nineteenth century. There is one fifteenth-century statue of the Virgin Mary, hidden in the hollow trunk of a tree, that was saved by the locals.

In the back of the grotto there is a stone, now topped with a statue of the reclining Magdalene, which is always dry, despite the humidity of the cave. Pilgrims identified this stone as Mary's bed, and were so fond of chipping off pieces as souvenirs that the stone was eventually enclosed by a metal gate.

The stained-glass windows depicting the life of Mary Magdalene are a modern addition, completed in the 1980s by Les Compagnons du Devoirs, a professional association of artisans and craftsmen. Today their website is full of career development advice for welders, pastry chefs, and carpenters, but they trace their legendary origins to Mâitre Jacques, one of the stone masons who built Solomon's Temple. During the medieval period, as part of a powerful guild system, their history intersects at various points (in legend and in fact) with the Knights Templar and Freemasons. The group still makes annual pilgrimages to St. Baume.

Today, the grotto is a functioning church with daily mass. The day I was there a group of teenagers preparing for their Confirmation came to hear a sermon about Mary Magdalene—presented as the loyal friend and follower of Jesus, and model of the Christian life.

The Dominican brothers that maintain the monastery remain philosophical about Mary Magdalene's presence at St. Baume. One quoted Père Vayssière, who was the guardian at St. Baume from 1900 to 1932: *"Je ne sais pas si elle est venu, mais elle est la."* ("I don't know if she *was* here, but she *is* here.")

Basilique Sainte-Marie-Madeleine, Saint-Maximin-la-Sainte-Baume

After thirty years of isolation, Mary Magdalene is said to have died in the arms of St. Maximin, who buried her body near Aix-en-Provence in the village that will later bear his name.

Today, the basilica of St. Mary Madeleine at St. Maximin has the feeling of a parish church that has sprouted into a Gothic monument. Built over a period of two hundred years, from 1295 to 1532, it is the only large-scale example of the Gothic style in Provence.

The nave of the church is dominated by an enormous pipe organ. The last in a succession dating back to 1500, it was commissioned in 1772 from Jean-Esprit Isnard. Directly above the organ you can still see the design for a stained-glass window. It was never completed for fear that the humidity would interfere with the functioning of the instrument. The organ may also have helped save the basilica from destruction during the French Revolution. Local tradition says that the church's organist appeased the region's revolutionary authorities (including Napoleon Bonaparte's brother Lucien) by striking up a lively version of "La Marseillaise" during an official visit. The basilica still holds regular organ concerts as well as a festival of organ music each summer.

The pulpit, a towering baroque construction in wood, is decorated with scenes from the life of Mary Magdalene. All the confusion surrounding her identity can be summed up in these panels. We see Mary of Bethany, sister of Lazarus, sitting at Jesus' knee while her sister Martha prepares dinner. We see the anonymous sinner mentioned in the Gospel of Luke, who washes Jesus' feet with her tears and dries them with her hair. We also see Mary of Magdala crying at the tomb, just before she sees the Risen Christ. All these women have been combined in the popular figure we now think of as Mary Magdalene. The pulpit is topped with what looks like a pile of whipped cream: a figure of Mary, supported by angels, rising up from her grotto to receive spiritual sustenance.

Despite the grand surroundings, the star attraction of the basilica of St. Maximin is the tiny crypt said to hold the "true" relics of Mary Magdalene. In 1279, Charles II, Duke of Anjou, perhaps jealous of Vézelay's wealth and prominence, "rediscovered" the relics supposedly removed by Vézelay's *furta sacra*. According to the new story, Vézelay's holy theft was a case of mistaken identity. Badilon had taken the wrong body, and Mary Magdalene lay undisturbed in her original resting place.

When you enter the crypt today, the first thing to notice is a golden angel wearing what looks like a scuba helmet. This strange bust contains a skull and a scrap of miraculously preserved skin supposedly taken from Mary Magdalene's forehead. Why her forehead? In the Gospel of John, when Mary is the first to see the Risen Christ, she reaches out to embrace him and he says, "Touch me not" (Latin: *"Noli me tangere"*). In many of the later paintings of this scene, Mary is kneeling before Jesus and he reaches out toward her forehead, at once to bless her and keep her away. You can see just such a painting, from the fifteenth century, in the chapel of St. Antoine on the left-hand side of the church.

The crypt also contains several early Christian sarcophagi (fourth to sixth centuries AD), one of which is said to be that of Mary Magdalene. Scientific studies of the relics say only that the body parts belong to a woman of Mediterranean origin, small stature, and about fifty years of age. The official church publication says it's a shame that carbon-14 dating would require such a large chunk to be removed for testing. Translation: preserve the mystery. Any excuse to keep hope alive.

Saintes-Maries-de-la-Mer

Continuing along the coast to Saintes-Maries-de-la-Mer we passed through the collection of wetlands, pastures, dunes and salt flats known as the Camargue. This is the region that produces much of France's famous *fleur du sel*. Mountains of sea salt were piled by the side of the road to dry in the sun, and a flock of pink flamingos waded in the shallows.

Saintes-Maries-de-la-Mer itself is a ticky-tacky little beach town, crowded with signs for snacks, ice-cream, and hot dogs. It also has almost nothing to do with Mary Magdalene. The Marys that give the town its name are Mary Jacob and Mary Salome, two lesser-known female followers of Jesus who were also present at the Crucifixion and opening of Jesus' tomb. According to legend, they arrived in Provence by boat along with Mary Magdalene, settling in this seaside village. It is to these two Marys, rather than their more famous ringleader, that the town's church is dedicated.

With tiny windows, high towers and ramparts, the church of Saintes-Maries-de-la-Mer resembles a military fortress more than a house of prayer. With a freshwater well running directly beneath the floor, the church was often used as a refuge when the town came under siege.

One legend relates how in 869, when the fortified church was being built, Saracen invaders carried off the archbishop of Arles, who was responsible for supervising the work. Residents of Arles quickly raised the ransom, and the archbishop was returned and set ceremoniously on his throne. Only after the Saracens dashed off with the cash did the prelate discover that the archbishop had died during his imprisonment, and the Saracens had, with great pomp and circumstance, returned a corpse to the throne.

Inside, the church is covered in ex-votos, the oldest dating from 1591. These are thank-you notes in the form of stone plaques, paintings, or written messages donated by people who feel they have been healed or blessed by the two Marys over the years.

One painting from the nineteenth century shows a couple bending over a crib. In the sky beyond, resting on a cloud is the boat containing the two Marys. The inscription reads: EX VOTO OF MARIE

MARIAVEL, MIRACULOUSLY HEALED, 25TH OF MAY, 1860. On the opposite wall is a photograph of a man, and below that, a photograph of his totaled car and an inscription: TO YOU GRACIOUS MARY, WHO SAVED OUR LIVES.

In 1448, two bodies were found buried beneath the church; they were quickly seized upon as the remains of Mary Jacob and Mary Salome. The bodies, now in wooden sarcophagi, are kept in a closed upper gallery and lowered onto the alter on certain feast days.

In the church's crypt is a black-skinned statue of St. Sara, patron saint of Gypsies. Legend can't seem to agree on her origins. For some, she is the black Egyptian servant of Mary Magdalene or Mary Salome; for others, she is a native queen of Gaul converted by the arrival of the two Marys in AD 42.

The statue is smothered in bright, colored robes donated by Gypsies from around the world. Each year on May 24, thousands of Gypsies arrive in Saintes-Maries-de-la-Mer to accompany the statue of St. Sara in a procession down to the sea. Following St. Sara's path down to the water, I turned my back on the snack bars and souvenir shops. The sea crashing in looks much as it must have two thousand years ago, when the legendary journey of these women began.

Rennes-le-Château

The village of Rennes-le-Château is a picture postcard of a town perched high in the Pyrenees. It is also the origin of one of the most bizarre and conspiracy-laden aspects of the Mary Magdalene legends, retold most recently in *The Da Vinci Code*.

In 1885, a new parish priest named Béranger Saunière arrived in Rennes-le-Château. He amassed a large fortune in a suspiciously brief time, and began an extensive renovation of the town's original eleventh-century church. During the renovation he found what he claimed were secret, coded documents hidden in a hollow pillar on the altar. He was advised to take them to Paris for an expert opinion. Once there, he fell in with a pretty fast crowd, dabbling in the occult and possibly having an affair with the famous opera singer Emma Calvé. After his return, his fortune continued to grow; he built himself a lovely villa, and a bizarre little library tower overlooking the valley, which he called the Tour Magdala.

Some, like the authors of *Holy Blood, Holy Grail*—on whose story Dan Brown relies—speculate that Saunière's fortune came from the Cathars, and that his secret text revealed Mary Magdalene's marriage to Jesus and their bloodline's link to the Merovingian kings. Others speculate that the restaurateur who later bought the property embellished the story to attract visitors.

The priests and monks I spoke with during my trip were quite clear that Saunière made his fortune from the forbidden practice of simony—selling private masses—and not from a famous buried treasure. The church itself was closed for the winter when we arrived, so one of the film crew walked down the road to have a chat with the current mayor of the town. He said he'd be happy to open it for us— for a thousand euros. Clearly, the entrepreneurial spirit of Père Saunière is alive and well.

Where There's Smoke . . .

Today, the sites associated with Mary Magdalene can be seen as props in a carefully constructed and cultivated legend—the devoted follower, the penitent hermit, the miracle-working saint. But the sites themselves, despite their hazy history, do offer real moments of rest and revelation. The quiet walk along a wooded path, the wide views over Provence, the silent crypt, or the approach toward a light-filled altar all continue to encourage the kind of contemplation that follows the spirit, if not the letter, of her story.

The question remains: where there's smoke, is there really fire? Why this church, this city, this cave? Even the most cynical traveler will finish a trip like this wondering if the legends that come to us from across the centuries hold at least the vestiges of something true.

8 Herstory Today

Mary Magdalene
in Popular Culture

I don't know how to love him . . . He's just a man, and I've had so many men before . . . I want him so. I love him so.

— TIM RICE, *Jesus Christ Superstar*

We were as close together as a bride and groom / We ate the food, we drank the wine / Everybody having a good time / Except you / You were talking about the end of the world.

— U2, "Until the End of the World"

Jesus had a son by Mary Magdalene and he rode the land like the man who went before young Jesus raised him loud, mother Mary raised him proud and he tracked the men who laid his father down.

— JEFFERSON AIRPLANE, "Jesus Had a Son"

Purring, Mary Magdalene hugged the man, [and] kept his body glued to hers . . . "Beloved wife, I never knew the world was so beautiful or the flesh so holy. It too is a daughter of God, a graceful sister of the soul. I never knew that the joys of the body were not sinful."

— NIKOS KAZANTAKIS, *The Last Temptation of Christ*

The Saint as Vamp
Mary Magdalene on the Silver Screen

BY DIANE APOSTOLOS-CAPPADONA

Mel Gibson, then promoting his new movie, *The Passion of the Christ,* explained to TV interviewers, "I threw mud on her; then, more mud. The more mud I threw the more beautiful she became." He was talking about Monica Bellucci, the actress who portrayed Mary Magdalene in his intensely personal film about Jesus' last days. However, the reality is that if we come to understand, to truly *see,* the meaning of Gibson's statement, we recognize that his comment can be viewed through a wider lens, both with reference to Mary Magdalene generally and to her presentation in film history. Among her many metamorphoses in Christian art and theology, Mary Magdalene has been transformed from a matronly saint to a sinner and from a sinner into a prostitute. Her personal integrity has been questioned and besmirched; and, yet, as the twenty-first century enters its first decade, Mary Magdalene has returned to the center of the stage of discussions, controversies, and cultural and theological inquiry. To paraphrase Gibson, then, we have come to recognize that the Magdalene's inner beauty shines through all the accusations, misreadings, and mud thrown on her.

Looking at the history of film, we can *see* the transformation of Mary Magdalene from saintly matron into alluring vamp and back again. Beginning with a brief discussion of what I term visual analogies and the way they work in religious film, we'll trace the development of Mary Magdalene's image in a variety of film categories, including biblical epics, morality tales, and stories with religious messages. This brief examination of the history of Mary Magdalene on the silver screen will provide insights into the power of images and the influence of the arts in our daily lives.

Diane Apostolos-Cappadona is an adjunct professor of religious art and cultural history in the Prince Alwaleed bin Talal Center for Muslim-Christian Understanding, and an adjunct professor in art and culture in the Liberal Studies Program of Georgetown University. She has long studied how religious images are conveyed in the mass media and, in particular, that of Mary Magdalene.

Visual Analogies and Religious Film[1]

A movie, regardless of its theme or mode of presentation (animation, action, etc.), is composed of a series of interrelated cinematic frames, "moving pictures," that create a continuum of identifiable images and corresponding story. The film's narrative relates, through dialogue and images, something about an event, a place, or a person (or persons) and simultaneously the images and symbols projected on the screen convey both overt and covert messages. While a movie's images and story are constructed by the filmmaker, the *seeing* is a work of inter-pretation by each individual viewer: each of us sees a motion picture or work of art differently. Our individual seeing is dependent upon the worlds—cultural, religious, social, political, and economic—into which we have been socialized and in which we live. Seeing is not pas-sive; it is an active engagement of the human senses with the intellect and vision. Seeing engages us in the activity of the transmission of knowledge. Knowledge is power. Images have power, and an essential part of that power is their ability to communicate authority and reality. They are the embodiments of the shared memory that forms the foun-dation for the social and political identity of a faith community and for the initiation of an individual as a member of that community.

In the medium of film, visual analogy is the prime source of the power that images wield. Each viewer has a history with the images he or she views, and the associations are especially profound when the images are religious ones. These are the pictures with which we were socialized as children: they are the illustrations in our Bibles, the art on our Christmas and Easter cards, the graphics we saw on Sunday school bulletins, and the patterned panes of stained-glass windows in our churches. Many of these images were derived from classical works

---

1. My original discussion of the concept of visual analogy with regard to the relationship between classical painting and film can be found in "The Art of 'Seeing': Classical Paintings and *Ben-Hur*" in *Image and Likeness: Religious Visions in American Film Classics*, ed. John R. May (New York/Mahwah: Paulist, 1992): 104–16. A later discussion of visual analogy with the development of images of women in re-ligious film appeared in "From Eve to the Virgin and Back Again: The Image of Women in Contempo-rary (Religious) Film" in *New Image of Religious Film*, ed. John R. May (St. Louis: Sheed and Ward, 1997): 111–27. My careful use of the term *seeing* throughout this present text reaffirms my commit-ment to the equality of image and text, and to the impassioned plea by my former student Lucinda Ebersole at the Seventh Cavalletti Conference on Theology and Film that film is a visual media.

of Christian art, though others—including late-nineteenth- and early-twentieth-century Bible illustrations—were created by artists specifically for religious pedagogy. Traditional Christian art evolved its depictions of biblical figures like Mary Magdalene as well as biblical events like the Crucifixion through a series of familiar symbols, costumes, scenery, backdrops, and even identifiable characterizations created by facial and bodily gestures. Over time, through artistic convention, recognizable codes developed: the Virgin Mary wears blue, Judas has red hair, Jesus appears in the center of the *Last Supper,* and Mary Magdalene is always seductively beautiful.

These visual elements were transferred, more or less consciously, from classical Christian art into cinema, where the familiar costumes and set designs, character portrayals, and overall visual atmosphere are translated from one medium to the other, and provide an aura of historical authenticity. Recognizable visual references imbue religious films with a history of shared cultural memory and religious identity, cueing the viewer to accept the depictions created by the filmmaker. Thus, we appreciate Gibson's or Cecil B. DeMille's portrayal of Christ or Mary Magdalene as "real" because their images conform to our existing ideas about the figures as we know them from our childhood Bibles and Sunday school bulletins. Often, director's and producer's notes—and in DeMille's case promotional photographs and interviews—tell us the artists whose work influenced the development of particular cinematic biblical narratives or figures. We know, for example, that the intense realism and dramatic lighting and composition of the Southern Baroque painter Caravaggio influenced Gibson and his cinematographer in the "imaging" of *The Passion of the Christ*.[2]

We now understand, based on what is sometimes called response theory, how and why certain images and symbols are perceived as real while others are rejected. According to response theory, those religious images and symbols that reflect the communal memory and

---

2. See my essay "On Seeing *The Passion:* Is There a Painting in This Film? Or Is This Film a Painting?" in *Re-Viewing "The Passion": Mel Gibson's Film and Its Critics,* ed. S. Brent Plate (New York: Palgrave-Macmillan, 2004): 97–108. For a specific discussion of the influence of Caravaggio's art on Gibson and his cinematographer Caleb Deschanel, see "A Savior's Pain: Caleb Deschanel," interview by John Bailey, ASC, and Stephen Pizzello, ed. Stephen Pizzello and Rachael K. Bosley in *American Cinematographer* (March 2004), available online at http://www.theasc.com/magazine/index.htm?mar04/cover/index.html-main.

embody the social and political identity of a faith community have singular power in forming our "eyes"; that is, the view from which we
evaluate what we see. The reality is that there is no innocent eye. We
are each trained from childhood to separate truth from fiction, reality
from fantasy, and our education about what is true and what is not is
especially compelling when it comes to matters of faith. So when we
can name characters by their costumes and places by their landscapes,
we believe we know the line of demarcation between the real story
and the Hollywood fantasy. When the costuming and set designs, then,
coalesce with what we recognize as "the real story" garnered from our
exposure to Christian art, we assure ourselves that what we see on the
screen is fact. Thus, the role of visual analogy affirms our cultural valu-
ing of Christian classical paintings, even as these works of art help con-
struct a believer's subliminal and conscious process of *seeing*.

Mary Magdalene Goes to the Movies

At least thirty major motion pictures categorized as biblical epics or
morality tales feature Mary Magdalene, but her presence can also be
seen in other films through a variety of female motifs, particularly
that of the "fallen woman" or prostitute with a heart of gold. The
countess Olenska in Martin Scorsese's *Age of Innocence*[3] is one such example of a woman living contrary to the sexual mores of her time,
though she appears in a secular story with only covert or implicit religious references. Here I've elected to look briefly at the image of
Mary Magdalene in the better-known biblical epics and specifically at
the influences upon and influence of DeMille's depiction of her in his
magnum opus, *The King of Kings* (1927).

In an introductory survey to Mary Magdalene in biblical epics, we

---

3. Other typical "fallen women" with a heart of gold include the nineteenth-century figures Camille
and Violetta, and the twentieth-century characterizations of the girls of the golden west like "Miss
Kitty" and Stella Dallas. For a survey of this iconography, see Linda Nochlin, "Lost and Found: Once
More the Fallen Woman," in her *Women, Art, and Power and Other Essays* (New York: Harper and Row,
1988): 57–85. If I were to include these secularized Magdalene figures in the movies in this essay, the
text might become both a deviation from the central argument of how such a significant interpretation as DeMille's came to be and also be overwhelming in its breadth, from Julia Roberts' *Pretty
Woman* to Greta Garbo's *Camille*.

need to recognize two central conventions: she must be portrayed by an actress who is beautiful and she is typically conflated with the anonymous "woman taken in adultery" from the Gospel of John. Although the movie versions of Mary Magdalene were created after the beginning of modern biblical scholarship, which is marked in part by the controversial theories of Joseph Ernest Rénan[4] and the so-called Protestant "quest for the historical Jesus," there would be little drama in the development of a Magdalene figure as clearly defined by the scriptural sources. The more than thirty major biblical epics in which I can identify Mary Magdalene chiefly present her as what I call the Magdalene mosaic, an amalgam of several biblical women together with various characterizations drawn from any number of historical sources. Only three films—DeMille's *The King of Kings* (1927), George Stevens's *The Greatest Story Ever Told* (1965), and Franco Zeffirelli's *Jesus of Nazareth* (1977)—present a version of the Magdalene in which she is separate from John's adulteress.

In the majority of biblical films, we find that Mary Magdalene is first and foremost a seductive creature whose primary role is temptress and sinner; examples of such films range from the little-known Italian epic *La Spada e Le Croce* (1959), in which Yvonne De Carlo portrays our beautiful seductress, to Scorsese's controversial *The Last Temptation of Christ* (1988), in which Barbara Hershey's tattoos and fulsome lips set a new standard for voluptuous portrayals of Mary Magdalene, to Gibson's *The Passion of the Christ* (2004), with his mud-spattered Monica Bellucci. Perhaps the greatest example of the Magdalene mosaic appears in Samuel Bronston and Nicholas Ray's 1961 *The King of Kings* (their remake of DeMille's film), in which Carmen Sevilla plays Mary Magdalene. The scene in which a stone-wielding mob chases Sevilla down a street until Jeffrey Hunter's gentle Jesus steps in to protect her presents us with a beautiful temptress whose carefully draped dress and remarkable jewelry highlight her physicality. Some of the very early movie Magdalenes—Julia Swayne Gordon in *Though Your Sins Be*

---

4. Joseph Ernest Rénan (1832–92), a French Orientalist and essayist, scandalized Paris when as professor of Hebrew at the Collége de France, he taught that Jesus was an "incomparable man." His research and study of the Hebrew scriptures led him to emphasize the humanity of Jesus in his most famous book, *Vie de Jésus* (*The Life of Jesus*). His controversial pronouncements were in tandem with the then emerging—and mainly Protestant—"quest for the historical Jesus."

as Scarlet (1911), Maxine Elliott in *The Eternal Magdalene* (1919), and Asta Nielsen in *I.N.R.I./Crown of Thorns* (1923)—likewise take your breath away with their extravagant period costuming and enticing postures. However, even when there is scriptural accuracy in the separation of Mary Magdalene from the unnamed "woman taken in adultery"—such as occurs with Joanna Dunham and Shelley Winters in *The Greatest Story Ever Told* (1965) or Anne Bancroft and Claudia Cardinale in *Jesus of Nazareth* (1977)—there is still an emphasis on the Magdalene figure as a beautiful but repentant "fallen woman." Fallen from what we may never know, but fallen she is.

Whether the film presents a composite figure or a scripturally accurate Mary of Magdala, each of these cinematic versions depends upon classical works of Christian art, borrowing authenticity by replicating her often dramatically minimal dress, her elaborate jewelry and hairstyle, and her posture and gestures. Films may draw, too, from traditions in which the repentant Mary is then transformed in her person/personae, evidenced by simplicity in her garments, lack of jewelry, makeup, and coiffure, and the silent emotion of her poses as she anoints the feet of Jesus (here Dunham and Bancroft are the grandest examples) or her tear-stained face at the crucifixion (Bellucci and Sevilla). Without doubt, the grandest of all cinematic Magdalenes was and is Jacqueline Logan, who, as we are about to see, set an unbeatable standard in DeMille's *The King of Kings*.

Mary Magdalene as Vamp and as Saint

No tattered streetwalker for the great showman Cecil B. DeMille. His casting of Jacqueline Logan as Mary Magdalene created both a glamorous on-screen courtesan and a superior example of dialogical visual analogy in religious film. The opening scene of DeMille's epic sets the stage for his seductress and her retinue of gorgeous slaves (including Sally Rand, with her famous fan), while offering to its multitude of viewers a standard definition of Mary Magdalene. Visual analogy here works two ways—classical art informs the depiction of DeMille's Magdalene and DeMille's Magdalene subsequently cements the identity of Mary Magdalene in the consciousness of his viewers.

DeMille's Mary Magdalene is at first wealthy, lustful, and elaborately arrayed. Annoyed that this Jesus of Nazareth person has influenced Judas Iscariot, her favorite customer, to the point that he no longer visits her regularly, the scantily clad Jacqueline Logan commands that her plume-decorated, zebra-drawn chariot be brought forth by her Nubian slave so that she can go to meet Jesus. Of course, we are first treated to a series of unforgettable images of Mary Magdalene in suggestive poses with a Roman soldier and on her portico as she remembers her encounters with Judas. She sets forth to confront Jesus in order to win back "her Judas," but instead Jesus compels her to repent of her sins. In a moment of extraordinary drama, DeMille's Jesus performs the most flamboyant exorcism of Mary Magdalene short of the medieval productions of the *Digby Magdalene*. She is thrown up, down, and around the ground in a variety of poses as the "seven deadly sins" exit from her in a swirl of energy and thunderous sounds. The experiential drama of this conversion scene overpowers the otherwise melodramatic love story between Mary Magdalene and Judas. She casts off her sinful life symbolically by casting off her jewels and her seductive costumes, which she trades in for an asexual sack. DeMille's formula that redemption has dramatic value only if we know why the sinner needs to be redeemed is fulfilled as we watch this transformation of Mary Magdalene from luscious vamp to saintly matron.

We know from photographs that document the making of *The King of Kings* and from DeMille's working journals, letters, and autobiographical notes that he was deeply influenced by the pictures he saw as a child in his family's edition of the Bible, which was illustrated by James Tissot (1836–1902), as well as by Bible illustrations by Gustave Doré (1832–83). Tissot's illustrations remained enormously popular in the United States as late as the 1950s and 1960s, and a careful review of them foreshadows a progression of cinematic biblical epics even up to Gibson's *The Passion of the Christ*.[5] Ironically,

---

5. Conversation with Judith F. Dolkart, Assistant Curator, Department of European Painting and Sculpture, Brooklyn Museum of Art, on 21 July 2005. Dr. Dolkart is preparing an exhibition of Tissot's original gouaches of his New Testament illustrations, James Tissot: The Life of Christ (14 September 2007 to 13 January 2008). The complete series of over four hundred works on paper were purchased by public subscription for the Brooklyn Museum of Art in 1900 following an international tour of these extremely popular images.

as DeMille's Magdalene garners her authenticity through visual analogy that relies on Tissot's and Doré's illustrations, she checkmates the image of Mary Magdalene in the minds of DeMille's audience. What do I mean by this? Simply that *The King of Kings* was one of the most popular and influential movies ever made, not only in terms of ticket sales but in its continued presence over the years in screenings on college campuses, in churches, and in theaters around the world. Praised in its own time as an accurate portrayal of the life of Christ, the *seeing* of this film had an indelible impact on the minds of the thousands of young people who saw it throughout the 1920s and 1930s. Ask them to describe Mary Magdalene, and see if you don't recognize Jacqueline Logan—bad girl turned saint! After all, seeing is believing.

The Saint as Pop Star
The Mary Magdalene Effect in Popular Culture

BY LESA BELLEVIE

There is no question about Mary Magdalene's mass appeal in our media age. She has been a prominent character in novels, songs, movies, pop art, television docudramas, and even comics. Those who imagine her often do it wildly, without bounds—as modern action hero, as poster-girl for sensuality, or even fallen angel turned vampire.

Why, though, has Mary become a figure of popular fascination while most religious and historical figures have not? Is it the flexibility of her character that makes her so full of creative potential? Is it the inherent drama in the concept of a repentant (and beautiful) prostitute? Is it the idea that she has been maligned, misinterpreted for so long? And, in the end, what are we searching for in her?

Lesa Bellevie, author of *The Complete Idiot's Guide to Mary Magdalene* and founder of the website www.Magdalene.org, ventures some answers. As she makes clear, the past two thousand years of fascination with the culture's favorite saint continues unabated, across an ever widening spectrum of media, and reaching audiences around the globe.

Mary, God greeted thee with heavenly influence!
He hath sent thee grace with heavenly signs.
Thou shall be honored with joy and reverence,
Enhanced in heaven above virgins!

—DIGBY PLAY, *Mary Magdalene,* fifteenth century

Perhaps the most recent major source of Magdalene fever (or fervor) is Dan Brown's runaway bestseller, *The Da Vinci Code*. But although the novel is receiving much of the credit for bringing her to the forefront in recent times, Mary Magdalene is no stranger to popular culture. She has been an important figure in the popular imagination for more than eight centuries, and from the thirteenth century onward, was so adored that full-blown dramas were often written in her honor. The Digby play quoted above is a fine example. Created in the late fifteenth century in the East Midland dialect of Middle English, it fits within the genre of medieval saints' plays and conveys perfectly a Mary Magdalene whose story of temptation, fall into sin, and ultimate sainthood, makes her a powerful figure of redemption. A sprawling play, consisting of more than 2100 lines and requiring a large cast, several backdrops, stages, and machinery, it would have been an enormous and expensive production. Mary Magdalene, with all of her attendant lessons, was clearly worth the effort.

Today, as in the Middle Ages, we continue to invest artistic energy into imagining who Mary Magdalene may have been. In many cases, our reasons may be the same as they were in the thirteenth century: to inspire as well as entertain and bring forth matters of religion without requiring an audience to step foot into a place of worship. Dramas about Mary Magdalene, then and now, have been effective ways of discussing the most taboo subjects of the time and promoting the ideals of forgiveness, love, penitence, and faith. Then and now, Mary Magdalene also stands as a figure to whom almost anyone can relate; someone whose simple humanity makes her fundamentally appealing—and ageless.

Mary, Imagined

Numerous artists have explored the idea of a relationship between Jesus and Mary Magdalene in a secular context. Singer Tori Amos, in her

2005 book, *Piece by Piece,* discusses her belief that Jesus and Mary Magdalene had been a couple. The song "Marys of the Sea" on her album *The Beekeeper* is based on medieval legends of Mary Magdalene's journey to France—often cited by proponents of a marriage between Jesus and Mary Magdalene—and demonstrates Amos's conviction that the story is true. Here is her reference to the place where Mary Magdalene was said to have landed:

> *Marys of the sea,*
> *The lost bride weeps,*
> Les Saint Marie de la Mer . . .

Tim Rice and Andrew Lloyd Webber's rock opera *Jesus Christ Superstar* broached the subject during a period of social and political turmoil. Mary Magdalene, receiving yet another "makeover" in order to reflect Western culture's shifting perspective on women, appears as a feisty yet loving companion to the Savior. First released as a record in 1971 and then produced on Broadway, by the time it hit movie theaters two years later, *Jesus Christ Superstar* already had an enormous following. Yvonne Elliman provided a standout performance as Mary Magdalene in all three formats, turning the song "I Don't Know How to Love Him" into a bestselling single. Although the song has been widely interpreted as reflecting a strictly physical ardor, it can also be seen as representative of the complicated mix of emotions with which the Mary character struggles. It encouraged audiences to imagine Jesus as a man as well as a messiah.

In 1972, the band Jefferson Airplane extrapolated an earthy, raucous family from the idea that Jesus and Mary Magdalene could have been wed. The song "Jesus Had a Son," from their album *Long John Silver,* leaps immediately past the subject of the union and begins with the existence of a son. The song tells us that "Jesus raised him loud" and "Mary raised him proud." Moving to the true purpose of the lyrical story, we then learn that the personal mission of Jesus' son was to avenge his father's death.

In Nikos Kazantzakis's 1951 novel *The Last Temptation of Christ,* Jesus is tempted with what he might have had—the life of a regular mortal man—as he hangs dying upon the cross. Central is the presence of Mary Magdalene, whom he marries in this hallucination before rejecting temptation and carrying out his mission of sacrifice. Kazantzakis describes Jesus' first imagined encounter with Mary Magdalene:

> She took his hand. Her fiery-red veil swelled as she walked hastily under the flowering, soon-fruitful lemon tress. Her fingers, entwined in those of the man, were burning hot, and her mouth smelled of lemon leaves. Out of breath, she stopped for a moment and looked at Jesus. He shuddered, for he saw her eye frolic seductively, cunningly, like the eye of the angel. But she smiled at him.

In 1988, Kazantzakis's book was translated to film by director Martin Scorsese and met with protests ranging from peaceful pickets to Molotov cocktails from moviegoers in the United States and Europe. Many people found a depiction of Jesus as a regular man, loving as any man would love, marrying and fathering children, offensive. The movie was condemned as blasphemous by Christians from all quarters, and some theaters even refused to show it.

Movement to the Divine

Almost twenty years later, The Da Vinci Code's highly accessible format and conspiratorial angle has brought the question to another level, one perhaps even more controversial. Where Kazantzakis's Jesus is only *tempted* by a marriage to Mary Magdalene, Dan Brown's Jesus actually marries her. Further, the Mary Magdalene in Brown's novel is more than wife and mother; she is co-equal with Jesus as a feminine manifestation of God. Interestingly, while Jesus becomes more human for being married, Mary Magdalene has been elevated to goddess.

Though perhaps we are entering a new period of social and religious reform, Mary Magdalene's "deification" did not begin with Dan Brown; it is a movement that has been slowly gaining momentum, with or without a presumed partnership with Jesus. Author Marjorie Malvern suggested in her 1977 book, *Venus in Sackcloth,* that artistic depictions of Mary Magdalene through history have much in common with those of goddess figures such as Pandora and Venus. In 1983, Barbara Walker's *The Woman's Encyclopedia of Myths and Secrets* radically revised history as we know it, casting Mary Magdalene as a priestess in a temple of a goddess called Mari. Margaret Starbird carried this idea one step further, suggesting that Mary Magdalene should be recognized as a goddess in her own right. In so doing, Starbird put forth a Christian mythology based on the reconciliation of masculine and feminine within God. In her vision, Jesus' mission was to "restore the feminine," an idea she believes has been systematically suppressed by a conspiratorial church.

Incorporating Starbird's ideas along with others, Dan Brown seems to have struck a resonant chord with readers. There is a ring of truth to it for many, even in the face of overwhelming evidence that its history is flawed. This elusive sense of authenticity is perhaps the book's greatest achievement, and one that heralds a social climate worth study. There seems to be more to the intense interest in the book than a love of conspiracy, more than an ignorance of history, or even an impulse toward New Age spirituality. *The Da Vinci Code* may be a seed that has fallen on ready soil, and the growing veneration of Mary Magdalene as an emerging divinity in her own right is merely *one* of its fruits. As has been true in the past, Mary Magdalene continues to serve as a popular culture bellwether, to either be examined or ignored.

Her Bad Reputation Lives On

There is, of course, much more to Mary Magdalene's presence in popular culture than our collective curiosity about her relationship with Jesus. Traditionally considered a reformed prostitute who achieved salvation, Mary Magdalene's "bad girl" identity still appears with great frequency in pop culture. It has long been acknowledged that there is nothing scriptural about Mary Magdalene's reputation as a harlot, but the Roman Catholic Church didn't officially change its stance on this until 1969. By that time the error was so firmly entrenched in Western thought that it seems unlikely that she will ever be free of the stain of sexual impropriety.

Popular music, in particular, has made great use of the penitent prostitute image, all via a minimum of words—perfect for a medium as brief as the modern pop song.

In a harlot's dress you wear the smile of a child
with the faith of Mary Magdalene
Yet you wash the feet of unworthy men

—ME'SHELL NDEGÉOCELLO,
"Mary Magdalene," *Peace Beyond Passion,* 1996

But far from confined to simply pop, Mary Magdalene, the scarlet woman, is a fixture in song lyrics across genre. Rock, R & B, rap, country, jazz, and even classical music make use of her mistaken identity. Lenny Kravitz, Linda Davis, Patty Larkin, the Australian band Redrum, the Scottish band Franz Ferdinand, and the American metal group Perfect Circle have all made mention of Mary Magdalene as a sinner, either directly or by referencing a character of the same name. And in "The Girl You Think You See," from her smash album *Anticipation,* Carly Simon offers to please someone, presumably a lover, by being a "Mary Magdalene."

Girls on Film

The medium of film allows the artist more time to characterize and give reasons for Mary Magdalene's brassy patina. One of these reasons can be traced to John 8. In this gospel story, a woman caught in the act of adultery is brought before Jesus. Hoping to catch him in a contradiction, the authorities ask Jesus what they should do with her since the law commands that she be executed for her crime. Jesus' famous answer, that the accuser who is without sin should cast the first stone, saves the woman's life. With no one left to persecute her, Jesus tells the woman that she is forgiven and should sin no more.

The woman in this scene is never named, but she is often associated with Mary Magdalene. Martin Scorsese's *The Last Temptation of Christ* showed Mary Magdalene (played beautifully by Barbara Hershey) cowering among a barbarous crowd before Jesus stepped in. Even Mel Gibson's 2004 blockbuster, *The Passion of the Christ,* known for its claim to biblical accuracy, presented Mary Magdalene (Monica Bellucci) as the woman caught in adultery. P. J. Harvey's hip, urban Magdalena character in Hal Hartley's 1998 film, *Book of Life,* describes the relief she experienced when Jesus prevented her certain execution.

Even more commonly, Mary Magdalene is "forced" to step in for the anonymous sinner in Luke 7. While Jesus dines with a Pharisee, a woman bursts in and begins crying on his feet. She then dries them with her hair and anoints them with expensive perfume. Affronted, the Pharisee exclaims that if Jesus really was a prophet, he wouldn't allow such a woman—a sinner—to touch him. But Jesus declares that this woman has shown greater love for him than the host and announces that her sins are forgiven "because she had loved much." This dramatic scene is repeated, with variations, in all four gospels, and in none of them is Mary Magdalene named as the woman who performs the anointing. Still, the fact that Mary Magdalene has been associated with the anointing woman is a case of mistaken identity that has followed her for more than a thousand years.

The error makes for dramatic cinema. In Franco Zeffirelli's 1977 miniseries, *Jesus of Nazareth,* Anne Bancroft's rough Mary Magdalene stirred audiences with the tender authenticity she brought to the anointing scene. More recently, Maria Grazia Cucinotta demonstrated poignant evidence of her character's conversion during the same scene in the Italian made-for-television movie *Maria Maddalena* (2002). Both actresses shed an abundance of tears, another popular association for Mary Magdalene passed down to us from the Middle Ages.

But how is it that so many artists and writers still ignore the probability that Mary Magdalene wasn't really a "fallen woman?" Is it because they haven't heard otherwise? Like Mary herself, there is probably a bit more going on than meets the eye. For almost fourteen hundred years, Mary Magdalene was celebrated as a penitent, a woman who represented an alienation and reconciliation with God as she rejected her (presumed) former life to follow Jesus. And it is still appealing to understand salvation as achievable by anyone, no matter how serious their sins. Many people look at the legendary Mary Magdalene as one of the few people in the gospels who seems truly human. She is someone with whom many feel they can identify: a person who made mistakes and eventually put herself on a higher road. Perhaps for these reasons, in spite of a theological decision to officially (but quietly) change her identity, her traditional reputation remains a compelling and complex subject of interest in popular culture.

Mary, Reimagined

In certain hybrid perspectives Mary Magdalene becomes something far greater, and occasionally, far *stranger*. In 1999, writer and director Chris Carter (*The X-Files*) pulled Mary Magdalene into his dark, supernatural crime drama *Millennium*. In an episode called "Anamnesis," a girl begins having visions of the Virgin Mary. Eventually the girl learns that the woman in the visions is actually Mary Magdalene and that she herself is a member of an ancient bloodline, a descendent of Jesus and Mary Magdalene. Gifted with supernatural powers as a result of her special ancestry, she discovers that her every move has been secretly guarded by shadowy protectors.

Horror writer (and former seminarian) David Niall Wilson, in his 1999 book, *This Is My Blood,* explores complex themes of redemption, good, and evil by placing a Mary Magdalene, fallen angel turned vampire, into a revised telling of Jesus' story. As unusual as this might seem, it isn't the only time Mary Magdalene has appeared in a vampiric context. A recent comic book called *Magdalena,* produced by comic book publisher Top Cow, has the female descendents of Mary Magdalene fulfilling a special role for the Vatican: supernatural warriors. In each generation a girl from this family is dubbed "The Magdalena" and fights against evils, including vampires. This series is so popular that a *Magdalena* movie is in the works. Finally, in the comedic cult movie *Jesus Christ, Vampire Hunter,* Mary Magdalene makes an appearance as a martial arts expert named Mary Magnum, who later becomes a vampire as well.

How deeply should we read into the appearances that Mary Magdalene makes in vampire-related fiction? Perhaps we need look no further than her recently acknowledged status as a maligned woman. There is a poignant sense of tragedy inherent to her story, understanding that her status as "fallen" is entirely mistaken. Given that one of the more popular themes in vampire fiction is the notion of being "cursed," or "damned," it doesn't take a great intuitive leap to understand why Mary Magdalene, at this stage in history, could emerge as a prime candidate for such an imagining. Rather than wilting beneath the slander that has been heaped on her, she emerges in popular culture with otherworldly strength and, sometimes, with righteous anger.

As such, Mary Magdalene is more and more frequently appearing—with or without vampires—as a martial arts superhero. In the 1999 smash hit *The Matrix,* the main female character, Trinity (played by Carrie Ann Moss), was clearly inspired by Mary Magdalene's legendary identity as Jesus' love interest. Laced throughout with Christian, Gnostic, and mythological references, the *Matrix* trilogy indulges a desire to remember Mary Magdalene, through the Trinity character, in a way that we would like to think of ourselves: independent, resilient, strong, and capable of faith. Not only does her presence offer emotional credibility to the film, Trinity also dons dark glasses and kicks her way through the bad guys alongside the film's savior-figure, Neo. Indeed, in the *Matrix* version of the resurrection, the savior is not able to cheat death on his own; it is the intensity of Trinity's love, and her belief in him, that brings him back. Turning every fairy tale on its head, this time it is the princess who wakes the prince with a kiss.

These last expressions of Mary Magdalene are perhaps the most telling of our modern preoccupation with her. Her ability to inspire doesn't end with her role in the gospels, or even with the popular reemergence of legends of her marriage to Jesus. She is being imagined in ways entirely unrelated to her traditional identities and integrated into unconventional arts. No longer is she the weepy penitent or the objectified fleshpot; she is a strong, savvy, and independent woman. She is capable of making her own sacrifice for the good of others. Could it be that the fascination with her imagined sexual misdeeds is finally waning? The next generation of artists seems to acknowledge that, like Mary Magdalene, everyone has skeletons in their closets. Even though we're bound to see ongoing references to Mary Magdalene's exotic past, at long last another kind of question is being asked. Regardless of the kind of person she was, what kind of person did she become?

The answers are surprising.

Piece by Piece

How Mary Magdalene, the Patriarchy, and Sinuality Have Influenced My Life and Career

BY TORI AMOS

Tori Amos is an internationally famous pianist and singer-songwriter who has been heavily influenced by mythology and religion. She is an avid student of the Gnostic Gospels and has used her reading of them to animate her 2005 hit album, *The Beekeeper.* (Beekeeping, she has said, is a source of female inspiration and empowerment.)

At the core of her belief and inspiration stands the figure of Mary Magdalene. For Amos, she is muse, teacher, Lost Bride, sacred prostitute, symbol of the struggle against patriarchy in both religion and politics, and the motivator in her search for "a way to reach orgasm and keep your spirituality intact." This attempt to integrate sin and sensuality has been a big part of her public image. Her worldwide tour for *The Beekeeper,* for example, was called the Original Sinuality Tour (renamed the Summer of Sin Tour in the United States). Also in connection with *The Beekeeper* CD, she published an autobiography, *Tori Amos: Piece by Piece,* which one reviewer characterized as "no mere star memoir . . . it's more like a soul-map of Amos's stride from pop tart to poet provocateur." All that and more is exemplified by these excerpts from the chapter in her book entitled "Mary Magdalene: The Erotic Muse."

"Jesus was a feminist, dear."

At nineteen years old I look up at my mom and with exasperation say, "Ma, I got no problem with Jesus, okay? Always dug the guy—still do. Do you really think the Magdalene would have entertained the idea of them as an item if he weren't for women's rights and equality in the workplace?"

"Yes, dear, I understand all that, dear, but you do seem to be carrying a lot of aggression concerning the Church."

"Damn right I am, Mom."

"Please don't use *damn,* dear."

"Okay, Ma. Darn tooting I am. But I am harboring a lot of f—ing rage over those Passive-Aggressive Manipulators of Authority that constitute The Patriarchy."

"That's better, dear. Articulate the breaking of the dam, the breaking of the emotional chains that have bound women for centuries—from your young feminist perspective. Use your music to tackle the infirmities of the patriarchal structure, which at its foundation has a cancerous moral flaw."

"Huh . . . ? Ma, are you all right?"

"Am I alright? Oh, darlin', I haven't felt so alive in years. Thank heaven your generation is rising to the call."

For a moment it seemed as if my mom were singing "Sister Suffragette," from the movie *Mary Poppins.* She was on a roll.

"In my own daughter, in other mothers' daughters across the land, there will be a thirst for knowledge. Yes, that is the way we will rattle the foundation of The Patriarchy's segregation. Their segregation of heart from mind, of actions from consequences, of man from woman, of power from imagination, and of passion from compassion."

"Jeez, Ma. I didn't know. I had no idea you still had it in you."

And she looked away. When she turned back she took my hand and whispered, "We all have it in us, but those voices can get lost and buried. Those thoughts you just heard have only been sleeping in me. And they sleep in everybody, dear. Don't let anyone tell you that these thoughts are dead. But they have been in a deep sleep. Your passion for the Magdalene is electric. So I don't want to discourage you when I say, a majority of the people in America are just not quite ready to open up to Mary Magdalene the way you have. But be vigilant."

"Why? What do you mean?"

"Be vigilant. Be vigilant against dangers. Be vigilant against the Magdalene's villains, against her vicious betrayers. And, dear, in most cases . . . they won't even know who she is or what she is. Some will, but many won't."

"For good or ill," my father would sermonize to me, "you are a daughter of the Christian Church." And you know what? That's probably the most accurate statement my father has made in respect to who I am as his daughter and my relationship with the Christian Church. I'm remembering the different bishops of the Methodist church, sitting around my mom's Sunday dinner and expounding on Jesus. Similar to Paul, known as St. Paul, these bishops were preaching their own theology, in Jesus' name. They, with their theological degrees, there with my father—who subsequently was to receive his doctorate from Boston University. Yes, we had quite a group discussing the Gospels around the dinner table. Were they preaching Jesus' message of gender equality? No. But probably the most glaring omission, to me, was when they would refer to Jesus as the Bridegroom.

So, stay with me here a second. Be with me at that Sunday dinner way back when, and hear the reasonings I was given. "We think of Jesus as the Shepherd, and we are the sheep." "We think of Jesus as the Vine, and we are the branches." And everybody—drumroll, please. Now I was about eight in 1970, as this last statement was said by a bishop—not a bad guy mind you: a very, very kind man. But being kind doesn't mean that you have any idea what you're spewing. So then he announced the final "truth" in his trilogy: "And last, we think of Jesus as the Bridegroom and the Christian Church as his Bride." Choke, cough, cough, choke. There went my candied sweet potatoes, regurgitated with the sour.

"Excuse me, sir." Through sips of water and a driving force within, I found my voice and looked at this very religious man and said, "Excuse me, but who did you say Jesus married?" And the bishop looked somewhat bewilderedly at my father, and my father jumped into the conversation and answered . . . I must say not so much as *patronizingly,* but with that glazed "I know my Jesus personally" kind of look. He answered, "We see Jesus as the Bridegroom married to the Church," both he and the bishop shaking their heads together in reverence. Oh, jeez, I said, "but who was Jesus' Bride?" And my father answered, "We believe the Christian Church is his Bride." "Well, what about Mary Magdalene?" The church leader looked a little uncomfortable, and I knew I was pushing it—but I couldn't stop. He and my father went into some speech about Mary Magdalene being a sinful woman, a woman of ill repute that got saved and blessed by our Lord and Savior Jesus Christ. Then she faded into the background as if she were just one of Jesus' many followers.

What they were saying kind of reminded me of a picture I had seen of young women fainting over male rock stars. And freeze frame. Take that picture. In that moment, I realized that my Mary had been minimalized by The Patriarchy. I realized that I knew that she truly was the Lost Bride. They were working just too hard to convince me otherwise. . . . Whatever I realized on that brutal Sunday back in 1970, I also realized that I was in a small minority that believed that the Magdalene was a sacred and important piece to the emancipation of Christian women. I had been born a feminist, but that day I knew I had to take the next leap. I know now that my avatar all along has been closer to Lisa Simpson than anyone else. Once I understood that, I had to make a huge leap as I had the taste in my mouth of regurgitated, soured candied sweet potatoes. I understood that the Magdalene was very much still in exile—even as women were burning their bras from coast to coast, I burned an idea into my head . . .

What is the sacred prostitute? What is the sensual spirit? The women's mysteries are ancient and preceded the Magdalene by many years. She was someone who walked the walk and integrated her teachings into her Being. . . . The way I understand it, many of Jesus' core teachings, which were uncovered in many of the scriptures found at Nag Hammadi, are really about reuniting the aspects of the Feminine—Wisdom and Consciousness, Sophia and Achamoth— together at the "Cross of Light."

In traditional Christianity the false split gave us two characters: the Virgin Mary and the Magdalene. Of course, within the psyche they must be joined, not polarized for a Christian woman to feel whole. The Virgin Mary has been stripped of her sexuality but has retained her spirituality; the Magdalene has been stripped of her spirituality but has retained her sexuality. Each must have her wholeness. I call this "marrying the two Marys."

There are so many people who come to my shows with this division in them. It seems that you can't be thought of as a Divine Mother type and have the respect of those around you if you're also the sacred prostitute. We divide and conquer on the deepest of levels, by cutting off our own spiritual Being from our own physical Being. Talk about painful. I lived it myself at one point. To have sex, I had to take on a character, because I couldn't be the me that I know and look at in the mirror and express all the different things I wanted to. Basically I didn't know how to "*do* what I just did under the covers" and then turn around and pick up my glasses and books and go to the library as the same person. I am both of those creatures; they are one person; but it was proving difficult to gather all those pieces and have them live together as one integrated Being. And, of course, I see it in the world all the time—the men go to the mistress and then to the wife. And the wife gets resentful because she is not allowed to experience or express that overtly sexual side of herself, and then the mistress gets vindictive because she doesn't get Christmas or Easter.

The piano is the bridge that resolves these elements. Music has an alchemical quality. And there's more than one voice on the piano. You have two hands. One can be playing a celestial melody while the other is doing quite the opposite. The joining of the profane and the sacred, or the passionate and the compassionate, happens right there on the keyboard. It reconciles a bond severed a long time ago. There's so much shame around passion's innate hunger, which sometimes can be deemed profane, but music can access its reality; that which has been sacred but has been severed.

That is what the sacred prostitutes understood. Termed the Hierodulae, these priestesses of the love goddess—whether you are calling her Inanna or Ashera or whomever—these sacred women knew how to transmute the sexually profane. Do I know how they did this? No. But I was taught that these sacred prostitutes could not have transmuted anything if they had "taken on" or become the sexual projection of the male whose company they were sharing. That would mean that they had *gnosis* of how to balance the sacred and the profane. They had an understanding of the sexuality that lives in the unconscious, which if not pruned and nurtured will take over a person's garden and choke all growth. Wasteland. Game over. Next player.

Sometimes, it seems, we're all looking for something outside ourselves because there's been this rejection of a piece of our consciousness. Mistakes can be made when taking on this division. A lot of people will say that they channel the Magdalene, but then they take the sacred into the realm of the profane and leave it there. I was taught that when you're working with archetypes you have to remem-

ber that you are connecting with an essence much older than yourself, whose character you must respect. We are not those creatures.
We each have a pattern inside. You can see when Aphrodite is working
through certain people. It's an aphrodisiac simply when they walk
into the room. You smell it in them. And it's not something they
learn. This is core, this is within. And you can't dissect it or examine a
blood sample. But if you're using this stuff and you don't integrate its
lessons and transform yourself the way the original myths described,
it can become quite a destructive situation. Passion's hunger can become addictive and abusive. That was something that took me many
years to learn.

If you walk down that road, then you must define the role of the sacred prostitute. You're walking into an arena where women do not
take on the projected image the men have of them during sex. Whoever the man wants to think this woman is, that is not at all who the
sacred prostitute is for one second. They know who they are. And
they have integrated this and owned this concept in their bodies,
without even a mortgage to pay. They own it. They had to do the work
to achieve this ownership.

I know that today there are women who have taken on the title of
sacred prostitute and are trying to walk that path. But what we're talking about occurred at a time when these women weren't called prostitutes: they were the Hierodulae, or the Sacred Women. Their role was
revered, and they trained their whole lives. They were initiated.

There have been many other performers brought up by very religious parents, and then when they are able to own this essence and
put it into their music, the sensual-sexual thing that they were not allowed to acknowledge and partake of in real life actually materializes
in the music. If anybody knew you were consciously partaking of the
sensual-sexual thing, you'd be ostracized. You would be thought of as
sinful. Elvis went through something like this, if you think about it.
Trace the roots of American popular culture, and the story is there.

With *Little Earthquakes* I started to face down the split between the
Marys, both personally and in the larger sense. I continued to explore
it during the *Under the Pink* phase. I think taking on the role of Ms.
God, or God's lover in the song I wrote called "God" (from *Under the*

Pink) was a big step for me personally in reuniting the two Marys within my Being. I began to realize that I needed the voices of both Marys to hold an anchor for the Mrs. God archetype I was to embody in order to sing this song. I'll ask myself the question that other people have asked me over the years: "Define which God, Tori. Which God is the God in the song 'God'? Do you mean God, God?" And my answer is "It depends on who you think God, God is."

In *The Gnostic Gospels,* Elaine Pagels writes,

> According to the Hypostasis of the Archons, discovered at Nag Hammadi, both the mother and her daughter objected when "he became arrogant, saying 'It is I who am God, and there is not other apart from me.' . . . And a voice came forth from above the realm of absolute power, saying, 'You are wrong, Samael' [which means, "god of the blind"]. And he said, 'If any other thing exists before me, let it appear to me!' And immediately, Sophia ("Wisdom") stretched forth her finger, and introduced light into matter, and she followed it down into the region of Chaos. . . . And he again said to his offspring, 'It is I who am the God of All.' And Life, the daughter of Wisdom, cried out; she said to him, 'You are wrong Saklas!'"

So to answer the question, this is the God to whom I refer in the song "God." I am not referring to Jesus' Divine Father termed the "holy Parent, the completely perfect Forethought, the image of the Invisible One, that is, the Father of everything, through him everything came into being, the first Humanity," again from Meyers. In this translation Jesus frequently refers to himself as "the Child of Humanity."

The beehive, formed of hexagons, was foundational for the visual piece of *The Beekeeper*. Once it was clear that we were working within the structure that was made of six sides, I began to subdivide the album into six segments. A large subtext of *The Beekeeper* is the garden, though our version of "the Garden of Original Sin" metamorphoses into "the Garden of Original Sin-suality." Our garden is made up of "the archetypal symbols for male and female, the V chalice and the Λ (blade)" (as mentioned by Starbird in her book, *Magdalene's Lost Legacy*). She goes on to say, "This feminine association of bees was known and honored in ancient times: priestesses of the goddess

Artemis were called melissae, and Demeter was called 'the pure Mother Bee.' In Hebrew the name of Deborah, one of the great Old Testament heroines, means 'queen bee.'"

Our sonic garden for *The Beekeeper* is made up of Desert Garden, Rock Garden, The Orchard, the Greenhouse, Elixirs and Herbs, and Roses and Thorns. This is where the story of original Sin-suality between male and female takes place.

"Marys of the Sea" was also inspired by the Gospel of Mary Magdalene translated from the Coptic with commentary by Jean-Yves Leloup. This Gospel sheds a lot of light on the inner relationship of the disciples. Peter's envy of Mary Magdalene is obvious when, in this Gospel, Mary is recounting what Jesus (the Teacher) had taught her in private. When she was finished, after Andrew (Peter's brother) expressed that he did not believe the Teacher had spoken these ideas, ". . . And Peter added: 'How is it possible that the Teacher talked in this manner with a woman, about secrets of which we ourselves are ignorant? Must we change our customs, and listen to this woman? Did he really choose her, and prefer her to us?' "

After Jean-Yves Leloup's explanation of this quote, which expanded my perception of this, the Gospel continues, "Then Mary wept, and answered him: 'My Brother Peter, what can you be thinking? Do you believe that this is just my own imagination, that I invented this vision? Or do you believe that I would lie about our Teacher?'"

In that moment it becomes crystal clear that this is a woman who just cannot win. She cannot win in history, as she has been relegated to her position as prostitute. She cannot win with her contemporaries, many of whom are disciples, because they are filled with jealousy over her intimacy with Yeshua or Jesus (the Teacher).

I have chosen to highlight Jesus and Mary Magdalene's intimacy in the song "Marys of the Sea." I was partially inspired to do this by a quote from the Gospel of Philip (59.9), which I quote here from Jean-Yves Leloup's introduction in the Gospel of Mary Magdalene: "With regard to the unique and particular nature of his relationship with Mary Magdalene, the Gospel of Philip insists, for example, that Mary is the special companion of Jesus (*koinonos*) . . . 'The Lord loved Mary more than all the disciples, and often used to kiss her on the mouth. When the others saw how he loved Mary, they said, "Why do you love her more than you love us?"' The Savior answered in this way: "How can it be that I do not love you as much as I love her?"

In the beginning I knew that the Magdalene was my teacher. But I couldn't get the information and I didn't know the walk. I didn't know how to do it. So you're casting your lines of questions into what seems a silent, visionless sea, and you know you're stupid because the sea can't be visionless. You're looking for signs all the time . . . but what do they look like? So there you go again, casting your line, looking for little signs. But do you need X-ray vision to even see them? Well, first of all, I had to re-define the clichéd term *freedom for women*. I've heard women who do X-rated movies say that they're liberated. That's their right. In a way, it's not different from the way I was approaching sexuality at the beginning of my career. But when a woman is being defecated on emotionally or physically, then we are up to our necks in the Profane, with Sacred nowhere near that casting call. The whole sensuality is gone. It's the brutality of power at its cruelest. We've missed what it's supposed to be about, which is the ecstasy, the coming together. Sex becomes about one person being the subject of somebody else's power, which so often is what Religion is about, too. I've never quite figured out if Sex is in Religion's harem or if Religion is in Sex's harem.

I've asked myself, *Is there a way to reach orgasm and keep your spirituality intact?* To me that is the orgasm of all orgasms, which is what I think I'm experiencing in performance. Not literally, but in an artistic sense. And what you ultimately want is to experience this when you join with your man or your physical counterpart.

Today I feel as if I walk a line of Mommy and the Sacred Prostitute. It's funny—because of where we live, [my daughter] Tash is going to a Christian school. She comes home with ideas about God. She said to me just the other day, "Mummy, do you believe in God?" And my instinct was to ask her, "Do you mean the God behind God?" And you know what I did? I said to myself, "Jeez, T, back off, she's only three and a half. This is your point of view, not necessarily hers." She says she wants to pray. So when I see that what Tash really wants to do is to just hold hands and say grace, "Let's go, I say, let's bless everything." And we do. She prays for absolutely everybody—dogs, children, mermaids, God, Mrs. God—literally everybody. We're also weaving in dear Mother Earth; she prays to her as well. She understands Baby Jesus and she understands there's God, but she understands there's a Mother, which hopefully for her will be the two Marys united. Since the two Marys have never been subjugated or divided with Tash's Being, then it makes sense that the two Marys were born married in Tash's little world. Mother Earth is sovereign. Mother Earth has awakened her daughters.

The Willing Secret

BY KI LONGFELLOW

Mary Magdalene affects people on all ends of the creative spectrum. Artists paint her; singers vocalize her faith, her great passion, her tarnished reputation. And, of course, writers write about her. It goes without saying that she makes good fiction. But more than simply a character or even a muse, Mary Magdalene seems for many a way to "come home." She is a means of integrating the creative and the spiritual in a way that fulfills on both counts—for the creator as much as his or her intended audience.

Ki Longfellow is one such author, whose painstakingly researched work, *The Secret Magdalene,* imagines Mary as a real woman, complete with joys and longings, great intelligence, and even a sense of humor. In addition to being a real woman, Longfellow hypothesizes that "Mariamne Magdale-eder" was a philosopher, teacher, prophet, and beyond: she "knew the all," a concept at the heart of Gnostic teaching.

A writer all her life, Longfellow believes that only when she began to write about Mary Magdalene did she fully realize her art and all of its implications. Like many who incorporate the Magdalene into their creative endeavors, she became consumed by her, feeling her emotions and relishing her wisdom and eloquence as she wrote. As she tells us here, Longfellow's experience in writing *The Secret Magdalene* became much more than an exercise in creative fiction. In many ways, it provided her own personal *gnosis.*

I wrote my first "book" at the age of four—eight whole pages, illustrated. So I think I can say I've spent my whole life honing my craft. Quite seriously, I also think I've spent my life preparing to write *The Secret Magdalene.*

Before the Magdalene, my first novels were arrows aimed at the usual targets: a taste of literary success, perhaps a little financial reward . . . enough at least to earn my living by what talent I had. And while I was interested in the tales I told—often amused, even at times excited by them—they were not dear to me. It was only when I found, mysteriously and inexplicably, the desire to devise my own version of the woman called Mary Magdalene that a story sprang from my own true heart.

And yet, I'm not even sure I wrote *The Secret Magdalene.* Not entirely. The voice of Mary Magdalene (called by the novelistic me "Mariamne Magdal-eder") is hers. Of course, all novelists find the characters they write about gradually taking on a life of their own, acting and speaking in ways that perhaps weren't originally intended by their author. In *The Secret Magdalene,* though, it felt as if things went a little further than this. Some sense of the Magdalene seemed to flow through me, forming on the pages fully clothed in magic, majesty, and wisdom. Day after day, listening to her unique voice quietly speaking in my head, the book came alive. I began to look forward to our daily "conversation." She started to surprise me. She said unexpected things so beautifully and so simply, I often stopped writing just to savor what had appeared on my screen. She became more than voiced thought; I felt her. I experienced reverie when she did, came over all giddy when she did, burned with curiosity when she did, grew fearful when she did. I came to admire her. She became my muse. Her wit, her intelligence, her vast learning, her ultimate lack of vanity, her sometimes foolishness, her despair and her hopelessness, and finally, her great gallantry as she lived a life few could withstand. At some point, I'm not sure when, I realized she'd chosen me, for I surely did not craft her. I never felt I was giving her as a gift to the world, but rather as if she gave herself as a gift to me.

I now strongly suspect that all I've ever done—all the writing, all the traveling, the long years of learning, all the important people in my life—are magical components of the ultimate reason for my artistic existence as Ki Longfellow: to write *The Secret Magdalene.*

Let me explain what I mean by "my own true heart." As a young girl, I experienced a moment of *gnosis.* Spontaneous, seemingly unsought . . . but there it was. So many things can cause sudden rapture. In my case it was beauty, a sense of beauty that swept through my mind and all of my senses, opening me to the bliss of the perfect, safe, and utterly loving cosmos. And I have never "recovered." Before this moment, I'd had intimations, understood Tennyson's more than thrilling line ". . . but trailing clouds of glory do we come." I'd sailed in little arks of awe. After this moment, I was not who I'd been. I am not saying I lost my mind, or that I lost my sense of self. I am very definitely not saying I became perfect, or even better. What I'm saying is that I gained a spiritual perspective that allows me to this day to find joy, even solace, in what seems, but is not, ordinary "reality." There is nothing ordinary about reality.

Gnosis has been called many things: Silent Intoxication, Cosmic Consciousness, Godsight. William Blake named it "Jerusalem." Walt Whitman, the "Body Electric." By Emily Dickinson it was called . . . oh, by Emily, as many names as she wrote poems, but mainly, I think, "Eternity." As for Jesus, he called it "the Kingdom of God." No one is lost and no one in need of being found. It is *gnosis* that is lost and *gnosis* that needs finding.

I am a storyteller, who had, to some degree, mastered her craft. As a storyteller, I could think of no better way to rediscover "Jerusalem" than through Mary Magdalene, she whom the Gnostic Gospels called "the Woman Who Knew the All."

But first I had to find her, and remove the pious paint of seventeen hundred years from her sorrowing face.

It took me seven years.

The Magdalene's is an ancient story, one told by the early Gnostics, and before them the Egyptians, and before them the Sumerians. Like all great stories, it asks eternal questions. "Who are we?" "Why are we here?" "Where is *here?*" And, "What happens to us when we die?" These are surely the very first questions asked by the very first humans gazing up at the ancient stars.

Because the Magdalene's is a universal story of the guiding myths of our lives, I wove the tale of Sophia, who is Wisdom, in and out of the Synoptic Gospel stories, always seeking a way to allow my Mariamne to speak. And over and under and all around the voice of the Magdalene, there is my story told as well. There is much of myself in the young Mariamne: my own youthful enthusiasm for philosophy and mysteries. When Mariamne and her childhood friend Salome surprise themselves with real magic and their own native psychic abilities while playing at spells and potions, they are exhibiting a bit of my own experience and fulfilling my own love of mystery and magic. When they race through the Great Alexandrian Library, I race with them. When Mariamne sulks over slights, delights in some new thing learned, despairs of purpose, argues a philosophical concept with someone like Philo Judaeus, is horrified by the man who contained Legions, feels jealousy when Jesus talks to the woman at the well, these are my moments, too. No writer leaves herself out of her work. It's not possible.

As for the actual life of a real Mariamne, she could have been and done a great deal more than we imagine now. All women were not bound to men. All women were not poor and exploited. Mary Magdalene could well have been wealthy. Her wealth could have come to her in a myriad of ways. If she had riches, she could easily have been independent. There was as well no need for her to have been a priestess in order for her to be learned. Books in the form of scrolls were available to those who could afford them. There were many women of means in her time, many women of high intelligence, and some of them chose to travel with and support a host of prophets and holy men as well as their followers. There was no need for the Magdalene to be married to Jesus if she served him in that capacity. But, yes, she could have been his wife. Or she could have been his wisest disciple. She could also have been his teacher. If you dig hard enough, there are scores of brilliant women hidden behind famous males.

I chose to make Mary Magdalene appear as both male and female in *The Secret Magdalene* for many reasons. I did the same for Salome. Circumstance and secrecy required them to be disguised as males. In this way they are allowed to move freely among fellow males as equal protagonists. Living the life of a male causes them to learn what it is to be the other gender so that each might grow in emotional wisdom. Assuming the role of a male also symbolizes the ancient thought that a seeker must become "male" in order to hear the teaching. While male, Mary Magdalene is known as John. While female, she is able to teach Jesus, or Yeshu as he would have been called, his own emotional lessons. When allowed to be female, Mariamne Magdal-eder would be able to relate to him in a sexual way and, at the same time, stand before him on an equal footing once he'd accepted her as "male"— meaning capable of understanding. Salome as Simon could travel with John the Baptist; she could become his favored disciple. And finally, they are both at times male and at times female to promote the simple idea that all humans are both male and female and that neither takes precedence over the other.

The Secret Magdalene is my idea of a *midrash,* new myth made of old, yet sparked throughout with the extraordinary voice of the Magdalene who is my Magdalene, and perhaps very much her own Magdalene, the one revealed in recently discovered ancient writings. I have given up wrestling with this problem. I leave it at the door of Creativity. When we walk through that door, it's no longer who is telling what to whom . . . it's just story, it's art, it's revelation. It's the work that matters.

Over the long years spent researching Jesus Christ and Mary Magdalene, not to mention their times (almost every contributor in the book you now hold in your hands gave in some way to *The Secret Magdalene*), I discovered compelling parallels between the mystery traditions of many ancient cultures and my own personal experience of *gnosis.* This was a revelation that shook me and transformed my story of the Magdalene into a universal myth, a symbol for the search for meaning common to us all. But when I came to read the Gnostic Gospels found in the Egyptian village of Nag Hammadi, I was floored. What I sensed, Mary Magdalene *knew* long before me. What I was trying to say in *The Secret Magdalene,* she had already said. It was here in these once secret codices that I learned she was called "the Woman Who Knew the All." As I sat in front of my books and my papers and my word processor, I hummed with revelation. Mary Magdalene, in some form, in some way, was speaking to me . . . as she no doubt speaks to any who turn a willing ear toward her.

Along with this, I hope I've found in the voice of Mary Magdalene a way to help resurrect the feminine principle in human affairs, and more importantly in spiritual terms, the reestablishment of the Goddess Principle, as it was commonly understood and accepted in ancient times. Again, the meeting of Mariamne and Jesus in *The Secret Magdalene* required her to assume the disguise of a male, John the Less, or John the Beloved Disciple, because in the Jewish culture of that time, a woman would otherwise never have found herself in the private company of an unrelated male. So in that sense, the power of the feminine principle had to be revealed to Jesus, by way of John/ Mariamne. Likewise, my novel, I believe, serves to coax our understanding of the mutuality of the feminine and masculine forces, combining to create a whole truth. The truth of God, or Source, as our Home and birthright, and the feminine principle as the outpouring of source, in the creative play of nature.

Over the course of centuries, Jesus has become God, but the Magdalene a "fallen woman." As we move close now to the dawn of her third millennium, she has also become in more than just popular fiction the "Holy Grail." More than goddess and wise woman, she is being elevated to savior, on par with the Christ. By this, I believe that like Jesus, Mary Magdalene is in danger of becoming beyond human, and therefore beyond our own powers to share in her realization which is *gnosis,* or "knowing the All." Just as Jesus would not be thought God but would have us "know" the god in us, her whole life was lived not to be called Goddess, but so that we might do as she did.

Ultimately, it seems I wrote *The Secret Magdalene* in an attempt to avert this danger. Mary Magdalene knew the All. What she knew, all can know. There must be a reason why she spoke to me, just as she speaks to this one and to that one. In our conversations, it was so clear she wished to teach. All I have done is help in the only way I could. I listened to her.

Mary Magdalene, Superstar

BY KATHLEEN MCGOWAN

Kathleen McGowan's story has the kind of conclusion that most writers can only dream of. After more than two decades spent researching and writing her trilogy, *The Magdalene Line,* McGowan began the process of searching for an agent. Although there was interest, no publishing deal was forthcoming, and she ultimately decided to self-publish the first volume of the trilogy, *The Expected One,* in March 2004.

The book attracted attention almost immediately. It ended up in the hands of a well-known literary agent, leading McGowan to a million-dollar book deal with Simon & Schuster. Meanwhile, the original, self-published version of her book goes for $100 on eBay.

Many novels focusing on their authors' vision of Mary Magdalene have been published in the last twenty years. McGowan's looks like it could become the best known and most widely read—in part because of her talent as a writer, in part because of her personal story, and in part owing to this particular moment when people all over the world and of many faiths have taken a new interest in this historic character about whom we know so little but imagine so much. For McGowan, who in her spare time is developing film and TV versions of her book and personal story, all of the newfound attention is just icing on the cake. Her relationship with Mary Magdalene, which began when she was ten years old, is not about fame and fortune. It's about courage, endurance, faith—and bringing a sense of grace, balance, and truth to the world. Her books, she feels, are, in the end, her contribution to this pursuit.

In this intriguing essay written especially for this book, McGowan tells the story of how Mary Magdalene "grabbed" her when she was ten years old and, after working as a journalist in Belfast, she "followed my heart" and pursued the oral traditions about Mary Magdalene in France and elsewhere in Europe.

I blame Andrew Lloyd Webber and Tim Rice. They started it.

When I was ten years old, my hip and progressive mother packed my older brothers and me into the Ford Falcon station wagon and headed off to see the film version of *Jesus Christ Superstar* in our local movie theater. It was love at first sight for all of us. We stopped at the record store on the way home and bought the vinyl version of the soundtrack—a pricey double album that was a little out of our family budget at the time, but the three of us begged for it until Mom relented.

That summer, we literally wore the grooves out of those records as we played them on our portable stereo. We acted out the entire drama from start to finish as we sang along with the soundtrack and danced around the patio. This ritual occurred literally every day for at least a month. The boys split up the lead roles and fought over who would play Jesus and Judas, but because I was the only girl and there was a solitary female character, that role was mine exclusively. We called it the Summer of Superstar, and I spent every day of July in my tenth year reenacting Mary Magdalene's devotion to Jesus while wrapped in my mother's red poncho. To this day, I do a wicked impersonation of Yvonne Elliman singing "I Don't Know How to Love Him." At that young age, I could never have guessed just what kind of mental and spiritual groundwork had been formed in my consciousness during that Summer of Superstar.

Cut to my late teens as I evolved from fledgling journalism student into idealistic writer and activist. I moved to Europe and immersed myself in the tumultuous politics of Northern Ireland throughout the 1980s. It was during this period that I developed an increasingly skeptical perspective on recorded, and therefore accepted, history. As an eyewitness to dramatic and often violent events, I realized that in every single circumstance the reported version bore virtually no resemblance to what had transpired before my eyes. The recounting of these occurrences in the media was often entirely unrecognizable to me; these documented versions were written through layers of political, social, and personal bias. My youthful idealism was crushed as I realized that the "truth" was lost forever.

Or was it?

I began to feel an overwhelming obligation to question history. With all that I discovered, I realized that I was now on the razor's edge of a potentially radical perspective—that I essentially didn't trust *anything* that had been written down as historical evidence!

So where did that leave me? I was a historian who no longer trusted history, a journalist who believed there were no credible sources available to me in libraries or on microfiche. Where was I going to find the answers I sought?

A family history of storytelling through my maternal Irish lineage led me to the ultimate answer: folklore. It sounds like a quaint and innocuous word, but it is a powerful and highly durable tradition, as ancient as humanity itself. My own experiences in Ireland reinforced my ultimate belief in the importance of the oral and cultural traditions that make up folklore, and why they are often the richest source of understanding we have of the human experience. During my days in Belfast, I interviewed members of secret political societies and members of underground paramilitary groups. The most valuable insight always came from stories that were related by insiders, firsthand accounts that included details of events and traditions that had been passed down from father to son, mother to daughter, for as long as anyone could remember. None of this information can be found in print anywhere. It is preserved solely in the minds of the local residents, for reasons no less immense than those of life and death.

These localized events on the Belfast streets became my microcosm. If they were continually reconstituted and altered by major press, what did this mean when that concept was applied to the macrocosm of world history? Wouldn't the tendency to manipulate the truth become greater and more absolute as we looked further back to the past, to a time when only the very wealthy, highly educated, and politically victorious were able to record events?

As a woman, I wanted to take this idea one step further. Since the dawn of written records, the vast majority of materials that scholars consider academically acceptable have been created by men of a certain social and political status. We believe in the veracity of documents simply because they can be "authenticated" to a specific time period. But carbon dating ink and paper cannot tell us anything about the perspective or potential agenda of the human hand that committed those words to paper. Rarely do we take into account that they were written during darker days when women held less status than livestock, or were even believed to have no souls! How many magnificent stories have been lost to us because the women who starred in them weren't deemed important enough, or even human enough, to merit mention? How many women have been removed completely from history?

Then there are those women who were so powerful and instrumental in world governments that they could not be ignored. Many who did find their place in the history books were remembered as notorious villains—adulteresses, schemers, deceivers, even murderers.

Were those characterizations fair, or were they political propaganda used to discredit women who dared to assert their intelligence and power? Armed with these questions and my escalating sense of mistrust for what has been academically accepted as historical evidence, I set out to research and write a book about infamous women. I called it *Maligned and Misunderstood* and started working with some of history's most notorious ladies, including Marie Antoinette and Lucrezia Borgia.

It was just one of many synchronicities that would change my life when in 1993 as I wrote the book, a revival of the rock opera *Jesus Christ Superstar* arrived in Los Angeles. I simply had to see the show in person, but at the time believed that this was just an act of warm nostalgia. As the actress playing Mary Magdalene took the stage and I sang along to the words I knew so well from my childhood, I realized that on some subconscious level I had been prepared to understand her story some twenty years earlier. As an adult woman, I was suddenly overwhelmed by the power and importance of Mary's legacy. Was it possible that she really was closer to Jesus than any other follower? And yet history preserves her legacy as that of a prostitute and a fallen woman. Was Mary Magdalene the queen of the maligned and misunderstood in history? I was beginning to think so.

I set out to gain a greater awareness of this New Testament enigma in terms of her importance as a follower of Christ. I knew that the reforms of Vatican II had made some effort to correct the injustice of Magdalene's tarnished reputation as it had been first created by Pope Gregory the Great in the sixth century when he conflated her story with that of an unnamed sinner. This was my starting point. But I discovered that the church's explanation, well intentioned though it may have been, was less effective than a retraction at the bottom of page thirty-eight for a story that has been headline news for many years. It became my intention to incorporate Mary Magdalene's story as one of many within the context of an entire body of work that spanned twenty centuries. But Mary Magdalene had a different plan for me, and began to make it known with irresistible force.

I was subsequently haunted by a series of recurring dreams that featured the intertwined lives of Mary Magdalene and Jesus. Unexplainable and often supernatural occurrences led me to investigate re-

search leads that took me to four continents. While I performed my
due diligence and read every historical and academic account I could
get my hands on, I found most of these disappointing. They asked
more questions than they answered, and only left me wanting more. I
followed my heart and my head as I explored the other research av-
enue that had never let me down—oral tradition. My interest in
Mary's folklore turned to obsession as I experienced fascinating ancient cultural traditions that have been preserved with love and a fervent passion throughout western Europe. I was invited into the inner
sanctum of secret societies and met with guardians of information so
sacred that it astonishes me to this day that they, and the information
they protect, exist—and have done so for two thousand years.

The folklore and traditions of Europe also provided new insight
into some of Mary's mysteries, those that have never been explained
in any way that I found palatable through traditional scholarship. A
rich and beautiful version of Mary Magdalene's life story was revealed
to me, one that depicts her clearly as not only the "apostle of the apostles" but as no less than a dynastic queen and the legal wife and
beloved of Jesus Christ. I believe with all of my heart that Mary Magdalene was not only a leader in the early church, but the individual to
whom Jesus entrusted his sacred mission. I tell this story in its en-
tirety, as well as the story of my personal journey of discovery, in my
fact-based novel, *The Expected One*.

Additionally, a treasure trove of information exists for the spiritual
seeker, most written from the second to fourth centuries, that is not
included in the traditional church canon. There are thousands of pages
of material to discover: alternate gospels, Acts of Apostles, and mis-
cellaneous writings that reveal details and insights into the life and
times of Jesus that will be completely new to readers who have never
before looked beyond the four evangelists. I believe that exploring all
of this material, including the folklore and traditions of Europe and
the Middle East, with an open mind and heart will build a bridge of
light and understanding among the many divisions of Christianity, and
beyond.

Fascinating details about the belief in Mary Magdalene's importance
can be found in the great art of the Renaissance and beyond, as great
masters painted her repeatedly. The majority of women in Botticelli's

allegorical paintings—like the expectant goddess at the heart of *Primavera* and the lovely woman in the scallop shell from *Birth of Venus*—are indeed representations of Mary Magdalene. This Mary is the muse of many other masters, including Ghirlandaio, El Greco, Poussin, and even Salvador Dali. She can be found in fairy tales, nursery rhymes ("Mary had a little lamb . . ."), and ancient troubadour songs written in tribute to this most virtuous and sadly unreachable lady. In many ways, the modern rock opera *Jesus Christ Superstar* is a new type of oral tradition—an artistic means of telling an important story through the passion and power of music. Indeed, I have since met with hundreds of fans of the Webber-Rice musical who credit the power of the music with turning them into devoted Christians! And while the portrayal of Magdalene in that modern work perpetuates the unfortunate idea of her as a prostitute, I credit that it also shows her as a woman of enduring faith and grace.

There are elements of Mary Magdalene's story as I tell it that cannot be corroborated through any readily acceptable academic sources. They exist as oral traditions and have been preserved in highly protected environments by those who have feared repercussions for centuries. My personal experience years earlier in Belfast helped me to understand the mindset of a culture that does not commit its beliefs to writing because to do so would only lead to persecution, arrest, and even death. The ancient followers of Mary Magdalene, known as the Cathars, lived with the fear of such retaliation, and for good reason: they were hunted down by the medieval church, brutally tortured and executed in the most horrific ways. Over a million people were massacred in the south of France for their "heretical" belief in the role of Mary Magdalene as the wife of Jesus and subsequently as the true spiritual founder of Christianity in the Western world. The Cathar people learned through unimaginable hardship that the only way to survive would be to keep their knowledge and traditions highly protected and secretive. They remain so to this day, where secret societies quietly preserve the pure faith of their people—the teachings of Jesus as they were brought to Europe by his beloved spiritual partner.

Through my years of research, I have discussed, questioned, argued, and even conceded many points with clerics and believers from a number of faiths. I am blessed to have friends and associates from many spiritual arenas, including Catholic priests, Lutheran ministers, Gnostic practitioners, and pagan priestesses. In Israel, I encountered Jewish scholars and mystics, as well as Orthodox guardians of Christianity's sacred sites. My father is a Baptist, my husband a devout Catholic, my mother a descendant of Ireland's most ancient traditions of goddess and nature worship. All of these individuals are a part of the mosaic of my belief system. Despite the myriad differences in their philosophies, each of these people blessed me with the same gift: the ability to exchange ideas and engage in dialogue freely and without anger.

And that is, for me, the essence of Mary Magdalene's story. She has taught me so much about courage, endurance, and faith over these years of exploration. I have found that Mary's message is one of love, tolerance, forgiveness, and personal accountability. It is a message of unity and nonjudgment for all people of all belief systems. It is my greatest joy that the consciousness of the world is being challenged and raised through the revival of Mary Magdalene's true story. It is her time to shine now, by returning us as humans to a state of grace and balance through her wisdom.

And that's where you'll find me if you'd care to join me as a pilgrim on the path of seeking and understanding, as one who wants desperately to learn how to create heaven on earth in the way that Jesus and Mary intended to teach us. I'm easy to spot—I'll be wearing red and singing along to the soundtrack of *Jesus Christ Superstar*.

9 Thoroughly Modern Mary

A Magdalene for the Twenty-first Century

If Jesus could entrust a woman to proclaim the greatest news of all, the Good News, why can women not preach homily in a Catholic Church today?

—BARBARA GRANTS, FutureChurch

I have found that Mary's message is one of love, tolerance, forgiveness, and personal accountability. It is a message of unity and nonjudgment for all people of all belief systems. It is my greatest joy that the consciousness of the world is being challenged and raised through the revival of Mary Magdalene's true story. It is her time to shine now, by returning us as humans to a state of grace and balance through her wisdom.

—KATHLEEN McGOWAN

Mary Magdalene for this time is a call-to-action figure. Like a Tina Turner or a Dixie Chick, it means get off your butt and vote; for making a difference in the time you live.

—JANE SCHABERG

Mary Magdalene's Spiritual Quest

BY DEIRDRE GOOD

As this essay makes clear, Deirdre Good's connection to Mary Magdalene is at once professional and intensely personal. At the professional level, one can hear the voice of one of the world's wisest scholars on Mary Magdalene and early Christian belief and experience. She does her research in the original Coptic, Aramaic, and other biblical languages and is a professor of the New Testament at the General Theological Seminary. This has led Good to believe that Mary Magdalene's spiritual vision provides a template for an intimate connection with Jesus, transcending death, time, and space. On a personal level, she says that for her, Mary Magdalene embodies a comforting and encouraging presence in the face of despair, the "only presence from which hope springs."

For both these professional and personal perspectives, Deirdre Good is in great demand as a teacher, lecturer, and commentator, with numerous media appearances to her credit. She also has edited *Mariam, the Magdalen, and the Mother,* a book comprising essays that come out of the academic and biblical scholar communities. Her most recent book is *Jesus' Family Values.* As contributing editor to *Secrets of Mary Magdalene,* Deirdre Good lent not only her expertise, but also this essay, which reflects her conviction that readers should have a sense of what Mary Magdalene stands for beyond the headline-grabbing controversies.

At the heart of the story of Mary Magdalene stands her encounter with the risen Jesus. When they meet in the garden, she becomes a witness to Jesus' Resurrection. As first witness to this good news, she preaches to the apostles and earns the designation "apostle to the apostles." But how and why she alone met Jesus, and what their exchange has meant and might mean merits investigation.

Few in antiquity, including disciples of Jesus, thought women capable of perception of any kind, let alone of one raised from the dead. Thus, Mary Magdalene's witness to the Resurrection reported in the gospels raises questions about anthropology and gender, namely, who perceives what and how can it be apprehended? What were (and are) ways by which women and men engage and recognize a resurrected Jesus? And finally, I will explore the way Christian tradition has understood the encounter between Mary and Jesus to convey a central idea of resurrection: that God's gift of risen life is expressed in recreating a bond between people. To make resurrection real and (re)establish their relationship, Mary Magdalene and Jesus must reach toward each other across death and through time and space. Resurrection is about human ties.

Seeing, Perceiving, Touching, and Hearing

First, I want to survey ways different sources emphasize different perceptions. How did Mary Magdalene apprehend the resurrected Jesus? Is the gift of perception hers and hers alone, or did others emulate it? Does she have a particular way of perceiving? Gospel writers, artists, musicians, and theologians suggest that through sight, perception, touch, and hearing Mary Magdalene engages the risen Jesus. In the New Testament Gospel of Matthew, two women apprehend Jesus' Resurrection through sight, hearing, and touch. On their way to announce news of the Resurrection, Jesus meets and greets them. Mary Magdalene and the other Mary stop, touch the feet of the risen Jesus, and worship him. They are told to tell the other disciples that they will see Jesus in Galilee. It is through the senses of sight and touch that resurrection is apprehended. Sight and touch lead to worship.

The Gospel of John goes one stage further. It makes much of Mary's recognition of Jesus through hearing rather than sight or touch. When Mary first sees Jesus, she thinks it is the gardener and she speaks to him as such. Sight is deceiving. Only when the risen Jesus speaks her name does she hear and turn in recognition of the voice. But she announces good news to the disciples by saying, "I have seen the Lord!" Of course, the "seeing" she speaks of could encompass perceiving and include hearing. So John's gospel describes Mary's apprehension of the Resurrection by means of sound and corrected vision.

In the same gospel, Jesus will soon appear to Thomas in order to address Thomas's demands for sight and touch: "Unless I see the mark of the nails in his hands and put my finger in the mark of the nails, and my hand in his side I will not believe!" he declares. See and touch me, Jesus says to Thomas when appearing to him. But Jesus adds a caveat, "Have you believed because you have seen me? Blessed are those who have not seen, and have yet come to believe." Sight and touch have their place and their limitations, Jesus infers. In the presence of Thomas, Jesus commends those whose perception of resurrection goes beyond Matthew's preference for sight and touch to encompass faith based not on sight and touch alone, but also through hearing.

Later artistic and musical renditions of the encounter between Mary and Jesus in the garden by the empty tomb emphasize both visual and aural aspects of their meeting. Such interpreters seek to render resurrection physically. In paintings, Mary looks at Jesus. She may be extending her hand toward him. He may be seen in grave clothes or as the gardener. One hand may hold a gardening implement. Another may be rendering the words "Do not touch me!" However, the closeness of these two figures links them together in strange contrast to Jesus' prohibition.

The well-known hymn "In the Garden" renders this scene musically. C. Austin Miles, its composer, relates how he came to write it: One day in March 1912, he opened his Bible to John 20 and seemed to become part of the scene in which Mary kneels before Jesus, crying "Rabboni" in recognition.

> As the light faded, I seemed to be standing at the entrance of a garden, looking down a gently winding path, shaded by olive branches. A woman in white, with head bowed, hand clasping her throat, as if to choke back her sobs, walked slowly into the shadows. It was Mary. As she came to the tomb, upon which she placed her hand, she bent over to look in, and hurried away. John, in flowing robe, appeared, looking at the tomb; then came Peter, who entered the tomb, followed slowly by John. As they departed, Mary reappeared; leaning her head upon her arm at the tomb, she wept. Turning herself, she saw Jesus standing, so did I. I knew it was He. She knelt before Him, with arms outstretched and looking into His face cried "Rabboni!"[1]

Miles continues that under the inspiration of this vision, he wrote the poem as quickly as he could and then later that same evening, the music for the hymn.

---

1. Cited in *Simple Gifts: Great Hymns: One Man's Search for Grace,* by Bill Henderson.

In the Garden

I come to the garden alone,
While the dew is still on the roses;
And the voice I hear, falling on my ear,
The Son of God discloses.
Refrain
   And He walks with me,
   And He talks with me,
   And He tells me I am His own;
   And the joy we share as we tarry there,
   None other has ever known.

He speaks, and the sound of His voice
Is so sweet, the birds hush their singing,
And the melody that He gave to me,
Within my heart is ringing.
Refrain

I'd stay in the garden with Him,
Though the night around me be falling,
But He bids me go; through the voice of woe,
His voice to me is calling.
Refrain

Many people know and sing this favorite hymn without recognizing its connection to Mary Magdalene. It gives collective voice to Magdalene in the role of every believer after the death of Jesus; that its language and sentiment are erotic and powerful.

In its recognition of the limitations of sight and touch, John's gospel helps readers deal with the physical absence of Jesus for first-century readers. At the same time, neither sight, sound, or touch are ignored or disparaged in the gospel: to Mary Jesus speaks so that he might be heard, and to Thomas Jesus appears so that he may be touched. Yet Jesus in the end commends faith that has not seen but yet believes. Is he praising those whose faith is grounded on something less aural and less tangible? By appearing to Mary Magdalene and

Thomas, John's gospel seems to acknowledge that faith longs for something aural and tangible. Artistic and musical interpreters of this scene have understood this longing.

Mary's vision of the resurrected Jesus as reported in the Gospel of Mary is apprehended through her mind. What we have of the gospel opens with Mary comforting the distressed disciples through words of consolation. The disciples then begin to discuss words of the Savior. Peter implores Mary to relate for the other disciples words of the Savior that she alone has heard. What she tells them is her vision of a resurrected Jesus. This account begins with her question to Jesus: does one see a vision with the soul or spirit? The Savior replies that it is neither the soul nor spirit but the mind that sees a vision. Jesus says to her, "Blessed are you for not wavering at seeing me for where the mind is, there is the treasure!" In describing and having Jesus praise Mary's rational powers of apprehension, the Gospel of Mary pushes the boundaries. It is rare to find women's powers of rational perception described let alone praised in any text in late antiquity.

Christian interpreters of John 20, probably unaware of the Gospel of Mary, went on to ask why it was women, among them the Magdalene, who encountered Jesus. This is a question about gender and the modes of perception of which women were thought to be capable. The theologian Aquinas, for example, suggests that it was women's supposedly greater capacity for love shown in their fidelity to Jesus at the Crucifixion and their early presence on Easter morning that will guarantee them, he says, a quicker share than men in the beatific vision. Aquinas thinks more highly of love than intellectual apprehension. This is a different value judgment. Perhaps Aquinas thought women more capable of greater love.

Different Gospels, Different Witnesses

Reports of the encounter between Jesus and Mary Magdalene found in the longer ending of Mark, in John's gospel, and also in the Gospel of Mary. In the Gospel of Matthew, as we have seen, two women, one of whom is Mary Magdalene, meet the resurrected Jesus. In Luke, several women interpret the empty tomb to mean the realization of

Jesus' prediction of crucifixion and resurrection that they announce to the apostles. But they do not see a risen Jesus.

According to an ending added to Mark, the oldest gospel, and John, the last of the four New Testament gospels to be written, Jesus appeared first to Mary Magdalene and then to others including the eleven disciples. In the addition to Mark, Mary Magdalene is identified as one from whom Jesus cast out seven demons. Her report is met with disbelief. In Luke, on the other hand, several women including Mary Magdalene bring spices to the tomb to anoint Jesus' body. In Matthew, Mary Magdalene and the other Mary go to see the tomb. There is no mention of spices. An angel of the Lord meets them there with the news that Jesus has been raised. On their way to tell the other disciples this news, Jesus met them and spoke to them. They grasped his feet and worshipped him. Jesus commissions them to tell "my brothers" to go to Galilee where they will see him. In Luke's gospel, the apostles to whom they relate news of the empty tomb disbelieve the women.

Each gospel account of the women's visit to the empty tomb emphasizes elements that are consonant with that particular gospel. The silence of the women at the empty tomb in Mark's gospel: "They said nothing to anyone for they were afraid" is a response to the numinous mirrored in Peter's reaction to the transfiguration of Jesus in Mark 9:6, "For they were afraid." Silence in Mark is the appropriate response to a manifestation of the divine, not a description of mute women failing to proclaim the Resurrection.

In Matthew's gospel, the fear of the women is linked with "great joy," an emotion that Matthew links to an epiphany or manifestation of the divine, as we see in the description of the Mages finding the place over which the star rested in 2:10, namely the place of Jesus' birth: "[the Mages] were overwhelmed with joy." Joy lends Mary Magdalene and the other Mary wings to tell the good news to the other disciples. The next action of both the women at the empty tomb and the Mages at Jesus' birth is to worship Jesus. Matthew describes the right human reaction to the divine: fear and joy followed by worship. This is a transformation of Mark's simple fear. It is not necessarily a description of what happened when the women went to the empty tomb.

The focus of Luke's Resurrection account, on the other hand, is on

men who heard the report of the empty tomb by women but who dis-
believed the women's account and could not construe its meaning. Jesus criticizes their limited understanding but attends to it carefully:
"O foolish men and slow of heart to believe all that the prophets have
declared! Was it not necessary that the messiah should suffer these
things and then enter into his glory? Then beginning with Moses and
all the prophets, he interpreted to them the things about himself in all
the scriptures." To a group of frightened disciples, Jesus seems to be a
ghost. Addressing their fears, Jesus encourages the disciples to look at
his hands and feet and touch him for, he says, a ghost does not have
flesh and bones as you see that I have. Having looked, the text goes on
to report that in their joy the disciples were disbelieving and still
wondering. So he eats a piece of broiled fish in their presence. Luke's
focus on shifting male understanding from disbelief of the women's
report to joyous disbelief to belief is accomplished by moving through
sight to touch to watching Jesus eat. An emphasis on eating is consonant with a gospel in which Jesus is born in an animals' feeding trough
or "manger" and in which Jesus is customarily found eating with tax
collectors, sinners, and many others throughout his ministry. It is the
means by which a connection to the earthly Jesus is reestablished and
by which the early Jerusalem community in Acts, the second volume
of Luke, will gather together in temple and homes for the breaking of
bread and prayers.

Why does John emphasize hearing as a way to perceive the resur-
rected Jesus in appearing to Mary Magdalene in John 20? Why does
John disparage sight as a mode of recognition when Jesus says to
Thomas in John 20:29, "Have you believed because you have seen me?
Blessed are those who have not seen and yet have come to believe."
Belief trumps sight and touch in John's gospel. A resurrected Jesus
may offer a breakfast of fish and bread to Simon Peter in John 21 but
he does not eat it himself. But nowhere is hearing disparaged.

John's emphasis on hearing as perception and hearing leading to
sight recalls ancient theories of sight contrasted to sound. Vision, as
Plato argues in several places, may be "the sharpest of our bodily
senses" (*Phaedrus* 250d) because it supposedly gives readiest access to
immaterial ideas through the comparatively pure medium of fire/
light (*Timaeus* 45), but hearing depends on a thoroughly material

medium, air, in which speaker and listener are both immersed. Seeing preserves separation between the object of sight on the part of the viewer and the subject doing the viewing, while hearing, on the other hand, calls into question a distinction between subject and object. When we hear sound, our logical minds may be bracketing off certain sounds as parts of speech and distinguishing them one from another, but all the while the ears are hearing the range of sounds in between. In a given word we hear the possibilities of other words that are almost present in the sounds of that word. What seems to be happening is, in effect, an echo that attends each word in a script and undoes the seeming fixity of sounded words.

John's gospel of course emphasizes sound and hearing for theological reasons.

The gospel's opening words evoke Genesis: In the beginning was the word, i.e., sound. The gospel describes Jesus as the word of God. To explain Mary's audible recognition of Jesus in John 20, many people quote Jesus' earlier words in the gospel describing sheep that know and respond only to the voice of the shepherd: "When (the shepherd) has brought out all his own, he goes before them, and the sheep follow him, for they know his voice. A stranger they will not follow, but they will flee from him, for they do not know the voice of strangers."

Jesus' words in John are clear but their meaning is not: they are often opaque. I find it helpful to recall Norman Peterson's reminder that only Jesus and the narrator know what's going on in John's gospel. Sometimes the narrator puts readers in the picture. This is the case here when the narrator of the encounter between Jesus and Mary in John 20 discloses the identity of the gardener to the reader *before* the gardener is recognized by Mary. Responding to the angels' question "Woman, why are you weeping?" she explains, "Because they have taken away my Lord, and I do not know where they have laid him." (John 20:14). Saying this, she turned round and saw Jesus standing, *but she did not know that it was Jesus.* Thanks to the narrator, the reader or hearer of the narrator's words knows what Mary does not. But Mary is not necessarily disadvantaged. We could instead say that the readers or hearers now can hear an acoustic echo behind anything the gardener says. It is like listening to Jesus in Bach's *St. Matthew Passion:*

before Jesus opens his mouth, violins create a halo effect around everything he says. Whatever is said, the listener knows to pay attention to the words because of the violins. You don't even have to hear what he says, you just know its Jesus about to speak. Now when "the gardener" speaks, the reader or hearer of John's gospel is in a position to anticipate that something more than gardening advice is being given. What we will hear is the voice of Jesus. We know and can anticipate Mary's recognition.

Jesus speaks to her in Greek: "Woman, why are you weeping? Whom do you seek?" To these questions she responds as if to the gardener: "Sir, if you have borne him away tell me where you have laid him and I will take him." She does not recognize the voice or the words but readers of John do. The gardener's second question, "Whom do you seek?" is surrounded by Bach's violins. It recalls the first words of Jesus in the gospel to disciples of John the Baptist: "What are you looking for?" This is not a simple inquiry. What they are seeking is in fact Jesus, identified by John the Baptist himself as Messiah. John's disciples leave him and follow Jesus.

Now, the hearers or readers of John and the gardener may be communicating but the woman and Jesus are not. This is the point at which John uses dialogue to facilitate revelation. John has done this throughout the gospel. The best example of this is in the dialogue Jesus has with the Samaritan woman at the well in John 4. Dialogue in the ancient world is an exchange in which gradual enlightenment takes place. Dialogue in John, on the other hand, is a means by which Jesus engages someone in conversation about the deeper meaning of ordinary things, like "who your husband is" (with the Samaritan woman) or "whom do you seek?" (with the woman in the garden). Readers knowing this kind of Johannine dialogue will appreciate its use here even if the woman in the garden does not. However, since the dialogue is not going anywhere, Jesus tries another language, namely Palestinian Aramaic. He addresses the woman directly: "Mariam!" Now *this* language she hears and understands, "Turning around, that one (f.) says to him in Hebrew 'Rabboni,' which means 'teacher.'"

Recognition takes place when Jesus speaks in a language Mary understands. It is not what he says but how he says it that creates recognition. It seems to me that Jesus' words take even the readers and hearers of John's gospel by surprise. I'm arguing that when they finally do communicate, both he and she are speaking in a different language. English translators try to clarify that he calls her "Mary!" That is their attempt to interpret Jesus' words. What he actually calls out to her is her name in Palestinian Aramaic: Mariam! This is a well-known name today. So what's my point? Listeners are surprised by Jesus' call in spite of the English translations. What seemed to be a hearer's advantage was only temporary. Now, we hear the two of them speaking together in a different language preserved in the Greek of John's gospel. Even if we know who "the gardener" is when he speaks to Mary, we haven't heard him speaking Aramaic in the entire gospel. He doesn't speak Aramaic from the cross and he doesn't use it to work miracles or pray to God as he does in Mark, for example. The exchange "Mariam!" and "Rabbi!" takes the two figures in the garden from our comprehension and leaves them as strangely other even as they communicate together in their language. However, this is entirely appropriate to a gospel in which Jesus' speech is usually opaque to listeners, even if it is the voice of God.

Reports of Mary Magdalene's auditory visions continue in music and story: *The Golden Legend,* a thirteenth-century collection of saints' lives written by the Italian Dominican monk Jacobus de Voragine, gives us an, albeit legendary, detailed description of her background and early character:

> Mary Magdalene is so called because of her connection with the town of Magdalum. She was born of noble parents who indeed were of royal descent. Together with her brother Lazarus and sister Martha she owned Magdalum, a fortified town two miles from Genezareth, Bethany, near Jerusalem, and a large part of Jerusalem itself . . ."

She meets Jesus who "set her all on fire with love for him, made her one of his closest associates, and lovingly defended her on many occasions." After Christ's ascension, she travels to France with her sister Martha and brother Lazarus, where she eventually retires to a life of solitude:

In the meantime blessed Mary Magdalene, wishing to devote herself to heavenly contemplation, withdrew to a barren wilderness where she remained in anonymity for thirty years in a place prepared for her by the hands of angels. In this wilderness there was no water, and there were no trees or grass, nor any comforts of any kind, so that it was clear that our Redeemer had meant to feed her not with earthly foods but with the sweets of heaven alone. Each day at the seven canonical hours she was lifted in the air by angels and actually heard, *with her bodily organs of hearing* [italics added], the glorious harmonies of the celestial chorus. So, filled day by day with this exquisite heavenly fare, she had not the slightest need for bodily nourishment when she was bought back to her cave.

The Voice of the Bridegroom

Another way Christian interpretation understood the core of Mary Magdalene's spiritual vision was to understand her as the bride in the Song of Songs: searching for her beloved, hearing him, finding him, holding him, and not letting him go. This counteracts the command "Do not touch me!" of Jesus to Mary in the gospel. We see examples of Mary Magdalene as the bride of the Song of Songs searching for Jesus from the second century to the late middle ages. It is a particular way of understanding Mary Magdalene's spiritual quest.

In the second century CE, Cyril of Jerusalem gave several baptismal lectures to candidates for Christian baptism. In the fourteenth baptismal lecture, Cyril clearly understands Mary Magdalene to embrace Jesus and that candidates for baptism should want to do the same. Cyril puts quotations from the Song of Songs in the mind and mouth of Mary Magdalene. In Cyril's account, the women of Matthew's gospel appear alongside Mary Magdalene in John:

The Bridegroom and Suitor of souls was sought by those noble and brave women. They came, those blessed ones, to the sepulchre, and sought Him Who had been raised, and the tears were still dropping from their eyes, when they ought rather to have been dancing with joy for Him that had risen. Mary came seeking Him, according to the Gospel, and found Him not: and presently she heard from the Angels, and afterwards saw the Christ. Are then these things also written? He says in the Song of Songs, On my bed I sought Him whom my soul loved. At what season? By night on my bed I sought Him Whom my soul loved: Mary, it says, came while it was yet dark. On my bed I sought Him by night, I sought Him, and I found Him not. And in the Gospels Mary says, They have taken away my Lord, and I know not where they have laid Him.

When the angels asked the women why they sought the living among the dead, Cyril adds:

But she knew not, and in her person the Song of Songs said to the Angels, Saw ye Him Whom my soul loved? It was but a little that I passed from them (that is, from the two Angels), until I found Him Whom my soul loved. I held Him, and would not let Him go.

My second example of this interpretation is from the so-called Biblia Pauperum, or "Bible of the Poor." The origins of this book are unknown but by the late Middle Ages, many examples existed. Reflecting a widespread method of interpreting the Bible by means of typology, in the Bible of the Poor persons, objects, and episodes from the Old Testament were seen to prefigure aspects of Christ's ministry. The book is a bookblock with pictures and text produced by impressions from carved wooden blocks. Between 1460 and 1490, the bookblock was a transitional form of publication leading to book printing by moveable type. Whether the book was really designed to educate the poor or whether it was intended to instruct clergy in their preaching is uncertain. However, printing facilitated spread of the book.

Three panels on a single page depict scenes thought to be typologically interrelated. In the example in Plate 16 we see Christ appearing to Mary Magdalene in the garden in the central panel. This is an interpretation of John 20. Christ holds a garden implement. In the panel to the left we see the king of Babylon visiting Daniel the morning after Daniel had been cast into the lion's den. Discovering Daniel to be alive brought the king great joy. The Latin above the panel continues: "Indeed the king prefigures Mary Magdalene [Latin: *Mariam Magdalenam*] when she went to the tomb. After she saw the Lord, she also rejoiced exceedingly because he rose from the dead."

The panel on the right is entitled "The Daughter of Sion discovers her Spouse." It shows the bride and bridegroom embracing each other. It is a reference to chapter 3 of the Song of Songs. The Latin inscription declares, "We read in the Canticle of Canticles, chapter 3, that when the bride had found her beloved, she said, 'I have found him whom my soul loves; I will hold him and I will not let him go.' This bride prefigures Mary Magdalene who seeing her spouse, that is Christ, wanted to touch Him. Christ responded, 'Do not touch me; I have not yet ascended to my Father.'" The inscriptions under the panel read: "The beloved bride now enjoys the much sought spouse" and "Showing yourself O Christ you console the holy Mary."

In this medieval illustration we see a widespread understanding that the bride in the Song of Songs searching for and finding her beloved prefigures Mary Magdalene in her search for and finding Jesus in the garden. What the bride (Mary Magdalene) says in the Latin scroll above her head (a medieval equivalent of bubble speak) is "I held him and I will not let him go."

These two examples indicate that far from suppressing an understanding of the erotic relationship between Jesus and Mary Magdalene, the church continued to depict it in instructional manuals for believers and in illustrated bibles like the Bible of the Poor. In the encounter between Jesus and Mary Magdalene the example of the bride searching for her beloved explains not only the presence of Mary Magdalene at the tomb in the garden but also the tenacity of her search and the fervor of her grasp. What we see in the embrace of Jesus and Mary Magdalene is a love transcending death.

Thus whether Mary Magdalene sees with sharper insight, hears a voice, perhaps the voice of her beloved, tries to or does touch, Christian tradition shows her quest for Jesus to be a universal one containing deep insight and affection that re-creates across space and time and even death a bond between them. Dan Brown should have looked further!

Separate, Not Equal at All
The Church and Its Goddess Problem

BY ANNA QUINDLEN

There is an important political dimension to the re-evaluation of Mary Magdalene as well as theological, social, and historical ones. Namely that is has given voice to an ever-increasing number of women who are now challenging the hierarchy of their church with this question: If Mary Magdalene was indeed the "apostle of the apostles," the person he "loved" more than his other disciples, and his close "companion," why are women still being marginalized when it comes to leadership in the church?

Anna Quindlen, Pulitzer Prize–winning author, columnist, and a Roman Catholic, joins the *cri de coeur*. In this column written for *Newsweek,* Quindlen points out that, while Jesus seems to have engaged in religious discourse with women throughout his life and after his death—even embracing women, despite the times—doctrinal conservatives in a variety of religions still refuse to do so today. Whether through fear, mistaken piety, or misogyny, women have been left out of the conversation in many still male-dominated religious groups. (The all-male composition of the twelve disciples is still used by the Vatican to exclude women from ordination.)

It is high time, she says, for the Church to embrace modern equality. Quindlen argues that a house divided will not stand, so unless religious conservatives come to terms with—and even appreciate—the female worshipper, they can expect to lose women as followers.

Here is where we begin: with Easter, the holiest day of the Christian calendar, with the visit by Mary Magdalene to the tomb in which Jesus is laid after the Crucifixion. The body is gone, and she runs to find the apostles Peter and John to tell them so. They look, run off, and she remains, distraught. A man approaches; she mistakes him for the gardener.

He says, "Woman, why are you crying?"

The very first word Jesus says after his Resurrection is our name. And perhaps that explains why Roman Catholic women who have been so poorly served by our church refuse to leave. The members of the hierarchy do not engage us in conversation, but their founder did.

You need only look at photographs of the pope and his cardinals to see the essential problem. A phalanx of identicals, the closest they come to daily contact with women is with the nuns who keep house for them. Half the world is out of bounds. The Catholic Church is not alone in this. Many religions have found some way to make women both apart and less, either by turning them into near occasions of sin or angels in the house. When a female Islamic scholar bucked tradition by leading a group of Muslim men and women in prayer at a ceremony last month in New York, some protesters insisted that restrictions on women's roles were a sign of respect, while a man who disrupted the event recommended stoning for those involved.

"There's a sense that the world is out of control and chaotic, and that if we can control our women then the world will be a safer place," says Randall Balmer, a professor at Barnard who is an expert on evangelical Christianity. "That's a real perception on the part of a lot of religious conservatives—Muslims, Catholics, Protestant fundamentalists."

In the years that he was running the Congregation for the Doctrine of the Faith, the new pope, then Cardinal Joseph Ratzinger, demanded a church press destroy copies of a book promoting the ordination of women, summoned American bishops to Rome to see that their pastoral letter on the role of women toed the church line, and was behind a move to get rid of altar girls. In a 2004 letter to the bishops, he explained that while feminists had seen fit "to give rise to antagonism," what his fellows should remember was the "genius of women," a genius that boiled down to all the old stereotypes: emotional, nurturing, warm. (In life, humans are blessed with individuality; in orthodoxy it is wiped away.) Proving that Scripture can always be made to say what you want, he quoted St. Paul—"in Christ there is neither male nor female"—as a reaffirmation of the differences between the sexes, when it appears to be exactly the opposite.

Cardinal Ratzinger once famously suggested that all religions, too, were second-class, except for his own, so perhaps he does not care about other communities of faith. The Anglicans manage to worship God with both female priests and married clergy; the Archbishop of Canterbury once brought his wife, the mother of his four children, to meet John Paul II. Judaism now prospers under the leadership of female rabbis in what one scholar called "the greatest change in Jewish life since the destruction of the temple in the first century." Can it be that the leaders of both groups are so wrongheaded, that only rigidly conservative thinkers have gotten it right?

The argument in orthodoxy is usually that women are separate but equal, an argument that made racial segregation—and flagrant inequality—possible for many years in the United States. Power is not relinquished easily; fear of the other is an enduring human handicap. "What orthodoxy is partly about is fear," says Rabbi Joy Levitt. "The world is moving very fast, and not all of it is positive." But ultimately many faiths came to the conclusion that strictures on women were the product of outdated norms and entrenched prejudice, not sacred texts. Their leaders embraced the possibility that modern equality could abet spiritual growth. Rabbi Levitt recalls the words of the founder of the Reconstructionist movement, Mordecai Kaplan: "Tradition ought to have a vote, not a veto."

Catholic women are not naive. They do not expect a new pope to wake one morning, wave a magic staff and make ordination possible and sexual responsibility individual. But it would be nice to have a pontiff consider the role of women in the modern church out of some communication with women themselves. The very fact that anyone would be able to write such a sentence illustrates how deep the chasm is between the church of the people and the church of the hierarchy.

For all those who ask why we stay, I say: because it is our church. Literalists like to harp on the gender of Jesus himself. What they overlook is the fact that in clear violation of the norms of his own time, the founder of the faith surrounded himself with women. In seeking the counsel, opinions and advice of female Catholics, church leaders would not be conforming to modernity, but modeling Christ. They argue that they cannot tailor church bedrock to suit social fashion. The truth is that they have tailored its bedrock to suit their blind spots. "Woman," the new pope might ask, "why are you crying?"

Following Mary

Magdalene Devotees Shape Their Own Religious Realities

BY JENNIFER DOLL

Across the country and the world, people are discovering Mary Magdalene and being inspired, through her, to reach out to others or to make an active difference in their own religious lives. There seems to be a sense of freedom that Mary Magdalene stimulates in her followers: the ability to determine what works and what doesn't for one's own spirituality. Mary Magdalene gives devotees a chance to see in her what they need, a kind of "religion by design" that is generating new movements in charitable work, art, writing, education, activism, and, of course, religion itself.

Robbi Sluder, forty-seven, of Austin, Texas, is one such person. Sluder had her first Magdalene experience at her in-laws' house on Easter eve, 1999. "They had a DVD on of the Gaither Vocal Band, this group of gospel singers," she says, "and Sandi Patty, whose voice is as magnificent as Celine Dion's, was singing." As she lay on the couch listening, Sluder realized that the words were being sung from the perspective of Mary Magdalene, and it became clear to her that Mary—not Peter or John, the disciples she'd heard the names of repeatedly throughout her Methodist upbringing—was the first person to have seen Jesus resurrected.

"It's like the curtain was pulled back," she says. "I looked up at the closet where I had my dry-cleaned white Easter dress, and my daughter's Easter dress, and all the Easter baskets I'd made, and I thought about the pretty church that I was going to go to the next morning, and I began to weep." Sluder considered her own life. "I thought, I've had it pretty good, but what about all the women out there on the streets who have no idea that God loves them and that they are valuable? If I could have done it that night, I would have gone out to Wal-Mart and bought things and passed them out to people on the streets."

Jennifer Doll is an editorial consultant, writer, and researcher who contributed to *Secrets of the Code* and served as managing editor for this book.

With the encouragement of her husband and a few friends, Sluder began to put a plan into action for the next year. She ordered Easter baskets and other inspirational gifts: Jesus Loves You bracelets, Jesus Is the Way of Light flashlights. "Every basket had an Easter egg with candy and some sort of stuffed animal to touch their hearts, bring them back to a more innocent time." Baskets also included personal hygiene items in sample or travel sizes, Sluder's cell phone number, and a "Mary note" explaining how the first Easter was celebrated.

Baskets ready, Sluder encountered a hurdle. "I had all this stuff done and I didn't know where to go!" She called the Salvation Army. There, a volunteer provided information on where her group of three men and five women might find prostitutes and guidance on how to approach and interact with them. That first Easter was a success. Sluder recalls holding hands with the women on a dreary rainy night, under the dark lights of a parking lot, and praying. "After it was over we thought, Wow. We came out to bless but we were the ones who were blessed. Our hearts were changed. Easter would never be the same." The project and group of volunteers expanded after that, and Sluder's team started visiting transition homes, correctional facilities, and men's clubs—reaching out to others through Mary Magdalene.

Sluder, who had always thought that Mary Magdalene was a prostitute, also began studying the Bible to find out more about her. What she learned surprised her. "I love that it never names her sins. But certainly she'd experienced hopelessness, depression, rejection, sadness. Who of us cannot relate to that? I began to see that Jesus chose her *because* of that. Mary is the access point. She's someone real, and anyone who receives our gifts can identify with her."

The Magdalene Project (www.themagdaleneproject.org) is now a full-blown nonprofit organization, functioning with the support of private donors, a board of directors, and more than three thousand nationwide volunteers. Headquarters is a fourteen-hundred-square-foot office in Austin, Texas, helmed by a paid staff member. All volunteers receive standardized training, and participating cities must follow the rules and policies of the mother organization. In 2001, the Magdalene Project was active in ten cities; in 2006, twenty-three cities will participate.

Living Her SpiritualityThrough Ministry

Pam Stockton, fifty-four, of Houston, Texas, first became involved with Mary Magdalene during the 1998 feast day celebration held for the saint at Brigid's Place, a nonprofit organization for women associated with Christ Church Cathedral (www.brigidsplace.org). Her interest piqued, she began taking classes at Perkins School of Theology at Southern Methodist University. Stockton says, "Studying Mary Magdalene has been a vehicle of transformation for me. I feel that she called to me through my studies; that's how our relationship started. But she calls other women, too. The 'Magdalene magnetism' is such that she reaches different women in different ways."

Stockton graduated from Perkins in 2006 and continues to be involved in feast day events as organizer and participant. She helped prepare for the festival in 2004, which brought Harvard's Karen King to speak to more than five hundred people, and for the one in 2005, featuring guest speaker Jane Schaberg of the University of Detroit Mercy. This year's speaker is Ann Brock, author of *Mary Magdalene, the First Apostle: The Struggle for Authority*. Feast day services are non-Eucharistic and often include imagined dialogues or reenactments. "In 2004 we dramatized Paul's command to the Corinthian women to veil themselves and be silent, and there were gasps from the congregation," Stockton says. "We're shocking people into the realization of what was, the way in which women's voices were silenced. That kind of thing is important."

In addition to feast day celebrations, Stockton participates in the church's Magdalene Community, which was founded by Reverend Betty Adam, spiritual director of Brigid's Place and resident canon theologian of Christ Church Cathedral. "Thirteen years ago, I had an idea for a woman's ministry," says Adam. "I felt that the church was not attending to the struggles of women and needed to lean into some of these issues. We're empowering women, talking about women's spirituality. While we are trying to develop our own spirituality and independence, we help others." Programs include Brigid's Hope, which provides incarcerated women with a place to stay when they leave prison, and Brigid's Paradigm, which builds houses for women and children using recycled materials. (St. Brigid started convents across Ireland in the early sixth century.)

Betty Adam has also organized a contemporary Magdalene community, which meets the first and third Friday of each month to study works such as the Gospel of Mary, and for Sunday worship at an interfaith chapel in Houston. In her spare time, Adam is writing a book titled *The Magdalene Mystique: Living the Spirituality of Mary Today,* due out in October 2006. "It's about the energy around Mary Magdalene, how the community develops, and what this means to us," she says.

Hearing Her Voice, and Speaking to Others

Joan Norton, fifty-eight, author, psychotherapist, and co-facilitator of the Magdalene Circle at the Women's Club of Hollywood, California, (www.marymagdalenewithin.com) says, "She came to me unbidden. I didn't come from a traditional religious background, I didn't have childhood stories or anything like that." However, Norton was a channeler, and like many of those who find Mary Magdalene, was not unfamiliar with loss (her sixteen-year-old daughter had been killed in a car accident in 1986).

One morning ten years ago as she set out to write, she heard the words of Mary Magdalene in her head. "Mary said she wanted to express gratefulness for her relationship with Jesus, and that she would tell me her story. It was an ageless wisdom coming through my mind. She talked to me every morning for a couple of weeks. The grief was intense, as were her feelings of love for Jesus."

The result was *The Mary Magdalene Within* and an active calling. "I feel that I am a source of education for other women about the lost story of the sacred feminine," Norton says. "It makes women feel strong and equal, empowered by owning our own Christian story."

A 2005 Mary Magdalene feast day celebration at the Women's Club of Hollywood inspired initial interest, and that September the Magdalene circle was born. The group, which now numbers about fifty women, meets one Sunday a month in a room at the Women's Club that is decorated with an altar, candles, flowers, and art, "So it feels like those good familiar feelings of church," says Norton. The group sits in a circle, opening first with prayer before moving on to study and discuss passages from the Gospel of Mary. "We have a guided meditation that brings the story into the personal lives of each woman. It's like a church service but with a lot of talk. Women are hungry for this material."

When I spoke to Norton, she was working on her lesson for the coming Sunday as well as planning Mary Magdalene's feast day for this year (the one in 2005, which attracted 150 people, featured an Essene minister, belly dancing, chanting, drumming, and food). She recently spoke at a Mary Magdalene event with author Margaret Starbird and founder and director of the online Esoteric Mystery School, Katia Romanoff. She is reflective about her increasingly public role. "I don't feel like I wrote that book, it just kind of happened. This is the path that has been chosen for me."

A Magdalene Rebirth Through Art

Sara Taft, seventy-one, is an artist, psychologist, and astrologer from Pacific Palisades, California. For her, Mary has been an inspiration and an affirmation, providing a parallel with a resurrection in her own life. Taft, who survived a liver transplant six years ago after being diagnosed with a life-threatening autoimmune disease, is currently exhibiting a show of paintings and narratives titled *A Legendary Biography of Mary Magdalene* (www.sarataft.com).

While she was still regaining her strength from the transplant, Taft journeyed to France to learn more about the divine feminine, and Mary Magdalene in particular. Coming from a patriarchal, Methodist family, this was all new to her. "It was like a revelation, an unfolding of the Christian story that I was seeing for the first time. I started to research and paint her, to become familiar with her, and as I would paint her I would weep. I wasn't sad, but I would weep."

Taft's paintings, which depict and narrate events in the historical and imagined life of Mary Magdalene, have appeared in galleries on the West Coast. The reaction to her work has pleased her. "The men were saying, 'We're going to read about this woman.' Catholic women

were saying, 'You've done this for all of us.' There were tears in people's eyes, not just women, across the board."

A Man's Magdalene: The Gnostic Approach

Mark Williams, forty-three, of Columbus, Ohio, is the Gnostic
teacher and coordinator of Magdalene Circle (www.magdalene-
circle.org), a moderate Gnostic group that, he says, "Runs somewhere between traditional Christianity and Gnosticism, focusing on
the divine feminine." He is also the single father of two teenage boys,
and previously held the spiritual post of youth pastor in a fundamental
Christian denomination, where he "struggled with things like women
not being able to serve." Williams returned to college to get a master's in theology, and there discovered the Gospel of Thomas.

"I went on the Internet and found that there still were Gnostics
around. I considered myself Christian and was not willing to give that
up," he says. "But I was feeling a disconnect between deep spirituality
and a nonjudgmental attitude." Williams found the connection he was
searching for in Gnosticism and in the figure of Mary Magdalene,
whom he believes speaks strongly to the human condition. Traditional
religious practices can lead to a sense of feeling like an outsider, he
says. "There's a mixed message of salvation through grace, but you're
all still not good enough. Mary brings this idea that it doesn't matter
that she was a woman; she struggled and was accepted, and had faith."

Inspired by what he found online, Williams began posting flyers in
local bookstores and leaving messages on various Internet forums. A
woman from the area who was doing the same thing contacted him
and they began to meet and study together. The group has since
grown to a dozen. "People who are following these paths are normal,
everyday people," says Williams. "In the past, people thought you had
to be a great theologian to do something like this. But you can be anyone. You can be a flawed person and find spirituality."

The group meets on Saturdays in an old house that's been converted
into a Unitarian church. In general, the focus is on how passages from
various Gnostic Gospels, including the Gospel of Mary, relate to the
personal, spiritual journey of each member. When I spoke to him,

Williams was also planning a summer gathering to take place on three acres of wooded lot outside of the church. Participants were to include a Gnostic Internet group of a hundred people as well as other religious groups, including Buddhist, Hindu, and Pagan. "There will camping, bonfires, and hour-long presentations sprinkled throughout the two days. Our goal here is to get back to where we belong. We believe that there are many paths," says Williams, who is planning to be a Gnostic priest, "Mine is the one that's right for me."

Education That Feeds the Soul

Another proponent of finding a religion that fits her personally is Katia Romanoff, forty-one, of Dallas-Ft. Worth, Texas. She is founder and director of the Esoteric Mystery School, an online educational community of approximately 250 active, studying members and an additional thousand or so who participate in discussion forums (http://northernway.org/school). Inspired by books like Margaret Starbird's *The Woman with the Alabaster Jar,* Romanoff first went online in 1999 and started a group discussion forum about the sacred feminine and Mary Magdalene. The group, Goddess Christians, still exists today with a thousand members. "We had people clamoring for lessons, study guides, affirmations, prayers. I threw some lessons together and in 1999 we created the Esoteric Mystery School," recalls Romanoff. Interestingly, the school's student population is about 40 percent male.

For Romanoff, a religious synthesis like hers has been a long time coming. "Religion needs to feed the soul," says Romanoff. "Mary Magdalene brings balance to the lopsided God-is-a-single-parent sort of thing. We need a heavenly mother. Who is God's wife? I remember asking that when I was six years old." But what if Jesus and Mary were never a couple? "If Jesus and Mary Magdalene were not married, they should have been," she says, "Because it resonates, it brings fulfillment, it lets us use the Christian framework we were all brought up under, and we can come back home this way. We can design our own version because that's what everyone else has done." That version includes a customized "Hail Mary," which begins: "Hail Mary Magdalene, the

Lord has wed thee." There's also a Balanced Lord's Prayer, a Mary Magdalene Rosary, and a special Order of Mary Magdalene Prayer book.

The Esoteric Mystery School is a legally incorporated church that can ordain members as ministers upon completion of the proper course work, and includes three major study halls, three degrees, and two to three hundred lessons focused on the works of such authors as Starbird, Jean-Yves Leloup, and Tau Malachi. Students pay a monthly fee of $25 for unlimited lessons and entrance into study halls, which are accessed online and via email. The online aspect creates a virtual religious community that is very new-millennium: Internet chats and gatherings on "the spiritual plane" at daybreak, high noon, and sunset help to link everyone despite the lack of physical meetings. The group also holds an annual convocation once a year, a chance to meet with students as far-flung as Africa, Canada, China, Europe, Indonesia, Mexico, Puerto Rico, and the United States.

A Church for the Future: Magdalene Activism

Chris Schenk, sixty, is the executive director of FutureChurch, a Catholic church reform community that began in Cleveland, Ohio, in 1990 with the goal of preserving the Catholic Eucharist by opening ordination to women and the married (www.futurechurch.org). For Schenk, there's something even larger than Mary Magdalene at stake: the future of the Catholic Church. "We're on a collision course with having no priests," she says. "By 2027, we'll have seventy-six priests for 235 parishes in Cleveland." By contrast, there are thirty thousand lay ministers in the U.S. church, 82 percent of whom are women.

In 1997, Schenk developed the Women in Church Leadership project in partnership with another Catholic renewal organization, Call to Action. "We sent out an email and mailing to people who'd purchased our women's resources and said, this July, here's what we'd like to do. Get your local biblical scholar to give a presentation on who Mary Magdalene was, and give it in prayer service where a woman presides." In the first year, twenty-three groups participated. Now, Schenk says, the numbers are in the three hundreds, with 60 to 70 percent of activities taking place on Catholic properties.

For Schenk, the public battle has been intensely personal as well. "I was on a mission to reverse the mistaken notion that Mary Magdalene was a prostitute. In fact, it was upon her that the proclamation of the Resurrection depended. As a Catholic woman all I'd known was that she was a public sinner; I wanted to change this understanding."

This year, along with events coinciding with feast days, Easter, Lent, and Holy Week, FutureChurch has developed a set of resources celebrating women throughout church history. "We thought that they were sweet, smart, and obedient and became saints," says Schenk, "But we didn't hear how strong they were, or what they actually did. There were in fact women bishops and priests. The church does indeed have a tradition of women's ordination." Of Mary Magdalene, she says, "She's the tip of the iceberg; she's the icon for women's suppressed roles in Christianity."

Is progress being made in the effort to have women ordained? Schenk's answer is cautious: "I guess it depends how you define it." On the plus side, women are getting educated for church ministry and as preachers at unprecedented rates. "Sixty percent of the eighteen thousand women studying for lay ministry—including masters of divinity, biblical studies, and the like—are women. This compares to three thousand men in seminary. It's changing it from within," she says.

For these eight people and thousands more, Mary Magdalene is changing things from within and inspiring change in the outside world as well. As the message spreads, aided by the popularity of books like *The Da Vinci Code,* we see what may be a revolutionary crossroads for religion. There's a new fusion between the spiritual and the personal; a freedom to create your own path and find your own way. There's also a deep need to reinstate a balance between the masculine and feminine, to reclaim what has been lost or covered up over time.

"People respond so positively, using words like *fulfilled, complete.* It is my greatest hope that we can continue the work and make this alternate form of Christianity a little more mainstream. It's not going to happen overnight, but at least it's started," says Katia Romanoff. Joan Norton is even more confident. During the channeling of *The Mary Magdalene Within,* she tells me, Mary revealed something else. "She knew that she would be left out until the time that we were strong enough to hold it," Norton says. "Now is the right time."

She Moves in Mysterious Ways
Mary Magdalene in the Internet Age

BY LESA BELLEVIE

Stories give meaning to the present and help us to imagine the future—and in the case of Mary Magdalene, a better future. This premise is just as compelling now as it was when the teachings of Jesus and the stories about Mary Magdalene first began to spread from one village to the next in biblical times. Our village is now global, with email sometimes replacing the oral tradition, but the stories themselves remain remarkably similar to the tales of those who sought guidance or relief from suffering during the Middle Ages by making pilgrimages to visit Mary Magdalene's relics in the south of France.

Today's favorite gathering place to discuss "what Mary means to me" is the Internet, and, within this home, www.Magdalene.org is the hearth. We asked Lesa Bellevie, the site's founder and webmaster, to tell us what her readers have had to say about Mary Magdalene. What stands out is how Mary, even in the third millennium, comes into the lives of many people unexpectedly, and how often the bond they feel becomes intensely personal. As she sifted through these personal stories and learned the ways in which women—and, yes, men—of a variety of faiths and backgrounds shared this common bond, Lesa also began to examine her own journey.

In 1997, I had a dream about Mary Magdalene. Although I had been raised in a Christian household, even reading the Bible in the evenings with my family, I had the same vague understanding of her identity that most people do: she was the prostitute in the gospels. The dream, which came—for the most part—out of the blue, was sufficiently odd and interesting that it prompted me to crack open my Bible, something I hadn't done for many years.

Try as I might, I couldn't find any reference to Mary Magdalene's illicit reputation in the pages of my King James. I scoured the concordance, tried different translations, but no luck; I could come up with no reasonable idea of why people would think of her as a redeemed harlot. What had begun as a simple exercise meant to satisfy curiosity became a more intriguing mystery. Who was Mary Magdalene, and how had she become a sinner?

One of my great joys in life is browsing used book stores. On one such excursion in early 1998, a friend handed me a copy of a book called *The Nag Hammadi Library in English*. I flipped immediately to the index and found, to my surprise, a treasure. Not only were there numerous mentions of her name, there was even a Gospel of Mary Magdalene. I had discovered Gnosticism, an early off-shoot of Christian belief that flourished in the first five centuries after Christ. Gnostics believed that a special revealed knowledge (*gnosis*)—not Christ's sacrifice—was the secret of salvation. In some Gnostic sects, Mary Magdalene was held in a position of high regard, as an apostle, as a leader, and as a companion of the Savior.

By trade, I am a computer software test engineer, and I've spent the better part of my career working on World Wide Web technologies. So my next move was natural: I went to the Internet to see what else I could learn about Mary Magdalene, both inside and outside of Gnosticism. To my dismay, I found very little. More committed to investigating this Christian figure with every passing day, I decided to create my own Mary Magdalene website. In 1998, www.Magdalene.org was launched. My goal was to create a repository of knowledge about Mary Magdalene that would be easily available for anyone else who had developed a fascination with the "other" Mary. At first I received comments on the site monthly, then weekly, and then almost daily. Reader emails, mostly from women, almost always had the same thing to say: "I thought I was the only one interested in Mary Magdalene!"

In short order, a number of the people I heard from joined together in a small online group by way of a mailing list. We shared our thoughts on Mary Magdalene, Christianity, and various related issues, forming friendships and support networks. At the time, it seemed the only connection among such diverse individuals—from teenagers to grandmothers, high school dropouts to Ph.D.s—was the fact that they had an interest in Mary Magdalene. As time progressed, however, trends began to emerge. Many were interested in Mary Magdalene because they were named for her, or because they had chosen her name at their confirmation in the Roman Catholic Church. Some, like me, had simply become intrigued by the commonly held belief (despite the lack of evidence) that she was a prostitute. Many felt a deep, spiritual draw to Mary Magdalene that they had difficulty articulating. The more I learned about Mary Magdalene, the more I felt the same way.

I've been fortunate to be in a position to hear so many stories from a cross-section of society. Although I don't always share the same opinions about Mary Magdalene as those who comment on the website, it's difficult not to appreciate the fact that she has enriched the spiritual lives of so many. In that, they, or perhaps I should say *we,* share common ground.

Looking for a New Way

One of the prevalent themes among women who find themselves pulled toward Mary Magdalene is a sense of alienation from traditional Christianity. This includes all branches of Christianity, not just Roman Catholicism. Finding themselves valued as bake sale leaders, Sunday school teachers, and pew-occupiers but not as elders, deacons, or pastors—many women come to feel that regardless of what they believe about Christ, their religion is flawed.

I share this experience. Raised as a Pentecostal, I learned that a woman was to be subject to her husband, and her place was in the home. Growing up in a culture charged by feminism, the conflict between believing that women could accomplish anything and believing that women could only bear children and keep a tidy house was overwhelming. I found solace in hearing the stories of other women in our online community:

> *My entire family is Catholic, though many have left the church—mostly the women, for various reasons . . . I stopped going to church because I felt that it was so very male-dominated that I couldn't even hear between the lines any kind of feminine aspect . . . Except for Mary the Mother, there was no strong female presence. We girls couldn't be altar boys—and that always bugged me.*
>
> —Mary, Northampton, Massachusetts

> *I left the [Church of Jesus Christ of Latter-day Saints] in the late sixties because of their stance on women. The issue of the priesthood did not matter as much as their insistence on women being subordinate to men, even to the point where domestic abuse was ignored.*
>
> —Loretta, Sylmar, California

I was brought up Lutheran, but I always felt that something was missing ... I had a problem with the way that women were portrayed in the Church.

—Elizabeth, Chestertown, Maryland

I found myself so dissatisfied with what was being taught in the Pentecostal church. I found it hostile in many ways to women and too dogmatic.

—Carol, Kansas City, Missouri

The women above all share the same point of origin to one destination: a devotion to Mary Magdalene as an independent and strong female role model in the gospels. Mary Magdalene tells us that Christianity isn't all about men; we're entitled to carry the good news as well, in ways other than pious obedience.

The more I learned, the more intrigued I became. I began to realize that changing the public perception about both Mother Mary and Mary Magdalene would be a powerful key in the advancement of women in society. I also began researching and writing about these two women with that goal in mind.

—Loretta, Sylmar, California

[Mary Magdalene] is truly an emblem for all—an emblem of gender equality, relationships based on partnership, a role model for women (and men) of all spiritual paths and experiences.

—Denise, Vernon, Connecticut

I think [Mary Magdalene's recent popularity] is great, especially if women are given more consideration and authority in the Church ...We are the rest of the population, and therefore we need to be heard.

—Carol, Kansas City, Missouri

Dreams, Death, and *The DaVinci Code*

In early 2003, no one in our little online Mary Magdalene community could guess that a book about to be published would completely change how the world viewed the subject of our devotion. Dan Brown's novel, *The DaVinci Code,* which came out in April of that year, quickly became a bestseller. Built upon Michael Baigent, Richard Leigh, and Henry Lincoln's 1982 book, *Holy Blood, Holy Grail,* as well as our community member Margaret Starbird's titles, *The Woman with The Alabaster Jar* and *The Goddess in the Gospels, The Da Vinci Code* pivots on the idea that Mary Magdalene was not only a divine feminine counterpart to Jesus, but also the mother of his children. This proved to be an attractive combination for many.

The number of people joining our online community began to grow steadily after the summer of 2003, and our "little" group became a major Internet stop for the discussion of Mary Magdalene. (At a relatively stable 100 members before the publication of *The Da Vinci Code,* at last count the group includes more than 750 participants.) Emerging among the latest subscribers to the group was a new path to Mary Magdalene:

> *I had no idea what* [The Da Vinci Code] *was about before I read it. It just sounded exciting. When I discovered . . . the theories surrounding the Magdalene, I was struck so hard that it changed my being. All of a sudden, everything came into focus—the connections, the abuse of women, the corruption of the Church—it became clear.*
>
> —Elizabeth, Chestertown, Maryland

> *After reading Dan Brown's novel* The Da Vinci Code, *I wanted to find out more about Mary Magdalene . . . Margaret Starbird's approach, the sacred marriage, seems very fresh to me on how it treats sexuality as a vital part of life which cannot be excluded.*
>
> —Martina, Berlin, Germany

> *When I read* The Da Vinci Code, *it was like a door had been thrown wide open . . .*
>
> —Kristin, Buffalo, New York

A particularly moving story comes from Erin of Fort Wayne, Indiana. She explains that her discovery of *The Da Vinci Code* and Mary Magdalene occurred at a vulnerable time in her life. She read the book just before the birth of her daughter, which occurred after a difficult delivery that threatened the newborn's life.

With the urging of hospital staff, I called for a priest, who was vacant and re-
moved. He was quite anxious to leave, actually, and provided little comfort.

In a desperation that many new mothers have experienced, Erin
promised God that she would lead a more spiritual life if only he
would help her newborn survive. Her daughter recovered, and Erin
committed herself to investigating some of author Dan Brown's
sources. She wanted to learn more about the unusual ideas contained
in his novel. This brought her to the books of Margaret Starbird,
which had a profound effect:

Margaret Starbird's work made so much sense to me. It felt as if it was all com-
ing together for the first time. In retrospect, my daughter's birth was a signifi-
cant part of my spiritual awakening to the feminine. I fulfilled my promise.

It isn't immediately obvious to most people that situations like
Erin's, with a life balanced on the brink of life and death, or mourning
an actual passing, can be catalysts to a discovery of Mary Magdalene.
But many come to their heartfelt respect for her after experiencing
the loss of a loved one. As the primary figure associated with the Crucifixion, entombment, and Resurrection of Christ, Mary Magdalene
models grief in a way that no other gospel figure does.

MaryEllen, an interfaith minister from Bucks County, Pennsylvania, says that a troubling dream of Mary Magdalene preceded the
death of multiple family members over the space of several years. Afterward, MaryEllen came to recall the dream as a visitation from
Mary Magdalene, in whose presence she subsequently found comfort.
Holding the view that Jesus and Mary Magdalene were involved in an
intimate relationship, she says:

She came to protect me and my mental stability from the additional stresses
that were coming my way. She knew that someday I would find her. She wanted
me to be mentally prepared to accept the skeptical views of people who do not
want to give up their ingrained beliefs and orthodox structures. She wanted me
to be curious and searching. I know she wants me, as well as so many others, to
help restore her to her rightful place, at the side of her Beloved.

MaryEllen's dream is but one of many I've heard through the years. Always amazed that my own experience is shared by so many others, I've come to see Mary Magdalene dreams as a deep impulse toward reconciling difficult and apparently opposing ideas: womanhood in the face of religious misogyny, or love in the presence of death. It is stunning to realize that Mary Magdalene moves in this way through the lives of so many. Here is the experience of Eleanora, of Seattle, Washington:

> *I thought Mary Magdalene was a prostitute until dreaming that I had made a shrine for her. It was so vivid. When I learned that there was much more to her than I had originally thought, I decided to make a small shrine in real life. After doing so, I began to dream of her more often. Many times the dreams were characterized by someone weeping deeply, and an incredible sense of loss. In one, someone had died and it seemed that those who were left behind were calling to Mary Magdalene in their grief. In the dream it was the power of Mary Magdalene's love for Jesus that allowed him to come back to life.*

Although I've only received permission to reproduce a few stories here, those that have been shared privately are equally poignant. At least one major Mary Magdalene scholar, working in academia, has attributed dreams of Mary Magdalene to her increasing awareness of the saint's importance.

Magdalene's Men

It's true that most people who express a deep devotion to Mary Magdalene are women, but there *are* men among them. Despite being in the minority, these men who have discovered a connection to Mary Magdalene are no less outspoken. Very frequently, the revived practice of Christian Gnosticism is at the heart of male veneration of Mary Magdalene. Some Gnostic texts written before the end of the fourth century, including a few in *The Nag Hammadi Library,* place Mary Magdalene in an elevated position among her peers. This leads many modern Gnostics to do the same.

My special interest in [Mary Magdalene] came about through my studies of Gnosticism. She's a very important character within Gnostic scripture; one of, if not the, most important of the Apostles.

—Jeremy, Seattle, Washington

After attending college for my master's degree I found I just couldn't do the fundamentalist Christian thing. I had always had issues with the judgmental- ism, and once I learned the history of the Church and found out about alterna- tive forms of Christianity, I couldn't go back. I became interested in Gnosticism and found the Sophian Gnostic tradition. Sophian Gnostics are very big on di- vine feminine and put Magdalene in a central role. I felt like she was finally where I had always believed her to be.

—Mark, Mount Vernon, Ohio

Contrary to popular misperception, men can be inspired by god- dess spirituality as well, particularly in light of its place in novels such as *The DaVinci Code.* One male journalist with whom I've spoken sev- eral times has expressed his love of Mary Magdalene as goddess in the Jungian term *anima,* the inner feminine within men that affects their relationships with women. Discouraged by a divorce, he credits Mary Magdalene's presence in his spiritual life with his gradual understand- ing of how to be a better husband and father.

Unwavering Christians

Where are all the Christians who are devoted to Mary Magdalene? Does she only appeal to people who have left the church and gone in New Age directions? Not at all. It does seem, however, that people who remain faithful Christians are much quieter about their dedica- tion, not shouting it from the rooftops, as it were. Very few have ex- pressed an interest in discussing their stories publicly. Among those perspectives I have heard from traditional Christians, acknowledging Mary Magdalene as the "apostle of the apostles" for her role as pri- mary witness of the Resurrection is one of the most frequently cited.

I really think the "Apostle of the Apostles" view of Magdalene is important in helping to bring the church up to speed with modern thinking concerning a "woman's place." I don't buy into any of the Da Vinci Code *or sacred feminine stuff surrounding Magdalene, but if that helps women find more equal footing within the Church, I don't see that as a bad thing.*

—Thomas, Bellevue, Washington

Yet another crucial perspective among Christians is an emphasis on Mary Magdalene's close relationship with Jesus. While allowing for some amount of intimacy in their friendship, these Christians do not feel a need to understand them as married partners.

To me, St. Mary Magdalene (I consider her a saint, as I am a practicing Roman Catholic, and she is recognized as such, with a viable feast day) represents love, total and unconditional; complete and utter surrender. [There is] no earthly pleasure compared to the ecstasy she must have felt at His feet, and at the sight of Him that Easter morning. To me that's what it's all about: loving the Perfect Man, the Perfect God, and having His love in return. To live in that love eternally—who could ask for anything more complete than that?

—Helene, Bloomfield, New Jersey

My own journey with Mary Magdalene is ongoing. After almost a decade, she has woven herself into my life at an integral level; she is there every day, every hour, and every minute. Somewhere between spiritual patron and Jiminy Cricket–style conscience, between hobby and devotion, she moves me all the more powerfully when I meet others who seem to be fellow pilgrims on the path. Whether they are Christians looking for a woman apostle or New Agers contemplating sacred union archetypes, whether they are scholars or mystics, they've all been touched by the numinous. And as people have had difficulty since the beginning of recorded history describing spiritual experiences, we continue to search for language to express the depth of our encounters with Mary Magdalene, whose identity, after almost two thousand years, remains unfixed. The fact that we have her in common, however, means that to some degree, no words are necessary. Like the ancient Gnostics, we just *know.*

Appendixes

The Mary Magdalene Bookshelf

BY THE SECRETS TEAM

A project the size and scope of a book like *Secrets of Mary Magdalene* requires prodigious research. As a result, our collective library has swelled to hundreds of volumes—from writings by serious scholars who have spent their careers bringing us translations and analyses of ancient records to self-help books touting Mary Magdalene as a "pleasure revolutionary." Authors include at least a dozen experts with varied interpretations of the goddess tradition and how modern society has suppressed it, as well as novelists and researchers who each in their own way wish to convince us that they have conclusive knowledge of the Magdalene's life, her relationship with Jesus, and her travels in southern France (and perhaps Egypt and Britain). Then there are those who believe she is literally the Holy Grail, originator of a royal bloodline and heroine of an action-adventure story and anti-history thriller that starts and ends at the Louvre. And we mustn't forget those who have thoughtfully opined on the various controversies about the meaning of her life—and the religious and intellectual use and abuse she has endured.

Sifting through all of these books and hundreds of websites left us first of all with a sense of admiration for the great deal of serious research and analysis that has gone into "finding" Mary Magdalene and tracing the remarkably deep impact her image has had on the course of Western civilization. Second, we were struck by the depth of religious and personal connections so many feel for Mary Magdalene, and the variety of forms in which they are being expressed. Third, and finally, we have found no evidence to contradict what many of the most insightful scholars and experts have been telling us: what people see in Mary Magdalene is largely a reflection of the attitudes and beliefs they bring to bear to interpreting her. There is no "one" Mary Magdalene, and there never will be, which is why our fascination with her is unlikely to end.

Any "best of" list would surely hold works by each of the authors we have interviewed, excerpted, or invited to write essays for this book. Nevertheless, with the help of Lesa Bellevie of www.Magdalene.org, we have cast the net wider to give you what we consider to be the best books for building a basic library on Mary Magdalene. The list reflects only our own judgment, of course, filtered through the lenses we ourselves have chosen. We expect that many scholars, experts, and lay readers whose judgment we greatly respect may disagree with some of our choices. We encourage you to weigh in and let us know your opinions on our website, www.SecretsOfMaryMagdalene.com.

Within each category, books are listed alphabetically, by author.

General Introductions and Overviews

The Complete Idiot's Guide to Mary Magdalene, by Lesa Bellevie. Don't be put off by the title. In between the breezy asides and highly informal style there is a tremendous amount of information, reflecting a judicious and comprehensive selection of insights on Mary Magdalene's legacy, what we do and don't know about her, religious and secular controversies, and her place in our history as well as contemporary culture.

Mary Magdalene: A Biography, by Bruce Chilton. Starting with an overview of what we know about her background, Chilton focuses on interpreting her "seven demons" and moves on to show how Mary Magdalene contributed her own "signature" to the origins of Christianity. Readers will also find some uplifting observations about Mary Magdalene's ability to inspire women in modern Christianity.

Lost Christianities: The Battles for Scripture and the Faiths We Never Knew, by Bart Ehrman. Ehrman explains how the early church fathers declared the four gospels as, well, Gospel—and all other early Christian texts as heresy. In the space of three hundred years, he tells us, religious organization and an alliance with political power overcame all opposition to its orthodoxy. Ehrman's latest book, *Peter, Paul, and Mary Magdalene: The Followers of Jesus in History and Legend,* is, as the subtitle summarizes, a work about the followers of Jesus and what their stories tell us about an emergent church.

The Gnostic Gospels, by Elaine Pagels. This is the classic for understanding the range of diverse Christianities in early years. Here, in the scholarly yet accessible writing style that earned her a National Book Award, Pagels untangles the threads of myth, theology, and politics that constituted early Christianity. Among her other notable books is *Beyond Belief,* where she wrestles with her own faith in the context of the *Gospel of Thomas,* and explores the reasons that Christianity became associated almost exclusively with the relatively narrow ideas in the New Testament as codified by the fourth-century Council of Nicea.

The Woman with the Alabaster Jar: Mary Magdalen and the Holy Grail, by Margaret Starbird. Starbird is almost single-handedly responsible for popularizing the notion that Jesus and Mary Magdalene were at the heart of a "sacred union" theology—which she believes is the true basis of Christianity, suppressed by the emergent and suffocating orthodoxy of the church. Although considered highly speculative by many scholars, she is also admired for the research she has done and for bringing this "lost" subject back to the fore. Her several books, including *Mary Magdalene: Bride in Exile,* are important titles for understanding the modern fascination with Mary Magdalene and her new mythology.

The Best of the New Scholarship on Mary Magdalene

Although some of these books are highly detailed, extensively footnoted, and sprinkled with the occasional dense paragraph (or even chapter), they are highly regarded, and justifiably so, for bringing the reader fresh—and often startling—insights about Mary Magdalene.

Mary Magdalene, The First Apostle: The Struggle for Authority, by Ann Graham Brock. The book explores what it means to be an apostle and why Mary Magdalene was never designated as one in the gospels, even though she is central to the Christian message. Brock, like other modern feminist scholars, uncovers evidence of an active effort to erase her as a witness of the Risen Christ in favor of Peter.

Mary Magdalen: Myth and Metaphor, by Susan Haskins. This definitive work examines Mary Magdalene's varied appearances in art, liturgy, theater, literature, music, and the popular imagination over the last two millennia. Haskins devotes the last portion of the book to more recent perspectives on Mary Magdalene.

The Gospel of Mary of Magdala: Jesus and the First Woman Apostle, by Karen King. King is one of the foremost scholars on the *Gospel of Mary,* an early second-century Christian text in which Mary Magdalene shares her vision of Christ with the other disciples. This is a serious introduction to what has been ranked as one of the most important Gnostic Gospels.

The Resurrection of Mary Magdalene: Legends, Apocrypha, and the Christian Testament, by Jane Schaberg. Expressed within a progressive feminist framework, and in a style of poetic observation and razor-sharp commentary, Schaberg brings the reader broad insight into the legends, archaeology, and Gnostic or apocryphal traditions that illuminate our collective memory of Mary Magdalene.

Other Works We Have Found Particularly Helpful

Gnosticism and Other Diverse Perspectives within Early Christianity

The Gospel of Mary: The Secret Tradition of Mary Magdalene, The Companion of Jesus, is a translation by Marvin Meyer with a useful commentary by Esther de Boer. Marvin Meyer is also known for his *Gospel of Thomas* and a new work that covers some of the latest finds, *The Gnostic Discoveries. The Gospel of Mary Magdalene,* by Jean-Yves Leloup, is popular for its emphasis on this gospel as a source of Gnostic wisdom. A complete compilation of the Gnostic Gospels, with commentary, can by found in *The Nag Hammadi Library in English,* edited by James M. Robinson.

Deconstructing the Magdalene Traditions

If intrigued by the idea of Mary Magdalene as the literal vessel for the blood of Jesus Christ and the role of secret societies (such as the Priory of Sion) in keeping the deepest secrets of the Western world, start with *Holy Blood, Holy Grail,* by Henry Lincoln, Michael Baigent, and Richard Leigh. Then move on to the work of Lynn Picknett (in this arena, *Mary Magdalene* and *The Templar Revelation*), who takes the view that Mary and Jesus were lovers and spiritual partners—and that everything the church teaches about her is "a deliberate attempt to cover up uncomfortable facts." Timothy Freke and Peter Gandy, in *Jesus and the Lost Goddess,* take the broad perspective, bringing in symbolism, goddess myths, and more to reveal a distorted Christianity and an increasingly important Mary Magdalene.

The Best of Magdalene Fiction

There are a number of writers who have combined their literary imagination with a great deal of research, thereby garnering praise from scholars, critics, and readers alike. Ki Longfellow's *The Secret Magdalene* places Mary Magdalene in first-century Palestine, educated better than most men (and dressing like one to be able to move about freely), and finding her life intertwined with Jesus. *The Moon Under Her Feet,* by Clysta Kinstler, explores a pagan version of the Christian story, with Mary Magdalene appearing as a sacred prostitute who engages in sexual rites with Jesus in a kind of Judeo-Hellenistic fertility cult. *Mary, Called Magdalene,* by Margaret George, pivots on Mary Magdalene's "seven demons" and creates a life for her that is filled, as a review says, with the complexities, tensions, sorrows, and joys of human nature. One of the most recent, and certainly the most highly promoted novel about Mary Magdalene, is *The Expected One,* by Kathleen McGowan, the first of a trilogy called *The Magdalene Line.* For McGowan, who was allowed into the world of secret societies during her research, Mary's story is about courage, endurance, and faith.

Other Perspectives to Consider

Deirdre Good's *Mariam, the Magdalen, and the Mother* is a collection of essays exploring in scholarly detail the religious and prophetic identity of Mary Magdalene and Mary, Jesus' mother, as Miriam figures. Katherine Jansen, in her *The Making of the Magdalen: Preaching and Popular Devotion in the Later Middle Ages,* describes the Middle Ages, when Mary Magdalene myths and legends abounded, many of them having a major impact on art and culture. Philip Jenkins represents the traditionalist view in his articulate and provocative *Hidden Gospels: How the Search for Jesus Lost Its Way.* A recent coffee-table book with magnificent reproductions of Mary Magdalene art is Jane Lahr's *Searching for Mary Magdalene.*

Mary Magdalene Appearances in the New Testament

BY BELIEFNET STAFF

1. References to Mary of Magdala During Jesus' Ministry

Luke 8:1-3: Afterward [Jesus] journeyed from one town and village to another, preaching and proclaiming the good news of the kingdom of God. Accompanying him were the Twelve and some women who had been cured of evil spirits and infirmities, Mary, called Magdalene, from whom seven demons had gone out, Joanna, the wife of Herod's steward Chuza, Susanna, and many others who provided for them out of their resources.

2. References to Mary of Magdala During the Crucifixion

Mark 15:40: There were also some women looking on from a distance, among whom were Mary Magdalene, and Mary the mother of James the Less and Joses, and Salome.

Matthew 27:56: Among them was Mary Magdalene, and Mary the mother of James and Joseph, and the mother of the sons of Zebedee.

John 19:25: But standing by the cross of Jesus were His mother, and His mother's sister, Mary the wife of Clopas, and Mary Magdalene.

3. References to Mary of Magdala After the Crucifixion

Mark 15:47: Mary Magdalene and Mary the mother of Joses were looking on to see where He was laid.

Matthew 27:61: And Mary Magdalene was there, and the other Mary, sitting opposite the grave.

Matthew 28:1: Now after the Sabbath, as it began to dawn toward the first day of the week, Mary Magdalene and the other Mary came to look at the grave.

Mark 16:1: When the Sabbath was over, Mary Magdalene, and Mary the mother of James, and Salome, bought spices, so that they might come and anoint Him.

4. References to Mary of Magdala at the Resurrection

John 20:1: Now on the first day of the week Mary Magdalene came early to the tomb, while it was still dark, and saw the stone already taken away from the tomb.

Mark 16:9: Now after He had risen early on the first day of the week, He first appeared to Mary Magdalene, from whom He had cast out seven demons.

John 20:18: Mary Magdalene came, announcing to the disciples, "I have seen the Lord," and that He had said these things to her.

Luke 24: But at daybreak on the first day of the week [the women] took the spices they had prepared and went to the tomb. They found the stone rolled away from the tomb; but when they entered, they did not find the body of the Lord Jesus. While they were puzzling over this, behold, two men in dazzling garments appeared to them. They were terrified and bowed their faces to the ground. They said to them, "Why do you seek the living one among the dead?

He is not here, but he has been raised. Remember what he said to you while he was still in Galilee, that the Son of Man must be handed over to sinners and be crucified, and rise on the third day." And they remembered his words.

Then they returned from the tomb and announced all these things to the eleven and to all the others.

The women were Mary Magdalene, Joanna, and Mary the mother of James; the others who accompanied them also told this to the apostles, but their story seemed like nonsense and they did not believe them.

Contributors

Dan Burstein (co-editor) launched Squibnocket Partners as an innovative, creative content development company in 2003 together with his business partner, Arne J. de Keijzer. In 2004, they created the *Secrets* series books, which have found a place as the leading, secular multiperspective guidebooks on the *Da Vinci Code* phenomenon. The books now include the *New York Times* and international bestsellers *Secrets of the Code* and *Secrets of Angels & Demons,* as well as *Secrets of the Widow's Son* and the present volume, *Secrets of Mary Magdalene.* Documentary films have recently been released based upon *Secrets of the Code, Secrets of Angels and Demons,* and *Secrets of Mary Magdalene.*

Maintaining an active full-time career as a venture capitalist in addition to his involvement with the *Secrets* series, Burstein is founder and managing partner of Millennium Technology Ventures, a New York–based venture capital firm that invests in innovative technology companies. He has served on the boards of more than a dozen early-stage companies and is currently a director of Applied Minds, a leading-edge research lab, and the Global Options Group, a publicly traded international risk management company. From 1988 to 2000, he was Senior Advisor at The Blackstone Group, one of Wall Street's leading private merchant banks. He is also a prominent corporate strategy consultant and has served as an advisor to CEOs, senior management teams, and global corporations, including Sony, Toyota, Microsoft, Boardroom Inc., and Sun Microsystems.

Burstein is also an award-winning journalist and author of numerous books on global economics and technology. His most recent technology-related book is *BLOG! How the Newest Media Revolution Is Changing Politics, Business, and Culture,* co-written with David Kline. Burstein's 1988 book, *Yen!,* about the rise of Japanese financial power, was an international bestseller in more than twenty countries. In 1995, his book *Road Warriors* was one of the first to analyze the impact of the Internet and digital technology on business and society. His 1998 book *Big Dragon* (written with Arne J. de

Keijzer) outlined a long-term view of China's role in the twenty-first century that has, so far, turned out to be prescient.

Working as a freelance journalist in the 1980s, Burstein published more than a thousand articles in more than two hundred publications, including the *New York Times,* the *Wall Street Journal,* the *Los Angeles Times,* the *Boston Globe,* the *Chicago Tribune, New York* magazine, *Rolling Stone, Paris Match, Le Nouvel Observateur, L'Expansion,* and many others in the United States, Europe, and Asia. Burstein has appeared on documentaries and news specials on the History Channel and CNN, and on numerous TV programs ranging from *Charlie Rose* to *Oprah!*

Arne J. de Keijzer (co-editor) is a writer, former China business consultant, and Dan Burstein's partner in Squibnocket Partners LLC. He is the author of an internationally bestselling travel guide to China, two books on doing business with China, and, with Burstein, *Big Dragon: China's Future— What It Means for Business, the Economy, and the Global Order.* Together with Burstein he created the *Secrets* series of books and was managing editor of *Secrets of the Code* and co-editor of *Secrets of Angels & Demons.* He was also a contributing editor to *BLOG! How the Newest Media Revolution Is Changing Politics, Business, and Culture.* Mr. de Keijzer's other work has appeared in publications ranging from *Powerboat Reports* to the *New York Times.*

Jennifer Doll served as managing editor for this book, a role she has carried out for various other publications. Currently an editorial consultant for *Reader's Digest,* she has also contributed her writing and editing talents to McKinsey & Company, *U.S. News & World Report,* and the Teaching Commission. She was a researcher and editorial associate for *Secrets of the Code.* In her spare time, she writes fiction and is at work on her first novel.

Joan Acocella is a staff writer for the *New Yorker,* where she covers dance and books. She has also written for the *New York Review of Books* and the *Wall Street Journal.* She is the author of the critical biography *Mark Morris,* as well as other books, including *Creating Hysteria: Women and Multiple Personality Disorder* and *Willa Cather and the Politics of Criticism.* She also edited the unexpurgated *Diary of Vaslav Nijinsky* and co-edited, with Lynn Garafola, *André Levinson on Dance.* From 1993 to 1994, she was a Guggenheim fellow. Ms. Acocella currently lives in New York City.

Tori Amos is a pianist and singer-songwriter who helped redefine the role of women in pop music in the 1990s. She is known for lyrically enigmatic and emotionally intense songs that tackle a wide range of subjects, including sexuality, religion, patriarchy, and personal tragedy. Her father was a minister, and she began her musical career at age five in his church. She was also the youngest person to ever attend the Peabody Conservatory of Music, until she dropped out to begin her pop music career. She published an autobiography, *Piece by Piece,* in which she recounts her rise to fame and also explores her obsession with mythology and religion. She is co-founder of the Rape, Abuse, and Incest National Network.

Diane Apostolos-Cappadona is a cultural historian and an adjunct professor of religious art and cultural history at the Prince Alwaleed bin Talal Center for Muslim-Christian Understanding, and an adjunct professor in art and culture in the Liberal Studies Program of Georgetown University. She was guest curator and author of the catalogue for the exhibition *In Search of Mary Magdalene: Images and Traditions.* Additionally, she has authored numerous essays related to Mary Magdalene, Christian symbolism, Leonardo da Vinci, and Gian Lorenzo Bernini. A popular speaker, Dr. Apostolos-Cappadona is a frequent contributor to the *Secrets* series. She has been interviewed for the documentary movie *Secrets of the Code* as well as a variety of television programs, including the *Today Show, A&E MovieReal, The Da Vinci Code, Secrets of Angels, Demons, & Masons,* and *Secrets of Mary Magdalene.*

Elizabeth Bard is a journalist and art historian based in Paris. Her art criticism and travel writing have appeared in the *New York Times,* the *International Herald Tribune,* the *Washington Post, Wired, Art News,* and *Time Out,* among others. She has served as the New Media editor of *Contemporary,* a London art magazine, since 2002. In the spring of 2004, she also began working as a guide for Paris Muse, a company of art historians offering private tours of the great monuments of Paris. She wrote about taking *The Da Vinci Code* tour of the Louvre for the paperback edition of *Secrets of the Code.*

Lesa Bellevie, whose "day job" is software test engineer, is the founder of www.Magdalene.org and author of *The Complete Idiot's Guide to Mary Magdalene.* The website, begun in 1998 as a way to collect everything she was able to learn about Mary Magdalene, has served as a resource and forum for connecting people worldwide. Magdalene.org was recently relented in 2005, with a new look and the foundations for a new project called Encyclopedia Magdalena. Bellevie has been frequently interviewed for local, national, and international newspapers and magazines, radio programs, and television documentaries. Among her current projects is a blog called The Magdalene Review (www.magdalenereview.org), in which she tracks media references and recent research about Mary Magdalene.

Ann Graham Brock is an author and lecturer whose special interests include New Testament and early Christian traditions, archaeology, and gender issues in' religion. Her most recent publication is entitled *Mary Magdalene, the First Apostle: The Struggle for Authority.* She has also co-edited five other books, and had scores of encyclopedia and journal articles published in German, French, and English. She has taught New Testament and world religion courses at the University of Colorado at Boulder, Trinity Lutheran Seminary, Cliff School of Theology, Harvard Divinity School, and Harvard University. She has appeared on the History Channel in its presentation of *The Twelve Apostles,* and the Discovery Channel in *The Real Da Vinci Code,* as well as several documentaries on British television.

James Carroll attended Georgetown University before entering St. Paul's College, the Paulist fathers' seminary, where he received his B.A. and M.A. degrees. He was ordained to the priesthood in 1969 and served as Catholic chaplain at Boston University until 1974. During that time he was a civil rights worker, an antiwar activist, and a community organizer, winning the first Thomas Merton Award. Publishing books on religious subjects as well as a book of poems, he was also a columnist for the *National Catholic Reporter.* Carroll left the priesthood in 1974 to become a writer, and in 1974 was playwright-in-residence at the Berkshire Theater Festival. Around this time he began writing novels, over time publishing ten. Carroll's works include *House of War: The Pentagon and the Disastrous Rise of American Power, Constantine's Sword: The Church and the Jews* (adapted into a documentary film in 2006), *An American Requiem* (National Book Award, 1996), weekly columns in the *Boston Globe,* and many essays, which have appeared in America's most prominent publications.

Bruce Chilton is Bernard Iddings Bell Professor of Religion at Bard College as well as chaplain of Bard College and executive director of the Institute of Advanced Theology. He has a master's degree from the General Theological Seminary as well as Columbia University, and a Ph.D. from Cambridge University. Chilton is also an ordained Episcopal priest, serving at the Free Church of Saint John in Barrytown, New York. His books include *Rabbi Jesus: An Intimate Biography, God in Strength, Rabbi Paul: An Intellec-*

tual Biography, Judaic Approaches to the Gospels, Revelation, Trading Places, Jesus' Prayer and Jesus' Eucharist, Forging a Common Future, and *Jesus' Baptism and Jesus' Healing.* He is also editor in chief of the *Bulletin for Biblical Research* and the founding editor of the *Journal for the Study of the New Testament.*

Richard Covington was a contributing writer to a *U.S. News & World Report* special report, "Women of the Bible."

Mary Rose D'Angelo is an associate professor in the Department of Theology at the University of Notre Dame. She teaches the course "New Testament and Christian Origins" and does research on religion, women, and gender in the ancient world. Author of *Moses in the Letter to the Hebrews,* she co-edited the book *Women and Christian Origins* and "Crossroads in Christology: Essays in Honor of Ellen M. Leonard" in the *Toronto Journal of Theology.* The author of additional articles on women, gender, imperial politics, theological language and sexual practice in the beginnings of Christianity, she is currently working on a project describing Roman imperial "family values" and ancient Jewish and Christian responses.

Jacobus de Voragine, an Italian monk, entered the Dominican order in 1244, and in addition to preaching with success in many parts of Italy, taught in the schools of his own fraternity. Attending various Councils, he rose steadily in the hierarchy of the Roman Catholic Church and was elevated to the rank of bishop in 1292. He died circa 1298 and was beatified by Pope Pius VII in 1816. De Voragine left several volumes of sermons, *Chronicle of Genoa,* and *Readings of the Saints.* Because of its immense and lasting popularity, the *Readings* came to be called *The Golden Legend.*

Bart D. Ehrman is the James A. Gray Distinguished Professor of Religious Studies at the University of North Carolina at Chapel Hill, where he has taught since 1988. An authority on the New Testament and the history of early Christianity, he has appeared on CNN, the History Channel, A&E, and various television and radio programs. He has taped several popular lecture series for The Teaching Company and is author or editor of thirteen books including, most recently, *Peter, Paul, and Mary Magdalene: The Followers of Jesus in History and Legend.* He has also written *Truth and Fiction in* The Da Vinci Code and the bestselling and critically acclaimed *Lost Christianities: The Battles for Scripture and the Faiths We Never Knew.* In the spring of 2006 he served as a consultant to the *Gospel of Judas* project at the National Geographic Society.

Deirdre Good, contributing editor to this book, is a professor in the Department of New Testament, General Theological Seminary, New York City. A widely published author and prominent lecturer, she is also a program consultant for television on religious history. She is editor of *Mariam, the Magdalen, and the Mother,* a collection of essays exploring the religious and prophetic identities of Mary Magdalene and Mary, mother of Jesus, as Miriam figures. She is also editor of *Reconstructing the Tradition of Sophia in Gnostic Literature* and *Jesus the Meek King.* Her newest book is *Jesus' Family Values.*

Maxine Hanks is a writer, lecturer, and feminist theologian whose research areas are women's studies in religion, Mormon studies, and Gnosticism. She has been a Merrill fellow at Harvard Divinity School and a research fellow with the Utah Humanities Council. Her first book, *Women and Authority,* reclaimed feminist theology and history in Mormonism. She has appeared in many publications and television programs as well as a guest lecturer at various schools. A former Mormon and Church of Jesus Christ of Latter-day Saints missionary, she became a Gnostic in 1996 and has since been active in local and national interfaith projects.

Susan Haskins is an author, editor, researcher, and translator. She has given lectures around the world, appeared on various television programs to discuss Mary Magdalene, and is currently translating from Italian and editing *Three Marian Writings* (texts on the life of the Virgin by three sixteenth-century Italian female writers). She is the author of *Mary Magdalen: Myth & Metaphor* and was also a contributor to *Secrets of the Code.*

Katherine Ludwig Jansen is the author of the award-winning book *The Making of the Magdalen: Preaching and Popular Devotion in the Late Middle Ages.* She is also an associate professor of history at the Catholic University of America. A researcher in the fields of medieval history, Italian history, women and gender and religious culture, her forthcoming book is entitled *The Practice of Peace in Late Medieval Italy.* Professor Jansen is a fellow of both the American Academy in Rome and Villa I Tatti, the Harvard Center for Renaissance Studies in Florence.

Philip Jenkins was educated at Cambridge University, where he obtained his doctorate in history. Since 1980, he has taught at Penn State University and currently holds the rank of Distinguished Professor of History and Religious Studies. His most recent book is *Decade of Nightmares: The End of the*

Sixties and the Making of Eighties America. Other books include *Mystics and Messiah: Cults and New Religions in American History, Hidden Gospels: How the Search for Jesus Lost Its Way,* and *The Next Christendom: The Rise of Global Christianity.* Professor Jenkins's articles can also be found in a wide variety of publications; he makes media appearances regularly.

Karen L. King is Winn Professor of Ecclesiastical History at the Harvard Divinity School, where she has also held the post of professor of New Testament Studies and the History of Ancient Christianity. Trained in comparative religions and historical studies, she pursues teaching and research specialties in the history of Christianity and women's studies. Her books have been widely acclaimed, the best known among them being *The Gospel of Mary of Magdala: Jesus and the First Woman Apostle* and *What Is Gnosticism?* Her particular theoretical interests are in religious identity formation, discourses of normativity (orthodoxy and heresy), and gender studies. She has received many awards for excellence in teaching and research; among them are grants from the National Endowment for the Humanities, Deutsche Akademische Austauschdienst, and the Graves Foundation.

Katherine Kurs is a member of the faculty of religious studies at Eugene Lang College of the New School University, and is also on the faculty of the General Theological Seminary. Her areas of specialization include contemporary American spirituality, urban-based religiosity, "lived religion," religious pluralism, and spiritual autobiography. The Rev. Dr. Kurs is an ecumenical associate minister at West Park Presbyterian Church and she maintains a private counseling practice. Her book, *Searching for Your Soul,* was named one of the best religion/spirituality books of 1999.

John Lamb Lash, an independent, eclectic scholar and co-founder and principal writer of www.Metahistory.org, is the author of several books, including *The Seeker's Handbook, Twins and the Double,* and *The Hero.* He sees in the figure of Mary Magdalene an opportunity to recover the genuine heretical features of Gnosticism. His forthcoming book, *Not in His Image: Gnostic Vision, Sacred Ecology, and the Future of Belief,* will recover what Lash calls "the Sophianic vision of the Mysteries."

Ki Longfellow is a novelist and screenwriter whose book *The Secret Magdalene* has been widely praised for its research and writing style. Under the name Pamela Longfellow she has published two novels, *China Blues* (an international bestseller) and *Chasing Women.* Both were optioned and adapted for the screen. She has also co-written, with her husband, a comic opera called *STINKFOOT,* which was twice staged in London to glowing reviews.

Kathleen McGowan began her writing career as a teenage journalist. At the age of twenty-one, she moved to Ireland to work as a reporter. During her time abroad, McGowan studied international folklore, mythology, and the art of storytelling. She has been a ghost writer and editor on full-length works of fiction and nonfiction and has also written in the fields of human potential, alternate therapies, spirituality, and metaphysics. McGowan has worked for The Walt Disney Company in marketing, worked as a story analyst and script doctor, and has completed her own film as screenwriter and producer, *Down to Gehenna. The Expected One* is her first novel, based on twenty years of research into the lives of Jesus Christ and Mary Magdalene.

Marvin Meyer is Griset Professor of Bible and Christian Studies at Chapman University and director of the Chapman University Albert Schweitzer Institute. He is also director of the Coptic Magical Texts Project of the Institute for Antiquity and Christianity, Claremont Graduate University. Dr. Meyer is the author of numerous books and articles on Greco-Roman and Christian religions in antiquity and late antiquity, and on Albert Schweitzer's ethic of reverence for life. Among his most recent books are *The Gnostic Discoveries, The Gnostic Gospels of Jesus, The Unknown Sayings of Jesus,* and *The Gospels of Mary.* His book *The Gospel of Thomas: The Hidden Sayings of Jesus* has been listed as one of the hundred best spiritual books of the twentieth century. Most recently Dr. Meyer has edited and translated *The Gospel of Judas,* with Rodolphe Kasser and Gregor Wurst. His books and articles have been widely translated and he is in frequent demand as a guest on national television and radio programs.

Elaine Pagels is the Harrington Spear Paine Professor of Religion at Princeton University. She graduated from Stanford University and completed her Ph.D. at Harvard University. There she was part of a team studying the Nag Hammadi Library scrolls, which became the basis for her bestselling *The Gnostic Gospels,* a popular introduction to the Nag Hammadi Library. The book won both the National Book Critics Circle Award and the National Book Award and was chosen by the Modern Library as one of the hundred best books of the twentieth century. In 1982, Pagels joined Princeton University as a professor of early Christian history. Her *New York Times* bestseller, *Beyond Belief: The Secret Gospel of Thomas,* focuses on the conflicts between the gospels of John and Thomas as a way of demonstrating Christianity's early diversity as well as its increasing willingness to narrow its doctrines to include only certain texts supporting certain beliefs. In addition to a MacArthur Fellowship award, Professor Pagels is also a recipient of the Guggenheim and Rockefeller fellowships.

Jeremy Pine is an American antiquarian who has been based in Kathmandu, Nepal, for thirty-five years. Specializing in antique textiles, he has had the opportunity to examine and research thousands of old pieces including woolens, silks, and carpets. From 1993 to 1995, Pine was expedition director for the Institute of Science in Moscow and the State Institute of the History of Material Culture in St. Petersburg. In that capacity he led three expeditions to Tuva to excavate ancient tombs for the benefit of the Hermitage Museum. The last two years were spent in the little known and remote Valley of the Silver Mountain, or Mongün Taiga, just north of the Mongolian border. In 1995 the team, Golden Griffin, excavated a rare thirty-five-meter-diameter Pazyryk tomb they discovered the previous year. Married, with two children, Jeremy has recently retired from business to become full-time curator of the Exile Carpet and its related treasures.

Nancy Qualls-Corbett is a practicing Jungian analyst in Birmingham, Alabama. A diplomat of the C. G. Jung Institute in Zurich, she is a senior training analyst in the Inter-Regional Society of Jungian Analysts. Nancy is the author of *The Sacred Prostitute: Eternal Aspect of the Feminine* and *Woman's Awakening: Dreams and Individuation.* She combines her love of travel and mythology in leading seminars to the sacred places of Egypt, Greece, France, and Italy.

Anna Quindlen is the bestselling author of four novels (*Blessings, Black and Blue, One True Thing,* and *Object Lessons*) and four nonfiction books (*A Short Guide to a Happy Life, Living Out Loud, Thinking Out Loud,* and *How Reading Changed My Life*). She has also written two children's books (*The Tree That Came to Stay* and *Happily Ever After*). Her *New York Times* column "Public and Private" won the Pulitzer Prize in 1992. Her column now appears every other week in *Newsweek.*

John M. Saul, who holds a Ph.D. in geology from MIT, joined forces with Henry Lincoln at Rennes-le-Château in mid-1974 to search for the "secret treasure" of Abbé Saunière then suspected to be hidden in one of the limestone caves dotting the area. It took a good five years to realize that "treasure" might be a code word designating a child or the children of Mary Magdalene. The author subsequently contributed to the research in preparing *Holy Blood, Holy Grail* but did not agree with the co-authors of that book that Pierre Plantard should be used as a source of information. With Janice A. Glaholm, also a geologist, he compiled *Rennes-le-Château: A Bibliography*, a fifty-two-page book whose introduction included a map that for the first time showed the five natural high points in the area of Rennes-le-Château, forming a near-perfect pentacle, or five-pointed star.

Jane Schaberg is a professor of religious studies and women's studies at the University of Detroit Mercy. She is the author of *The Resurrection of Mary Magdalene: Legends, Apocrypha, and the Christian Testament,* a landmark work in feminist cultural and Christian testament studies. She has also written *The Illegitimacy of Jesus: A Feminist Theological Interpretation of the New Testament Infancy Narratives,* and her poetry has appeared in such journals as *Atlanta Review, Appearances, Pittsburgh Review,* and *Interim.*

Margaret Starbird holds a master's degree from the University of Maryland and has studied at Christian-Albrechts University in Kiel, Germany, and at Vanderbilt Divinity School. In great demand as a leader of workshops and a commentator in the media, she has written extensively on the concept of the sacred feminine and sacred union. Her books—which Dan Brown acknowledges as major influences on his exploration of the same themes in *The Da Vinci Code*—include *Magdalene's Lost Legacy: Symbolic Numbers and the Sacred Union in Christianity, The Goddess in the Gospels: Reclaiming the Sacred Feminine, The Feminine Face of Christianity, Mary Magdalene: Bride in Exile,* and her best-known work, *The Woman with the Alabaster Jar: Mary Magdalen and the Holy Grail.*

Merlin Stone, a teacher of art and art history as well as a widely exhibited sculptor, became interested in archaeology and ancient religion through her art. She has produced pieces on the Goddess for both radio and the stage, and conceived and organized Goddess festivals in both New York and Toronto. Her book *When God Was a Woman* was the result of more than a decade of research, and has become a classic. First published in the United Kingdom as *The Paradise Papers,* it was republished in the United States in 1976 under the present title.

Acknowledgments

This book has been a fascinating journey, and many guides along the way have helped make it so.

As ever, the people to whom we owe the greatest debt are our families: Helen and Hannah, Julie and David. They know how much they mean to us, but the importance of their love, wisdom, and support as we venture through the odyssey necessary to create one of these books cannot be overstated.

We are deeply grateful to Deirdre Good and Diane Apostolos-Cappadona, two extraordinary scholars whose generous and cheerfully rendered advice helped guide our way through the maze of new thinking and new writing about Mary Magdalene. They unstintingly shared with us their rich ideas and deep understanding of history, theology, ancient languages, scriptures, art, and much more.

Elaine Pagels has been an inspirational force in the background of several of our recent projects, and we deeply appreciate the contribution of her important introductory essay for this book.

We are fortunate to have a close partnership with our publisher, CDS Books/The Perseus Books Group. CDS/Perseus has supported and encouraged us every step of the way. For their help on this, the fourth in our series of *Secrets* books, we are especially grateful to David Steinberger, Roger Cooper, Steve Black, Robert Kimzey, Jennifer Fried-Dedman, Chris Nakamura, and Peter Costanzo.

Thanks also to the many talented people working behind the scenes who helped produce this book, especially David Wilk, our shepherd from the very beginning of the *Secrets* series, and Danny Baror, world-class agent. We have benefited from the expertise and tireless assistance on all matters large and small from Christine Marra (valued den mother once again), Jane Raese, Gray Cutler, Leigh Taylor, Paul Berger, David Shugarts, Lottchen Shivers, and Johanna Pfund.

The center of gravity of this book is the "Mary Magdalene Round-table." To our knowledge, no one has ever before convened such an in-sightful and wide-ranging group to think out loud together about Mary Magdalene and her role in history, as seen from the vantage point of today's world. For their enthusiastic participation and valu-able contributions to this unique event, we express our deep appreci-ation to Diane Apostolos-Cappadona, Lesa Bellevie, Deirdre Good, Susan Haskins, Elaine Pagels, Jane Schaberg, and Katherine Kurs. We also want to thank Stuart Rekant, Rob Fruchtman, Lori Nelson, and Erika Dutton of Hidden Treasures Productions, which filmed the roundtable. They have created a compelling companion to this book in the form of a documentary film, *Secrets of Mary Magdalene,* that will have widespread global television and DVD distribution.

We have again been fortunate to have had the collaboration of some of the world's great scholars, thinkers, and writers. The list is a verita-ble who's who in Mary Magdalene expertise. In addition to the schol-ars acknowledged above, our thanks to Joan Acocella, Tori Amos, Elizabeth Bard, Ann Graham Brock, James Carroll, Bruce Chilton, Richard Covington, Mary Rose d'Angelo, Bart Ehrman, Maxine Hanks, Katherine L. Jansen, Philip Jenkins, Karen King, John Lash, Ki Longfellow, Kathleen McGowan, Marvin Meyer, Jeremy Pine, Nancy Qualls-Corbett, Anna Quindlen, John Saul, Margaret Starbird, and Merlin Stone.

And speaking of collaboration, we extend our sincere thanks to Jennifer Doll, managing editor of this book. She, in turn, says, "Thanks to my family, Marilou, Bruce, and Brad Doll, for their sup-port and feedback throughout this process. Also, special thanks to Sarah Griffin and Mike Haney for their editorial advice and support, and appreciation for the pleasure of having worked with Betty Adam, Kathleen McGowan, Rosamonde Miller, Joan Norton, Katia Ro-manoff, Chris Schenk, Robbi Sluder, Pamela Stockton, Sara Taft, Lila Sophia Tresemer, and Mark Williams."

Personal acknowledgments from Arne de Keijzer: Warmest of thanks to my brother, Steve, and my extended family: Dick and

Shirley Reiss, Bob and Carolyn Reiss, Marni Virtue, Jelmer and Rose Dorreboom, Brian, Joan, and Breeze Weiss, Lynn Northrup, and Sandy West. And a special note of appreciation for "D," loving, supportive, and generous patriarch, and for Bob, valued friend and virtual brother for nearly thirty years; both will appreciate the irony of getting a special salute in this particular book.

Personal acknowledgments from Dan Burstein: A special thank you to my many friends and business partners who have helped us in the creation, promotion, and distribution of the *Secrets* series, including Marty Edelston, Judy Friedberg, Chuck Hirsch, Joan O'Connor and the extended O'Connor-Aires family, Gilbert Perlman, PalTalk, WetPaint, Alchemist Films, the Endeavor agency, Hidden Treasures, Waterfront Media, BzzAgent, U.S. News & World Report, and our many international publishers all over the world.

We are often asked who does what in this writing partnership. The answer is both, and all. For this book, Dan Burstein had the original inspiration and advised, edited, wrote, and acted as chief marketing officer. Arne de Keijzer developed the concept into a working outline, recruited and worked with the contributors, forged it into a book, and advised, edited, wrote, and acted as chief of assembly. As we said: both, all.

Dan Burstein and Arne J. de Keijzer
August 2006

Visit us at www.SecretsOfMaryMagdalene.com and
www.SecretsOfTheCode.com